REAL WORLD
DIGITAL
VIDEO
SECOND EDITION

PETE SHANER
GERALD EVERETT JONES

PEACHPIT PRESS
BERKELEY, CALIFORNIA

REAL WORLD DIGITAL VIDEO, SECOND EDITION

Pete Shaner
Gerald Everett Jones

Peachpit Press
1249 Eighth Street
Berkeley, CA 94710
510/524-2178
800/283-9444
510/524-2221 (fax)

Find us on the World Wide Web at: www.peachpit.com
To report errors, please send a note to errata@peachpit.com
Peachpit Press is a division of Pearson Education

Editor: Charles Koppelman
Production Editor: Hilal Sala
Compositor: Happenstance Type-O-Rama
Indexer: Karin Arrigoni
Cover production: Alan Clements
Cover Illustrator: Nathan Clement
Cover design: Aren Howell
Interior design: Mimi Heft
Interior Illustrator: John Farnsworth

ISBN 0-321-23833-8

9 8 7 6 5 4 3 2 1

Printed and bound in the United States of America

*Dedicated to Charlotte and Hal Shaner, who taught
a young director what to look at and how to see.*

CONTENTS AT A GLANCE

TABLE OF CONTENTS

PREFACE TO THE SECOND EDITION

It's little more than a year since *Real World Digital Video* first hit the bookshelves, and already we needed to update sizable chunks of the manuscript—to keep it out of the Ancient History section!

Peachpit Press had the foresight and the marketing fortitude to commission this new edition much sooner than most publishers. After all, the first edition was selling quite well from the Computer Multimedia section of bookstores, and we were even beginning to conquer some of those die-hards over in Film Production.

Too much was changing—and not only camcorder model numbers, software versions, technical specifications, and prices. As in the first edition, we make references to products mostly for purposes of comparison. Be sure to check for the latest specs and prices in trade magazines or on the Web before you make any final buying decisions.

The big news over the last year was introduction of the first prosumer 24P camcorder, confirming our suspicions that "film-look DV" is a hot topic, and getting hotter. We tried it both ways: shooting movie mode in-camera, and converting standard video in post. Based on that real world experience, we have some powerful advice for you. (For more information, see "What's the Best Way to Achieve 24 fps?" in Chapter 11.)

And, as moviemakers who always strive to show rather than just tell, we did two new productions for the companion DVD:

- *Alan Smithee's Hollywood Tips:* We used digital chroma-key compositing to superimpose a wise-cracking directorial tyro over some amateur footage. It's not only a lesson in professional-style cinematography, it's also a kick to watch because your own mistakes can't possibly look this bad.

- *How to Make Digital Video Look Like Film:* Watch one of our favorite talking heads declaim while we switch among various film-look techniques on the fly. See for yourself how 24P and some other tricks make a big difference on the screen.

These two clips join our theatrical short *When Harried Met Sally* and our campy lesson on shot design, *Ten Ways to Shoot a Chair,* each a 2003 Bronze award-winner at the WorldFest-Houston International Film Festival. Also on the DVD, you'll find helpful, chatty on-camera interviews from movieland pros and one of the first-ever multicamera DV concert videos. To top it off, there are all-new motion-graphic menus, just to start you thinking about what you can do with DVD Studio Pro 2 and After Effects.

No sooner did we start revising Chapter 1 than we caught ourselves harping on story, story, story as the test of talent for any videomaker. Did we cut those preachy passages? Heck, no. We gave them their very own chapter. (For more on the importance of story and script, see the all-new Chapter 2: "Yes, You Need a Script.")

And we fact-checked, cross-referenced, worried over, and updated everything else. We moved some of the techie stuff to the back of the book—adding to Appendix A on DV Technology and getting up close and personal with NLE system design in Appendix B. Nothing's gone—it's just in a better place.

ABOUT THE AUTHORS

Pete Shaner graduated from USC film school with a commitment to finding ways to tell his own stories without having to submit to the creative compromises imposed by the Hollywood studio system. In pursuit of his dream, he formed his own production company in the mid-nineties, raising nearly half a million dollars to produce, write, and direct his first feature film, a romantic comedy called *Lover's Knot*. Produced on 35mm film and released in 1996, this venture actually made money for its investors. (You can buy the VHS on Amazon.com.) Pete was well into preproduction for his second film when he heard about the CineAlta, a new high-definition, 24-frames-per-second video camcorder that Sony was developing for George Lucas. Pete arranged to rent the camera as a kind of beta test, to shoot *Nicolas*, a romantic thriller, before Lucas used it to make *Star Wars: Episode II— The Attack of the Clones*. With image quality rivaling what he could have achieved on 35mm film, produced at a fraction of the cost, working digitally gave Pete a creative freedom he couldn't have afforded otherwise, and he was hooked.

In addition to making his own films, Pete has taught directing and movie production at UCLA Extension, emphasizing the use of digital media.

Gerald Everett Jones is the author of numerous technical and business books, including *Easy Photoshop Elements* and *How to Lie with Charts*. Prior to working on this book, he had experience in developing graphics software, writing and producing industrial film and video projects, and writing screenplays. After studying film craft at UCLA with Pete (and catching the same digital video bug), he proposed the collaboration that resulted in *Real World Digital Video*.

ACKNOWLEDGMENTS

A team of dedicated professionals labored diligently to bring you this book. The authors particularly want to thank Marjorie Baer, Executive Acquisitions and Development Editor, Peachpit Press, for holding a vision of what digital video can mean to the real world; Charles Koppelman, editor, for his gentle persuasion and friendly advice, and for helping us look our best in print; Maureen Forys for an impressive book design; Hilal Sala for her masterful production coordination; John Farnsworth for rendering our crude sketches as stunning illustrations; and Jay Payne for shepherding the DVD.

Grateful acknowledgment goes to our colleagues and fellow wizards who contributed content, resources, and technical advice: Craig Abaya, Director of Intensive Programs, San Francisco State University Multimedia Studies Program; Michael Alberts, Ambidextrous Productions, Inc.; Nir Averbuch, Muzikhead Productions; Bruce R. Cook, Ph.D., Professor of Cinema Studies, Los Angeles City College and CEO of New Millennium Media; Lynn Fredricks, E-On Software; Greg Huson, Secret Headquarters Editorial; Bob Jeffords, Directors Guild of America; Thomas C. Muniz, CIO, IMPART, Inc.; Robert Payne, storyboard artist; Vivek Paramesh, Comco, Inc.; Randall Peede, Advanced Systems Group; Tom Reynolds, Executive Vice President, R A Media Company; Debbie Rich, Digital Anarchy; and Steve Weiss, CAS.

Thanks to the vendors who graciously granted permission to use copyrighted material: Robert Christie, Senior PR Strategist, Professional Video Products, Sony Electronics Inc.; Paul Clatworthy, PowerProduction Software Inc.; Frank Colin, Vice President Product Development, Final Draft, Inc.; Steve Foldvari, Sony Pictures Digital Inc.; Stephen Gallagher, Publisher, *Filmmaker: The Magazine of Independent Film;* ; Michelle Kohler and Tonya Sorn, Shure Incorporated; Andrew Little, Red Giant Software LLC (Magic Bullet Suite); Richard Manfredi, SmartSound, Inc.; Charles Parra, President, Denecke, Inc.; Lana Posner, Producer; Taina Rodriguez, Business & Legal Affairs, RCA Records; Brian Schmidt, Product Manager, DVD Studio Pro, Apple Computer, Inc.; Claire Smith, Citizens Bank; Mike Virgintino, PR Manager, Canon U.S.A., Inc.; David N. Walton, Professional Publicity Department, JVC Professional Products Company; and Comcast Digital Media Centers—Los Angeles.

And sincere thanks for their professionalism and enthusiastic participation to our photo models and video production cast and crew: Nicholas Altman, Philip Burgers, Paul Candice, Caleb Cindano, Ric Frazier, Elizabeth Fujimaki, Richard Haase, Rebecca Hirschfeld, Ainsley Hudson, Dave Hurley, Philip J. Gallegos, John Gilmore, Andrew Gorry, Tony Jenkins, Anthony Kaufman, Jenifer Kingsley, Ren Knerr, Heather LaFace,

Peter Meech, Eddie Ed O'Brien; Ann Park, Michael W. Rue, Georja Umano, Derrick Warfel, and Josh Williams. We're grateful to Lance Schmidt, Visual Marketing, for logistical support, as well as to Mark Zamel, Zamel & Associates real estate management for providing shooting locations. Special thanks to Bruce Hornsby and Deep South Entertainment for permission to use his performance of "Try Anything Once" (used courtesy of The RCA Records Label, a unit of BMG).

Heartfelt personal thanks to Georja Umano Jones for her kindness, patience, and belief. And we appreciate the support and encouragement of Matt Wagner of Waterside Productions, who brought us all together.

INTRODUCTION
Pictures from the Revolution

Thanks to digital technology, the tools of video production can now fit on a desktop. A briefcase can easily hold a palmcorder and a notebook computer, with room left over for your cell phone and the slate you use to mark the start of a shot. New technologies for video distribution fit on that desktop or laptop, too—tools for streaming video across the Web and authoring interactive DVDs, for example. And with each passing season, prices fall and the technology improves. Altogether, these developments mark a truly revolutionary era in video storytelling. Seasoned professionals are discovering new creative techniques that the technology makes possible, both in the editing studio and on the shoot. Meanwhile, capable, affordable equipment lowers the barriers to entering the field. Video cameras and editing applications are finding their way into the hands of independent film-makers and journalists, corporate communications departments, students and educators, and even family documentarians.

Isn't there some story you're dying to tell? Some public figure or issue that sets you off? Do you dream of making a career behind the camera or at the editing console? Do you long to see your name or your product on the screen? By writing this book covering both

Best Train Set

Legendary filmmaker Orson Welles once remarked that a movie studio was the best set of electric trains a kid could ever have. There was only one catch: His trains cost millions of dollars. Today, for less than $10,000, you can own a digital train set Welles would have envied. The variety of DV tools available now—cameras, editing systems, postproduction software, and distribution media—is dazzling. And in many ways, DV offers more power than Welles' studio-sized filmmaking toys, at a fraction of their cost.

But making movies isn't just about technology. While Welles had a striking technical flair he is mainly remembered for his almost irrational passion for cinematic storytelling.

the latest technology and the essential production skills needed to use it effectively, we hope to empower and inspire you to produce videos that win awards, influence people, earn money, and fulfill your artistic aspirations—and that tell *your* story.

MASTERING THE MEDIUM

One thing the technological revolution hasn't changed is the importance of the specialized know-how that video production professionals bring to their craft. It may be true that now almost anyone can gain access to the tools of production, but learning to use them to communicate effectively still takes experience and an extensive skill set. Minus the craft of the professional moviemaker, much of the work that's now so easy to produce will be downright unwatchable.

Today's best filmmaking, whatever the venue—television news, commercial movie house, film festival circuit, corporate boardroom, or Web site—is born out of a marriage of technology and a visual vocabulary that's been evolving for over a century—along with the arts of cinema and television. Skilled professionals know how to apply these tools and techniques to create dramatic fiction movies, sales pitches, training demonstrations, advertising, political interviews, fundraising solicitations, educational documentaries, and lots more.

This book approaches digital video from the perspective of a media professional working in the real world. It emphasizes not only what's new about the technology but also what's become traditional in the craft of filmmaking: timeless principles of engaging storytelling, painting with light, working with actors, interacting with interview subjects, enriching the viewers' experience with sophisticated sound, and putting it all together with a sense of rhythm, pacing, and personal style. Whatever your ultimate ambitions may be for your video creations, this book is intended for anyone—at any level of skill or expertise—who is eager to use the digital video medium to tell a story.

What Is DV?

Not all digital video is DV. There are actually quite a few different electronic technologies today that use streams of binary data to record, transmit, and display pictures and sound—like on a TV. To media professionals, DV is a specific recording standard—like its analog videotape predecessors VHS, Hi8, and Betacam SP.

*This book deals with both digital video as a creative medium and the DV recording standard. When we're talking about the art and craft of video production, we'll spell it out as **digital video**. When we mean the recording format, we'll say **DV**.*

Thinking in DV

It's possible that you've already had some experience making movies using analog video, or film, or both. If so, you'll find many of your skills are directly applicable to working in digital video.

However, there are critical differences. DV requires a different mindset, and it offers a universe of new opportunities for creativity. For example, you might expect to light DV differently from film, but do you realize shooting in DV can also affect the ways you work with your actors? Our emphasis throughout this book will be on showing you how working in DV differs from working in traditional media.

If you don't have any real-world experience making movies, relax and enjoy the ride. By the time you're done with this book you'll have learned everything you need to know to plan your production, lock down a budget, choose your equipment, shoot and edit your footage, all the way to releasing your finished work.

This book is structured to mirror the video production process step-by-step. We start where you've probably started already, thinking about the kind of project you want to create. Since different assignments call for different shooting styles, different equipment, and different creative solutions, we'll begin by looking at different approaches to video storytelling—interviews, documentaries and training videos, and scripted presentations.

We'll emphasize the importance of story, *the* non-technical but altogether essential element of success, and we'll describe how professionals—whether feature screenwriters or corporate documentarians—turn stories into shooting scripts, storyboards, shot plans, schedules, and budgets.

Caveat Emptor

When you go out to shop for equipment you want to have some idea of what things cost, so we list prices for some of the more popular products. But with a marketplace that's evolving as fast as DV is, it's impossible to remain current for long, and these prices may have changed—perhaps significantly—by the time you're ready to buy. Always check current pricing and the newest comparable products before making any buying decisions.

Incidentally, if you haven't yet purchased a camcorder or a desktop editing system—or if, like many pros, you prefer to rent your gear—you may want to hold off on making any final decisions for now. We've got important advice for you on how to match these tools to your style of shooting, your creative approach, and your budget. (For more information, see Chapter 3, "DV Technology and the Camcorder" and Appendix B: Selecting and Building an NLE System.)

The next section begins with an overview of DV technology to help you choose and operate a camcorder, then goes on to survey the features you'll need most for getting good results on different kinds of projects.

With camera in hand, you'll learn professional techniques for planning a shoot, choosing equipment and personnel, working on the set, designing effective lighting, and capturing good sound. We'll warn you about production pitfalls, help you build an editing system (after first encouraging you to work with an experienced editor), and take you through editing, postproduction, and distributing your work in various media. Finally we'll sketch in the future of this fast-developing technology.

What's on the DVD?

The DVD that comes with this book plays on any DVD player, or any PC or Mac equipped with a DVD drive. It includes video presentations produced especially for this book to illustrate the three basic types of projects and shooting styles: interview, training video, and scripted show.

The disc also includes additional resources: on-camera interviews with DV experts; demo versions of editing, sound, and production software for PC and Mac; and an assortment of production forms and templates that you can use as is, or modify for your own projects.

WHAT LIES AHEAD

This is an ambitious book: It's about selecting tools, getting value for your money, advancing your career, satisfying your curiosity, having fun as you work, discovering new work methods, experimenting in a new medium—and putting your story on screens all over the world.

So, please tell your parents, friends, and loved ones that you might be late for dinner.

You have a new world to explore.

—Pete Shaner
—Gerald Everett Jones,
   www.lapuerta.tv

CHAPTER ONE

All You Can Achieve with Digital Video

The promise of the "democratization of video" goes far beyond inexpensive camcorders and desktop editing systems. It means easier access to the tools of mass communication—and freedom of expression.

- Don't like the way the big networks are covering (or not covering) local events? Get it on tape, add your own commentary, and create a community video webzine.

- Starting a small business and can't afford TV ads? Shoot your own and buy inexpensive *spots* on local cable in key markets.

- Can't get a major studio interested in your quirky independent movie? If you're savvy about going digital, you might only need a small fraction of the millions a film production could cost. And if you don't need their money, they can't tell you what to shoot.

> **SPOT:** Advertising industry term for a television or radio commercial, usually referred to by its length (30-second spot, 60-second spot).

So feel free. What do you want to express? What do *you* want to achieve?

TYPES OF PROJECTS YOU CAN SHOOT WITH DIGITAL VIDEO

No matter what your particular media project involves, no matter if you're a seasoned industry professional or a would-be moviemaker with a new script under your arm, digital techniques will help you achieve fast, affordable, professional results.

In many ways digital video is not unlike film or analog video. The main difference is that digital video is more plastic—it allows, even encourages, experimentation. And whether you're interested in trying new techniques or simply want to put your story on the screen, it won't cost nearly as much in time or money.

Nonetheless, before your project becomes a digital video production, it starts out as an *idea*. So before you become too concerned with how long your project will take, what it will cost, or what equipment you should use, let's talk about storytelling and moviemaking, and how these time-honored professions intersect with digital technology.

Here are just a few of the possibilities:

- Home movies
- Video diaries
- Performance art
- Experimental videos
- How-to demonstrations
- News coverage

- Corporate videos
- Commercials
- Documentaries
- Interviews
- Fiction movies

Home Movies

Don't laugh! Most media professionals start by making home movies or amateur video. You buy a camcorder and point it at the people closest to you. There's at least one young Hollywood producer who got his first experience with digital video by editing *shots* he made of his toddler's attempts to walk. There's nothing trivial about this stuff. It's real life, just the way it happens. A wedding video, for example, captures the love and commitment of two people who have decided to make a life together. That's a unique and powerful thing.

> **SHOT:** A single, continuous film exposure or tape recording.
>
> **MONTAGE:** From the French, meaning "to assemble." An edited sequence of rapidly following, usually unrelated, shots.

To begin with, digital video can enrich the home-moviemaking process by allowing you to shoot freely, with no worries about the cost of film processing or the time required to digitize analog video into your desktop editing system. Also, you can add effects and multimedia elements with your desktop computer. For example, you might scan pictures from the family album and build them into a *montage*, add titles, or incorporate original music.

Sure, you could do these things before—but with DV, adding these extra touches is now amazingly quick and easy.

Video Diaries

Now that every desktop computer can be equipped with an inexpensive *webcam* no larger than a golf ball, there's a whole new way to capture your true confessions. *Video diaries* are just what the term implies—uncensored streams of autobiographical material. It's a time-honored filmmaker's technique for people to talk into cameras as if to a best friend, and now you, too can star in the intimate story of your own life.

WEBCAM: Any video camera equipped to output compressed video (MPEG2) for distribution on the Internet.

VIDEO DIARY: Uncensored streams of autobiographical material captured with a webcam or camcorder.

SPY CAM: Webcam used for continuous surveillance of a remote location.

Certainly, you could do much the same with an inexpensive analog camcorder. But digital video technology extends the possibilities to include convenient archiving on DVDs and instant electronic distribution (if you dare) on the Web.

Another variation on the video diary has evolved from the not-so-glamorous tradition of the industrial security camera—as webcams have become remote peepholes onto everyday activities of dorm rooms and street corners. (A webcam used in this way as a presumably benign surveillance device is called a *spy cam* or just a *cam*.)

A third variation is *video chat*—two-way communication via Internet-linked webcams.

VIDEO CHAT: Two-way conferencing via linked webcams.

As video becomes an increasingly integral part of the Web, expect cams and video diaries to merge with *blogs,* or web logs. You can find good examples of blogs and cams at *www.leoville.com,* the personal website of TechTV personality Leo Laporte.

BLOG: A succession of daily web page postings, exchanges between a website operator (author of the blog) and other users with common interests; web log.

All these Web-based uses of digital video are examples of large-scale democratization. Not many years ago, before public access to the Internet, only large corporations could afford the private networks necessary to hold such global electronic exchanges and conferences.

If you're interested in experimenting with video diaries, bear some things in mind about the technologies involved. If you capture yourself with a webcam, you'll end up with the kind of compressed video used on the Web. It's far from broadcast quality—not that you'd want to bare your soul on national TV. But if you want higher quality, use a camcorder instead and capture to tape rather than to the hard drive of your computer.

However you capture your diary, you'll end up with hours and hours of it. The main practical use for it will be as an archive. Except for snippets you might email to friends, you probably won't want to invest the time required to edit much of it. Consider that a professional editor assigned to assemble a two-hour feature film probably starts with at least eight hours of good-quality material—and can take weeks just to cull the best *clips*. A video diary or spy cam could easily generate hundreds of hours of the stuff. And even you might not have the patience to sit through it all, much less try to assemble it into a more structured presentation.

> **CLIP:** Any short segment of recorded video.
>
> **PERFORMANCE ART:** One-person theatrical show, often confessional or intimate in nature.

But it's all good and all fodder for your imagination and creativity. And if you come to think your video diary experiments could have real audience appeal, you might step into—*performance art.*

Performance Video

Not all one-person shows rise to the level of performance art, but every actor and performance artist has a *sample reel* that he or she uses to apply for commercial roles. Shooting and editing those sample reels can be a steady source of income for professional videographers. With digital video making the process easier and more affordable, performers themselves (or friends of performers) can try their hands at building much-needed sample reels.

> **SAMPLE REEL:** Highlights of an actor's (or videographer's) work, typically a series of edited clips.

For example, there's a group of aspiring stand-up comics and musicians in Los Angeles who put on a show in a church basement every Friday night. They videotape their shows, providing a way to critique themselves while building a library of clips for their sample reels (Figure 1.1).

Ideally, performers will customize the content and length of their reels for each submission. With digital editing software on your desktop, and a library of performance clips on your hard drive, it's a snap to customize sample reels and make *one-off* copies to tape or disk. And as with home movies, the ability to integrate multimedia elements in the edit makes for better-looking, more professional samples.

> **ONE-OFF:** A single, custom-made video copy (called a dub of a tape or DVD) as opposed to multiple dubs made from a master tape or data file.

Not only are actors and other performers becoming more involved in creating their own sample reels, the quality of the results is improving. With digital editing, it's much more common to see these reels incorporate quick cuts, animated graphics, and other slick visual effects, as well as professional-looking titles. That's important, because busy casting directors have short attention spans (you've got no more than two minutes to grab them). So, another reason to get started is that many of your peers and competitors are already doing it.

Figure 1.1 Stand-up comedians at "Friday Night Live" in L.A. try new routines for their peers and tape the show, both to analyze their performances and to select the best clips for their sample reels.

Experimental Video

If fictional video is a short story and documentary video is an essay, experimental video is poetry. Video art may be the largest unexplored area in new digital media.

There's a Humanities Workshop in which students are required to shoot a one-minute video piece on any subject. Although most students filmed skits and pranks, one group shot multiple views of ink flowing through water. It sounds like a lame idea , but it was experimental, highly visual—and fascinating. The ink-flow movie illustrates how open-ended any definition of video art must be.

Increasingly, modern art museums are including video *installations* as part of their permanent collections. As digital editing makes it easier to combine live video sequences with *computer generated imagery (CGI)* and animation, video artists are beginning to realize the potential of the medium.

> **INSTALLATION:** A museum exhibit by a single artist that may include multimedia elements.
>
> **COMPUTER GENERATED IMAGERY (CGI):** Synthetic pictures, special effects, or animation produced by manipulating graphic objects (including previously captured digital pictures) in software.

How-To Demonstrations

One of the most popular, longest-selling titles in video stores is a show called *Dorf on Golf,* in which comedian Tim Conway demonstrates how *not* to play the game—step-by-step. Similar, if more serious, how-to demonstrations have been a mainstay of video production for years, aimed at commercial, educational, and corporate audiences. Increasingly, video tutorials and interactive multimedia are replacing printed user manuals. Well-produced videos can be a much more effective training tool than a book of diagrams with numbered circles and arrows.

Digital media (and editing) make it feasible for companies to produce video support materials themselves, without spending a fortune and having to raise the price of the product. For instance, you can easily include live product demonstrations, training exercises, and simulations—and then add digitally generated text overlays, on-screen highlighting of parts or controls, and animations to help simplify complexities of product operation.

News Coverage

Professional videographers and editors working in broadcast news were early adopters of digital video, dating from the introduction of the first digital videotape formats in the mid-1980s. If you're working in television news, you probably already have a lot of experience using digital technology.

However, you may not know about the latest, low-priced camcorders and editing software. These tools are aimed primarily at consumers and budget-conscious pros, but they are making inroads into the professional broadcast industry. TV networks are just as interested in saving time and money as consumers are. (For more information on some of the technical issues involved in using the popular DV format in broadcast applications, see "Color Space" in Chapter 3, and "What Is Color Space and Why Is It Important?" in Appendix A.)

For non-pros who are interested in covering the news, it's a brave new world. Schools, community groups, local governments, individuals, and organizations can use inexpensive digital tools to capture the events *they* consider significant, and portray them as they see fit.

Until recently, alternatives to broadcast newsgathering were limited to public-access television. Unfortunately, in many parts of the country public-access stations reach few people and use production resources limited to ancient analog video gear. Now, with the

Web, public access is a whole new ballgame. You can easily reach audiences across the street and around the globe. The means of capturing a breaking news story can now be hidden in a pocket or purse. In fact, we live at a time when people interested in capturing current events often carry compact camcorders in the glove compartments of their automobiles. And to make sure the police have their own records, many squad cars are now routinely equipped with videocams that roll automatically whenever the officers make a traffic stop.

The events of 9/11/01 may be the most documented in history—simply because so many professional and amateur videographers were at the scene, most of them using digital video equipment. The news can now be in the hands of the people, and we are only beginning to see the impact video democracy will have on public discourse and debate.

DV in Professional News Gathering

Most videographers and editors in the broadcast world already have several years' experience with one of two video formats: Betacam SP (high-quality analog) or DigiBeta (Digital Betacam). Unfortunately, the high prices of these camcorders and editing systems put them beyond the reach of most individuals.

Some—though certainly not all—of the new DV camcorders and editing systems rival these high-end systems in quality, at a fraction of their cost.

DV camcorders should be particularly attractive to news crews because they are remarkably compact, relatively lightweight, and portable. And desktop DV editing systems now make it possible to edit a news segment on your laptop as you're flying home from a shoot.

Nonetheless, many broadcast engineering departments are still suspicious of DV. They seem unaware that DV encompasses two different sets of technical standards—one for consumers and the other for professionals. Consumer DV recordings aren't suitable for broadcast (at least without a conversion step). But professional-spec DV gear is just as light and portable, and does produce broadcast quality output.

For the technically minded, the problem with consumer DV is that it does not record broadcast-spec color space (it does 4:1:1 instead of 4:2:2); it permits the timing of audio tracks to drift as much as one-third of a frame; and it uses timecode spec that isn't up to studio standards. (For more information on how these specs will affect your selection of camcorders, see "Consumer vs. Professional DV" in Chapter 3.)

Marketplace confusion doesn't help. While some DV camcorders are truly professional in specs and output quality, other comparably priced models adhere to the non-professional consumer spec. You have to look closely at the data sheets of these camcorders to spot the differences.

Bottom line: If you make some informed gear choices, you can shoot and edit broadcast-quality video with lightweight, modestly priced, professional DV tools.

Interviews

Interviews are typically unrehearsed encounters with newsworthy people. Generally (but not always) based on a question-and-answer format, their purpose is to draw out information on a topic the audience is curious about.

Shooting an interview can be a great last-minute, last-resort option for just about any informational purpose when you've run out of time and need to get something *in the can*. Production planning, lighting, and sound recording are relatively simple if you're just shooting one interview subject. You don't even need a script, just a list of questions.

> **IN THE CAN:** Successfully capturing a desired shot; cinematographer's term for a completed take.

As with other types of shooting styles already mentioned, DV makes it easy to add supporting visuals to make an interview more interesting. Clip libraries, multimedia sources, and graphics can make the difference between a presentation viewers will watch and one they'll turn off.

 *Look at short interviews with movie industry experts—editor Michael Alberts and sound technician Steve Weiss (**Figure 1.2**). Both men worked with co-author Pete Shaner on the first 24P hi-def feature film, Nicolas, and have extensive experience in digital formats.*

Figure 1.2 In his on-camera interview, sound technician Steve Weiss tells how to capture professional-quality sound on the set and advises how to match different types of microphones to the job. The interview is a good example of how you might shoot an expert without an on-camera narrator or resorting to the person simply reading a speech.

Corporate Videos

Far more professional moviemakers are gainfully employed producing corporate video, or industrial film, than working on blockbuster movies in Hollywood.

Videotaped product demonstrations can be effective sales tools for media-savvy businesses. Corporate videos also include how-to sales training, investor relations and institutional fund-raising, visual support for annual meetings, taped speeches by company officers, and employee orientation. And increasingly, brochures and policy manuals are out—while videos and multimedia Web sites are in.

Use of digital media archives, video clips, and other multimedia elements will become increasingly commonplace as corporate videomakers assemble custom video presentations quickly for specific purposes, clients, or events.

> **HD (HIGH DEFINITION):** High-resolution digital video producing a wide-screen (16:9) display with resolution at least four times that of conventional video. Also called hi-def.

If you're a professional corporate film- or videomaker, and you're not already up to speed on digital video, you probably have considerable experience in film, analog video, or one of the older digital formats. Much of that knowledge will be directly translatable. And learning to use DV and *HD* technology will not only enhance your career, it may be the best way to ensure that you keep working as these formats take over the business.

If you're a businessperson, or work at a business that could use video support, now is the best time to take up the new digital tools.

DV in the Business World

Not so many years ago, video production was so expensive and so technical that you had to hire pros to do it. That's still a very wise choice, especially when your corporate image will be judged by the quality of the results. But in that bygone era, only CEOs and top-level sales managers could command the many thousands of dollars it cost to create and distribute a video message.

Digital video will cause a proliferation of on-camera interviews in the corporate world with CEOs, marketing directors, and all manner of businesspeople now that DV makes it so inexpensive to capture them on tape.

Managers and professionals at all levels will try it—because it's affordable and they *have the tools to do it themselves.* If you've grown tired of receiving e-mail with Microsoft PowerPoint attachments, for example, wait; more stuff is coming your way. As network bandwidth becomes greater and cheaper, these attachments will increasingly contain video clips.

So let this be an appeal to your sense of corporate survival: *You want to know this stuff.* If you have the budget to hire pros, you'll be able to supervise them better. If you have no choice but to do it yourself, at least the results won't be an embarrassment.

Working with Clients

When you're creating a presentation for a paying customer, digital video has some real benefits. Previewing results on the set is easier than with film, with no great cost or delays. Also, shooting several versions is nowhere near as expensive as it once was. If a client joins you on the set and wants to see it done another way, there's no cost premium. Let the tape roll. Do one for him, one for your boss, one for you—then pick the best one in the edit. And making changes at that late stage will be easier, too.

Working with Outside Producers and Vendors

Corporate video does not have to be amateur video. It's not the equivalent of home movies in the workplace. Or, it shouldn't be. Standards of quality in the business world are very high—as high or in some cases higher than in Hollywood. That's because a company's sales and reputation are on the line. The fact that there will be more peer-level video communication—much of it, no doubt, hastily produced and poor in quality—doesn't mean that overall standards of quality will get lower. Particularly when communication involves the public—consumers and shareholders—only the best will do.

If you find yourself charged with the responsibility of producing a high-visibility product and your primary job description isn't video production, think seriously about finding the money to hire professionals. At the very least, reading this book should help you judge when it's absolutely essential to seek some expert help.

Commercials

Since broadcast television and some cable channels rely on commercials, you might expect that digital video would be having a major impact in this area. Well, think again. Commercials still represent the highest cost-per-minute of any type of film or video project, including big-budget movies and network TV shows. Maybe that's why most major advertisers still want their spots shot on film—even though digital video can rival film in quality (especially on the small screen). In the grand scheme of things, saving money and time are relatively low priorities for big-money advertising clients. Apparently their perception is that film provides the highest-quality look. Eventually, that perception will fade, especially as the general public becomes more exposed to high-definition digital imagery—

and as tools for making video look like film become more powerful. (For more information on the hi-def format, see "HD" in Appendix A.)

One reason some major broadcasters mistakenly perceive DV as a substandard medium is that not all DV meets broadcast quality standards. This isn't necessarily a barrier to producing fine-looking commercials on DV. If you're aware of the technical issues when you shoot and when you convert your DV master to meet broadcast specs, you'll be fine. (For more information, see "Releasing on Television" in Chapter 12.)

For now, the low-cost DV format is mainly used by local cable advertisers and for *public-service announcements (PSAs)*. Thanks to DV, these spots look much better than low-budget ads done in analog video (as to color and sharpness, in particular). And as production expenses come down, more local businesses are considering advertising on television. Whether you own one of those companies and want to set up an in-house production team, or you're a videographer looking for a market, DV opens exciting possibilities.

> **PSA (PUBLIC-SERVICE ANNOUNCEMENT):** Informational television spot presented on behalf of a government agency, charity, or nonprofit organization.

Documentaries

A documentary is a fact-based journalistic program—usually without actors or scripted dialogue—intended to inform, persuade, or entertain. Its structure or story can be imposed before shooting or might be discovered afterwards, during editing. If you have an agenda, political or otherwise, or if you simply want to try building a story in the editing room, the documentary form will excite and challenge you.

Shorts

In bygone days, movie exhibitors showed short subjects—fiction films, documentaries, or "art films" that ran from 10 to 20 minutes—between double-feature presentations to give the audience time to visit the restroom and snack bar. Nowadays, trailers and coming attractions serve that purpose. Since exhibitors prefer to maximize revenues by showing a feature attraction as many times as possible, shorts have all but disappeared in most commercial venues.

Happily though, the format isn't dead. Some film festivals, and the Academy Awards®, still have special categories for short subjects, and even a few festivals are dedicated exclusively to shorts. Moreover, some distributors package collections of new shorts and show them at independent theaters around the country.

Shorts are ideal opportunities for students and experimental filmmakers to produce small-scale movies. They provide a great way to practice and experiment with your craft, and possibly attract attention—as long as you understand that you probably won't make any money. (Some media pundits feel that Internet sites such as atomfilms.com will revive the demand for short subjects. Time will tell.)

Some of these genres overlap. For example, news stories, corporate videos, and documentaries can all follow an interview format.

In a sense, a news story is a documentary. However, the audience assumes that a news story presents actual events as they unfolded—edited for length, perhaps, but structured more or less chronologically. Documentaries don't necessarily follow that rule. Like news stories, they capitalize on the immediacy of the image. That's one reason video documentaries can be so effective as a means not only of reporting but also of persuasion. Historically some documentaries have been powerful tools of propaganda: The audience believes it is watching unrehearsed events as they unfold, and they may think they are drawing their own conclusions. In reality, the moviemaker chooses which events to show, arranges them in a sequence to support a particular point of view, and may even add a reinforcing commentary. The audience draws its own conclusions, but the moviemaker has stacked the deck.

Most documentaries are shot and edited on low budgets, which makes them ideal candidates for DV production. In fact, professional documentarians have been among the first adopters of digital video, partly for economic reasons and partly because of the ease with which lightweight camcorders can be deployed in the field and operated with a minimal crew. Also, the time savings of digital *nonlinear editing (NLE)* supports this style of work, which relies so heavily on discovering and building a story in the edit.

> **NLE:** Non-linear editing (digital editing, as in Final Cut Pro, Avid, and so on).

 Ten Ways to Shoot a Chair, *a brief demonstration of visual composition and camerawork, takes an instructional documentary approach: The audience has a sense of being guided by a skilled teacher as he explains visual possibilities. Capturing events as though they are unrehearsed (whether or not they actually are) can give your show an immediacy and excitement that's difficult if not impossible to capture any other way. The French call it* cinema verité, *meaning "filmed truth."*

In the history of cinema, feature-length documentaries only occasionally become commercial successes in theatrical distribution. Right now we may be in the midst of one of the great documentary resurgences of all time. Michael Moore's 2002 release, *Bowling for Columbine*, achieved critical acclaim and had a long, profitable run in movie theaters. Interestingly, the members of the Writers Guild of America gave it a "Best Original Screenplay" award, significant recognition for a movie that was largely "written" in the editing room. Soon afterward, *Winged Migration,* a documentary about wild birds, had a major commercial run, as did *Spellbound* and *Capturing the Friedmans.*

Before these successes, reality TV, or nonfiction television, came into its own, with highly rated shows like *Survivor* and *Big Brother.* These are "documentaries" presented in weekly

LOCATION: A physical place where you plan to shoot, such as a park, an office building, or your own living room.

serial format. Networks are eager to experiment with this form because *location* production saves on costs of developing formal scripts, building elaborate sets, and hiring professional actors. Audiences tuned in, perhaps because they saw the plot formulas of sitcoms and dramatic series growing stale.

Although the reality TV fad has waned somewhat, the genre is probably here to stay—along with other nonfiction staples such as game shows and talk shows.

If you're not an industry pro but are nonetheless an avid fan of reality TV, you probably know more than you think you do about producing effective documentaries.

Fiction Movies

Fiction, or narrative movies tell stories—and storytelling is probably the oldest use of moviemaking. Aside from some experimental, low-budget pieces, video hasn't been used to produce theatrical movies until quite recently. Even most made-for-TV movies are still shot on film. The television shows that are increasingly being produced in HD are sitcoms, longform (hour-long) dramas, and soaps. However, this is changing fast. The first feature-length fiction movie to be shot entirely in the DV format, Thomas Vinterberg's *The Celebration,* premiered in 1998, followed by Lars Von Trier's *Dancer in the Dark* (2000) and *Anniversary Party* (2001), written by, co-directed by, and starring Alan Cumming and Jennifer Jason Leigh. George Lucas' widely publicized *Star Wars: Episode II—Attack of the Clones,* shot entirely with HD digital cameras, opened in 2002. Soon afterward, writer-director Robert Rodriguez, renowned for breaking into the business with the ultra-low budget 16mm feature *El Mariachi*, shot *Spy Kids 2: Island of Lost Dreams* on HD. The live actors in the next movie in the series, *Spy Kids 3-D: Game Over,* were shot in HD and then combined digitally with CGI to create its fantasy-world in three-dimensions.

For our take on the process of creating a story, see "What's *Your* Story?" in Chapter 2. Shooting a digital feature is far less expensive than using film (you save on film and processing costs, and the cameras are cheaper to buy or rent), but that's not the only reason fiction filmmakers are looking more closely at digital moviemaking. Thanks to new camera features and post-processing software, it's becoming almost impossible for audiences to tell whether a movie originated on film or video—a key factor in getting audiences (and distributors) to regard digital features as professional and commercial. (For more information on post-processing digital video to look like film, see "Post Processing Filters" in Chapter 11.)

Story, Story, Story

Real estate moguls preach that the three fundamentals of property value are location, location, and location. In movies—indeed, in all types of video presentation—it's all about story.

If your movie fails at the box office, it will be because its story didn't grab the audience. No amount of technical virtuosity can save a bad or unappealing story, and nothing short of an inaudible dialogue track can completely kill a good one.

Case in point: The DV feature Tadpole *caused something of a stir in movie industry circles. It played to enthusiastic audiences at the Sundance Film Festival, but on release it didn't perform well at the box office. Some observers interpreted this result to mean that audiences found the DV product somehow substandard. The reason may have been more fundamental. The central story of the film was a potentially incestuous relationship between a boy and his stepmother—a topic that might have intrigued a jaded festival audience but simply didn't play in Peoria. Although it was well acted and not badly shot (given its low budget), it wasn't a story a general audience was willing to pay to see.* Tadpole *is now available on DVD, so take it home and judge for yourself. (Don't miss playing the director's commentary to hear Gary Winnick talk about his challenges shooting low-budget DV in New York City.)*

It's not just your choice of subject that determines whether the story will be appealing. Screenwriting instructors often quote writer-producer Stephen J. Cannell as saying that a good story poorly told sounds like a bad story. Storytelling skill, the craft of spinning a yarn, is at the core of making good movies. True, you can assemble some seemingly unrelated clips in the editing room to make a documentary—but that process of selection and sequencing must result in a story line—or it will be a waste of time to watch.

While we're at it, let's not let the videographers who are working in other genres off the hook. Even a corporate video must tell a story that conveys some crucial business message.

Perhaps the most important question as you plan your new production is: What action do I want the audience to take? What do I want them to feel—empathy for my suffering hero? The thrill of overcoming impossible odds? What do I want them to do—buy my product? Invest in my company? Vote for my candidate?

If you don't know the answer you may not have a story to tell. Without a story, you don't have a compelling reason to communicate, and there's no point spending the time and expense producing a video. Granted, like the proverbial tormented artist, you might have a story locked inside you somewhere—and it might take the arduous process of actually writing the script or editing the documentary to bring it out. That's a difficult way to find your story. If you must do it that way at least keep at it until you have the best story possible.

 A fiction short, When Harried Met Sally, *tells the story of office worker Josh, who struggles to finish a last-minute report in time to satisfy a demanding client—and keep a date with his fiancée to celebrate their anniversary. Like our* Ten Ways *short, this video was post-processed for a film look.*

BASIC VIDEO SHOOTING STYLES: NEWS OR FILM

No matter what kind of digital video project you're planning, early on you'll have to choose between two very different styles of shooting, each representing a unique set of challenges for you as a videomaker. This decision will affect everything else you do. Your choices are:

- News style: no script, no crew, run and gun.

- Film style: script, crew, take your time and get it right.

SCENE: Basic unit of visual storytelling that advances the plot or imparts useful information to the audience.

GUERILLA FILMMAKING: Shooting with one camera and a minimal budget and crew, typically done outside the movie studio system by independent producers who want to tell unconventional stories; film-style shooting done as if by a news crew.

This is not about how you stage your *scenes,* nor how they look, nor about the form or purpose of your presentation. It's how you gear up and shoot.

It's not unheard of to shoot a feature in news style or to use film style to shoot a news clip—it's just unusual. In fact, there's a cult term for shooting an entire feature using run-and-gun news style—*guerilla filmmaking*

In one sense, your choice of shooting style will be a matter of aesthetics, based on the look you want. On another level, it comes down to schedule (deadline pressure) and budget (how big a crew you can afford to put in the field).

For now, we're going to focus on shooting both news and film styles with a single camera or camcorder. This is by far the most common technique. There's nothing to stop you from shooting either style with multiple cameras, but usually the only places you'll see multiple cameras in use are broadcast television studios, and during live coverage of sporting events. It's also standard operating procedure for professional videographers shooting weddings and live performances.

> **TIP:** *The basic rationale for using multiple cameras is to capture an unrepeatable event from different angles so that you can choose different shots during live broadcasting or in the editing suite. Some makers of low-budget DV movies have used multiple camcorders for similar reasons—to save time and budget by getting several angles on the subject at once. But for impressive Hollywood-style results, a scene should be lit so that only one of the angles looks just right.*

Shooting News Style

Often called ENG for "electronic news gathering," single-camera news style is the most straightforward way to go after a story (**Figure 1.3**). Veteran news people call this style "run and gun." The term conjures the image of a videomaker-as-soldier-of-fortune—camcorder operator and sound-and-lighting crew, all in one. Obviously, you can use this shooting style for almost every type of project, not just news.

At its simplest, shooting news style is a lot like making home movies: point, shoot, and hope for the best.

The main challenge in shooting news style is simply to get the shot—to follow the action and get it on tape, pretty or not. The biggest disappointment for news-style videographers is *not* a shot that's poorly lit or incorrectly exposed—it's a shot they miss entirely, knowing it will never come again (something of a show-stopper if your assignment is capturing a news event). If you're actually shooting for the evening news (as opposed to shooting an interview, say, in news style), you have the additional pressure of having to edit your segment in time to meet a broadcast deadline.

Figure 1.3 In the simplest kind of news-style videography, the camcorder operator is a one-person crew and must monitor sound (through the headphones), watch lighting, and adjust focus and other camcorder controls.

TIP: *Although beginners will be tempted to turn on all the camcorder's automatic controls under the pressure of shooting news style, the pros know better. Automatic camcorder controls such as auto-focus, auto-exposure, automatic white balance, and automatic audio gain control will impose technical and aesthetic choices on you that will be difficult, if not impossible, to correct in* post. *(For more information on how to control your camcorder in fast-paced situations, see "News Style" in Chapter 3.)*

POST: Slang for "post production."

Shooting Film Style

Digital video technology encourages news-style shooting: The new camcorders are so light and inexpensive that you can take them almost anywhere, any time, without much planning. But no matter what kind of project you're shooting, you'll be able to improve its technical quality if you're willing to incorporate some film-style techniques.

The main objective of shooting film style is to control the situation as much as possible (**Figure 1.4**). That's why film-style shoots (all fiction films, and even many documentaries) generally use scripts of one kind or another and employ a crew to handle sound and lighting. Working from a script, *storyboard*, or shot list, you can precisely plan the placement of camera and lights. (Not least important, having a good script and shot plan will also help you decide what gear to take with you in the first place.)

STORYBOARD: A series of hand-drawn illustrations of the director's intended shots, based on his or her visual interpretation of the script.

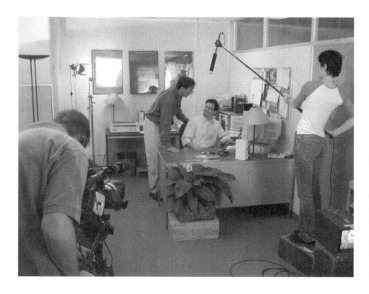

Figure 1.4 Shooting film style generally requires a script, or at least a list of planned camera setups. Each setup will require a specific complement of lighting and sound equipment, as well as crewmembers to place, rig, and operate it.

Would using multiple cameras help? Well, sometimes—especially if a stunt or special effect is so complex, destructive, or expensive it can only be performed once. But most filmmakers and videographers prefer a single camera for artistic reasons.

As cinema art evolved, filmmakers (and especially *cinematographers*) began thinking in terms of "painting with light," creating an evocative lighting design for each camera *setup* to create exactly the desired mood.

Using light to create highlights unique to each scene isn't a purely aesthetic exercise, either. It has a crucial storytelling function—*controlling the light can show the audience where to look.*

It also stands to reason that you shouldn't plan on shooting film style unless you can afford the required lighting and sound equipment and a crew to operate it.

> **CINEMATOGRAPHER:** The crewmember primarily responsible for both the technical and artistic aspects of lighting and photography or videography; sometimes called the *director of photography (DP)*, even if the production is video.
>
> **SETUP:** Camera placement within a particular setting and scene.

 REALITY CHECK: *One of the reasons video gets a bad rap from the art police is that many videographers don't take the time to light their scenes properly. Cheap tape and camcorders with low-light sensitivity can make you lazy about lighting. If you want your video to look as impressive as film, you have to light it like film. For more information on lighting video for a professional look, see "Lighting Techniques" in Chapter 6.*

Put simply, film-style shooting delivers a higher-quality product, but it takes time (and lots of it).

What's Your Role?

Unless you're a lone ranger, run-and-gun videographer, the answer to this question is neither easy nor obvious. The more complex your production, the less likely it will be that you can do everything yourself. Moreover, it's nearly impossible for any one person to pay attention to everything that's going on during a *take*.

> **TAKE:** Each recorded attempt to capture a shot.

If you're planning your first video project, it's neither practical nor wise to plan on doing it all by yourself. If you're primarily interested in storytelling, perhaps your role should be writer-director. If it's mainly the technical side of videography that appeals to you, go ahead and operate the camcorder—and hire a producer, an editor, and/or a theatrical director to watch your back. If they're looking for their first digital video experience, they may be willing to work for free, or at least for deferred payment.

All but the lowest-budget productions employ a small army of people with specialized jobs, including art director (with art department in tow), location manager, wardrobe supervisor, sound technicians, makeup and hair stylists, caterers, transportation crew, and many, many more. Still, you have to choose which hat you want to wear, so here are the most obvious choices.

Producer

Perhaps the best definition of a producer is someone who makes things happen. Generally, a producer hires people and equipment to get a project made. But in the realm of feature films, a producer can also be an investor; the person who owns the rights to the story; a businessperson employed by, or affiliated with, the studio; or the star's personal manager. (There's an organization called The Producers Guild of America that advocates a stricter definition for the role of producer, specifically the *line producer*, a professional contractor for media services.)

LINE PRODUCER: A movie professional who develops, or supervises development of, schedules and budgets, then contracts for crew, equipment, supporting actors, extras, and post production services.

If you're the primary mover and shaker on your project, by default you're its producer. You're the one who must worry about expenses and legal obligations. You also get to take credit for its success or failure—in the marketplace or the critics' corner. You might as well take the title, too.

Director

In the world of features, a director concentrates much of his or her energy on actors' performances and is largely responsible for how the story is told.

However, in practical terms a director's role is much broader. Crew, actors, and production staff all look to the director for the last word on any detail, creative or logistic: Do you like her hair? Is this lighting effect what you're after? What about his performance on the last take? Is this fabric okay? Do you want to try to get in one more setup before the sun goes down?

A director isn't necessarily a hands-on expert in any of these areas, but ultimately he or she is still expected to have an opinion—the deciding one—on what other skilled people do. If you're responsible for making the ultimate creative decisions on your digital video production, whether you're working news style or film style, you're a director.

Videographer / Cinematographer

Then again you may aspire to be a videographer or camcorder operator. On a Hollywood set, the cinematographer gets the final word on lighting and supervises several other people who actually operate, focus, and move the camera. (The professional society in the U.S.

for cinematographers is the American Society of Cinematographers, ASC.) The cinematographer is ultimately responsible for the images on film or tape. Robert Rodriguez was both director and camera operator on *El Mariachi* and felt strongly that this style of shooting enhanced the artistic and commercial success of the 1992 movie. (It also kept the shooting budget around $7,000—-astonishingly low, especially for a *filmed* production.)

 REALITY CHECK: *In his case-study book* Rebel without a Crew, *Rodriguez admits that the studio spent hundreds of thousands more repairing and enhancing his soundtrack before releasing the movie to theaters.*

Some low-budget directors take up the camcorder simply because they can't afford to hire help. Others aren't prepared to delegate the critical responsibility for capturing images to anyone else. Ace cinematographer Laszlo Kovacs once said that letting someone else operate his camera felt like playing the piano by telling someone which keys to press over the telephone.

If you take responsibility for the way the scene is lit and composed, then you're a cinematographer/videographer.

Editor

After the shooting is done, an editor will piece together the shots captured during production. Most movies are made, and most stories finally begin to work, in the editing suite. This is a hugely important, creative, detail-oriented job, and someone other than the director often does it.

 REALITY CHECK: *There's adventure and economy in doing it all yourself, but writers can learn from directors and both can learn from editors. Especially on an ambitious project, a skilled creative partner can be your—dare we say it?—reality check.*

How Long Will It Take?

Here's the basic rule of thumb: Plan on shooting between four and eight script pages per day—if you can get your script into standard screenplay format. (See "Script Elements and Formats" in Chapter 2.)

Even though screenplay format was created for features, there's nothing to prevent you from adapting it for any type of scripted movie or video presentation, including how-to demonstrations, corporate videos, documentaries, and interviews. You can even script a home movie or performance art project if you like. It might seem like more trouble than it's worth, but once you have even a rough script, you can use it to estimate a shooting schedule for these projects.

Shooting four to eight script pages a day can be tricky, depending on the complexity of your script or shooting requirements. Your project may go significantly over schedule if your script requires:

- An unusually large number of locations

- An unusually large number of camera setups

- Complex lighting

- Complex sound rigging

- An unusually large cast and/or crew

- Complicated physical action (stunts, demonstrations, moving vehicles, aircraft, machinery, and so on)

- Multiple cameras

- Shots involving destruction or damage of props, wardrobe, or sets (requiring replacement or repair before the next take)

- Nonprofessional actors or on-camera subjects

- Inexperienced crew

- Unrehearsed or spontaneous action

Studio film productions generally allow anywhere from six weeks to several months for shooting a feature-length movie. That's long for a digital video production. Low-budget DV (or HD) features typically adhere to one of two schedules: two consecutive seven-day weeks (14 shooting days) without a break, or three six-day weeks (18 shooting days) with two days off. Of course, some films come in under that deadline, and others will need more time.

 REALITY CHECK: *Working with no days off, or only one day off a week, can be a mind-numbing grind that eventually shows up in poorly done footage. Avoid this if at all possible. The crew and cast will appreciate it, and will work harder because they're rested.*

Ultimately, scheduling is a complex, time-consuming process—one that's difficult to approach without considerable experience.

We won't offer many specifics on pre-production planning or scheduling until you reach Chapter 8—by which time you'll have a better grounding in digital video equipment and techniques. Even if you're a pro and think you already know how to do scheduling from your experience with film or analog video, take a look at the intervening chapters first. Digital video technology may change some of your assumptions.

Scheduling Postproduction

Tough as it is, estimating the number of shooting days is relatively straightforward compared with estimating editing and post production time. The schedule for this phase of production will depend on the skill of your editor, the quality of video you shot, and the degree of sophistication you seek in cutting, special effects, and soundtrack. (For more information, see "No Need for Perfection" in Chapter 10.)

Editing and finishing a feature in digital video will take you at least several months. A documentary feature may take longer, especially if you're building its story and structure during the edit.

Other kinds of scripted projects will follow comparable schedules, based more or less on length. A ten-minute fiction short will require at least a couple of weeks to edit—longer if you do it yourself and if it's your first experience with the software.

Obviously, news stories won't follow these guidelines because the very nature of breaking news imposes strict limits on the length of time you have for postproduction. If you're working under really short deadlines (for instance, if you're trying to shoot and edit a segment in a single afternoon) you'll be limited by the time it takes to upload your video recordings from the camcorder into the editing system. In the DV format, upload time can range from 1:1 (that is, one hour of transfer time per one hour of program) to 4:1 (15 minutes of transfer time per one hour of program) with more expensive, high-performance gear.

Experimental videos are, well, experimental and don't follow any rules, in postproduction or any other time.

Postproduction and editing on commercials can be quite time-consuming—largely because commercials often require complicated special effects for maximum impact.

What Will It Cost?

As is true for scheduling (and for all the same reasons), you'll have to wait until Chapter 8 for most of the specifics on budgeting. However, the overview is fairly straightforward: Your budget is the cost per day of the resources you need (people and equipment) multiplied by the number of days you will need them. And it's just as true whether you're shooting or in post.

Two decisions will have a major impact on your budget:

- Cast and crew: professionals or pals?

- Equipment: rent or buy?

Cast and Crew

If you have the funds to hire professionals, this part of the budgeting process is fairly straightforward. And obviously, using pros will make your project go faster and easier.

If you're working on a low- or no-budget project, you will have to entice friends, relatives, or aspiring professionals to work in front of the camera, and behind it, for something other than money.

 REALITY CHECK: *Experienced directors from Clint Eastwood to Anthony Minghella keep working with the same crew (and often, the same cast) simply because they have built relationships which work. The heat of production tends to solidify deep personal bonds. The long-term result is good chemistry, shorthand communications, and fun. Production is hard enough without having to work with people you can't stand.*

It's better, and more professional, to hire actors on the basis of deferred pay than to ask them to work for free. Deferred payments to the actors can become due if and when you place the movie in commercial distribution and receive some money. Unfortunately for the low-budget moviemaker, crewmembers don't generally work this way. (They are not in the game for fame.)

Equipment

For budgeting purposes, you must decide whether it makes more sense to rent or buy your production and postproduction gear: digital camcorder, lighting and sound equipment, and desktop editing systems.

In the professional digital video environment, it's far more common to rent high-quality production gear and expense it to the project than to buy it outright. The exceptions to this rule are network news organizations and independent producers who shoot continually and can afford to maintain an in-house equipment pool because it's constantly in use.

For most videomakers, especially those who are working on restricted budgets, renting makes more sense than buying. For one thing, you can generally afford to rent better equipment than you can buy. Another reason to rent is that it guarantees you'll get the most modern equipment.

 REALITY CHECK: *Yes, it's generally cheaper to rent, but always do the math: Depending on the purchase price of a camcorder or editing computer and the length of time you need to keep it, you might be dollars ahead buying it at the beginning of production and reselling it just as soon as you're done.*

The same holds true for postproduction. You can buy a good desktop editing system for between $2,000 and $5,000, provided you, or someone on your project, have the requisite editing skills or are prepared to acquire them. However, it may be more cost-effective to hire the services of an editor and/or editing suite. A professional editor with his or her own editing system may cost as little as $100 per hour—or as much as $500 per hour if you want expertise, artistic judgment, high-end equipment, and speed of execution. If you're on a low- or no-budget shoot, you can probably hire an apprentice-level editor, with his own desktop editing system, for as little as $50 per hour.

> **TIP:** On longer projects, it's customary to negotiate a weekly rate of between $1,500 and $4,000 as a package price for a professional editor and system.

The Bottom Line

There are so many variables (running time, project type, production values, cast and crew size) that it's almost pointless to try and generalize about budgeting.

As noted in this book's introduction, you can buy all the equipment you need—camcorder, lighting and sound equipment, and desktop editing system—for under $10,000. However, the total cost of a production will include significant labor expenses—including cast, crew, and postproduction personnel. That's why low-budget videomakers look for alternatives to paying people out-of-pocket.

For instance, take one of the most common projects, a feature. It's possible to produce a perfectly professional, low-budget DV feature for less than $50,000 if you defer cast and crew salaries. However, if you pay union wages, expect that figure to be much higher. Union feature productions start at about $1 million. See Chapter 8 for a more detailed breakdown of budgeting issues—but read the intervening chapters first.

FINDING THE MONEY

Everything we've talked about so far takes money – and we're not even into the pricey stuff yet. The road you're on has two forks: either someone else pays the bills, or you fund this trip yourself. If it's the first fork, you're home free; all you have to worry about is staying on budget and being clever enough to do what you want without the money people calling the shots. (If it's a corporate video, that's different; the client is always right.) If you're on the other road, having to find the money yourself, then you have another big challenge on your hands. You can do it. Like everything else in this business, it just takes passion and perseverance. Whether the money comes from foundation grants, distribution pre-sales, rich relatives, or your boyfriend's credit cards, there are two things you must have: a realistic budget and the irrepressible desire to "sell" your project to people with resources. In the Reference section at the end of the book we've listed books and web links that can help you master the fundraising game.

EXPERIMENTING WITH DIGITAL VIDEO

When directors such as Sergei Eisenstein and D. W. Griffith were making some of the first silent features at the beginning of the last century, there were few precedents for how to tell a story with moving pictures. There was no vocabulary of cinema, no language for on-screen storytelling. Concepts such as montage, flashback, crosscutting, fantasy sequence, and dissolve had yet to be discovered. These filmmakers defined those techniques, and more.

The medium of digital video has inherited that vocabulary, but it's also a unique technology, an artistic and informational medium all its own. We don't yet know the full extent of what the combination of digital video cameras and computers will achieve, but we expect there are many new techniques and lots of moviemaking language yet to be invented. Digital postproduction has already contributed novel effects like *morphing*, *ramping*, *pixellation*, and *fractals*.

MORPHING: Visual transformation in which the shape of one object seems to blend continuously into the shape of another.

RAMPING: Smoothly changing the playback speed of a clip; for instance, from normal speed to slow motion to fast motion and back again.

PIXELLATION: Enlargement and exaggeration of the individual picture elements, or pixels, that make up a digital image for a block-picture effect.

FRACTALS: Mathematical formulas used in CGI systems to create effects like synthetic fog, clouds, trees, and mountains.

Experimenting with digital video is irresistible, possibly because there's no longer such a brutal cost. Director Lars von Trier reportedly used 100 DV-format camcorders running at the same time to shoot sequences for his 2000 feature *Dancer in the Dark*. Affordable DV technology allowed him to try something that would have been unthinkable on a film budget.

Wim Wenders reportedly said that the inexpensive DV tape medium made it possible for him to shoot a *thousand times* more footage for *Buena Vista Social Club* than he needed, giving him the luxury of having that many more choices in the editing room. (Of course it can also be a headache to deal with all that footage! Every pleasure has a price.)

Steven Soderbergh chose to shoot hand-held DV for parts of *Full Frontal* because he felt that the lightweight camcorder would make it possible for him to work more closely with the actors as he followed them around the set. (He also had the digital footage post-processed heavily to achieve a garish, electronic look that contrasted sharply with filmed segments.)

For these experienced feature filmmakers, digital video offered a way to tell their stories and experiment in a new medium on modest budgets. We don't expect to see all movie production suddenly become dirt-cheap; after all, stars' salaries are going up, not down. But if you're willing to do without big-ticket items such as mega-stars, lavish sets, and complicated special effects, you no longer need to convince a studio to invest millions of dollars before you can make your film.

Certainly, the marketplace will continue to rule. An explosion of cheap, digital video fare will probably result in too much product chasing too few distribution channels. What else is new? But someday very soon, near-global digital distribution may change that picture, too.

Manipulating Digital Imagery

One of the truly breathtaking developments of the digital revolution is the ease with which you can create visions that are downright unreal. And you don't need to be a trained artist. Even today's garden-variety desktop computers are fast enough to manipulate video imagery without special-purpose hardware. And the software is getting increasingly sophisticated, with lots of built-in technical wizardry that you can apply at a stroke.

What a stimulus to the imagination!

> **COMPOSITING:** Combining two or more video images to create a new image.

There are two basic types of video manipulation: The first type, transformation, changes some characteristics of a camera-captured image. Pixellation, decomposing the picture into colored blocks, would be an example. The second type, *compositing*, combines two images to form a third. Superimposing a live actor on a fantasy background is an example of compositing (**Figure 1.5**). Supering titles over any other image, usually a less spectacular but much-needed effect, is another example.

A third category of wizardry doesn't involve manipulation but can also achieve convincing unreality—synthetic imagery, the end product of CGI. Synthetic images are pictures generated mathematically from geometric shapes; pictures that never passed through a camera.

Figure 1.5 One of the main uses of postproduction software beyond assembly of clips in story sequence is to combine images in a process called *compositing*. Here the image of a live actor has been combined with a fantasy background to put her—and the viewers—in a place they've never been. Putting live actors on synthetic backgrounds reduces set construction costs. It also takes creativity beyond the physical world.

And there's nothing to prevent your using these techniques in any combination.

In fact, in the digital video software business these days, integration is the name of the game—all with the goal of making it easier to use different software tools and effects in combination. For example, one of the mainstay programs for doing transformations and compositing is Adobe After Effects. Complex, sophisticated "canned" effects created by computer artists are available within the After Effects programs as menu selections (**Figure 1.6**). For example, the motion effect Wiggler can cause individual letters in a title to jiggle and dance. It took an experienced animator a considerable amount of time to create the effect, but now that it's available as a tool in After Effects, anyone can apply it to any title frame with a few mouse clicks.

It's also a trend for software manufacturers to offer suites of related programs that work seamlessly with one another. For example, Adobe has its Video Collection suite, including After Effects for compositing and titling, Premiere for editing, Encore DVD for authoring, and Audition for sound editing. (An enhanced version of After Effects, as well as Photoshop for manipulating still imagery, are included in a Professional version of this suite.) Not only are these applications packaged and sold together, they are also designed to be used in tight coordination, permitting you to switch easily among different tasks without perceiving that you are switching among different applications.

For more information on software tools for manipulating digital imagery, see "Adding Eye-Popping Special Effects" in Chapter 11.

Figure 1.6 This pull-down menu in Adobe After Effects lists just a fraction of the many pre-built animations and transformations you can apply in postproduction with a few mouse clicks. When new effects appear on the market, you see them everywhere (especially in TV commercials). After awhile they inevitably get overused, becoming visual clichés.

Developing Your Own Style

What can you achieve with digital video? Experience and experimentation are the only ways to know for sure—and one goal of experimentation should be to develop your own unique style as a video storyteller. Style is your unique way of seeing the world and interpreting it with moving pictures and sound.

Making videos has very few firm rules; it's an art, after all. But, as you explore and experiment, here's one rule you should remember:

Have a reason for everything you do.

And herein lies a crucial point: People who understand the technical issues, options, requirements, and possibilities of digital video technology will generally have better, more reliable reasons for their production decisions.

Using the Tools at Hand

Whether you're a professional who feels the need to enhance your skills, or someone with virtually no experience in media production, start thinking about what you can do *now*. Go ahead, experiment. Sooner rather than later.

You can buy a reconditioned DV camcorder for a few hundred dollars. Apple iMovie editing software is standard on newer Macs, Windows Movie Maker 2 with PCs. Or, you can get a fully functional version of Avid Free DV, well, for free. You can light your shots with ordinary floodlights or halogen floor lamps.

Start.

Here's a tip for getting motivated: Buy a blank Mini DV cassette. It will cost you less than $10 at your local supermarket. Put it someplace where you can't avoid seeing it every day: your desk, your nightstand, the console of your car, next to this book.

It won't be long before you'll be burning to put your story on that cassette. Either that or it'll drive you nuts.

CHAPTER TWO

Yes, You Need a Script

Certain European filmmakers, Federico Fellini among them, became famous for the improvisational quality of their movies. However, even these renegades from the traditional studio system relied on scripts and detailed production plans. Within the limits of predetermined locations and situations, these directors permitted actors to vary their lines and actions, achieving a feeling of spontaneity. But that's not the same as shooting without a script.

Even "unscripted" projects like documentaries need some kind of script, though it might be just a shot list or storyboard.

Why use a script? Professionals all know why—three big reasons:

- It's a way to evaluate your story before you shoot it. It's easier and cheaper to work out problems on paper than on the set or in the editing room.

- At the beginning of a project the script can be the magnet for drawing in the people you need to get things started. The script can be the basis for a working agreement among investors (or clients), crew members, actors, and production personnel about the importance of the project's message, its artistic merit, or its commercial potential—and for gaining a consensus about the actual work to be done.

- A script is a work plan, a production tool, and a guide for all the steps that follow. If you skip writing a script, it will be more difficult to create a reliable schedule and budget. If you start with a written plan, even a simple list of locations and shots, you'll be on much firmer ground.

If you don't have a script, it's almost impossible to do a *breakdown*, schedule, or budget. How can you possibly finish on time and on budget if you have neither

> **BREAKDOWN:** Process of deconstructing a shooting script into production elements such as locations, sets, interior or exterior, day or night, actors, props, live special effects, and so on.

29

a schedule nor a budget? Without a script, how will you know what equipment you need, how many people, and for how many days? For more information on the breakdown process, see "Breaking Down the Script" in Chapter 8.

SCRIPT ELEMENTS AND FORMATS

A script is a written plan for shooting and editing a movie or video. Fiction films, sitcoms, and television spots all follow scripts. Even game and variety shows have scripts for everything but the spontaneous responses of participants.

> **SETTING:** In a script, the description of a location, including whether action takes place exterior (outdoors) or interior (indoors), and whether it's day or night.

Generally, any presentation or show longer than a few minutes must be constructed as a sequence of scenes. For each scene, a script must describe four essential elements: *setting* (the location and time of the scene), characters (actors or interview subjects), action (what the audience will see), and dialogue (what the characters will say).

Motion-Picture Script Format

Standard motion-picture script formatting (**Figure 2.1**) was codified during the old studio production system. Using this format forces you to think about, and specify, where the action will take place, what the camera will see, and what the actors will do and say—all in a form that supports the process of breaking the work down into lists of physical elements.

A standard-format script also allows you to make a rough estimate of total running time— the length of the edited and finished production. It also gives you a good idea of how many days it will take to complete your shooting.

As we pointed out in Chapter 1, plan on shooting between four and eight script pages per day. Figure one formatted script page equals approximately one minute of running time in the finished movie.

For more information on scheduling, see "How Long Will It Take?" in Chapter 1 and "Scheduling and Budgeting for Digital Video Production" in Chapter 8.

> **TIP:** It takes some practice to learn how to properly describe action in a script. For example, if you're scripting a cooking video, dropping in an overly concise description like, "Emeril demonstrates how to make béarnaise sauce," will destroy any production scheduling estimates you make based on that script page. This sequence could well fill several minutes of running time and take all day to shoot. A better approach is to describe each step in the procedure as a series of shots, formatted correctly on the page—selecting a saucepan, melting butter in the pan, sifting and stirring flour into the butter, and so on.

```
                          "WHEN HARRIED MET SALLY"

                  FADE IN:

Scene heading ──── INT. URBAN OFFICE BUILDING - JOSH'S CUBE -- DAY

     Action ──── JOSH sits in front of his computer.  A document is open on
                  his screen and he's typing from a rough draft written on a
                  yellow legal pad.  He wears a telephone headset.  His phone
                  RINGS with a bubbly chirping sound.

   Character ──────────────────────────────── JOSH
Parenthetical ──────────────────────── (into his headset)
    Dialogue ──────────────── This is Josh.

                  A gentle FEMALE VOICE is heard over the headset.  It's
                  SALLY, Josh's longtime girlfriend.
Offscreen voice ──
                                 SALLY (O.S.)
                        Hey...whatcha doin...?

                                 JOSH
                        Finishing the Red Star proposal.

  Transition ───────────────────────────────────────────── CUT TO:

                  INT. SALLY'S CUBE -- CONTINUOUS

                  Sally talks on the phone.  She also works in a cubicle, but
                  like all cubicles, it's impossible to figure out where it
                  is in relation to anything.

                                 SALLY
                        You got it done?!

                                 JOSH (O.S.)
                        Yep.

                                 SALLY
                        Then we've got two reasons to
                        celebrate today.

                                 JOSH (O.S.)
                        I can't wait.
```

Figure 2.1 The intention of motion-picture page formatting is designed to support production planning. Here's an example from *When Harried Met Sally*.

REALITY CHECK: *For purposes of breaking down a script, it's customary in the movie business to subdivide page counts for each scene into eighths. You might assume that studio production managers chose this fraction because of some correspondence to the length of shooting days. However, the practice actually evolved because folding a script page in half three times divides it quickly and neatly into eight parts.*

> **Exceptions to the Rule**
>
> *The rule of thumb that estimates running time based on the number of script pages won't work for experimental videos and news gathering, mainly because it's impossible to predict specifics for these kinds of projects from a script.*
>
> *Nor do the rules apply to commercials. Partly this is because commercials are exceptionally short (30 or 60 seconds), very fast-paced, and advertisers don't mind spending more time getting a perfect image and performance. But another reason you can't use the standard rules of thumb for commercials is they often use a different (A/V) script format.*

A/V Script Format

AUDIOVISUAL (A/V) FORMAT: Two-column script format traditionally used for corporate video and commercials.

SIDE: An actor's script page showing only the character names and dialogue; any script page. Also refers to script pages used on set, sometimes even reproduced on half-size paper, with only that shooting day's scenes, in their shooting order. Easy to fold up and stick in your back pocket while working. Probably derived from the German word for page (Seite).

DIRECTOR'S FORMAT: European term for two-column A/V script format.

Television commercials, and industrial film and video production use a professional script format called *audiovisual (A/V)* style (**Figure 2.2**). An A/V script has two columns, video on the left, audio on the right. A/V scripts don't generally follow the one-page-per-minute rule; one page may run two minutes or more.

One reason for the popularity of this format is that it's easy to mask off the video column on a copier and make dialogue-only sheets (known as *sides,* regardless of script format) for actors, as well as to create exported text files for Teleprompter machines. In Europe, A/V is known as *director's format*, perhaps because it's also easy to do the opposite—strip off the dialogue so that the director can study the shot list.

Some beginning screenwriters find the motion-picture script format complex and intimidating. You can become so bewildered by the mechanics of formatting that you lose the flow of the story. You'll get used to it over time. For writers who want an alternative, we recommend working first in A/V format, then possibly converting the script to motion-picture format when you are ready to start breakdown and budgeting.

TIP: Use the script format that's generally accepted by the industry segment you're working in. If you're unsure, ask to see a sample script from a previous production.

"WHEN HARRIED MET SALLY"

VIDEO	AUDIO
IN A CUBE OF AN URBAN OFFICE BUILDING, JOSH SITS IN FRONT OF HIS COMPUTER. A DOCUMENT IS OPEN ON HIS SCREEN. HE'S TYPING FROM A ROUGH DRAFT WRITTEN ON A YELLOW PAD. HE WEARS A TELEPHONE HEADSET. HIS PHONE RINGS WITH A BUBBLY CHIRPING SOUND.	JOSH (INTO HIS HEADSET): THIS IS JOSH.
A GENTLE FEMALE VOICE IS HEARD OVER THE HEADSET. IT'S SALLY, JOSH'S LONGTIME GIRLFRIEND.	SALLY (O.S.): HEY...WHATCHA DOIN...? JOSH: FINISHING THE RED STAR PROPOSAL
IN SALLY'S CUBE, SHE TALKS ON THE PHONE. SHE ALSO WORKS IN A CUBICLE, BUT LIKE ALL CUBICLES, IT'S IMPOSSIBLE TO FIGURE OUT WHERE IT IS IN RELATION TO ANYTHING.	SALLY: YOU GOT IT DONE?! JOSH (O.S.): YEP. SALLY: THEN WE'VE GOT TWO REASONS TO CELEBRATE TODAY. JOSH: I CAN'T WAIT.

Page #1

Figure 2.2 An example of the script from Figure 2.1, formatted in two-column style using Final Draft A/V software. The video description is on the left, audio on the right. Unlike motion-picture format, this layout does not force you to include scene-heading information (essential for break-downs) and doesn't necessarily deliver any consistent page-to-running-time equivalency.

REALITY CHECK: *Remember, motion-picture format forces you to include information essential for production breakdown—such as whether the scene is interior or exterior, day or night. Although there's nothing to prevent your including these details in an A/V script, the format itself doesn't demand that you do. After you've become familiar with the breakdown process, you'll appreciate why the seemingly cumbersome motion-picture script format is so useful.*

SCRIPT FORMATTING SOFTWARE AND PREPRODUCTION PLANNING

SLUG: Slang for scene heading in a motion-picture script.

As filmmaking professionals know, you can buy computer software for writing a screenplay in standard script format. Most of these programs use an underlying document template, plus keyboard shortcuts and point-and-click controls for applying appropriate styles for character names, dialogue, and so on. As you type, the best programs anticipate what comes next, automatically starting a new scene with a *slug* line or starting a dialogue paragraph after a character name, for example.

One of the most popular of these programs is Final Draft, which is available for both Macs and PCs (*www.finaldraft.com*). In addition to the features just described for formatting scripts as you type, the program can also:

- Print and label sides for specific actors

- Support file sharing and annotation, as well as track revisions by teams of writers (especially needed for staff-written television series)

- Format scripts according to templates, not only for screenplays but also for Broadway musicals, stage plays, sitcoms, and one-hour TV dramas

- Provide script-page samples for popular TV series

- Generate synthetic speech for each character in the script to simulate script readings

- Import, export, and convert script files of other word-processing programs, as well as exchange files with its two-column version, Final Draft A/V

Some script formatting software is designed to work closely with other computerized production tools. For example, if you use Entertainment Partners' Movie Magic Screenwriter to create your script (or if you export a script in .SEX—no kidding!—format from Final Draft), you can import that file directly into Movie Magic Scheduling—which can automatically perform many script breakdown tasks such as extracting and sorting lists of locations, grouping day and night scenes at a given location, and so on (**Figure 2.3**). To proceed from scheduling to budgeting, you can export that schedule file into Movie Magic Budgeting.

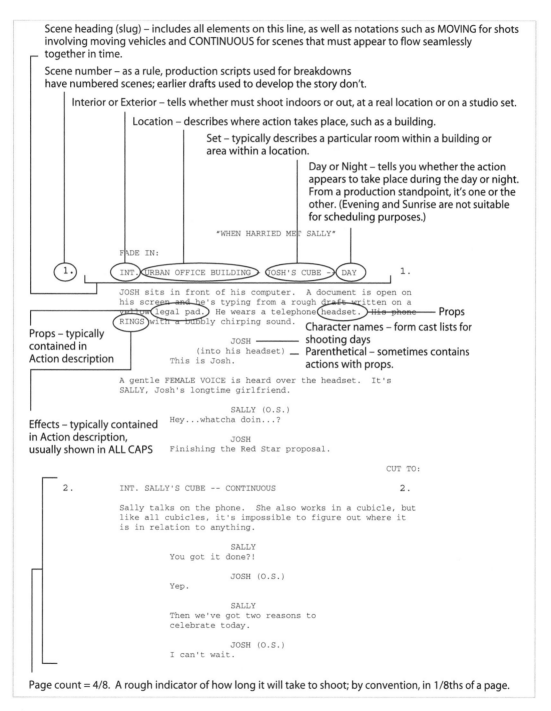

Scene heading (slug) – includes all elements on this line, as well as notations such as MOVING for shots involving moving vehicles and CONTINUOUS for scenes that must appear to flow seamlessly together in time.

Scene number – as a rule, production scripts used for breakdowns have numbered scenes; earlier drafts used to develop the story don't.

Interior or Exterior – tells whether must shoot indoors or out, at a real location or on a studio set.

Location – describes where action takes place, such as a building.

Set – typically describes a particular room within a building or area within a location.

Day or Night – tells you whether the action appears to take place during the day or night. From a production standpoint, it's one or the other. (Evening and Sunrise are not suitable for scheduling purposes.)

"WHEN HARRIED MET SALLY"

FADE IN:

1.   INT. URBAN OFFICE BUILDING — JOSH'S CUBE — DAY   1.

JOSH sits in front of his computer. A document is open on his screen and he's typing from a rough draft written on a yellow legal pad. He wears a telephone headset. His phone RINGS with a bubbly chirping sound.

Props — typically contained in Action description

Props

Character names – form cast lists for shooting days

                    JOSH
             (into his headset)
        This is Josh.

Parenthetical – sometimes contains actions with props.

A gentle FEMALE VOICE is heard over the headset. It's SALLY, Josh's longtime girlfriend.

Effects – typically contained in Action description, usually shown in ALL CAPS

                    SALLY (O.S.)
        Hey...whatcha doin...?
                    JOSH
        Finishing the Red Star proposal.

                                              CUT TO:

2.   INT. SALLY'S CUBE -- CONTINUOUS   2.

Sally talks on the phone. She also works in a cubicle, but like all cubicles, it's impossible to figure out where it is in relation to anything.

                    SALLY
        You got it done?!

                    JOSH (O.S.)
        Yep.

                    SALLY
        Then we've got two reasons to
        celebrate today.

                    JOSH (O.S.)
        I can't wait.

Page count = 4/8. A rough indicator of how long it will take to shoot; by convention, in 1/8ths of a page.

Figure 2.3 Here's the script page shown in Figure 2.1 with production elements highlighted. The process of extracting these elements from a shooting script in preparation for creating a production schedule is called *breaking down the script,* or *script breakdown.*

Many producers build their own scheduling and budgeting spreadsheets with programs like Microsoft Excel. Entertainment Partners (*www.entertainmentpartners.com*) also offers a newer budgeting program, EP Budgeting, which integrates with its Vista accounting package for producers, studios, and networks. For more information on scheduling and budgeting, see "Scheduling and Budgeting for Digital Video Production" in Chapter 8.

> **TIP:** If you're using older screenwriting software that formats your script in a separate, subsequent batch operation after you've typed it in some plainer form, you're doing too much work. Get an upgrade.

How to Script "Unscripted" Projects

Even though documentaries and news shoots aren't scripted in the traditional sense, you'll still need some sort of a plan as a basis for scheduling and budgeting your video production. Creating that plan helps you control the situation and provides a logical flow to your shooting and editing. One approach for documentaries and for news is to write a script describing what you *think* will happen, even though events may not follow to the letter.

Scripting Interviews

If you're shooting an interview, your "script" might simply consist of a list of questions you want to ask your interview subject, and the appropriate background notes for each answer. A list of questions won't follow the one-page-per-minute rule, unless you write a script that simulates the subject's expected responses as dialogue.

Scripting Documentaries

If your project is a documentary, your "script" might be a list of locations and people you plan to cover during each day of documentary shooting.

Documentary filmmakers sometimes take a leaf from the interviewers' book of techniques and construct a shooting script based on subjects' responses to preliminary interviews. The documentary script then attempts to structure and illustrate these responses as a series of locations and shots—which can serve as the basis for breakdowns, schedules, and budgets. It's not foolproof, but it's certainly better than showing up on location with a camcorder and no plan at all.

There's a catch, of course. Scripting reality shows like documentaries with a shooting plan gives you greater predictability and control, but it runs the risk of sacrificing spontaneity. An unscripted shoot is riskier but may capture more delightful surprises.

THINKING ABOUT YOUR PROJECT

As you begin to write a script or outline for your project, it's the perfect time to start thinking about all the elements of your production—budget, schedule, equipment, crew, and how you plan to tell your story. If you're a professional moving into digital video, much of this section will be familiar. Even so, it's good to be reminded to think ahead, particularly about your intended distribution method.

Thinking Ahead to Distribution

Before you become immersed in the details of the production process, consider how you intend your work to be exhibited. In effect, you must put your mind into the future and imagine who is viewing your show and where, then work backward to determine all the steps it took to get there. Each of those steps will have its particular requirements in terms of cost, time, technical issues, and quality.

For each of these alternatives, we offer in-depth advice in Chapter 12, Distribution and E-Publishing. For your planning purposes at this early stage, here's an overview:

Videotape. You'll have the least demanding set of choices technically if you only plan to make analog videocassette copies and ship them to users. Your challenge is to end up with a high-quality master tape to give your chosen duplicating facility. Essentially, if it looks good visually, it is good.

DVD. Although releasing on DVD might seem much the same as distributing on tape, it's not. There's an extra mastering step, which has its technical challenges. Study the step called "DVD Authoring" in Chapter 12. Also, a relatively low-capacity DVD you can burn on your PC doesn't hold enough data for a feature-length theatrical movie. To get higher-capacity discs, you must contract with a pressing plant, and it won't be economical to make just a few copies.

> **TRANSFER:** Conversion of film or analog material to digital video, or vice versa.

Broadcast television. Commercial TV imposes technical requirements that have to do with standards of image and sound. Basically, colors can't be too bright, sound too loud, nor titles too close to the edge of the frame. A show that looks and sounds fine when *transferred* to tape might not necessarily pass muster by a network engineer. Most inexpensive DV camcorders don't meet broadcast specs. You can make up for the deficiencies in post production, but it will take time, money, and technical tweaking.

Theatrical film. If the goal is to exhibit your digital movie in commercial theaters, you may or may not need to undertake the expense of converting it to film before you have a commercial distribution deal. (See "Converting Video to Film: Should You Bother?" in

Chapter 12.) That decision can depend, in part, on how close you are to making a deal with a distribution company. You can submit your video to most film festivals in electronic form—on digital tape or disc. But in any event, you must plan every detail of your production with the technical and aesthetic requirements of film in mind. Particularly for film conversion, it's necessary to work backward and to plan as carefully as possible. From the very beginning, you need to work closely with a lab that does video-to-film transfers or one of the vendors that specializes in transfers exclusively. We recommend doing tests, rent the same model camcorder you intend to use, shoot some tape, and pay for conversion of the video into short filmstrips. (Renting makes it practical to try several different cameras.) Evaluate the test strips as you make your decisions on crucial camcorder settings (such as frame rate) and lighting design.

 REALITY CHECK: *Know your intended market. If you plan on foreign distribution (an essential component of any movie sales strategy) a sizeable portion of the foreign market will demand 35mm film prints.*

Producing a theatrical film that's also suitable for broadcast means ending up with two different master recordings, each optimized for its proper medium; this is an extra step you need to plan for.

Internet. If you intend to distribute your show on the Web, there aren't any stringent technical guidelines, as yet. There just isn't enough bandwidth available to present high-quality video to the public. One way or another, you'll have to degrade the quality of the show to make it playable. As you adjust the technical characteristics of video files you create for the Internet, you'll have to balance image quality and viewing size against smooth playback.

The Digital Video Production Process

The major steps in the digital video production process—how you put your story or message on the screen—are quite similar to those of film or analog video (**Figure 2.4**). The difference is that much of the process goes faster, and some of the traditional steps (such as film lab processing) don't happen at all.

Script. A script provides a way to refine your story and specifies essential elements of production. For fiction films it's a necessity, and for presentations such as documentaries, even a shot list or shooting plan can be an invaluable planning tool.

Breakdown. Working from the script, you'll list all the elements required for production: locations, cast members, props, shots, and so on. You'll also determine the number of crew members and kinds of equipment you need, based on descriptions of settings in the script, appearance of real locations you intend to use, and the extent of lighting and on-location sound you need.

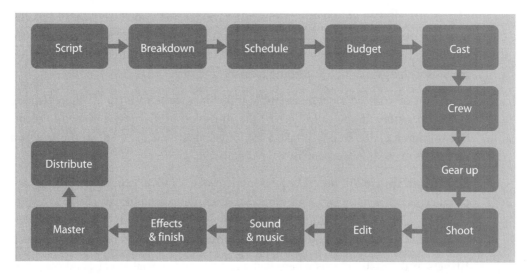

Figure 2.4 Digital video production includes most of the familiar steps for shooting film or analog video but, until final output, eliminates all steps requiring transfers to or from other media.

Schedule. If your script follows standard format, you can use it to make a rough estimate of the number of shooting days you'll need. This works for most types of productions, not just fiction movies, assuming you can create a reasonably accurate script. The length of time you'll need for editing and finishing your project will vary, depending on the length of your script and the degree of sophistication you expect from special effects and sound.

Budget. Creating an accurate budget for a film is a specialized and advanced skill. As with scheduling, the sophistication you require in postproduction will affect cost, as will your expected distribution method—videotape, DVD, broadcast, Internet webcast, or film.

Cast. This step includes auditioning actors and selecting a cast. Casting a fiction movie can be so time-consuming that even low-budget producers often hire a casting director. If you're shooting a documentary or some other nonfiction project, you'll probably do preliminary interviews and briefings during this step.

Crew. Identifying the number of crew members you'll use is often a compromise between how large your project is and how much money you have to spend. The larger the project, the more people you'll need to hire—if you can afford them. And the larger your crew, the greater your related costs for transportation and food—two areas where you can't skimp. The smaller the project, the more jobs you'll probably end up doing yourself.

Gear up. Just prior to shooting, you and your key production personnel will select lighting, camera, sound, and grip equipment. If you're hiring a professional crew, many of them have their own equipment and will rent it to you at a rate (daily or weekly) that is packaged with their services.

Shoot. The thrill (and terror) of capturing images and sound on tape begins here. Your schedule must be detailed enough to tell you which actors, crew, equipment, and props you'll need at specific locations on specific days. Be prepared to rebuild a collapsed house of cards if things don't go according to plan.

Edit. You or your editor will assemble individual shots to form a coherent presentation and build a story. If you didn't get all the shots you need, or if you need to reconstruct a bad soundtrack, this step will take a lot longer than you planned. In the worst case, you may need to re-shoot missing or flawed material.

Sound and music. Audio is a crucial element of the movie experience. Editors and sound technicians construct most of a soundtrack after the fact, adding music and multiple layers of sound effects to the dialogue recorded on set. Ironically, while they do this to provide realism, the sound track may be the most intricately fabricated part of moviemaking.

Effects and finish. This is where you add titles and special effects, and correct colors so they look more natural, more film-like, or fit better with the mood you wish to convey.

Master. You'll need to prepare your finished production for its intended distribution medium by way of a master source for copying; this master could be on videotape, DVD, or film negative. An emerging format, "digital intermediate," is being used on major motion pictures to make release prints from a digital file that is created by scanning un-cut negative.

Distribute. And you thought you were finished! Unless you pre-sold your project for distribution, getting your work out into the world means selling, marketing, and promotion. This can be difficult and tiresome. But planning ahead and following through after it's all in the can is essential if you want audiences to see your work.

What's *Your* Story?

By "story" we mean the unique content of your video presentation, whether it's fact or fiction. There are plenty of ways to ruin a movie in production, but bad storytelling is the most common.

Screenwriting is a huge subject, one we have no intention of summarizing here. There are lots of classes you can take, and plenty of books you can read. You can probably gain the same level of skill by experimenting with a documentary approach—relying mainly on digital production and editing to "discover" a fully formed story—but that kind of trial-and-error can be time consuming and expensive, and is probably best employed *before* you start a professional project.

Legal Protection for Writers

Scripts and story ideas do get "borrowed," even stolen. And it can happen to anybody. In a famous case, humorist Art Buchwald claimed he wrote but was neither paid nor credited for the story of Coming to America (he won). To protect your work, register it with the Writer's Guild of America (WGA). It's simple and inexpensive ($20 for nonmembers), and you can either mail it in or upload your document file online (www.wga.org). Other online creative registries permit you to register short stories, Web pages, patentable ideas, computer programs, poems—any written work. These services include National Creative Registry (www.protectrite.com) and WriteSafe (www.writesafe.com).

When you believe you have a finished script, you can register it with the U.S. Copyright Office (www.loc.gov/copyright). Copyright registration can apply to outlines, treatments, and synopses, as well as to finished screenplays. Even though copyright technically applies to anything you put on paper, it's not customary to make application for anything but a completed work, such as a novel, stage play, or screenplay. For more information on how copyright applies to scripts and videos, see "Copyright" in Chapter 12.

Registration with WGA, NCR, or WriteSafe establishes the exact date of authorship, which is when the term of copyright begins—even if you don't apply for copyright right away. Most professional screenwriters register their major drafts with the WGA—before anyone else has seen them—as a way of establishing the originality of the material.

According to copyright law, only your personal and unique written expression is protectable. Ideas and titles are not. (Motion picture distributors, however, register titles with the Motion Picture Association of America to avoid marketing conflicts.) In the industry, a brief, one- or two-sentence description of a story—called a logline—is considered an "idea" or "concept." Even if written down, a logline by itself would be difficult if not impossible to protect. However, some courts have held that even when discussing ideas for movie and television projects, you may have certain rights that are rooted in contract, not copyright, law. When you meet with an executive at a network or studio, there can be an implied contract that the company agrees to compensate you if it decides to produce the project you're suggesting. To protect your interests in such situations—especially if you don't yet have a script—you'd be wise to register a treatment that describes your story or project in some detail before taking any meetings with prospective producers. However, if the producer makes you sign a release form prior to taking the meeting, read it carefully. It may contain language by which you waive these rights.

OUTLINE: One- or two-sentence descriptions of major scenes of a script, often numbered . A feature-length movie will have about 30-40 major scenes.

TREATMENT: Long narrative that describes the plot of a screen story, scene by scene, perhaps with excerpted dialogue. The form used for presenting movie projects to executives and investors who do not want to deal with the technicalities in a formatted screenplay.

SYNOPSIS: Typically less than a page, a short summary of a screen story.

LOGLINE: One- or two-sentence description of a screen story; idea for a movie; concept.

If you haven't learned the craft of telling a story with pictures and sound, we can recommend some good books and seminars on the subject. Our favorite for movie screenwriting is Lew Hunter's *Screenwriting 434,* based on the course he gave for years at UCLA. To learn more on how writers and directors tell stories with pictures, pick up Bruce Block's *The Visual Story: Seeing the Structure of Film, TV, and New Media.* If you want to learn fundamental screen story structure, get *Screenplay: The Foundations of Screenwriting* by Syd Field. Read it to learn the classic approach to plot construction, then put it away—you don't want to stick too closely to its formulas. If you have a difficult time getting started, or staying motivated, check out *How to Write Movie in 21 Days* by Viki King. Chock full of exercises and reassurance, this book may not get you a full-length feature in three weeks, but it will get you over writer's block. Then there is *The Elements of Screenwriting* by Irwin R. Blacker, which is in the tradition of Strunk and White's *The Elements of Style.* Hard to find, this little book packs a wallop, especially on subjects of character, action, and dialogue. You'll find full citations of these and other books in the "References" and "Web Links" sections at the back of this book.

> **TIP:** *There are countless volumes on how to write a screenplay, but one book predates most of them. The Art of Dramatic Writing (1946) by Lajos Egri, was originally intended for playwrights, but you'll probably find it in the personal library of every successful Hollywood scribe. Egri himself admits his ideas aren't particularly original. He cribbed them from Aristotle.*

Basic Story Structure

As you study visual storytelling, there's a temptation to focus so much on technique that the essential notion of what a story is—and must be—gets lost in the details. Whether you are telling a love story, showing someone how to fold a shirt, or creating a montage of intriguing imagery, your story must have three parts:

A beginning. A middle. And an end.

Your challenge in the beginning is to hook your audience, capture their interest, and motivate them to watch. You set up a problem, pose a question, present a dilemma, or create a tension you propose to solve (or resolve) by the end of the experience.

In the middle, you elaborate on or wrestle with the issue you introduced in the beginning. You add complications, obstacles, fascinating details.

The ending of your presentation must answer the question you posed, resolve the conflict, achieve a new balance.

Most important—however you resolve the issue—when the lights come up, your audience must have a clear sense of why you wanted them to watch. That's a pretty good definition of whether they will find the experience "satisfying."

Remember, this advice applies to all kinds of presentations—not only to narratives but also to music videos and abstract art (which, to satisfy, must build to a *visual climax*).

> **VISUAL CLIMAX:** Nonverbal resolution of a screen presentation that gives it a sense of completeness or finality.

Key Questions About the Story

Here are some questions you should ask yourself to test the viability of your story. If you can answer yes to all of them, you're ready to pick up your digital video tools and get to work.

Do You Feel Strongly About the Subject?

If you don't have passion for your story, no one else will. If you're selling a product or service, you must believe in it. If you're observing and reporting with your camera, be bold and follow the action wherever it leads.

Whatever excites you is what you want to get on tape—and that's what an audience will want to watch.

Passion is important for a more practical reason: you'll need it to get through the production process. Even though digital video tools make the job easier than ever before, producing a video project of even modest length will be a soul-searing, time-consuming, labor-intensive activity. It will probably take longer, require more effort, and cost more than you expect. If you aren't strongly motivated to tell your story, you might not be able to muster the persistence, or the diligence, to finish your video production.

Will It Change the Way People Think or Feel?

All movies and all videos carry a message of some kind—and no entertainment, however trivial, is without one. A light-hearted comedy, a bit of entertaining fluff, expresses a philosophy of life, an attitude about coping with reality. Commercials convey powerful propaganda about lifestyle and consumerism. Even abstract video art, if it's good, evokes feeling and mood, or stimulates thought.

Relish the notion that your work can express, motivate, and persuade. That thought will get you up in the morning, no matter how early the crew call.

Is Your Perspective Unique?

Novice screenwriters often worry that people will steal their ideas. However, ideas in themselves aren't unique (or even legally protectable). Shakespeare stole from Plutarch, and everybody steals from Shakespeare.

So the question isn't whether your story has been told before—because it has. An old joke in the movie business has the producer saying, "Give me a new story that's stood the test of time." What the producer wants, really, is a fresh retelling of an old story. Your execution of the ideas in your story, and your viewpoint on that story, can be unique—and might well make a valuable contribution to our culture.

When it comes to storytelling, people (and producers) are a lot like children being put to bed: they want to hear a familiar story told *as if for the first time.* If you can pull that off, knowing you've thrilled an audience is the biggest thrill you will ever have as a teller of video tales.

Is It Visual?

THX, DTS, and Dolby sound notwithstanding, moviemaking is, above all, a visual art form. When the audience views your finished video, will they get the gist of the story with the sound turned off? Some film buyers, especially those thinking about international markets, actually watch videos in fast-forward, with the sound off, to see whether the action is understandable and interesting without the benefit of dubbing or subtitles. Will your video story pass that test? To find out, see if you can tell your story in the panels of a comic strip (**Figure 2.5**).

Inexperienced videomakers, whether they're making fiction films, documentaries, or training videos, often depend far too much on dialogue and "talking heads"—which is what filmmakers call close-up shots of actors, or anyone else, giving a long speech. It's also a pejorative term for a boring sequence. Talking heads are deadly. Actor-producer Jodie Foster says she believes audiences rarely remember specific words of dialogue in a scene, but they always remember its emotion. Talking heads can be interesting—which is why dialogue close-ups are a mainstay of television drama—but only if the underlying emotion is compelling.

As an experiment, try to convey blocks of dialogue visually. Even the snappiest repartee won't strike the audience as much as a single, evocative image of a delighted face.

Does It Suggest Action?

Action is inherently visual, and visuals are inherently interesting. The audience becomes involved because something is happening. If your idea doesn't suggest action, it may be a poor subject for a video story. For example, "a guy and a girl and a car" isn't a story; it's a situation. Neither is "a tough guy." That's a character description. However, "a tough guy and a girl steal cars and fall in love" has the makings of a story because it suggests a series of visual actions.

In dramatic stories, action is the result of conflict between characters. Conflict doesn't necessarily mean violence. A difference of opinion is a type of conflict. If disagreements weren't interesting to watch, the television talk show format would disappear.

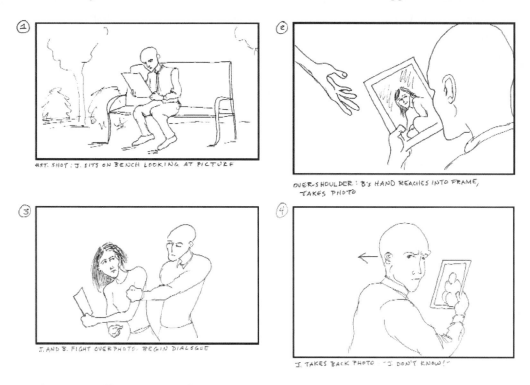

Figure 2.5 Will your story work as a comic strip? A production storyboard, which illustrates the director's intended shots, attempts to find out. (For more information, see "From Storyboard to Shot List" in Chapter 5.) (Image courtesy Robert Payne.)

Is It Achievable with the Resources You Have?

The mission of this book is to help you answer this question. Thanks to the cost savings digital video makes possible, more people than ever before will be able to answer yes, it is achievable.

Digital economies aside, you need to give some thought to the scale and scope of your intended project, and then do a reality check. In Woody Allen's *Hollywood Ending*, an art director stuns the studio head when he insists it will be necessary to build a full-scale replica of the Empire State Building on a sound stage—then yields to pressure and agrees to accept just the first 20 floors.

So let your imagination run free, but remember: unless you have a very rich relative, you must be able to pay for re-creating your vision in some readily accessible part of the real world.

CHAPTER THREE

DV Technology and the Camcorder

Most digital video starts with a camcorder, and choosing the right one may be the single most important decision you have to make on your project.

Which camcorder would an experienced cinematographer advise you to use? What features would a skilled video editor urge you to look for? What would a professional camcorder operator tell you about which automatic controls she uses most often—and which make her job harder?

Before you buy or rent a camcorder, you need to know the answers to those questions, and a lot more. You'll find them in this chapter.

RESOLUTION: Sharpness and detail in a film or video image; spatial resolution.

COLOR SPACE: The range of colors a camcorder or video device can reproduce.

Some of this information, which ranges from video formats to image *resolution*, *color space*, and TV broadcast standards, is fairly technical. You'll find more detail in Appendix A, "Digital Video Technology in Depth," where videomakers with a driving need to know as much as possible about the technology can turn for enlightenment.

Many of you may be tempted to skip this overview of DV technology, especially if you already own a DV camcorder. But take it from a couple of pros: The more you know about DV technology, the better prepared you'll be to buy, rent, shoot, and edit successfully.

Although the abbreviation "DV" obviously stands for "digital video," and *could* refer to all digital video formats, we'll follow standard practice and use it only when we want to refer to *DV*—the popular format that's currently democratizing video. DV is the least expensive, fastest-growing format on the market, and is also the native format used by most desktop editing systems. For the money, DV offers the best value you can find.

We'll use the term "digital video" to refer to DV plus all those other formats that are *not* "DV."

ABOUT DV

Development of the video recording standard known today as DV began in 1993. The first DV camcorder—the Sony DCR-VX1000—appeared two years later, and the DV industry has been on a rocketship ride ever since.

> **DATA BIT:** Basic unit of binary digital computer code; a 0 or a 1, represented by switches in electronic circuits or by memory locations in storage devices that are set to "off" or "on," respectively.

One reason DV became technically feasible was because new compression techniques made video data files much more compact at the same time that processing chips in camcorders and PCs were becoming more powerful. A DV tape recording or computer file requires only one-fifth the *data bits* of the uncompressed digital signal, and the picture quality is almost undegraded. (For more information, see "DV Technology: Under the Hood" in Appendix A.)

Consumer vs. Professional DV

There are actually two separate specifications for DV: *consumer* and *professional*. Some of the key differences are summarized in **Table 3.1.** Simply stated, consumer DV recordings don't meet television broadcast specs, and professional DV recordings do. The people who care most about this distinction are television producers, engineers, and news crews. For most filmmakers and corporate videographers, especially those who aren't interested in broadcast distribution, the technical differences are relatively trivial.

The significant distinctions between consumer and professional DV camcorders come down to technical specifications, usability features, price ranges, and lens options. So-called "prosumer" equipment offers a mixture of consumer and professional features and specifications. For more information, see the sidebar "The Prosumer Buzzword" later in this chapter.

Table 3.1 Key Differences Between Consumer and Professional DV Camcorders

	Consumer	Professional
Color space	4:1:1	4:2:2 (Broadcast spec)
Audio sync	Unlocked: ±1/3 frame	Locked
Timecode	DV data format	SMPTE/EBU studio standard
Advanced editing support	No	Yes
Rugged?	No	Yes
Price range*	$500–$2,000	$6,000–$40,000
Lenses	Built-in	Interchangeable

* Prosumer units cost $2,000–$6,000

DV Media: Mini DV and DVC

The DV technical standard specifies ¼-inch magnetic tape—but no particular size for the cassette the tape comes in. Currently, DV tape comes packaged in two cassette designs: Mini DV (**Figure 3.1**) and Standard DVC.

Today, "Standard DVC" is something of a misnomer because Mini DV is by far the most popular DV tape format with a cassette measuring just 66 mm wide by 48 mm high by 12.2 mm thick, and capable of holding up to one hour of recorded material. (A 30-minute size is also available but is not as common.) The small size of Mini DV makes it easy to carry, and its price is economical: less than $10 each, or less than $5 each in bulk.

Mini DV cassettes are quite an improvement for pros who are used to handling book-sized media. Of course, there's a downside. Technology has now made it possible for you to lose a whole day's shooting in the pocket of the coat you just sent to the cleaners.

The DVC cassette is physically larger than the Mini DV, holds between 3 and 4.5 hours of material, and the tape stock is more durable than the tape used in a Mini DV cassette, which means it will withstand repeated shuttling and playback.

You may be perplexed to see Mini DV cassettes with "DVC" on the label, which is a reference to the tape width, not to the size of the cassette package. Most camcorders are designed to use one size cassette or the other, Mini DV or DVC; only a few professional units will accept both sizes.

> **NOTE:** Some proprietary, non-DV digital formats, such as Digital8 and Digital-S, use different size tape but still make DV-compatible recordings. For more information on these formats, see "Proprietary DV Variants" and the sidebar "Digital8 and Betacam SX: Hybrid Formats" in Appendix A.

Figure 3.1 The majority of today's DV camcorders, whether consumer or professional, use Mini DV cassettes.

Ultra-Compact Recording Media

You'll see some consumer DV camcorders equipped with other types of recording media besides cassettes:

- Memory Stick—Developed by Sony and known generically as a *flash memory module*, this solid-state wafer is about the size of a couple of postage stamps. Some camcorders use memory sticks as auxiliary recording media for holding still pictures. Depending on the size of the stick (4–128MB) and the capabilities of the camera, you might be able to also store a few seconds of video.

> **FLASH MEMORY MODULE:**
> A solid-state storage chip that can be inserted into digital photographic cameras and video camcorders for purposes of holding still images and short video clips; Memory Stick.

- MicroMV—Also developed by Sony, this is a tiny cassette about the size of a book of matches designed for camcorders no bigger than a pack of cigarettes. Although the cassette is 70 percent smaller physically than the Mini DV, it can still hold up to an hour of video.

- 8cm DVD—Some camcorders can accept these recordable optical discs, which are about 3 inches in diameter (**Figure 3.2**). The camera can record up to 30 minutes of video directly on the 1.7 GB disc, which you can load directly into a DVD player or computer optical drive.

Figure 3.2 This consumer-model camcorder from Sony records onto an 8cm DVD that can be loaded directly into a home player. (Photo courtesy Sony Electronics Inc.)

However convenient these cameras and data formats might seem, don't use them for anything but home movies, email clips, and Webcasts. All of the ultra-compact formats capture video as MPEG-2, the same compressed files used to make DVD recordings. MPEG-2 is not as easily editable as uncompressed DV, and the results might look unprofessional. For more information on MPEG-2, see "Creating a DVD, Step by Step" in Chapter 12.

Other Output Options

Two other output options available with some camcorders deserve mention:

- HDD—Recording directly to a hard-disk drive (HDD) is an option with some professional DV and HD cameras (**Figure 3.3**). The main advantages are high capacity and reliability. Since the HDD units tend to be much bulkier than cassettes, this type of recording is mostly used in-studio. In fact, HDD is the only recording medium available for the Thomson Viper, an HD camera, because its 4:4:4 color space requires lots and lots of storage. (See the next section, "Color Space.")

- Bluetooth—A type of wireless LAN used to link hardware units at distances of less than 35 feet, Bluetooth communication is a feature on some DV camcorders. It's handy for connecting cameras to computers for sending video directly out onto the Web. Remember, however, that Bluetooth offers relatively narrow bandwidth, about 2 Mbps, which makes it suitable only for home-movie-style applications.

Figure 3.3 An option for DVCAM professional-level cameras is an external hard drive, which can take the place of recording on multiple cassettes for long shooting sessions or events. (Photo courtesy Sony Electronics Inc.)

Color Space

Consumer DV uses fewer data bits than professional DV to describe color, causing some hues to appear dull while others may seem too bright. Colors in professional DV are more lifelike. Consumer color space is defined as 4:1:1. Professional color space is defined as 4:2:2. Don't worry about what those numbers mean for now. (For more information, see "What Is Color Space and Why Is It Important?" in Appendix A.)

The most important practical impact of the different color spaces is that before you can broadcast a consumer DV program, you have to convert it to the professional spec. The conversion process isn't hard, but some people think that a converted video doesn't look as good as one that originated on professional DV in the first place.

Audio Sync

In professional DV, audio and video are absolutely in *sync:* a sound on the audio track is locked to the specific instant in the video *frame* during which it occurred. Editors rejoice at such perfection. In consumer DV, sync can drift by as much as ⅓ frame. This is rarely a big problem, but most professional editors doing meticulous sound edits prefer to work with professional DV.

> **SYNC SOUND:** Audio recorded during a take that corresponds to video action; frame-accurate soundtrack.
>
> **FRAME:** One still image within a motion sequence captured by a camcorder or movie camera.

 REALITY CHECK: *Some veteran editors will assure you they can work with consumer audio—and then they'll boast to their colleagues about how much extra time they billed for fixing your mistakes!*

Timecode

Timecode is a numeric index that identifies a specific location on a videotape by hour, minute, second, and frame (HH:MM:SS:FF). It's the editor's most reliable tool for quickly finding a desired take among hours of recordings.

Professional DV employs the same, strict SMPTE/EBU (Society of Motion Picture and Television Engineers/European Broadcast Union) timecode standard used in broadcasting, which can act as a control code for professional equipment like a studio video deck. Consumer DV camcorders generate timecode that is usable by desktop editing software but may not work with studio machines. After you've spent half an hour completing a sequence that would have taken five minutes with SMPTE timecode, you'll appreciate the difference.

These differences in timecode matter most to videographers who are working at studio-based production facilities. It could be downright embarrassing to proudly shove the cassette with your dailies into a deck in the edit bay, only to be scolded about not providing usable timecode. (For more information on timecode in editing, see "Selecting and Uploading Clips" in Chapter 10.)

> **TIP:** Those film editors who actually handle film (as opposed to working with it in converted digital format) locate scenes by way of edge-code numbers printed on the film workprint. You can think of video timecode as electronic edge-code numbers.

Usability Features

Professional DV camcorders have a variety of features designed to speed the work for professional videographers and editors. (They are also designed to sell you the associated editing gear that interfaces with the camcorder, of course.) These conveniences include high-speed data connections that reduce upload times to the editing system, and electronic markers that permit you to flag just the good takes, to name just two. Professional gear is also more rugged than consumer gear and is less likely to be damaged by tough field conditions and the rigors of travel.

Price Range

Consumer DV camcorders range from $500 to $2,000, and thanks to those affordable prices, are very popular. These units are aimed at the home market where, sales executives believe, amateur videographers just want to point and shoot. To maximize ease of use, consumer camcorders are designed with relatively few manual controls and lots of automatic features. They're fine for shooting that special family event, or even a short training presentation, but if you have professional plans for your DV camcorder, you'll want more control over the results (**Figure 3.4**).

> **NOTE:** Not long ago, when the world was a simpler place, an important indicator of a camcorder's quality was the number of charge-coupled devices (CCDs) it had. CCDs are image-sensing chips that convert incoming light to electrical signals. Less expensive cameras had one chip; more expensive models had three (designated 3CCD). Optics in the three-chip cameras separate white light into three component colors—red, green, and blue—one color for each chip. However, industry buzz has it that tomorrow's cameras may go back to single-chip design, with a new generation of image-sensing technology. Today, it's still generally true that 3CCD camcorders provide the best image quality. For more information on image sensing, see "CCD Technology" in Appendix A.

> **CCD:** Charge-coupled device; image-sensing chip in camcorders.

Figure 3.4 Consumer-model DV camcorders usually have a built-in, nonremovable lens, flip-out viewfinder screen, and automatic features to promote point-and-shoot videography. The latest models are designed for portability and convenience, small enough to fit easily into a pocket, purse, or briefcase. (Photo courtesy Sony Electronics Inc.)

Professional DV camcorders start at around $6,000, including a *zoom lens*, and can run as much as $40,000, or more (**Figure 3.5**). However, very few professional videographers actually buy their own camcorders. They either borrow them from a network equipment pool or rent them for the duration of a shoot. Renting doesn't mean they'll use whatever camcorder happens to be available. Pros always have strong opinions about the specific makes and models they prefer.

ZOOM LENS: Lens with continuously variable focal length; zooming in increases magnification and makes the subject seem closer, while zooming out does the opposite.

The Prosumer Buzzword

You've probably seen the term prosumer *in ads and product reviews. From an engineering standpoint, there's no such thing as a prosumer DV spec. The term (which combines the "pro" from professional and the "sumer" from consumer) is strictly a marketing category and refers to a class of DV equipment that offers a mixture of consumer and professional specifications—a mix that varies widely from one model to the next.*

Prosumer camcorders lack some professional features but generally deliver good-to-excellent results along with relatively affordable prices. Many videomakers have found them to be great devices for turning out professional work on an amateur budget. However, take care: Just because a salesperson tells you a camcorder is a prosumer unit, that doesn't mean it will do the job for you. Since there are no rules for which features must be included in a prosumer unit, prosumer has just one reliable meaning—"medium-priced."

Prosumer DV camcorders, which range in price from $2,000 to $6,000, are becoming increasingly popular with serious, budget-conscious videographers—a group that includes independent filmmakers, corporate training and marketing departments, and every professional who wishes to own rather than rent his or her equipment (**Figure 3.6**). In 2003, the first prosumer HD camcorder appeared on the market, JVC JY-HD10U (**Figure 3.7**). It's a handheld model, featuring a single-chip CCD, and built-in lens, for a suggested list price of $3,995 (about a tenth what you'd have to spend for the lowest-priced professional model).

Figure 3.5 Professional DV camcorders like this one are tools of choice for shooting location news and other demanding field assignments. This model is the JVC GY-5000U, featured in the product comparison in this chapter. The base model has consumer color space; professional broadcast spec is available as an extra-cost option. (Photo courtesy JVC Professional Products Company.)

Figure 3.6 The Canon XL1S prosumer camcorder is popular with filmmakers thanks to features designed to support "film look" video. Although it has some professional features, it belongs to the prosumer category because of its consumer-format color space. This camera is featured in our comparison. (Photo courtesy Canon U.S.A., Inc.)

Figure 3.7 The JVC HD10U was the first prosumer camcorder to offer high-definition video and frame rates. (Photo courtesy JVC Professional Products Company.)

Lenses

Every serious moviemaker knows you should always use the best lenses you can afford. Typically, consumer camcorders come with built-in lenses, while professional units offer interchangeable lenses. The optics of interchangeable lenses are superior to built-in lenses, and they offer more precise controls over wider ranges of exposure and focal length. In fact, as far as pros are concerned, the most important reason for preferring one camcorder over another is the quality and variety of lenses available for that model.

 REALITY CHECK: Adjustable camcorder lenses with precise markings on the barrels are known as "cinema-style" lenses, for reasons that will become apparent when we describe how camera operations work on a film crew. For more information, see "Lenses and Lens Operation" in Chapter 4.

> **CINEMA-STYLE LENS:** Photographic lens designed for a motion-picture camera.

MATCHING A DV CAMCORDER TO YOUR SHOOTING STYLE

You shouldn't choose a camcorder based on its feature set alone, however impressive it might be. Camcorder features are only important in relation to your style of shooting. You'll have very different sets of requirements for shooting in:

- News style

- Film style

- Multicamera style

News Style

Whether you're actually covering news or simply can't afford to field a crew, here are the camcorder features you'll probably want for running and gunning:

- A bracket (called an *accessory shoe*) for attaching a photo floodlight

- A built-in microphone

- The size, weight, and balance that work best for you

> **ACCESSORY SHOE:** Bracket on a camera for mounting floodlights or flash accessories; if it also provides power, it's called a "hot shoe."

- Camera mounts for shoulder braces and specialty rigs

- A wide-ranging zoom lens (no time to change lenses)

- Broadcast-spec color space and SMPTE/EBU timecode

- Automatic controls (although you'll begin to avoid using them as you gain skill operating manual controls)

- Low-light sensitivity

- Advanced editing support

Film Style

Because shooting film style usually means single-camera setups, meticulously planned, lit, and executed, you'll need:

- Manual overrides for automatic controls

- *Progressive scanning* (one aspect of "film look"; for more information, see "Making Video Look Like Film" later in this chapter)

- An assortment of interchangeable lenses

- Manual, mechanical focus control

- A separate/detached zoom control

- Camera mounts for tripods and dollies

- Professional-style audio connectors

- 24P *scanning mode*, if your output is film, or a film look

PROGRESSIVE SCANNING: Capturing the entire video frame in one scan, as opposed to dividing it into fields.

SCANNING MODES: Scanning modes are delineated with a combination of a frame rate (usually 24 or 30) and a letter that refers to scanning method ("I" for interlaced, or "P" for progressive).

For instance:

30I: 30 fps, interlaced (i.e., normal NTSC).

30P: 30 fps, progressive (used for "film-look" video).

24P: 24 fps, progressive (most like film).

Multicamera Styles

For studio productions such as newscasts and game shows, as well as for sporting events and weddings, you'll want camcorders (or cameras) that feature:

- Outputs for studio *switchers* and *VTRs* (including component-color signals)

SWITCHER: Control console in a TV studio where the director selects which camera's image will be recorded or transmitted.

VTR: Videotape recorder.

- Multicamera synchronization (including SMPTE timecode)

- Output matched to other cameras in the studio (so colors and details look the same when you switch camera angles)

- Support for advanced editing systems

- Selectable film or video look (*interlaced* or progressive scanning and variable *frame rates*). (For more information on scanning, see "What Are NTSC / PAL / SECAM Broadcast Formats?" later in this chapter.)

> **INTERLACED SCANNING:** Method used by NTSC and PAL/SECAM to capture and display one video frame as two alternating field patterns.
>
> **FRAME RATE:** The number of still images a film or video camera captures every second; frames per second (fps); picture rate.

ACCESS TO CONTROLS

Especially if you're shooting one-person news style, you must be able to work all the controls easily as you cradle the camcorder in your hands, or rest it on your shoulder. You'll probably prefer camcorders that divide functions between your right and left hands—with all of them easy to reach, so that you don't have to take your attention from the eyepiece to make adjustments.

Camcorders vary considerably in the placement of their controls. As you hold the camcorder, note the location of the controls you'll use most frequently. Obviously, one of the most important ones is the Record Start/Stop button—usually bright red in color.

 REALITY CHECK: *You won't know whether you're comfortable with the controls until you've done some shooting. Try holding the camcorder in various positions (cradled in your hands; on-shoulder; on a tripod). Can you reach the Record button without taking your eye off the viewfinder? How about the zoom control? Are the controls easier to use in one position than another? If you're left-handed, does the arrangement of controls seem awkward?*

CAMCORDER RESOLUTION AND PICTURE QUALITY

Let's take a closer look at the internal workings—and image-capture capabilities—of DV camcorders, as they pertain to resolution. (In conventional filmmaking, this would be equivalent to a discussion of camera capabilities and film stocks.) This technical information will be crucial for choosing and deploying the right tools for shooting, data transfer, editing, and distribution.

Digital camcorders are often rated in terms of resolution, and you will eventually need to make a decision about what kind of resolution you require from your camcorder. However, resolution is a complex subject. Even defining it can be tricky.

Spatial resolution generally refers to the number of individual dots, or *pixels* (short for *picture elements)* that compose an image. Most of the time, when people refer to resolution, they mean spatial resolution. However, resolution can also be used as a general measure of a video picture's sharpness and detail. *Chromatic resolution* refers to the range of colors each pixel can show; in effect, it's another term for color space.

> **SPATIAL RESOLUTION:** The number of pixels used by a camcorder or video display.
>
> **PIXEL:** Picture element; smallest area of color in digital video picture.
>
> **CHROMATIC RESOLUTION:** The number of colors a camcorder or video display is capable of recording or showing.

No doubt you've seen digital still cameras advertised with "megapixel" capability. For sake of simplicity, if digital pictures were square (which they usually aren't), megapixel spatial resolution would mean an image 1,000 dots wide by 1,000 dots high, totaling a million pixels, hence "mega-."

NOTE: *Film doesn't have pixels. The resolution of film depends on its arrangement of photosensitive chemicals (or grain). One of the key techniques to making video look like film involves adding "noise" to the video signal to simulate the appearance of film grain. From an aesthetic standpoint, the noise adds texture to solid colors.*

That may sound like a lot of pixels, but it's still not nearly as good as film. Film has a resolution higher than the human eye can see. Until recently, video didn't even come close. To match the resolution of a single frame of 35mm film, you'd need about 2,000 × 2,000 pixels.

Some high-priced still cameras do offer 4-megapixel capability or better, but at present there are no megapixel DV camcorders. You need an HD (high definition) camcorder to get into the megapixel range. (For more information, see "HD" in Appendix A.) It's not that electronics manufacturers can't make multi-megapixel devices—they obviously can, and cheaply. But with video, the challenge comes in dealing with the sheer volume of data involved in capturing 24–30 megapixel frames per second (fps).

The more data a camcorder has to process for each frame, the faster it must work, and the more expensive its electronics need to be. So resolution is not only a measure of quality, it's also a good way of predicting cost. High-resolution digital cameras, whether still or video, fetch high prices.

Professional still cameras need maximum resolution to capture images which can then be blown up onto large sheets of film. But there's a limit to the spatial resolution that a digital camcorder requires. For North American SDTV (standard definition television), that's 640 × 480 pixels; for HDTV, it's either 1920 × 1080, or 1280 × 720.

You'd think, then, that a DV camcorder would need no more than 307,200 pixels (640 × 480) and an HD model would need no more than 2,000,000 (1920 × 1080).

EFFECTIVE PIXEL COUNT:
Number of pixels on a CCD that show up in the active picture area—the image on the screen.

In reality, however, the *effective pixel counts* of DV and HD camcorders vary considerably. To understand why, and to make an informed decision about which camcorder with what resolution to buy or rent, some explanation of CCD technology is in order. (For more information, see "CCD Technology" in Appendix A.)

Comparing Resolution and Picture Quality in the Real World

There's a lot to think about when the time comes to choose a camera: resolution, color space, CCD design, aspect ratio, price, and all the rest. So just as an exercise, let's compare three real-world camcorder models to see how they stack up—the Canon XL1S, the JVC GY-DV5000U, and the Panasonic AG-DVX100 (**Figure 3.8**). These are some of the most popular camcorders among professional videographers and represent interesting tradeoffs between price and performance (**Table 3.2**). When it comes to technical specifications, the Canon and the Panasonic are prosumer DV camcorders, while the JVC is a professional unit; but any of these models might well compete for your attention.

Figure 3.8 The first prosumer camcorder to offer 24P (film look) scanning mode was the Panasonic AG-DVX100, which is also featured in the product comparison in this chapter.

Table 3.2 Comparison of Some Key Specifications of Three Popular DV Camcorders

	Canon XL1S	**JVC GY-DV5000U**	**Panasonic AG-DVX100**
Chip configuration	3CCD	3CCD	3CCD
CCD size	1/3 in	1/2 in	1/3 in
Effective pixel count	250,000	380,000	380,000
Color space	4:1:1	4:1:1 (4:2:2 option)	4:1:1
Shooting modes	30I/30P	30I/30P	30I/30P/24P
Zoom lens	Interchangeable	Interchangeable	Built-in
List price with zoom lens	$4,699	$6,795	$3,795

Effective Pixel Count

When you inspect a camcorder's spec sheet, the first things you'll be tempted to check are the chip size and *total pixel count*. However, "total pixels" isn't necessarily a good measure of resolution. You really need to know how many pixels actually show up on the screen. This is the "effective" pixel count. Some manufacturers provide this data, some don't.

> **TOTAL PIXEL COUNT:** Number of pixels on a single CCD, whether the camcorder uses one or three chips.

> **TIP:** *The term "total pixels" can be confusing in itself. Used correctly, it means all the pixels on just one CCD chip—not the sum of all three! So, any salesperson who says a 270,000-pixel 3CCD camcorder has nearly a million pixels is literally right, but is misleading you about its resolution.*

Canon gives the total number of RGB pixels for the XL1S as 270,000, and its effective pixels as 250,000. JVC's model has 410,000 total pixels on 1/2-inch chips, with 380,000 effective. Panasonic claims to have the same number of pixels as JVC, but on smaller, ⅓-inch chips.

> **INTERPOLATION:** Mathematical approximation process by which digital circuitry estimates the values of missing pixels.

All of these camcorders are available in the North American TV standard, which requires 307,200 pixels in the displayed picture. You can see that the Canon unit has fewer pixels than it seems to need, the JVC and the Panasonic more. As with any camcorder which has fewer than the required number of pixels, the Canon unit uses a digital *interpolation* process (essentially, a kind of mathematical approximation) to produce the missing pixels it needs for the final output. The result can look surprisingly good. All three cameras offer a variety of automatic image-processing functions, which no doubt use some of the extra chip real estate.

Seeing Is Believing

Judging from the combination of effective pixel count and chip size, you might conclude that the JVC camcorder is clearly superior. Some experienced videographers think so. However, *your* eye might well favor the Canon or the Panasonic. All of these cameras offer consumer 4:1:1 color space, but if you're producing solely for videocassette, DVD, or film transfer, the higher broadcast standard (requiring 4:2:2) need not concern you.

Canon claims its pixels are relatively large and give a better picture. It also offers a proprietary process for digitizing color called Pixel Shift that's supposed to improve picture detail. Do those features make up for JVC's larger CCD chip size and higher pixel count? Where do you factor in the JVC's higher price? Even though these considerations are technical, the answers can be artistic and financial: Which output looks best to your eye for your purposes, and how much can you afford to spend?

The list price of the Panasonic is attractively low by comparison. But before you jump for it, there's something else to consider. Unlike the Canon and the JVC cameras, the zoom lens on the Panasonic is not interchangeable—it's built into the camera body. Although this Leica lens is very good, it can't beat the wide selection of cinema-style lenses available for the other two cameras. (JVC offers a selection of Canon and Fujinon lenses for its ½-inch CCD video cameras.)

You can't decide which camera you prefer by looking at a spec sheet. When camcorders are roughly comparable in features and price range, as these are, you have to compare outputs, features, and feel—in the real world. But here's a hint: Filmmakers seem to favor the Canon or the Panasonic, news crews the JVC.

> **TIP:** *The previous version of the JVC camcorder, the GY-DV500U (one less zero in the model number), had a significantly lower list price—with true broadcast 4:2:2 color space. Officially, it's been discontinued, but you'll still find it in rental houses.*

WHAT ARE NTSC/PAL/SECAM BROADCAST FORMATS?

One of the biggest challenges for DV and digital TV (DTV) is that for the foreseeable future they must remain compatible with analog television (ATV) standards that were established half a century ago.

As a videomaker, you need to understand this arcane system well enough to make the right choices about equipment that may be compatible with some standards but incompatible with others. (For the most part, filmmakers don't have to worry about this stuff, aside from framing their shots for the small screen.)

ATV broadcast formats apply to network transmissions, cable systems, camcorders, VCRs, and DVD decks. And to make matters worse, there are different ATV broadcast standards for different parts of the world.

NTSC: North American broadcast television standard; initials stand for National Television Standards Committee.

PAL: British broadcast television standard; initials stand for Phase Alternating Line.

SECAM: French and Asian broadcast television standard; initials stand for Système Electronique Couleur avec Mémoire, which translates as Electronic Color System with Memory.

DV camcorders are designed to work with either NTSC (the North American TV standard) or *PAL/SECAM* (the British and French/Asian TV standards). Although there are multiformat VCRs and DVD players, camcorders come in one format or the other, not both.

TIP: You can't generally play an NTSC videotape on a PAL VCR, or vice versa. However, you can import both kinds into your digital editing system, and once a DV recording has been loaded, you can easily convert it to any output standard you like. That's one of the many reasons DV is overtaking analog video so rapidly. You can intermix NTSC and PAL DV clips in the same presentation, then output the finished show to either standard without fretting too much about the details. To achieve the same results in analog video, you'd need to employ time-consuming conversion steps at both input and output stages.

The basic differences between NTSC and PAL/SECAM come down to frame rates and scan lines. (They also differ in color space, a topic we've already mentioned in this chapter and cover in greater depth in Appendix A.)

Frame Rates

The standard frame rate for motion-picture film cameras anywhere in the world is 24 frames per second (fps). If only video were so simple!

Hz: Cycles per second; Hertz.

RASTER: Zigzag pattern painted by the electron beam as it scans the photosensitive phosphors on the inside face of a cathode ray tube (CRT).

NTSC displays pictures at nearly 30 fps—the actual number is 29.97. PAL/SECAM uses exactly 25 fps. These frame rates are based on the local frequency of alternating current (AC) electrical power: 60 *Hz* in the States; 50 Hz in most of the rest of the world. Early television engineers used the AC frequency to control *raster* scanning (**Figure 3.9**).

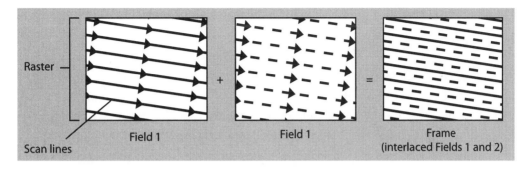

Figure 3.9 TV's complex system of scan lines and interlaced fields is inherited from the early days of television. The scanning beam is turned on during the left-to-right trace that creates visible scan lines, and turned off during the right-to-left (horizontal flyback) and bottom-to-top (vertical flyback) traces.

Fields and Scan Lines

In theory, new digital TV sets could make a clean break with the past. The technology exists for making video broadcasting simpler, but it won't happen anytime soon. Anyone who produces video is stuck with the complicated legacy of decades-old analog television. If it were otherwise, millions of older sets all over the world would go blank, and no one in the industry is ready for that to happen.

Early TV picture tubes couldn't hold an image for very long before it started to fade, so television engineers added an additional complication to reduce flicker: They divided each frame into two fields, each composed of alternate sets of scan lines (first odd-numbered lines, then even-numbered lines).

Under this method, NTSC scanning becomes a succession of horizontal scans at close to 60 fields per second. The scan lines of the second field are painted in between the scan lines of the first. The result is a near-30 fps shown at nearly 60 fields per second—with little or no flicker. PAL/SECAM TV sets do 50 fields per second to achieve 25 fps.

The alternating scan lines of the two fields that compose each frame are said to be *interlaced*.

In the world of analog video, the number of horizontal scan lines on the screen is one way to measure picture resolution. And once again, NTSC and PAL/SECAM employ different specs: NTSC uses 525 horizontal scan lines; PAL and SECAM use 625.

WHAT DO YOU NEED TO KNOW ABOUT SCANNING MODES?

We've discussed scanning, but we haven't looked at how different scanning modes might affect your selection of a DV camcorder. Not every camcorder supports every scanning mode. Depending on the nature of your project, especially its intended release media, you will need to make sure your camcorder supports the needed scanning mode.

Camcorders use two possible scanning modes:

- Interlaced (mainstay of ATV)

- Progressive (considered more "filmic")

Interlaced

Interlaced scanning will be with us for awhile, since broadcast technology has to remain backward compatible with the old ATV standard. That means if you're aiming your video project at release on NTSC video, you'll probably shoot in 4:3 aspect ratio, 30I (30 fps, interlaced). Any consumer or professional NTSC DV camcorder will do the job.

> **NOTE:** When you're studying product literature and trade magazine articles, you may see the scanning-mode designation 60I, which means "60 fields per second interlaced." It's therefore equivalent to 30I, or "30 frames per second interlaced." In general you may see 60I used more commonly to refer to HD cameras. Perhaps the rationale is that a high-def field exceeds the resolution of a normal standard-def frame. To be consistent, this book sticks to the frame rate, not the field rate, when discussing scanning modes.

Curiously enough, HDTV was originally intended to be compatible with old sets, which meant interlaced scanning. This plan was abandoned as impractical, but one of two predominant HDTV broadcast formats still uses interlaced scanning. It's designated 1080I because it has 1,080 scan lines. So, one scanning mode only available on HD camcorders is 1080I—with a variety of frame-rate options. This HDTV format is designated by the number of scan lines rather than by fps, which can vary by broadcaster.

> MULTISCAN: Referring to computer and television monitors, and TV sets, that can operate at a variety of scanning modes, or frame rates.

> **TIP:** If you're shooting HD for broadcast, the required frame rate and scanning mode will be set by your network client; broadcasters use different formats based on the bandwidth of the satellite channels they lease or control. HDTV sets operate in multiscan mode, adjusting their scanning rates automatically to that of the incoming signal.

Progressive

If you are planning to release your project on film, or want your video to *look* like film, you will probably set your camcorder to use progressive scanning mode, in which interlacing is turned off and the camcorder captures the entire picture one frame at a time, like a motion picture camera. Progressive scanning eliminates artifacts due to interlacing and blurs rapid motion a bit, which contributes even more to a film look.

The most common progressive scanning option for NTSC camcorders is 30P—30 fps without interlacing. Even if you are producing primarily for video, this mode can give a filmed look to your production. A show shot in 30P and converted to NTSC in post will look more like a film that was converted to television.

Another option, which first appeared in HD and is now appearing in prosumer DV camcorders (starting with the Panasonic AG-DVX100), allows you to shoot at 24 instead of 30 fps. This mode is called 24P, which stands for 24 fps progressive. The 24P mode provides a one-to-one match with motion-picture frame rate, and makes for better transfers. Watch for 24P scanning to become an increasingly common DV camcorder feature.

 REALITY CHECK: You don't necessarily need to shoot in 24P mode to achieve film-look video motion. We'll give you tips on film-look shooting and finishing throughout this book. For more information on your options in post, see "Applying Film-Look Filters" in Chapter 11.

The other most commonly used HDTV mode, found only on HD camcorders, is 720P, which progressively scans 720 lines—at various frame rates (like the interlaced HDTV format, the number of scan lines is fixed but fps can vary by broadcaster).

Making Video Look Like Film

Most of the time you will want your video to look like...a video. But sometimes, whether you are tailoring your production for film transfer or simply trying to create a television show that has a glossy, high-quality film look, you will want to make your video look more like film. This can be accomplished by using a combination of DV camcorder settings and postproduction techniques. Film-look characteristics include:

Resolution. *If you require theater-quality, 35mm film resolution, shoot in HD. In comparison, transferring a standard DV video to film for big-screen theatrical exhibition looks like 16mm. That's not necessarily bad: It can give your production an interesting cult-movie quality. If you get a chance to see 28 Days Later which was shot in PAL DV, on the wide screen, you'll see what we mean. This movie had a budget large enough to shoot on film, but its producers chose DV to get the look they were after.*

Continued on next page

Making Video Look Like Film (continued)

Film grain and video noise. *Film resolution is much higher than DV, and even a bit higher than today's HD, but since the photosensitive particles in the film emulsion are distributed randomly, grain structure is often visible in projected film, especially in low light. If you want to capture that look, you can actually add "noise" to the video image during post, providing a grainy, film-like texture. If you want to make a video production look like an old newsreel or home movie, one type of digital processing will even add random scratch marks to your footage.*

Contrast range. *This is the variation from the brightest to the darkest areas in a scene. The contrast range of film is about 100:1. The contrast range of video, limited by the current state of the art in CCD and related technologies, is only about 30:1. The blacks in a film look blacker than they will in video; the whites look whiter, and you can see more detail in both shaded and sunlit areas. In video, if you expose for a dark face in the shade of a tree, the brightly lit areas will be washed out. If you expose for the brightest areas, the face under the tree will turn to mud. So, to give your video a film look, you must pay careful attention to keeping your lighting even. Although you can handle some contrast-range problems through color correction in post, the best way to address this issue is by lighting the scene very carefully in the first place.*

Color space. *If you're shooting primarily for film transfer, color space doesn't matter. However, due to variations in specific lenses, chips, and circuitry, each camcorder will give a somewhat different look. Plan on shooting tests with different camcorders, doing transfers to specific film stocks, and evaluating the results.*

Motion capture. *Progressive scanning modes (30P or 24P) will look more film-like than interlaced modes, because they provide some blurring of fast-moving objects—an effect audiences associate with film.*

Depth of field. *Depth of field defines the range of distances that will remain in focus within a single shot. In general, video offers greater depth of field than film. While it may seem counter-intuitive, most cinematographers consider that to be video's disadvantage. The cinematographer's goal is to show the viewer where to look, and controlling focus is one way to do that. If everything in the shot is in sharp focus, it's harder to direct the viewer's attention. To achieve a shallower, and more film-like, depth of field, look for a vidcam with a large CCD—or optical target area. (You can also use lower f-stop settings and longer lenses.) The bigger the chips (or the optical target area) in the camcorder, the more shallow the depth of field you can achieve. For more information on lighting scenes to achieve depth, see "Use Rim Light for Depth" in Chapter 6.*

> ***TIP:*** *You can buy an adapter developed by P+S Technik that lets you use standard motion-picture lenses on some prosumer and professional camcorders. With the adapter in place, the CCD chip is no longer the initial optical target. Rather, the image is focused on a ground-glass screen that's the same size as a 35mm frame, after which the resulting image is reflected onto the chips. The larger optical target creates a shallower, and more visually pleasing, depth of field—permitting the videographer to use those motion-picture lenses to their best advantage.*

Continued on next page

> **Making Video Look Like Film** (continued)
>
> *If you don't have access to a 24P NTSC camera, would a PAL video camera do better for shooting film look? This question lies at the heart of a fierce controversy. Ask low-budget filmmakers who aspire to make Hollywood productions, and the answer you'll hear most often is, "For sure." PAL's 25 fps frame rate is so close to film's 24 fps that transferring from PAL to film is assumed to be easier and presumed to look smoother. In addition, PAL offers 20 percent higher resolution—625 lines per frame instead of 525—which looks better on film. Finally, some people think PAL's 4:2:0 color space looks more film-like. This is why some North American filmmakers pay a premium to rent PAL camcorders for their projects, even though they are relatively difficult to find outside Europe.*
>
> *However, another set of filmmakers (including the authors of this book) aren't convinced. A lot depends on the "look" of the individual camcorder and the expertise of the lab doing the tape-to-film transfer. (For more information on video-to-film transfers, see "Releasing on Theatrical Film" in Chapter 12.)*

NOTE: *The typical scanning mode of NTSC consumer DV camcorders is 30I. Some prosumer and professional camcorders can shoot at 24P, 30I, 30P, or 60P. HD cameras can shoot at 30I, 30P, and 60P. HD models intended for motion-picture production, including the Sony CineAlta and Panasonic AJ-HDC models, can shoot at 24P.*

DO YOU NEED AUTOMATIC CAMCORDER CONTROLS?

If you read the ads, you'll notice that manufacturers seem to feel that automatic camcorder controls are a must-have feature for most videomakers.

However, even if you're an inexperienced user, it won't take you long to discover that automatic controls and image processing features are usually more trouble than they're worth. If you're hesitant to buy an otherwise attractive camcorder because it lacks automatic controls, our advice is to go ahead and buy.

All professional camcorders give you the ability to turn automatic functions off and use manual controls instead. But it's a challenge to find low-cost or budget-level camcorders with manual overrides for automatic functions.

The Price You Pay for Image Processing

DV camcorders at all price levels offer various sets of automatic controls, including auto exposure (AE), auto-focus (AF), auto white balance (AWB), and automatic audio gain control (AGC) or automatic level control (ALC). AE and AF take the place of making manual lens adjustments, AWB compensates for variations in the color of lighting sources, and AGC is an automatic audio volume control.

Unfortunately, most automatic features sacrifice quality for the sake of convenience. No digital processing circuitry, no matter how sophisticated, can read the mind of a videographer.

For example, consider what happens in a DV camcorder when you use its "automatic electronic image stabilization" feature:

The lighter the camera, the more difficult it is to move it smoothly. Automatic electronic image stabilization compensates for camera jiggle by selecting a smaller-than-normal portion of the CCD to frame the image. If the image drifts or jiggles toward the edges of the CCD, the camcorder's processor selects the new boundaries as the correct image framing.

However, by using a smaller-than-usual portion of the CCD's active picture area, this function sacrifices resolution and steals pixels from the CCD. It delivers a picture that's less sharp than if you had turned off the feature and simply found a way to hold the camera more steadily.

Want another example? If you pan across a bright light source, AE won't be able to adjust fast enough. The circuitry will undercompensate, then overcompensate, and by that time you'll be off the bright light, and the exposure will need to auto-adjust again.

More examples:

Autofocus gets confused in action-packed scenes. It may focus on objects at the center of the frame, not on the main character who is making a hasty exit at frame right.

CCDs in Low-Light Conditions: Feature or Flaw?

Low-light sensitivity seems like a camcorder plus, but if you use it you'll be stuck with images film-makers would call grainy.

Sensors on a CCD don't give up their electrons easily. A stimulating voltage (or bias) must be applied to the chip to get the sensors "hot." It's possible to increase a CCD's sensitivity to light by raising the bias, thereby reducing the intensity of light required to stimulate electron flow.

Some DV camcorders allow you to use this trick to adjust the CCD sensitivity for low-light conditions. Sometimes that's a handy option, but there's a catch: Turning up the sensitivity tends to make the chip "noisy," because some of the electron output is caused, not by light, but by the bias voltage itself.

This is a perfect example of why camcorders with automatic features can deliver disappointing results. Many consumer-model camcorders compensate for low-light conditions by automatically increasing the CCD bias. The camera's designers think you'd prefer any picture at all—even a noisy one—rather than taking the time to light the scene better.

If a camcorder comes with this low-light feature, and there's no way to turn it off, either don't buy the camcorder or find a way to increase lighting on your subjects.

Auto white balance is designed to take a guess, based on the assumption that the brightest areas of a scene should be white. What if they're supposed to be hot pink?

Automatic audio gain control will crank up the audio gain as soon as the scene goes quiet. The result? You'll make a clear, digital recording of the house air-conditioning system. The opposite happens when actors shout: AGC can't crank the volume down fast enough, and audio distortion results.

Other automatic features are just as likely to get in your way. Examples include shadow enhancement or reduction, picture sharpness control, color correction (other than white or black balance), and digital transition effects (such as fades and dissolves). All of these effects are best handled in post.

Do you need automatic camcorder controls? Let's put it this way: Do you need training wheels on a bicycle?

OPTICAL VS. DIGITAL ZOOM

Zooming is another name for changing the focal length of a lens, as when you zoom from wide angle to telephoto. Zooming is the first lens adjustment novice videographers learn, because it can add interest, even drama, to a scene—and it's easy.

Some consumer camcorders, especially low-cost models, supplement their limited zoom lenses with a digital zoom. For instance, if the optics of the lens only provide limited zooming range (say 10X), and you want to zoom beyond that, an image-processing circuit inside the camcorder selects a smaller portion of the CCD image area and enlarges it electronically. The electronic zoom involves interpolating pixels, a process that always sacrifices resolution.

Digital zooming makes it possible for even the most inexpensive cameras to offer what *sounds* like major magnification. Of course, it's a cheat. Compound zoom lenses and their high-quality optics can be very expensive; image-processing circuitry is cheap—and the results look it.

AUDIO OPTIONS

When you're on location or on the set, your main concern with audio is usually getting a clean track of the person who's talking. Most of the sophistication of audio—including sound effects, stereo dimension, and music—is added during postproduction.

Another reason not to worry about your camcorder's audio capability is that you don't need to use it. To achieve the best audio quality, some videomakers use an external DAT recorder, not the camcorder's built-in audio. (For more information about external audio recording, see "Should You Record Separate Sound?" in Chapter 7.)

However, there are several audio features you should think about. As we've already mentioned, professional DV recorders have audio lock for timecode-accurate soundtracks—a feature consumer camcorders lack. (For more information, see "Using a Clapper Board and Timecode" in Chapter 7.) Also, higher-priced camcorders do use better electronic components and professional-style audio connectors, which can make a difference in sound quality.

DV Camcorder Audio Recording Modes

Four standard audio-capture modes are built into every DV camcorder to help you get that clean dialogue track. They are the same whether your camcorder is a consumer or professional unit, so paying more for your camcorder won't give you better audio specs.

DV camcorders sample audio by pulse code modulation (PCM), the same method used in computer music synthesizers. Options for PCM sampling rates are expressed in thousands of cycles per second (kHz) and the number of data bits per sample:

- Studio-standard stereo (highest quality)—Two 16-bit channels sampled at 48 kHz. This is default mode, and you'll rarely have a reason to switch away from it. When you get into the editing suite, ideally all your audio sources should be at 48 kHz.

- CD-quality stereo (medium quality)—Two 16-bit channels sampled at 44.1 kHz. At one time you needed this lower-quality format so you could match the frequencies of CD sources, such as music and sound effects. These days, desktop editing software easily resolves any differences in sampling rate, and it will sound better if you up-convert the CDs to 48 kHz instead.

- Stereo (lower quality)—Two 16-bit channels sampled at 32 kHz. Don't use it. Stay at the highest, default rate.

- Four channel (lowest quality)—Four 12-bit channels (typically, left and right stereo sync sound, plus two channels for dubbing) sampled at 32 kHz. You'll use this mode when you intend to go back and do a voice-over recording on another track—for example, adding commentary to a news clip. It's also handy for doing the same thing while you're in the field.

GETTING DV INTO YOUR COMPUTER

> **PROTOCOL:** Data communication specification for the sequence of transmission.

The cables, connectors, and *protocols* by which you upload recordings from a DV camcorder into a PC are officially designated IEEE 1394. However, this high-speed data link usually goes by more familiar trademarks like Apple FireWire and Sony iLINK.

All DV camcorders have an IEEE 1394 connector for handling uploads, but the connection requires a FireWire or iLINK interface card on the computer side. For convenience in uploading to computers that don't have IEEE 1394 connections, some camcorders provide other types of high-speed connections like Fast Ethernet, USB2, and wireless LAN. A higher-bandwidth Fast FireWire is also available, and proprietary Sony video hardware supports a faster version of iLINK.

All of these high-speed connections—IEEE 1394, Fast Ethernet, or USB2—carry pictures and sound in a single data stream.

> *TIP: Like their analog forebears, many digital camcorders have a connector labeled "Video Out." This is an analog signal, and it's only useful purpose nowadays is to drive conventional TV sets, VCRs, and monitors. Video engineers call this output* composite video *because it carries all the image information on a single line. A separate output line labeled "Audio Out" carries the analog audio signal; there will be two paired outputs (Left and Right) if it's stereo. If a camcorder has both Video Out and S-Video (or Y/C) jacks, using S-Video will give you a much better picture on a monitor. Don't use Video Out or S-Video outputs to capture DV for editing, even if your computer has an analog video capture card—you'll lose the benefits of going all digital.*

YOUR MISSION

Now that we've told you all about what goes on inside a camcorder, you know enough to be dangerous—especially if you've read Appendix A. You can see right through spec sheets and make high-powered salespeople sweat.

Is there more to learn? Absolutely. We can't tell you whether the camcorder you just saw advertised on special or gleaming in the store window offers the best value for your money and for your particular project.

But now you know how to find out, so go ahead and make 'em sweat!

CHAPTER FOUR

Using Your Camcorder Like a Pro

So much for technology. Now it's time to get ready to shoot. We're about to introduce you to the controls and operational features of a DV camcorder and its accessories. We'll also point out some things to think about when you're getting to know your camera or looking it over at the rental house. And we'll pass along a few professional tips and techniques for using your camera to its full potential.

HOW TO GET A CRASH COURSE WITHOUT TRASHING A CAMERA

It's a bad idea to take your new camcorder out of the box for the first time on the morning you start shooting your video. For one thing, it might not work properly. But even if it does, any piece of complex technical gear has foibles, bugs, and "design trade-offs." It's best to learn about them early—when you're shooting test scenes, for example—so you won't waste valuable time while actors and technicians stand around with the clock ticking.

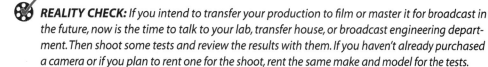 **REALITY CHECK:** *If you intend to transfer your production to film or master it for broadcast in the future, now is the time to talk to your lab, transfer house, or broadcast engineering department. Then shoot some tests and review the results with them. If you haven't already purchased a camera or if you plan to rent one for the shoot, rent the same make and model for the tests.*

Read the Manual

Tedious as it might seem, you really should read the camcorder manual—from cover to cover. Many people use just 10 percent of their camcorder's features simply because they don't know what the thing can do. If you're using a rental unit (or a reconditioned one) and didn't receive a manual, documentation for most prosumer and professional models is available on the technical support sections of the manufacturers' Web sites.

Scan the Magazines

If you're getting acquainted with your camcorder—especially if it's a model that just hit the market—check to see what reviewers in trade magazines like *Digital Video Magazine* and *Camcorder & Computer Video* have to say about the camera. Find out if they picked up on any design flaws or idiosyncrasies. If so, the review might include work-arounds for them.

Check the Web

Magazine Web sites often have searchable archives of articles. You can also log into camcorder outlets and DV user groups on the Internet.

Visit a Rental House or Trade Show

One great way to get a guided tour of your new camera is to go to a video equipment rental house and ask for a demonstration. Technical support reps at rental houses are usually much more knowledgeable than sales clerks at stores. And they often have precious, undocumented tips because the service desk is a clearinghouse for professional gossip. Another possibility is to attend a DV trade show and talk to videographers who've used the camera.

> **TIP:** To familiarize professionals with new camcorder products, manufacturers often hold free hands-on clinics. You'll find notices about these briefings at the manufacturers' Web sites and in DV trade magazines.

ERGONOMICS

Perhaps the single most important characteristic of a camcorder is how it looks and feels when you pick it up. Hopefully, you've tried out the camera before buying or renting, but even if you haven't, give yourself some time to get used to it.

Physical Size, Weight, Balance

Camcorders are lighter than ever, but there's a catch: Although it's easier to hold lightweight camcorders for extended periods of time, you may find it difficult to keep them steady during a take. Heavier camcorders have more inertia, which promotes smoother movement.

Keeping the camcorder steady is also a matter of balance, and the biggest factors in camcorder balance are the size and weight of the lens and the counterbalancing weight of the camera body itself.

Lens optics are made of glass, and glass is heavy. Most good camcorders have a compound zoom lens that weighs several pounds all by itself. The camcorder body, the part that houses its electronics and recorder, is relatively light. As a result, camcorders with zoom lenses tend to be front-heavy, and holding them steady during a shoot can be a challenge.

Use Back-Weighted Cameras for Shooting News Style

Front-heavy cameras can be particularly annoying if you are shooting handheld, news style, which is one reason news-style videographers prefer to work with their cameras on their shoulders (**Figure 4.1**). In the old days, when cameras were briefcase-size and weighed 10 pounds or more, this was the only practical way to carry them. However, even with the new, lighter models, many videographers still find it easiest to keep the camera steady with its back resting on their shoulders.

Figure 4.1 Veteran news videographers prefer to carry their camcorders slung over the shoulder. This provides better balance and lets them operate the controls easily using both hands.

Right hand holds camcorder and presses Start/Stop (Record) and Zoom switches.

Left hand focuses the lens and adjusts focus and exposure controls, which may be located either on the barrel of the lens or on the left side of the camera body.

For this reason, some manufacturers who make camcorders intended primarily for news crews have added extra weight at the back to counterbalance the front-heaviness of the lens—a so-called *shoulder-mount body*. A back-heavy camcorder tends to stay in place on your shoulder as you move about. JVC's GY-DV5000U is an example.

By contrast, the body of Canon's XL1S is relatively light, causing it to be front-heavy with any of its big lenses attached. To make the XL1S more suitable for over-the-shoulder news-style work, you'll probably want a weighted shoulder pad (**Figure 4.2**), which provides a comfortable resting place for the camera on your shoulder as well as a counterbalance for the weight of the lens.

Camera Balance for Shooting Film Style

If you're shooting film style, the camera will usually be *locked down*—set on a tripod or some other mount—and you won't need to worry about its weight, except when you're moving it from one setup to another. (Of course you might want to shoot hand-held for effect.)

> **LOCKED DOWN:** Immobilized camera on a stationary mount, such as a tripod.

Wireless microphone receiver

Weighted shoulder pad

XLR audio jacks

Figure 4.2 You can buy a weighted shoulder pad for the Canon XL1S, which compensates for the front-heaviness caused by its large lens. This attachment (shown here mounted on the camera) also has professional-style XLR audio jacks and a wireless microphone receiver. (Photo courtesy Canon U.S.A., Inc.)

NOTE: To a veteran cinematographer, "locked down" means tightening the screws so hard that the camera is absolutely unmovable on its tripod or mount. But you'll also hear less picky types use the term to simply mean "stationary," as opposed to handheld or mechanized movement.

HEAD: The mechanism on top of a tripod or dolly that holds the camera and allows you to move it.

But even if the camcorder is on a mount, weight is still a consideration for another reason: It affects the quality, size, weight, and expense of the camera mounts you must buy or rent. A heavy camcorder needs a relatively expensive tripod and *head* to safely support the camcorder and provide smooth movement.

Moreover, balance is still a big factor even if the camcorder is mounted on a tripod. If the weight is distributed unevenly, it will affect how easily and smoothly you'll be able to pan, tilt, and move the camera on its mount. Professional tripods have a movable base plate that you can slide backwards or forwards to precisely align the camera's center of gravity over the tripod attachment point.

Viewfinders, LCD Screens, and Monitors

Camcorders offer two basic methods to help you frame your shot: *viewfinders* and flip-out *LCD* screens. Film-style shooters tend to prefer viewfinders. News-style videographers find that flip-out screens allow them to hold the camera more steadily when they're making hand-held shots, especially with smaller cameras. (LCD screens are also handy for checking menu settings when it's not convenient for you to be looking through the eyepiece.)

Viewfinders

You'll recognize the viewfinder by its eyepiece, a small lens surrounded by a rubber shield called an *eye cup* (**Figure 4.3**). The eyepiece shields the image from surrounding glare.

The viewfinder focuses on a tiny LCD screen inside the camera body that displays the video picture. The image is a miniature of the shot you'll capture if you press the Record Start/Stop button. The viewfinder *status display* also shows alphanumeric text and symbol overlays that tell the operator about camera settings, lighting conditions, and the charge level of the battery.

VIEWFINDER: Lets you see the current view through the lens of a camcorder. Status information is usually displayed as well.

LCD: Liquid crystal display that shows the current view through the lens of a camcorder. The LCD may be either internal (seen through the viewfinder) or external (on a small door that flips out from the camera body).

EYE CUP: Rubber shield surrounding the eyepiece of a camera viewfinder

STATUS DISPLAY: Alphanumeric readouts that appear in the camcorder viewfinder (and sometimes on a field monitor) showing f-stop, battery level, current timecode, Rec/Pause/ Standby, and more.

Figure 4.3 Sighting through the camcorder's eye cup lets you see the viewfinder display: a shot through the lens, overlaid with alphanumeric text that gives you information on current camera settings. (Photo courtesy Canon U.S.A., Inc.)

Depending on the camera, the viewfinder display will be black-and-white or color. Most film-style videographers prefer black-and-white viewfinders, since it's easier to judge focus and other picture details with a black-and-white display.

> **OVERSCAN:** Camera viewfinder function showing a larger image area than will actually be recorded.

Film-style videographers should also look for camcorders whose viewfinders can be set to *overscan,* showing an area that's slightly larger than the final frame of the recorded picture—a standard motion picture feature you'll now find on some prosumer and professional camcorders. That extra area surrounding the picture will help you spot moving subjects before they enter the frame. The fraction of a second warning you gain might give you just enough time to point the camera or change focus. This is particularly useful for anticipating an actor's entrance. (This feature is not currently supported on any flip-out screens that we know of. But you can get much the same effect by not pressing your eye up hard against the eyepiece—that way you can see things in your peripheral vision.)

External LCD Screens

Many camcorders offer an additional preview device—an external LCD screen that flips out from the body of the camera like a car door (**Figure 4.4**). Compared to the internal LCDs used in viewfinders, these external LCD screens are relatively large—one or two inches across. The display is usually in color.

The flip-out LCD screen lets you shoot hand-held with the camcorder in front of your body, rather than pressed to your head. This technique makes for a steadier picture: when you press the eyecup of a viewfinder to your face, then walk and shoot, physical contact with the bobbing of your head jars the camcorder. If you use the flip-out screen, you can cradle the camcorder in your hands, away from your face. The muscles at your elbows are natural shock absorbers, smoothing the camcorder's ride and steadying the image. This is just what the director ordered for run-and-gun news gathering, especially if you're using a small camera.

TIP: Most flip-out screens are mounted on a swivel so you can rotate them for viewing as you stand facing the camera lens. This feature can be useful if you don't have a crew and you're standing in for a close-up, or if you're shooting your own presentation. You'll notice that rotating the screen also causes the image to be presented not only upright, but also mirrored. This might seem odd at first, but clever camcorder designers realized that subjects are more used to seeing themselves in a mirror. In fact, it can be quite difficult to keep yourself in frame if you turn mirroring off (which you can do through the menu), in which case you'll see yourself the way others see you—with your hair parted on the "wrong" side!

LENSES AND LENS OPERATION

The lens of your camcorder will probably have more of an impact on picture quality, and your control of it, than any other single feature.

Lens Terminology and Functions

Camcorder lenses come in various *focal lengths*: wide angle, normal, and telephoto. These terms refer to how close the lenses make objects appear in the frame. Wide-angle lenses include a wider field of view than normal lenses and make objects seem far away. Telephoto lenses give a narrower picture and make objects seem close.

> **FOCAL LENGTH:** Range of distances over which a lens can be focused to achieve a sharp picture.

Figure 4.4 This is a DVCAM unit designed for news crews. In addition to the handy flip-out LCD screen, a swivel attachment lets you point the built-in mic directly at sound sources that aren't directly in front of the lens. (Photo courtesy Sony Electronics Inc.)

Removable vs. Built-in Lenses

Most consumer and some prosumer camcorders have built-in, nonremovable lenses. Almost all professional models (and some prosumer units) are designed for removable, interchangeable lenses.

 For more information on lens selection, see "Ten Ways to Shoot a Chair" in Chapter 5 and on the DVD.

An inexpensive consumer camcorder with a built-in zoom lens could be perfect for shooting news style, since you'll rarely have time to change lenses anyway. Even if you have a professional camcorder with interchangeable lenses, you'll probably rely mostly on a single, multi-purpose zoom lens for news-style shooting. (Of course, the zoom lens on a professional camcorder is likely to be of much higher optical quality than the one on an inexpensive consumer unit.)

If you're shooting film style, there's ample time to change lenses and pick exactly the right one, even though prosumer and professional camcorders generally come with a zoom lens as standard equipment. Lenses are precision instruments, and selecting the right lens is like picking a wrench to do a delicate auto repair: you'll do a better job using the just-right-sized tool than an adjustable one. (There's also a creative dimension to selecting lenses, much like picking a brush of a particular size for the next stroke of your painting.)

Since film-style videographers like to be able to choose just the right lens for each shot, the single most desired camcorder feature for this group is a large selection of removable lenses (**Figure 4.5**).

Figure 4.5 The XL1S offers an assortment of interchangeable zoom and special-purpose lenses. If you're shooting film style, this is an essential factor in choosing a camcorder. (Photo courtesy Canon U.S.A., Inc.)

Exposure and Focus

Getting good exposures isn't just a matter of setting your camera correctly; how you light a scene is extremely important. But the camcorder certainly plays a role. The main way of controlling exposure on the camcorder is to adjust the *aperture*, iris, lens opening, or *f-stop*—all of which mean the same thing.

> **APERTURE:** Size of lens opening used to control exposure; iris.
>
> **F-STOP:** A numeric index defining aperture size. Camcorder f-stop settings generally range from f/1.6 (the widest opening, allowing the most amount of light to enter the lens) to f/16 (narrowest opening, least light).
>
> **MONITOR:** External display connected to a camcorder that shows the viewfinder image on a larger screen so you can frame the shot and judge its quality.

The iris can open or close to a specific aperture size or f-stop. On some photographic-style lenses, you select f-stop settings by rotating a ring on the lens barrel. On other camcorders, you rotate a dial, or iris wheel, on the camera body. On most camcorders, the current setting appears in the viewfinder and *monitor* status displays (**Figure 4.6**).

The higher the f-stop number, the smaller the aperture, and the less light striking the CCDs. (For instance, f/2.8 is a large opening that lets in more light than f/16, which is a small opening.) The ideal setting, whether you're shooting video or film, will be in the midrange between f/4.0 and f/5.6—called the "sweet spot."

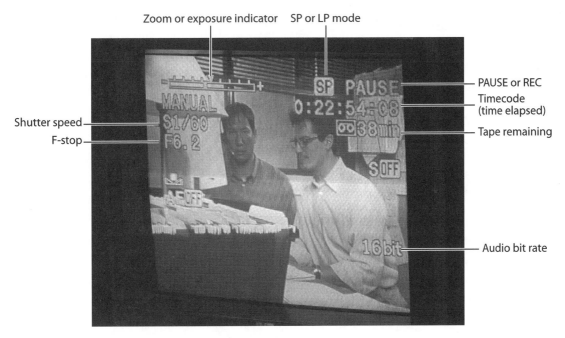

Zoom or exposure indicator   SP or LP mode

Shutter speed

F-stop

PAUSE or REC

Timecode (time elapsed)

Tape remaining

Audio bit rate

Figure 4.6 The alphanumeric status display shows the camcorder's current f-stop setting, among many other things.

Video CCDs respond best between f/1.6 and f/11. F/1.6 is the widest aperture for low-light conditions, and f/11 is about the smallest, for bright lighting. (If you need a setting outside this range, you'll need to adjust light levels instead.)

> **TIP:** You may see t-stop settings listed in lens spec sheets. T-stops are numeric indexes for the actual performance of a specific lens. You needn't concern yourself with t-stops unless you are comparison-shopping for lenses for a special purpose, such as shooting in low light. T-stop indexes work like f-stops: Larger numbers mean smaller openings.

Most camcorders have an auto-exposure (AE) feature. If you're serious about the quality of your work, you will turn it off and set exposures manually. Even so, some consumer-level camcorders don't give you full control over the exposure. They set the exposure for you and then allow you to open or close the iris by only one or two f-stops. This feature is usually called *AE shift*. Stay away from cameras with this feature if you want true manual operation. (For more information on using a light meter to set correct exposures, see "Light for Narrow Contrast Range" in Chapter 6.)

Focusing is what makes the picture sharp (or fuzzy, if you do it wrong—or if you're going for a slightly soft look to hide the star's wrinkles). On almost all camcorder lenses, you adjust focus by rotating a focus ring, a circular fitting that wraps around the barrel of the

> **AE SHIFT** Semi-automatic camcorder function that you adjust one or two f-stops up or down from the setting calculated by the camera's autoexposure circuit.

lens (**Figure 4.7**). Some inexpensive still cameras come with fixed-focus lenses that can't be adjusted, but you won't find them on camcorders. However, some palm- and pocket-sized camcorders with lenses built into the body can be focused manually only by disabling the camera's autofocus feature.

> **TIP:** Want to make sure your shot is in focus? Zoom in on your subject as close as you can go. Adjust focus until the image in the viewfinder is sharp. Now, readjust the zoom to frame the shot you want. The shot will be in focus anywhere within the zoom range.

How Lens Aperture Affects Depth of Field

Depth of field defines the range of distances that will remain in focus within a single shot. For example, in a medium shot with a normal lens, objects three to six feet away might appear sharp. Objects nearer than three feet and farther away than six will be blurred. Telephoto lenses tend to have a shallower depth of field (a narrow range of distance can be in focus), and wide-angle lenses tend to have a greater depth of field (nearly everything in focus).

In any case, setting depth of field is an important artistic decision, part of composing a good shot. But it's not just a matter of changing lenses. The size of the aperture makes a big difference: Smaller f-stop settings (say, around f/11) will give greater depth of field than larger apertures (for instance, f/1.6). In addition, dim lighting gives shallower depth of field than bright. (We've summarized these factors in **Table 4.1**.)

Focus ring   Zoom ring

Figure 4.7 The barrel of the telephoto zoom lens on the XL1S has two knurled, black, moveable rings. The ring closest to the operator controls zoom; the one farthest forward controls focus. Notice that (unlike photographic-style lenses) this lens has no distance markings on the rings. However, the current distance setting appears in the alphanumeric viewfinder display. (Photo courtesy Canon U.S.A., Inc.)

Table 4.1 Factors Affecting Depth of Field

Depth of Field	Lens Focal Length	Aperture	Lighting Level
Shallow	Telephoto	Wide open	Dim
Great	Wide angle	Stopped down	Bright

The focal length of your lens, the size of your aperture, and the level of lighting all affect depth of field. However, apparent differences in depth of field will be more pronounced on film than on video, because video cameras tend to put almost everything in focus. (For more information on depth of field and optical target size, see the sidebar "Making Video Look Like Film" in Chapter 3.)

 REALITY CHECK: *When used for closeups, long lenses (with shallow depth of field) not only flatter the face, but can also direct audience attention to the actor's eyes. In this type of setup, the depth of field can be so shallow that one eye will be in focus, leaving the ear and the hair soft. Due to video's inherently greater depth of field than film, this effect has been more typical of movies shot on film.*

Additional Camcorder Settings

You may encounter some other types of features and settings that can affect exposure.

Shutter Speed

You may be familiar with what *shutter speed* does in still photography. Don't expect adjusting this control on a movie camera does the same thing; and once you've come to terms with what shutter speed means in a motion picture context, forget that too: Neither still photography nor movie photography will prepare you for how shutter speed works in videography.

> **SHUTTER SPEED (STILL PHOTOGRAPHY):** Varies length of time film is exposed to light.
>
> **SHUTTER SPEED (MOTION-PICTURE CAMERA):** Varies the frame rate (fps).
>
> **SHUTTER SPEED (VIDEO CAMCORDER):** Varies length of time CCDs are exposed to light during each frame; does not affect the frame rate.

In a still camera, adjusting the shutter speed changes how long the shutter is open. High shutter speeds mean shorter exposures, which freeze motion better. They also reduce light levels, which means you need to open the aperture wider to let in more light. Simple.

In a motion-picture film camera, shutter speed controls the number of frames the camera captures each second. Increasing the shutter speed means you're recording more than the normal 24 frames per second, which achieves a slow-motion effect when the film is projected at normal speed.

 REALITY CHECK: To study how varying the frame rate in a motion picture camera can affect the perception of fast-moving action, take a look at the opening fight scene in Gangs of New York. For example, to emphasize the reactions to blows rather than the impacts, follow-through motions have a horrifying, staccato quality. To achieve similar effects in video, you might have to experiment with varying both the shutter speed and the shutter angle (discussed in the next section). If creative motion effects are your goal, you'll need to select a camcorder that offers these controls.

> **SLO-MO:** Slang for "slow motion."

Few video camcorders, consumer or professional, can shoot true slow motion. Their frame rates are fixed by their television standard—NTSC (30 fps) or PAL (25 fps). (*Slo-mo* effects are typically done in post.) A shutter-speed control, if one is available, only regulates the length of time the image of each frame stays on the CCD, much like a still camera.

> **TIP:** An HD vidcam that can shoot slow motion (indeed, a range of variable frame rates) is the Panasonic AK-HC900.

Adjusting the shutter speed on a video camcorder does have a striking effect, and it will allow you to fine-tune the look of moving objects in your video. At some shutter speeds motion appears jerky, at others erratic, and at some settings, motion looks smooth as silk.

For instance, in interlaced scanning mode, a camcorder shutter normally operates at 1/60—one exposure for each field. Changing it to 1/30, a longer duration (one exposure per *frame*), might make moving objects look blurred. Changing to a higher shutter speed, such as 1/200, might make the action go by in fits and starts when you play it back.

If you adjust the shutter speed, you must also adjust the aperture to expose the scene correctly. This is true for all three imaging methods: still photography, motion-picture photography, and videography.

Shutter Angle

Movie cameras have a control called *shutter angle*, which affects the physical orientation of the rotating mechanical shutter to the film. Since most camcorders don't have mechanical shutters, it probably seems odd that some of them offer a shutter-angle control.

> **SHUTTER ANGLE:** Vidcam setting that emulates the staccato-motion effect of varying the physical angle of a motion-picture camera shutter.

The effect of adjusting shutter angle is much the same in film and video: it changes the appearance of motion on the screen. It's an unpredictable effect, and you'll need to experiment with it to see what it looks like.

Reducing the shutter angle reduces both the amount of light and the length of time each frame is exposed, making action appear more jumpy. Videographers sometimes reduce shutter angle by increments of 45° or 90° when they want to make action seem more intense. However, at some settings the scene may flicker badly because artificial light sources actually pulsate with the frequency of electrical power.

An excellent example of the aesthetic effect that shutter angle creates can be seen in the combat scenes of *Saving Private Ryan*. These scenes were shot with a different shutter angle from the rest of the film, giving them the feeling of an altered sense of reality.

Video Gain

At low-light levels, as in a room lit only by a flashlight, video camcorders have an advantage over film cameras: they can increase their sensitivity to light. One way to accomplish this is to increase the excitation, or bias voltage, applied to the CCD itself; some cameras do this automatically. (For more information, see the sidebar "CCDs in Low-Light Conditions," in Chapter 3.) Another way is to manually turn up the *video gain*, or electronic amplification of the signals coming from the CCD. Both methods have the same effect.

> **VIDEO GAIN:** Degree of amplification of CCD output, measured in decibels.

Either way, the cost is video noise, a fuzzy-picture quality much like the grainy quality film gets when underexposed. (Some videographers like the effect, but your client might just think you don't know how to light a scene.) Many camcorders feature automatic gain control (AGC). Make sure you can turn it off; in some less expensive models, you can't.

> **TIP:** Don't confuse video AGC with its audio counterpart, which makes automatic adjustments to audio levels. (See "Audio Level Controls," later in this chapter.)

Record and Playback Settings

Most of the time you don't need to worry about what's going on inside the camcorder, but, if they're available, the following controls are worth knowing about.

Record Controls

The following settings control how the camcorder's image-processing circuits handle the output from the CCD before it goes on tape.

Full Auto Mode

This setting, which is sometimes simply called *Auto,* means just what you'd expect: the camcorder makes all the technical decisions (such as autofocus, auto-exposure, and sharpness enhancement) while you run, gun, and keep the action in frame.

As we've said before, when you get serious about videography, we encourage you to shuck those training wheels and turn Auto mode off. News-style videographers (or guerilla filmmakers chasing an actor through the streets) may occasionally turn it on to help keep things from going to pieces in a totally frantic situation. Film-style shooters will want more control.

> **AUTO:** Camcorder full automatic mode in which most if not all critical camera settings are determined by logic circuitry.

Modes for Extreme Conditions

Camcorders offer automatic modes that compensate for harsh lighting conditions: Spotlight, and Sand & Snow modes, for instance. When you select one of these modes, image-processing circuitry allocates more or less signal bandwidth to the bright parts of the picture so you don't blow them out.

If you are shooting news style with a photo floodlight, try turning on Spotlight mode (which assumes your subject is brightly lit) and see how it looks. Sand & Snow (which assumes the background is brighter than your subject) is obviously handy if you're shooting at the beach or on the ski slope.

> **ZEBRA PATTERN:** A slanted-bar symbol that appears in the camcorder viewfinder indicating overexposed areas. Also called *zebra stripes*, or *zebra*, it is superimposed over just those parts of the scene that are overexposed; a feature on some prosumer and all professional camcorders.

Film-style videographers, whether working at the beach or ski slope or anywhere else will get better results if they turn off these features and use the *zebra pattern* to help determine the correct exposure. (For more information, see "Use the Zebra Pattern" later in this chapter.)

Manual Mode

Manual mode is where the real film-style videographers live. It means you make all the choices yourself. Obviously, this requires practice and skill, especially to keep up with fast-moving action. But if you know what you're doing, you can capture just those images that will achieve precisely what you intend.

Shutter vs. Aperture Priority

Unless you're shooting in manual mode, you'll probably select either shutter priority or aperture priority, two different kinds of semi-automatic exposure control. If you choose shutter priority, you pick the shutter speed manually and the camcorder sets the exposure (f-stop). Aperture priority is just the reverse: you pick the f-stop and the camcorder sets the shutter speed.

News-style videographers will generally use aperture priority in low light, and shutter priority to capture fast-moving objects. And film-style shooters will be in full manual.

SP/LP Mode

In the Mini DV format, SP mode sets your camcorder to record at 3/4 ips (inches per second). To expand the recording time you get on a given tape, you can switch to long play (LP) mode. All DV camcorders have this feature. In LP mode the tape speed is slower— 1/2 ips—and the camera switches to a narrower track that increases recording time. Recording on a standard Mini DV cassette at LP speed, you get 90 minutes as opposed to the usual 60.

Don't use LP mode. Here's why:

- When you increase the recording density, you also increase susceptibility to imperfections or damage on the tape.

- DVCAM or DVCPRO decks may be unable to read LP recordings.

- Tape manufacturers make special Mini DVs designed to provide 80 minutes in SP mode or 120 in LP mode. Because the tape stock used in these tapes is thinner, and the density of magnetic material is higher, it is less durable and reliable than standard tape.

You might need LP mode if you're shooting a long-winded CEO news style and you know there won't be an opportunity to change tapes. However, if you absolutely must have unbroken continuous recordings lasting more than an hour, a better solution is to buy or rent a professional-level camcorder that uses Standard DVC cassettes, which can hold three hours or more.

Shooting-Mode Settings

On many prosumer and most professional camcorders, you can select the shooting mode to change the video frame rate. (For more information on why and when you might want to do so, see "What Are NTSC/PAL/SECAM Broadcast Formats?" in Chapter 3.)

You can generally choose from three shooting modes: normal, frame, and photo.

Normal Mode (News Style)

On an NTSC camcorder, normal mode is 29.97 fps, interlaced, which captures two fields every $\frac{1}{29.97}$ second—also called *drop-frame mode*. You may also see it written as "30I,"

DROP-FRAME MODE: Standard NTSC frame rate of 29.97 fps.

even though the frame rate isn't truly 30. News-style videographers who are producing in NTSC should stay in this mode.

> **TIP:** *NTSC video is often said to run at 30 fps, but in fact it runs at 29.97 fps. The term for this slightly slower rate is "drop-frame" video. All consumer and most prosumer NTSC DV camcorders record at 29.97. Other models can record either 29.97 or true 30 fps. Even if you have the ability to switch between modes, don't. Stay in "normal" drop-frame mode; your editor will thank you.*

Frame Mode (Film Style)

Switching to frame mode changes scanning from interlaced to progressive, capturing images as full frames (as movie cameras do) rather than as two separate fields. On an

NTSC camcorder this mode is called 30P, and it's one of the ways you can give your video a film look.

Photo Mode

In photo mode, you can use your DV camcorder as a still camera. Handy enhancements to this feature may include a self-timer, which counts down the number of seconds until the shutter snaps, and support for a flash-photography attachment. Some camcorders capture the still image to a removable memory card; others record a few seconds of the still image on the DV tape itself.

> **NOTE:** Photo mode in a camcorder isn't the same as single-frame or stop-frame mode in a motion-picture camera. Photo mode actually takes several video frames and interpolates the result to give you a composite picture, reducing or eliminating any recording artifacts. It's therefore not feasible to use photo mode to shoot animation with a camcorder.

Playback-Mode Controls

Switching the camcorder to playback mode lets you review your recording and upload it to a computer for editing.

The buttons that control video playback follow the same familiar pattern you'll find on VCRs and audio cassette decks: Fast Rewind, Play, Stop, Fast Forward, and Pause.

> **IC INDEX:** Feature on some camcorders that logs each take's starting point and its timecode location on the tape by creating an electronic table in an embedded chip, or integrated circuit (IC), in special Mini DV cassettes.

Some camcorders also have a search mode which will fast-forward the tape between still-photo takes, or different recording dates, based on the camcorder's timecode.

If your camcorder supports the *IC Index* feature, you can use special Mini DV IC tapes to record the starting point of each new take. Then you can shuttle rapidly to the beginning of a scene during playback or upload.

> **TIP:** It's not a good idea to shuttle Mini DV tapes back and forth unnecessarily in your camcorder. The magnetic coating of the tape can become damaged, causing loss of data in spite of redundant storage (recording of the same take on multiple tracks to permit recovery from data loss). Upload the show to an editing system; then you can review it to your heart's content. For the same reason, it's a bad idea to reuse Mini DV tapes. Once you've uploaded a tape, keep it as a data backup. And while we're on the subject of bad things to do, it's a bad idea to review scenes in the camcorder right after they've been shot. Doing so increases the chances you'll create a break in the timecode (an editor's nightmare), or accidentally erase something you meant to save.

Audio/Video I/O Connections and Settings

You won't need to pay much attention to these: Default settings are usually best. But now and then you will need to know what your options are.

Audio Modes

As noted in Chapter 3, the DV recording standard offers four options for recording audio:

- AES/EBU standard, stereo (highest quality)—two 16-bit channels (48 kHz)

- CD quality stereo (medium quality)—two 16-bit channels (44.1 kHz)

- Stereo (lower quality)—two 16-bit channels (32 kHz)

- Four channel (lowest quality)—four 12-bit channels (32 kHz)

Most videographers keep the audio set on the highest-quality sampling, 48 kHz. The only reason to ever select four-channel mode is if you want to go back and record a separate voice-over narration on track 3 or 4. If you do this often, look for a camcorder with the *one-touch audio dubbing* feature.

Microphone Connectors

A critical audio feature on a DV camcorder is a tiny, seemingly mundane thing—the style of its audio input connectors.

Mini Plugs

Most consumer and many prosumer camcorders have mini audio input jacks. These accept the same little plugs you'll find on the headphones of a portable tape or CD player (**Figure 4.8**).

There are four problems with mini plugs:

- The mini plug can wobble in the jack, breaking the connection.

- The tiny mini contacts don't pass high-frequency sound very well. That means bird songs and the consonants of human speech may not make it into your audio recording. If the track sounds muffled, there's no inexpensive way to fix it in post.

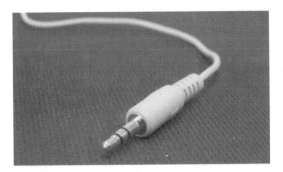

Figure 4.8 Low-cost audio gear typically uses these mini-plug connectors. Unfortunately they don't assure good mechanical connections and have trouble passing high frequencies.

Figure 4.9 The XLR plug, a three-pronged heavy-duty connector, is standard in the professional audio world. Most professional camcorders accept this type of plug for audio input.

- Most professional-level audio gear uses high-quality, three-prong XLR plugs (**Figure 4.9**). If your camcorder has mini audio jacks, you won't be able to make connections to this equipment without an adapter. And even if the adapter lets you make the physical connection, high frequencies could still be lost at the mini end.

- Most consumer audio cables aren't properly shielded, meaning they pick up noise (usually an annoying hum) from nearby sources of electricity, such as power cords.

XLR Plugs

XLR connectors are by far the best Audio In jacks to use—but you won't find them on many consumer or prosumer camcorders (not even the XL1S).

RCA Plugs

The familiar RCA plug (**Figure 4.10**) is still in use on many camcorders. It's actually older than the mini, but it's a bit better at passing high frequencies. Even so, it's not as reliable as the XLR plug.

Figure 4.10 Some consumer and prosumer camcorders accept RCA plugs, an older style of consumer audio connector. They're better than minis, but not as good as XLRs.

Audio Level Controls

You can control the amplification of audio inputs to the camcorder by way of audio level controls, sometimes called audio gain or *REC level*. Most camcorders offer an Auto (AGC) feature for setting audio levels automatically, but you shouldn't use it except in situations of dire need. AGC will boost the gain when the scene is quiet, and turn it down when a truck goes by. The result is an uneven audio track that's nearly impossible to fix in post. Even if you're shooting news style and relying on in-camera audio recording, avoid AGC if at all possible.

Video I/O Connections

The video outputs on a camcorder are fairly straightforward.

Composite

A composite (NTSC or PAL) Video Out jack can be found on just about every camcorder. It's an analog video signal on a single line you can use to view output on a monitor or to record it on a VCR. *This is not a digital output.* Don't use it for uploading your show to a computer.

Check to see whether the composite video output includes the alphanumeric status display. That's good if you want to run it to a monitor, bad if you want to dub a reference-quality recording onto a VCR. Some camcorders permit you to turn off the status display if you're dubbing.

Component RGB

High-end professional camcorders may provide component analog RGB video output, with separate jacks and lines for Red, Green, and Blue signals. (For more information, see "Color Models: RGB to YUV" in Appendix A.) You probably won't need it, but it could come in handy if you ever want to connect the camcorder directly to a high-end video projector or a broadcast studio control booth.

Y/C

Also called S-Video, the Y/C video output is an analog signal, but it offers a higher-quality alternative to composite. This two-channel connection separates the luma (Y) from the chroma (C) signal, thereby reducing video noise. It's handy for connecting to field monitors and making quick analog recordings for reference purposes. As with component outputs, the viewfinder status information may or may not be present in the signal.

Digital I/O

You'll use this connector to upload your recordings to a computer. (For more information, see "Getting DV into Your Computer" in Chapter 3.) All camcorders that follow the DV recording standard offer digital output for uploading. To initiate a transfer from the camcorder side, connect the cable, put the camcorder in playback mode, and press Play.

PROFESSIONAL CAMERA TECHNIQUES

Here are some tips for camcorder operation that you probably won't find in the manual. There's only one catch: Many of these techniques are primarily applicable to professional models with interchangeable lenses, and some prosumer models that work the same way, but not all camcorders have these features.

Choosing Between 30I and 24P

With the introduction of 24P mode in prosumer camcorders, even videographers on modest budgets can think about shooting at the same frame rate as film. But don't automatically assume that's the way to go. Shooting plain-vanilla NTSC (30I mode) has its benefits.

We'll discuss the postproduction consequences of this decision in a later chapter. (See "Postprocessing Filters" in Chapter 11.)

We bring up 24P at this early stage to give you another reason for thinking ahead to the results you want in the end.

The reasons to think about it now—when you're selecting and familiarizing yourself with a camera—is to consider the choice from aesthetic and stylistic points of view. When the lights come up, how do you want your audience to feel? Frame rate and the perception of motion do affect them on a subliminal level. So, the choice isn't about being right or wrong. It's like many decisions you'll make along the way: does this choice enhance the mood I want to create?

Traditionally, audiences have come to associate certain types of projects with video, others with film. Video has typically been used for interviews, field reports, educational presentations, live events, and sports. A video image not only captures fast action more smoothly than film does, but also its faster frame rate (enhanced by the sampling of two fields for every frame) imparts a sense of immediacy, of "being there." In classic video, the audience feels transported to a place where something is happening *now*.

By contrast, film has been used for storytelling. It's the medium of Hollywood. The blurred motion resulting from its slower frame rate might capture action less accurately than video does, but some people feel it has a texture that video lacks. Audiences have come to expect that a film is not a live experience, but a contrived story. They think of a film as a work of art that was assembled meticulously for later viewing.

With digital tools, it's now possible to make low-cost video look like film. But if that's your objective, the decision involves much more than simply shooting at 24 fps. Going for a film look invites all the other expectations audiences have of Hollywood product—careful, artistic lighting; a musical score that enhances the emotional dimension; layered sound effects that create a rich, realistic audio environment; and even other-worldly special effects. These elements—just as important as frame rate to achieving a convincing filmed look— take time and money.

So, if you don't have adequate time or money, you may not be able to choose a film look. If, for example, you're covering a live event, if the subject is somehow current and news-worthy, or if you're shooting the CEO's speech and you won't get lots takes, striving for a film look might be a needless complication, and the wrong impression to give the audience.

Think of it another way, this time in purely technical terms: shooting in 30I will rarely be a mistake. Software tools such as Red Giant's Magic Bullet will convert 30I footage to 24P in post, as well as help you adjust colors to look more filmic. If, on the other hand, you shoot in 24P and convert to the 30I broadcast standard, the conversion will do nothing to correct the blurred motion effects you captured at the lower frame rate.

 Is it better to shoot in 24P, or to shoot in 30I and then apply Magic Bullet in post? In either case, the result will be a 24 fps experience. But you be the judge as to whether one or the other looks better or suits your purposes. On the DVD, we've included a side-by-side comparison of clips shot and post-processed both ways. See "How to Make Digital Video Look Like Film."

Certainly, if you decide to shoot in 30I and post-process for film look, you'll have a wider selection of cameras and lenses in all sizes. You might be disappointed, for example, to choose the Panasonic AG-DVX100 for its 24P feature, only to find the nonremovable Leica lens too limiting on the set.

 REALITY CHECK: *Be aware that Magic Bullet will not convert 30P to 24P, last we checked; if you want to apply film look later with this tool, you must shoot 30I.*

When to Choose Cinema-Style Lenses

Some camcorders come with cinema-style lenses, complete with precise mechanical movement and numeric indexes on the barrel to indicate focal length, f-stop, and zoom position

(**Figure 4.11**). Other lenses have no markings. Canon, for example, offers both unmarked and marked lenses in its accessory options for the XL1S.

Choosing one style or the other is a decision rooted in the different cultures of news-style videographers and film-style DPs. Your choice will be influenced to a great extent by whether you have a camera crew, which crew member operates the camera, and how he does so.

SERVO: Electric motor that translates applied voltages to discrete motion in precisely controllable steps.

Unmarked lenses aren't designed that way because the manufacturer is trying to save money. Those lenses are unmarked because their electromechanical movement isn't precisely repeatable from one take to the next. In fact, the focus and zoom rings aren't even connected to the lens mechanisms. They are electronic dials that send signals to a *servo* that adjusts the movement up or down. If you mark the barrel with a grease pencil, and return the ring to that position, the lens probably won't repeat the original setting.

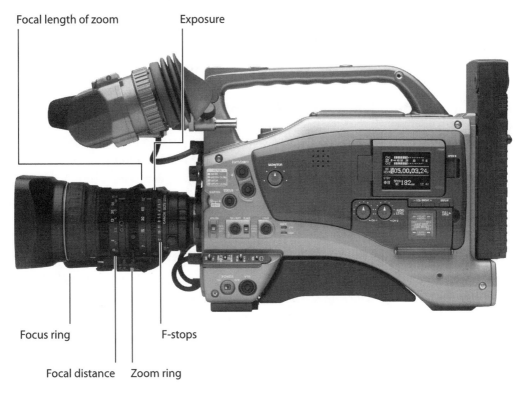

Focal length of zoom   Exposure

Focus ring   F-stops

Focal distance   Zoom ring

Figure 4.11 The lens on this JVC GY-DV5000U has mechanical focus and iris adjustments as well as photographic-style lens markings. Most film-style videographers prefer this type of lens because settings are precise and moves are repeatable. If a film-style crew includes a first camera assistant, he or she will rely on the lens markings rather than the readouts in the viewfinder or on the monitor. (Photo courtesy JVC Professional Products Company.)

If you are the only person operating the camera, especially if you're shooting over-the-shoulder news style, you'll be looking in the viewfinder throughout a take. Lens markings won't matter since you won't be able to see them. You'll want a lens that sends its settings for the current f-stop and zoom position to the viewfinder status display. By contrast, on a film-style shoot, another person besides the camera operator—usually the First Camera Assistant —has her hands on the lens. She will control focus, exposure, and zooming—and since she's not looking through the viewfinder, she must rely on lens markings to adjust settings. The DP or First Camera Assistant may even use a grease pencil to mark the lens barrel so he can make sure retakes use the same lens settings.

Advanced Zoom Techniques

Twisting the zoom ring isn't the only way to control zooming. Most camcorders have a semi-automatic *continuous zoom* control. It's usually a rocker switch (**Figure 4.12**) or a pair

> CONTINUOUS ZOOM: Changing magnification or demagnification via the semi-automatic zoom control.

of pushbuttons labeled In and Out, or + and –, or T (telephoto) and W (wide). For example, to zoom in you press and hold the rocker switch (or the In or + button), and the camcorder increases the magnification until you let go of the switch.

Choose the Right Camera Controls for Precision Zooming

Getting a smooth, controlled zoom can be tricky. For one thing, on camcorders that use the unmarked, electromechanical lenses, zooming is subject to all the problems of imprecision we just discussed. But that's not all. The zooming action of most cameras isn't linear. The speed of the zoom may vary depending on how hard or how fast you press the switch: More pressure, or a quicker action, causes faster zooming. It's very important to give yourself time to practice on your camcorder so you can achieve the rate of speed and smoothness you want without visual jerks and jarring effects that will annoy the audience.

You should also experiment with your camcorder's various zoom controls; they often work differently. For instance, the XL1S comes with two zoom controls. The larger zoom rocker switch near the lens barrel is pressure-sensitive, but the smaller switch on the handle isn't. Also, you can vary the sensitivity and speed characteristics of the large switch through the camcorder's menu settings.

No matter which camcorder you use, even if it's on a tripod, you might jiggle it just by putting your finger on the zoom control—especially if you're using a shake-sensitive telephoto setting to begin with. Try using the zoom switch on the camcorder's remote control, if it has one; it lets you operate the zoom without touching the camcorder.

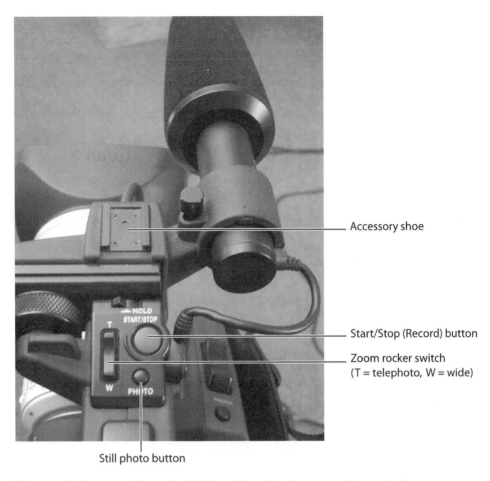

Accessory shoe

Start/Stop (Record) button

Zoom rocker switch
(T = telephoto, W = wide)

Still photo button

Figure 4.12 For convenience, the XL1S provides a handy zoom rocker control.

Use Zoom Accessories

If you need precise zooming, start by using one of the photographic-style lenses with mechanical adjustments and markings. These lenses often come with zoom accessories made for motion-picture cameras.

One type of mechanical zooming accessory is totally manual: a smooth, gear-driven crank that attaches to the front of the camera. The crank is easy to use and totally linear in response, which makes it easy to get fancy zooms with precise control.

For truly artful zooming with mechanical lenses, you can get a motorized zoom attachment with a remote LANC (Local Application Control bus) controller. The LANC is a digital control that permits you to pre-program complex zooms and then execute them with a press of the button—without having to touch the camera.

Zoom, Autofocus, and Image Stabilization

Autofocus (AF) and image stabilization are ways to keep the image sharp and steady as the camcorder or its subjects move. (For more information, see "The Price You Pay for Image Processing" in Chapter 3.)

The AF circuit on most camcorders looks at color boundaries between adjacent pixels, assuming these are the object's edges, and adjusts focus until it finds the setting that yields the greatest contrast in values. This works reasonably well as long as nobody is moving or you're not panning, tilting, or zooming the camera.

Zooming is confusing for AF, and its wild, erratic attempts to self-adjust the focus are all too visible. Video technicians call this *hunting,* and it's very distracting to watch. Attempting to zoom with image stabilization turned on is even worse: the zoom itself becomes erratic.

Whether you're shooting film style or news style, it's best to turn AF and image stabilization off (if you can), hold the camera as steadily as possible, and adjust focus manually, judging the shot through the viewfinder or in the monitor. Once in a long while, if you're in a desperate run-and-gun crisis, AF and image stabilization might save your shot. But if these features are turned on, try to avoid zooming.

Use the Zebra Pattern for Correct Exposure and Contrast Range

For all but the fastest-breaking news-style work, and for all film-style videography, the most reliable tool for monitoring the exposure level of a shot is the zebra pattern. You can find the zebra feature on most prosumer and all professional cameras.

Used correctly, zebra stripes are the best way to make sure you don't overexpose parts of your shot.

Zebra stripes are a black-and-white optical effect that appears in the viewfinder and on the monitor to highlight overexposed portions of the image (**Figure 4.13**). To adjust for proper exposure, rotate the f-stop ring or dial to reduce the size of the aperture until the stripes disappear.

Figure 4.13 The highlights just above the actor's head in this scene are *blown out*, or totally overexposed. If the camcorder's zebra pattern is switched on, stripes will appear in these areas in the viewfinder. As you stop down, at some point the stripes will disappear, indicating that the brightest parts of the image are no longer overexposed. However, at this f-stop setting, the rest of the scene may well be underexposed. The best solution is to adjust lighting to remove the highlight, or increase brightness on the rest of the scene.

Once you've done this, as long as the faces in the scene appear well lit, you're ready to shoot. If the faces don't look right, leave the exposure alone, adjust the lights, check the zebra stripes again, and reset the f-stop.

> **TIP:** You're the boss, and you can choose to ignore the zebra stripes. For example, if everything in the scene looks great except for a hot highlight, you might make an artistic decision to permit the overexposure (let the highlight blow out). The result will be a white area of the image that contains absolutely no image detail. Therefore, no matter how much you might adjust brightness or contrast in post, you will not find any visual information there. At the risk of overstating the obvious, remember that permitting blown out highlights is an irreversible decision.

> **BLOWN OUT:** White area within a video image that is totally overexposed and contains no picture detail.

The IRE Setting

When the zebra function is on, stripes appear in the viewfinder wherever the light intensity is greater than a preselected numeric value. That value is called an IRE (International Radio Engineers) reference. Camcorders that can display zebra pattern also allow you to change the preselected IRE value.

A value of 100 IRE is pure white. In the NTSC system, black is not zero but IRE 7.5 because of limitations of early television transmitters. (PAL systems set black at 0 IRE, however.)

Most of the time you don't have to fool with the IRE setting, but it's a good idea to check the spec sheets to see how the factory has set the default zebra IRE on your new camcorder. Many camcorders are preset to 78 IRE, far less than pure white, to keep you from blowing out the highlights on people's faces, which range from 70 to 85 IRE, depending on skin tone.

If you shoot news style, an IRE setting of 78 is a good idea, provided you aren't so busy you have to rely on AE—in which case the zebra function will be disabled.

Setting Black Balance

The white-balance control on a camcorder is crucial to getting good-looking color in your shots. It's closely related to setting and rigging lights. (For more information, see "The Importance of White Balance" in Chapter 6.)

The opposite setting—*black balance*—also exists, but you will rarely have to deal with it. A camcorder sets its black balance—the absence of signal on all three primary colors—when you turn the unit on. This automatic feature is fairly reliable and probably won't need attention unless you haven't used the camcorder in a long time, or it's gotten physically cold or hot while being transported.

> **BLACK BALANCE:** Camcorder color compensation adjustment when red, green, and blue signals are all effectively zero.

If you've set the white balance, but the colors in your scene still look odd when you play them back, try setting the black balance. Cover the lens with its lens cap, and with the camera on, press the Black Balance button (if there is one), or adjust the video gain until the image in the viewfinder or on the monitor looks black. Then, take the lens cap off and repeat the manual white-balance procedure.

SHOOT SOME TESTS

You'll only know your new camcorder well enough to trust it under field conditions–after you've worked with it under field conditions. So shoot lots of tests. Tape is cheap, and that old saw about an ounce of prevention is time-tested wisdom.

We know a man who bought a DV camcorder in order to record meetings at his social club. He bought a lightweight tripod to hold the camera, since several speakers were scheduled and he didn't want to hold the camera that long. He knew that Mini DV cassettes hold only 60 minutes of video, so he had a pocketful of them. He figured he would reload between speakers.

After the first speaker had gone on for almost an hour, there was a short break. But when our videographer attempted to eject the used tape he discovered to his dismay that this particular camcorder loaded from the bottom. And since it was securely screwed to the tripod, the bottom-ejecting loading door wouldn't open.

Needless to say, he took the camcorder back to the store the next day and exchanged it for a top-loading model.

Both authors have had similar experiences. Take our advice and run some tape through your new camera before you're on the set and it's too late.

> **TIP:** Electronic gear is relatively delicate compared to mechanical equipment. Heat, dust, vibration, and humidity destroy chips—and like many of us, camcorders crave air conditioning. If you're heading out into the world with your brand new camera, take reasonable precautions to protect it from harm. Identify a good service facility in the area in advance. If it's a critical shoot, you might consider bringing two cameras. And if you must shoot in unusually harsh conditions— sweltering heat or freezing cold—you could go retro and shoot on film instead. Interestingly, there are some new compact 35mm cameras designed specifically to let filmmakers shoot "DV style"—highly portable with available light. (You still have to shell out for the stock and processing, though.) To see a film shot with this lightweight gear, take a look at Lost in Translation, directed by Sofia Coppola.

YOUR CAMCORDER—AN EXTENSION OF YOU

Professional racecar drivers and professional cinematographers have something in common. A racing driver doesn't have time to think about which controls to use; the driver simply acts. As a videographer, your camcorder should be an extension of your senses of sight and sound. You won't discover the full extent of your visual storytelling skills until you're so familiar with the controls that you can make an adjustment without thinking first.

CHAPTER FIVE

Shots and Shot Plans

Telling a story visually is the essence of cinematic art. Although the audience gets much of its information from dialogue, the experience of film and video captivates our brains with imagery, much as dreams do.

Ideally, pictures—not dialogue—should carry your story. In fact, at some film schools first-year students have to do all their projects as silent movies, which forces them to think visually. Videomakers who fail to learn this lesson generally make movies and presentations that are little more than radio with pictures.

> **SHOT PLAN:** Diagram showing camera setups and positions of actors required to capture all shots needed for a scene.

Shot plans and storyboards are twin techniques that help you visualize how you're going to tell your story with a sequence of images. A storyboard shows how each shot will look on the screen. A shot plan lets you diagram individual shots to show camera setups and other technical choices you intend to make to get those shots.

PLANNING YOUR SHOTS

Planning your shots is only one part of a larger story development process that begins with your script or presentation outline, and carries through to the decisions you make in the editing room. We surveyed the basics of writing a script in Chapter 2. Continuing at that overview level, this chapter follows through on translating your story into a logical sequence of pictures. This is a creative process built upon practices in film and television craft that have evolved over the last century.

 We treat the subject of shots and shot design in the video Ten Ways to Shoot a Chair *(Figure 5.1).*

Figure 5.1 Our survey of cinematography is set in a fictional classroom where Professor Hightower instructs Holly, a young student, on the techniques of shot size, lens selection, camera angle, and camera movement.

Turning Theory into Pictures

Shot design involves several disciplines:

- **Art.** Different types of shots affect the artistic, perceptual, and emotional impression you make on an audience.

- **Technique.** Your knowledge of the optical characteristics of various lenses and the ways camcorders capture images will affect how you design your story.

- **Organization.** Your shot plan affects how you tackle the production job and who you select for your crew, as well as how you develop your shooting schedule, stage your setups, and direct camera operations.

The principles of shot design and the techniques of drawing shot plans apply to all types of shooting, whether news-style or film-style. Granted, in news-style shooting you'll probably have little or no time to make formal plans, but you'll get better results if you know how to design film-style shots and setups well in advance of the first shooting day.

From Storyboard to Shot List

Accomplished videomakers develop distinctive styles, not only in terms of aesthetics (how shots look and how stories are told) but also in how they apply technical aspects of cinematography and directing to their work.

One important way videomakers differ from each other in their approaches to shot planning is the extent to which they rely on storyboards (**Figure 5.2**). As discussed in Chapter 2, a storyboard is a preproduction planning tool that arranges sequences of shots as thumbnail sketches on a page. (See **Figure 2.5** in Chapter 2.)

Figure 5.2 (Top) Here's a storyboard frame created with Storyboard Quick. You can manipulate pre-drawn characters and position them on drawn backgrounds or, as shown here, against imported location photos. (Bottom) Compare with the corresponding scene from *When Harried Met Sally*.

Drawing Stick Figures? Try Storyboard Quick

Director Tim Burton would probably rather draw a storyboard than write a script, since he was trained originally as an animator. But for those of us who aren't skilled at thinking with a pencil this way, there's PowerProduction Software's Storyboard Quick. This program is essentially a clip-art manipulation tool designed specifically for generating and printing finished-looking storyboards.

Storyboard Quick is available for both Macs and PCs. (For more information on this product, surf to www.storyboardartist.com.)

The purpose of a storyboard is to give you a sense of whether your shots work for visual storytelling. Continuity, conflict, and character ideas should come across at a glance, without having to read the dialogue (which is usually written with key actions summarized underneath each storyboard frame).

> **SHOT LIST:** List of individual shots, including settings, subjects, and key actions.

One type of *shot list* is simply a written summary of the frames in your storyboard, recapping types of shots, settings, subjects, and key actions for each scene (**Figure 5.3**).

Shot	Type	Description
	Shot List for "When Harried Met Sally" Scene 3	
1	Wide Master favoring Josh	Josh talks to Atwater, types, makes phone call, then talks to Phil. Phil enters cubicle
2	Med Josh	Same as above. When Phil enters, reframe for two shot
3	CU Josh	Clean single on Josh for entire scene
4	CU Atwater (reverse of shot 3)	Atwater enters and exits cubicle (let him into and out of frame)
5	CU Phil (reverse of shot 3)	Phil stands at door of cubicle, then enters (let him into and out of frame)
6	Insert of keyboard	Tight CU of keyboard as Josh types
7	Insert of monitor	Tight CU of screen as error messages appear

Figure 5.3 Developing a shot list is an essential planning step, whether you storyboard your scenes or not. Eventually you'll group your shots by setup and in the order you intend to get them—not in story sequence.

If you don't want to go to the time and effort of developing a storyboard, you should at least make simple shot-plan diagrams, which is another way to develop shot lists. Some directors—so green they don't know better or so experienced they can do without them—don't use storyboards or shot plans at all, but work directly from a script and visualize it in their heads. That's like building a house without a set of blueprints. Such an approach might work for a one-person runner-and-gunner. But when you need to communicate your vision to some other member of your crew, you'll wish you had it all on paper.

This chapter follows a logical progression: script to storyboard, to shot plan, to shot list. However, you don't necessarily need a storyboard *and* a shot plan. For example, if you're shooting an action movie, you'd be wise to use a storyboard to help you visualize your shots before you think about sets or locations. But if your video involves people talking in a room, and it relies heavily on dialogue, first seeing the physical space and its props can be more important than storyboarding ahead of time. In these situations, you might first draw up a shot plan—concentrating on placement of actors and camera in the space—then use that shot plan to produce your shot list.

Structured vs. Improvisational Approaches

The extent to which you can plan your shots depends on how much experimentation you intend to encourage on the set. Sticking closely to a preconceived shot plan is a *structured approach*, the way Alfred Hitchcock worked, for example, or how Steven Spielberg directs. Permitting variations on the plan, or starting a shoot with no plan at all, is an *improvisational approach*; Francis Ford Coppola and Robert Altman often work this way.

> **STRUCTURED APPROACH:**
> Adhering strictly to a storyboard or shot plan.
>
> **IMPROVISATIONAL APPROACH:**
> Permitting experimentation on the set in terms of actors' performances and/or shot design.

Steven Spielberg is renowned in the industry for his highly structured approach. Once a script is approved, he has a storyboard created for every shot of every scene in the script. And when he's shooting, he goes for the shots in the storyboard—frame for frame, if possible.

Robert Altman works at the other extreme. He's famous for encouraging improvisation and experimentation on the set. In consultation with his DP, he chooses a camera setup that will capture the desired action. But the framing of shots, the movement of actors, the exact lines they will say, the number and variety of takes—these are all subject to change, depending on the chemistry of the moment.

If you're a relatively inexperienced moviemaker, you'll find the discipline and paperwork of the structured approach can help keep you on budget and on schedule. If you're a long-time director who knows how to cope with the unpredictability of the production process, you stand a better chance of getting away with an improvisational shooting style.

In any case, for more information on the practical impacts of these antithetical approaches in preproduction planning, see "Casting and Improvisation for DV" in Chapter 8.

TELLING STORIES WITH PICTURES

Before you get involved with designing individual shots, there are some overall principles of visual storytelling you need to think about.

Don't Forget Establishing Shots

Planning your shots will succeed if you think about how they'll flow together in the edit. Transitions between scenes are particularly important.

> **ESTABLISHING SHOT:** Image that introduces the audience to a new setting in which the next action takes place.

For example, when you begin a new scene, the audience must recognize and understand the new setting. You need to provide a shot to establish the new location, usually called an *establishing shot*. It might simply be a shot of the building a character is about to enter.

So when you're planning your shots, be sure to include transitions. When you're editing, you may find that a transitional shot isn't necessary—it may be possible to cut directly from one situation to another without confusing the audience. But it's good to have the option.

 REALITY CHECK: *It's the mark of a polished screenwriter to anticipate transitions in the script, even if the director or editor eventually might choose some other technique to bridge scenes. The idea is to carry the eye—and the interest—of the audience from one scene to the next. A really slick transition permits an actor to step from one time and place into another, as if stepping into the next room. For example, in one scene, we see an arrested suspect being ushered into the rear door of a squad car. As the officer closes the door, we cut to the barred door of a jail cell slamming shut behind the prisoner.*

Pay Attention to Continuity

Continuity is visual common sense, and it refers to how shots match up with one another when they are assembled. An assembled sequence should give a unified, convincing impression of uninterrupted time, space, and action. For example, showing an actor as left-handed in one scene and right-handed in another is a break in continuity. If she wears a purple dress in one shot and yellow pants in the next shot (of the same scene), that's another break. Ultimately, continuity is an editing issue, but you can't get it right unless you plan your shots with the concept in mind.

> **NOTE:** As with other aesthetic aspects of shot design, moviemakers have been known to disagree on the importance of maintaining continuity. To paraphrase director Oliver Stone (who used stronger language): "Continuity is for people with no guts."

On a fully crewed movie set, a person called a *script supervisor* watches each take, makes notes on problematic details (such as non-matching clothing), and advises the director of possible breaks in continuity. If your production can't afford a full-time script supervisor, continuity should be the concern of the director or camera operator.

There are three key principles of continuity to keep in mind when designing your shots.

> **SCRIPT SUPERVISOR:** Production staff member who observes shooting to assure compliance with the script and avoid breaks in continuity; also provides the editor with shot-by-shot script notes and the director's preferred takes.
>
> **STAGE LINE:** Imaginary line between two actors on a set; setups should not cross the stage line.

Don't Cross the Stage Line

The stage line is an imaginary line drawn between two actors on the set (**Figure 5.4**). To assure visual continuity, make sure all your camera setups are on the same side of the line, often called "the axis" in filmmaking. If you fail to follow this rule (also known as "the 180 degree rule"), characters may seem to swap positions on screen during the same scene, which can be disorienting to your audience. If you stay on the same side of the stage line, Adam will always be on the left side of the screen and Amanda will always be on the right, no matter how you frame them. This is a little hard to visualize if you're new to the concept, but experienced moviemakers know how important it is.

Figuring out the stage-line rule can become complex if the scene includes three or more actors. In this situation, there are effectively multiple stage lines, one between each pair of actors. One simplified approach is to find a central element—a table, for example—and shoot the scene from just two setups, one on either side of the table, respecting a single stage line drawn through the table's center.

But ultimately, there aren't any hard and fast rules for handling the stage line in multiple-character scenes. Your best guideline is your own intuitive sense of continuity, gained from watching movies all your life. Here's our best advice, which is more of a guideline than a strict rule: Actors should always appear to be looking toward the person they're talking to, even if that person isn't in the frame. If the listener is offscreen, decide where he is in relation to the speaker and maintain that imaginary stage line. If the actors' eye contact doesn't seem logical, find an alternate setup. This is where a detailed storyboard helps, especially as you discuss the problem with the actors and the DP.

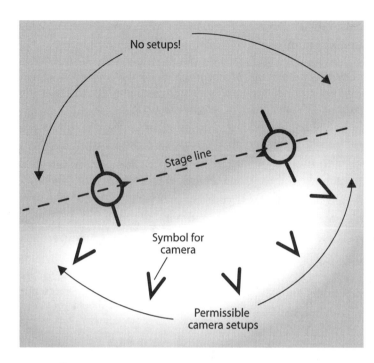

Figure 5.4 The stage line connects two actors in a scene and divides the playing area in half. Plan to make all your camera setups on one side of the line or the other. Directors with experience in live theater can think of the stage line as marking the edge of a proscenium stage. The audience can't go behind the footlights. (The symbol that looks like the top view of a parrot is the filmmaker's convention for the subject: The "wings" are arms and the "beak" is the nose, indicating the direction the subject is facing.)

 REALITY CHECK: *If you've ever wondered why people in movies or on television only sit around three sides of a table, it's to make working with the stage line easier. If you use all four sides, at least one of the actors will always have his back to the audience. And you'd have to shoot the scene from more angles, further complicating the stage-line problem.*

Some moviemakers—disciples of Oliver Stone, perhaps—deliberately experiment with crossing the stage line. But be prepared for a challenge in the editing room if you decide to try it.

Respect Screen Direction

Screen direction refers to how subjects move within the two-dimensional space of the frame. Stated as a basic rule, respecting continuity of screen direction requires maintaining a consistent point of view and frame of reference for the audience. For example, if a character is walking from left to right in the first shot of a sequence, and you cut away for the second shot, when you return to the character in shot three, he should still be walking left to right and not right to left.

> **RULE OF SCREEN DIRECTION:**
> Motion of actors within the frame must preserve continuity from one shot to the next.

Another illustration: Think of an actor walking down the sidewalk. Her goal is the front door of an apartment building, but that door isn't shown in the first shot. In the first shot, we see her walking from right to left. In the next shot, we see her friend waiting expectantly for her at the building entrance. To preserve continuity of screen direction, the friend must be looking to screen right, expecting her approach. For best effect, the building entrance should be on the *left* side of the frame, to establish it as the ultimate goal of the walker's journey from right to left. Also, compose the shot so that most of the *air*, or empty space in the frame, is in front of the expectant friend. The audience will get the idea that the walker will enter the frame there.

> **AIR:** Cinematographer's term for empty space within the composition of a shot.

If you want to show the actor approaching the building entrance in a series of shots, you must always show her moving from right to left. The only way to change screen direction without confusing the audience is to interpose a neutral shot—one with the actor coming right at the camera (or moving directly away from it). Then you can show her walking left to right in the next shot. However, if you now cut back to the friend waiting at the entrance, he must be looking to screen left.

Some aspects of screen direction are rooted more in moviemaking convention than in reality. For example, if you're cutting back and forth between two sides of a telephone conversation, it will look more natural if one character holds the phone to her left ear, and the other to his right.

As with other principles of continuity, some filmmakers deliberately violate screen direction. Don't risk confusing your audience this way—at least, not on your *first* project.

Avoid Time-Dependent Elements (The Problem of the Burning Cigarette)

Sometimes the best way to fix continuity problems is to avoid them in the first place. A perfect example is the so-called burning cigarette problem, which refers to the difficulty of preserving continuity when you're shooting any time-dependent process that you can't control—a burning cigarette, ice cream melting, or a slow leak in a tire that's going flat. For instance, if the actor's cigarette is burned down to the butt in the first shot, it will be a break in continuity to see him holding a freshly lit one in the next, unless you interpose a shot of him lighting up a new smoke.

Naturally, there are ways of dealing with these problems. A production assistant can start several cigarettes burning at various times, and hand one of appropriate length to the actor just before a take. You can use multiple dishes of ice cream, kept cold offscreen at various stages of thawing. You can repeatedly inflate the sagging tire to match previous takes.

However, unless the effect is essential to your story, a much better fix is to simply eliminate problem elements from the scene before they become a problem! When you're planning your shots, look out for elements that might create continuity problems and try to replace them with less complicated alternatives.

DIRECT AUDIENCE ATTENTION

When you're designing your shots, you can employ various techniques to help direct the audience's attention.

Color

All things being equal, viewers will focus on the brightest (or most unusual) color in the shot. For instance, you could put your main character in a pink top and dress everyone else in beige. Similarly, in a sea of white hats the audience will watch the black one. Or you could make the clue on a cluttered coffee table big, shiny, and orange.

Videographers find that color is a particularly good way to draw attention, especially since the contrast range of video is relatively narrow, and simply increasing the illumination on your subject to draw attention isn't always an option. (For more information on using color in coordination with your lighting plan, see "Use Color to Direct the Eye" in Chapter 6.)

Faces and Eyes

From birth, human beings are conditioned to look into and study other people's faces. It's no different in the movies. Actors' faces are the most interesting objects in any shot, the eyes most of all. (For information on matching *eye lines* in closeups, see "Over-the-Shoulder Shot" later in this chapter.)

> **EYE LINE:** Imaginary line connecting two actors' eyes as they look at one another.

Focus

An effective way to draw audience attention is by camera focus, particularly if the camera changes focus (or *racks focus*) during the shot. This is a common technique in film, but selective focus is more difficult to achieve in video because of video's greater depth of field. (For more information, see the "Making Video Look Like Film" sidebar in Chapter 3.)

> **RACK FOCUS:** Named for the flat gear called a "rack" (half of the rack-and-pinion focusing mechanism on old-style movie cameras), to change focus during a shot.

TIP: To optimize the effect of selective focus in video, try using a telephoto lens with a wide aperture in dim light. You can also use a camera adapter such as the P+S Technik Pro35Digital Image Converter, which increases the effective target size of the CCD to about the size of a 35mm frame, permitting use of motion-picture lenses. For more information, surf to www.pstechnik.de.

Moving Actor or Object

The audience will follow whomever or whatever happens to be moving in a shot. If several objects are moving in a frame, the audience will be drawn to the one moving the fastest. And as we've mentioned earlier in this chapter, some of your best editing choices join two disparate actions that seem to blend into one continuous movement across the cut. In effect, by following the action, the viewer's interest is being pulled into the new scene.

Exceptional Object

Unique physical characteristics of objects—size, shape, or texture—can make them stand out. The audience will quickly spot a vintage car in the midst of a traffic jam, even if it isn't in the center of the frame.

TEN WAYS TO SHOOT A CHAIR

From a creative viewpoint there are countless ways to shoot a chair—or any other subject—but from a technical viewpoint we'll concentrate on just ten (**Table 5.1**).

The ten basic ways to design a shot derive from varying framing, lens selection, camera angle, and camera movement. The creativity of cinematography and the impact of visual storytelling come into play when you apply these factors in different combinations to manipulate audience perception and emotions.

You can use any combination of framing, lens selection, camera angle, and camera movement to design a shot. Each of these variables has a different effect on the way the audience perceives the subject or action.

Table 5.1 Variable Factors in Shot Composition

Framing (Size of Subject)	Lens Selection (Focal Length)	Camera Angle
Closeup	Wide angle	Low angle
Medium shot	Normal	Neutral
Long shot	Telephoto	High angle
Camera movement	Camera movement	Camera movement

TYPES OF SHOTS

Shots can be classified in many ways, depending on their function in the visual storytelling process. For instance, a given shot might be a *two-shot*, a dolly shot, and an establishing shot—all at the same time.

> **TWO-SHOT:** A shot that frames two actors.

Size of Subject

The first variable in classifying shots is the apparent size of the subject of the shot.

Closeup

The *closeup (CU)* generally frames an actor's head and shoulders, emphasizing her facial expressions and emotions (**Figure 5.5**). Variations include a *medium closeup (MCU)*, which is a bit wider, and an *extreme closeup (ECU)*, which shows only a portion of the face, cutting off either the chin or the forehead.

The traditional way to frame a closeup is to leave some space above the actor's head. But in a variation named for the studio that specialized in promoting star quality, the *Warner's closeup* is so tight, the frame line intersects the top of the actor's head.

Medium Shot

A *medium shot (MS)* shows the actor from the waist up (**Figure 5.6**). A medium shot is the perfect choice for showing upper-body movement, such as gestures in dialogue scenes, or for showing two or more actors having a conversation.

The closeup and the medium shot are most frequently used to frame a scene in visual storytelling.

Long Shot

A *long shot (LS)* shows the actor's entire body along with a good deal of her environment (**Figure 5.7**). Use long shots to emphasize action (running or combat, for example), to frame groups of people, and to orient the audience to the physical space of a set or location. A variation called the *extreme long shot (ELS)* looks at the subject from very far away, as if the viewer were spying unobserved from a great distance.

Figure 5.5 The closeup is a mainstay of moviemaking since it emphasizes emotion in the face. If the scene includes vigorous body movement, you'll either have to move the camera to follow the action or go to a wider shot.

Figure 5.6 The medium shot is appropriate for showing dialogue, gestures, and body language, provided that there isn't a lot of action in the scene.

Focal Length

Another way of classifying shots is by focal length, which is determined by which lens you select. No matter how you frame your shot or how big your subjects appear in it, you have a variety of choices for focal length.

Wide Angle

A wide-angle lens captures a wider field of view than the human eye (**Figure 5.8**). It offers great depth of field—almost everything in the shot, near and far, will be in focus. And it exaggerates distances so objects appear farther away than they really are.

You can use a wide-angle lens to distort the facial features of your subject by shooting her in closeup (**Figure 5.9**). Some comedy directors think wide-angle shots of dialogue scenes heighten the sense of fun.

Telephoto

Shots made with a telephoto lens magnify the subject, bringing it closer and flattening the image. Telephoto shots have shallow depth of field, which usually means that if the subject is in focus, the background will be soft, or blurred. A telephoto lens minimizes facial contours and can flatter an actor's face in closeup (**Figure 5.10**).

Figure 5.7 The long shot is commonly used for establishing shots and opening shots of scenes. It shows body-length views of the actors and gives the audience a chance to see a location. You might start a speech in a long shot, but these shots aren't very good for filming dialogue; you'll want to cut to a tighter shot for most of the actor's speech.

Figure 5.8 A shot done with a wide-angle lens is sometimes called a wide shot (WS).

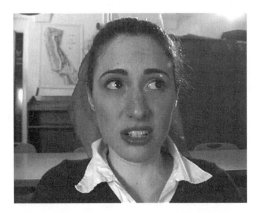

Figure 5.9 A wide-angle closeup is seldom flattering to the face and forces you to place the camera so close the actors may feel uncomfortable. Unless you are going for this odd effect, use a longer lens and move the camera back.

Figure 5.10 If you're going for a closeup of a star and want to make her look as good as possible, use a long lens. A telephoto lens compresses the contours of the face in a pleasing way. Add a diffusion filter to eliminate freckles and small blemishes.

Normal

A normal lens approximates how a scene would actually look to the viewer's unaided eye.

Varying the Camera Angle

A third set of shot descriptions refers to the angle of the camera in relation to the subject. You can use one of these camera angles in combination with any subject size and any lens choice. Camera angle adds an emotional charge to a shot and can make even a dull medium shot taken with a normal lens seem unusual and striking. Here are your options.

Low Angle

Looking up at the subject from a camera position near the floor, a low camera angle makes the subject loom over the viewer (**Figure 5.11**). The effect can be one of power and domination.

Neutral Angle

A shot at eye level is a neutral angle and gives no particular emotional perspective to our view of the subject.

High Angle

A high camera angle looks down on the subject from above (**Figure 5.12**). The effect exalts the audience over the subject, diminishing the actor's power or importance. You'll often see a high-angle long shot used at the conclusion of a movie as a kind of God's-eye-view, implying a larger perspective on the human events we've just witnessed.

Figure 5.11 The effect of a low-angle shot is to make a person look powerful or domineering.

Figure 5.12 A high-angle shot can make a person seem weak or powerless.

Moving the Camera

You can add camera movements to any shot we've discussed so far. Camera movements can be complex, involving many different motions, changes of speed, and changes of direction in the same shot. High-budget productions sometimes use computer controlled camera mounts for special-effects work so that complicated movements will be smooth, repeatable, and error free.

Pan

In this move, the camera is mounted on a tripod and rotates from side to side—left to right, or right to left—on the same level. You could use panning to survey the landscape in a long shot or to follow the action in a tennis game (**Figure 5.13**).

Tilt

Again, the camera is mounted on a tripod, but this time it tilts up or down. You might tilt to follow the flight of a rocket, capture the descent of a monkey from a tree, or progressively reveal the height of a building (**Figure 5.14**).

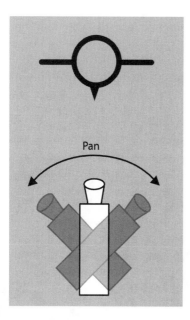

Figure 5.13 In a panning shot, the camera swivels from side to side on the tripod head, staying in the same horizontal plane.

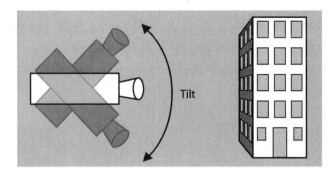

Figure 5.14 Tilting the camera swivels it upward or downward on the head, staying in the same vertical plane.

Zoom

In a zoom, the camera doesn't actually move, it just *seems* to move. A zoom is a lens adjustment that changes the optics from a wide-angle to a narrow-angle configuration, or vice versa, during the shot, thereby increasing or decreasing the magnification of the subject. The view with increased magnification is a *telephoto shot*.

Another term for zooming in is *pushing in*. The opposite move is called *pulling out* (**Figure 5.15**).

> **TELEPHOTO SHOT:** Done with a long lens, a narrow-angle closeup taken from a great distance.
>
> **PUSH IN:** Zoom in.
>
> **PULL OUT:** Zoom out.

 REALITY CHECK: *You can push in on the lens between takes to quickly set up a closeup without changing camera positions. This is a time-honored low-budget technique, especially in episodic television, where tight shooting schedules are the norm. Perhaps because of its extensive use on TV, movie directors and DPs tend to disapprove of the practice. Yes, it's a quick and dirty alternative to doing a new setup, but at the end of a long shooting day when light is fading fast, we wouldn't hesitate to use it to get one more precious shot.*

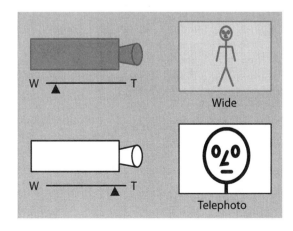

Figure 5.15 In a zoom shot, the camera position doesn't change. The operator adjusts the lens continuously from wide (W) to telephoto (T) when zooming in, and from T to W when zooming out.

Dolly

Named for a camera mount that rolls on tires or tracks, a dolly shot wheels the camera in toward the subject (a *dolly in*) or away from the subject (a *dolly out*). Dollying in on an actor has the same effect as walking up to the person: it increases the sense of intimacy. Dollying out produces a sense of withdrawal, even alienation (**Figure 5.16**).

Truck

Moving the camera parallel to a moving subject while keeping a constant distance is called *trucking*. A common use of trucking is to keep up with an actor as she walks or runs (**Figure 5.17**).

Crane

Named for the piece of equipment that raises or lowers the camera, a *crane* shot may also require panning, tilting, or zooming to keep the subject framed as the camera goes up,

CRANE: Counterweighted lever for raising or lowering a camera.

down, forward, or back. An upward-moving crane shot gives the audience a sense of soaring, downward movement of swooping or invasion.

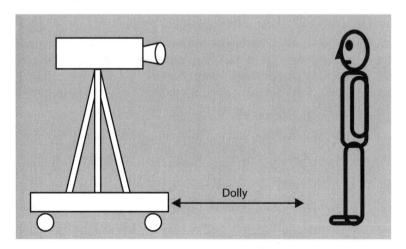

Figure 5.16 The camera rolls toward the subject when dollying in, away when dollying out.

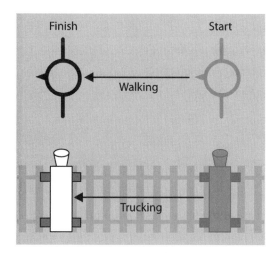

Figure 5.17 In a trucking shot, the camera rolls parallel to the actor.

Some camera dollies have a mechanical *boom arm* that can be used to create a small-scale version of a crane shot. (In general, a crane can extend upward to about 15 feet, a boom arm about six.) Using the boom arm of the dolly is referred to as *booming up* or *booming down* (**Figure 5.18**).

> **BOOM ARM:** Dolly-mounted crane.
>
> **BOOMING:** Raising (booming up) or lowering (booming down) the camera on a boom arm; crane shot.

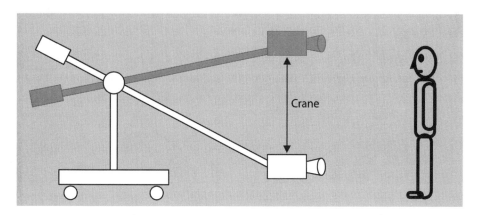

Figure 5.18 In a crane shot, the camera is raised or lowered. Other adjustments, such as tilting, will probably be needed to keep the subject in the frame.

Dolly Counter-Zoom

The complex camera move called a *dolly counter-zoom* (best known from Alfred Hitchcock's *Vertigo*) is a favorite of student filmmakers because its effect can be thrilling, and it's fun to do. But it's not easy to do well!

> **DOLLY COUNTER-ZOOM:** Zooming out while dollying in, or zooming in while dollying out.

You can execute the dolly counter-zoom in one of two ways:

- Dolly in on the subject while zooming out.

- Dolly out while zooming in.

Both methods use a zoom lens to change focal length while shooting—and while moving the camera.

The first method changes from a telephoto closeup to a wide-angle closeup. The effect is to signal a character having a frightening revelation. It's a staple of horror movies (accompanied by the all-too-familiar *reek-reek-reek* effect on the soundtrack).

The second method—moving out while zooming in—changes from a wide-angle closeup to a telephoto closeup. The effect is to give the sense that the world is closing in on a character—a criminal cowering on hearing the jury's verdict, for example.

Executing a smooth dolly counter-zoom can be challenging because the shot won't be convincing or effective unless the dolly and zoom movements occur at exactly the same time, at exactly the same rate, in perfect coordination.

The dolly counter-zoom has an intoxicating effect on aspiring DPs and camera operators, but if it doesn't work, you'll be smart to cut it in the editing room. As you might imagine, the sure sign of a rookie is a dolly counter-zoom that has no reason for being there other than the moviemaker's urge to try it.

Hollywood movies make extensive use of camera movement, including crane and dolly shots. These kinds of setups can be expensive, considering the cost of hiring and operating a crane, or the time and labor involved in laying a track for a dolly. Camera movement is another hallmark of that film-look quality audiences expect—along with artistic lighting, selective focus, rich audio, and lots of other high-priced effects.

 REALITY CHECK: *You can do camera moves even if you don't have the budget to rent a dolly or crane. Go handheld, use hand-carried mounts, or improvise with a shopping cart, child's wagon, skateboard, or even sit the camera operator on a blanket and pull him along a slick floor. For more information on doing these shots successfully, see "Moving the Camera During a Shot" in Chapter 9.*

USING SHOTS AS STORYTELLING ELEMENTS

So far in this chapter, we've discussed the technical categorization of shots, touching only briefly on how you might use them to tell stories. Now let's look at shots from a functional point of view.

Certain kinds of shots and combinations of shots have become filmmaking traditions (or clichés): the flattering closeup shot with a telephoto lens at neutral angle, for example, or the scene-opening combo of long-shot, medium-shot, closeup. But you don't have to be constrained by those choices just because they are mainstays of both talented directors and studio hacks.

In fact, you can apply any set of technical choices we've discussed to any of the following storytelling functions.

Establishing Shot

An establishing shot introduces the audience to a new setting. Traditionally, it would be an LS or ELS of the geographic location where the scene will take place. But if the scene is taking place in a diner, the establishing shot could just as easily be an ECU of a waiter's hand pouring a cup of coffee.

Master Shot

In the traditional approach to scene *coverage*, a *master shot* is an MS or LS of an entire scene, from beginning to end. If the editor uses it to open the scene, it can establish the actors in the setting. Inserted elsewhere in a sequence, it gives the editor a reliable alternative to closeup dialogue shots.

COVERAGE: A complete enough set of shots for a scene so the editor has every angle she needs to make the edited scene work.

MASTER SHOT: Continuous take of an entire scene, showing all the actors.

Two-Shot

A two-shot simply means that two actors are included in the frame; two-shots are generally framed as MS. If the scene involves only the two characters, a two-shot could be a master. Or, a two-shot could be a tighter shot of a wider master, to draw the audience into the emotional conflict between two characters in a scene involving many people.

Over-the-Shoulder Shot

This shot centers one actor in the frame as viewed *over the shoulder (OTS)* of another. In a traditional approach, it's a closeup of the speaker's upper torso, including the listener's shoulder and the side of her head. This framing lets you show some of the listener's body movements as she reacts to what's being said—nodding her head, for example. But it's just as valid for the person facing the camera to be the listener. His silent reactions to the speaker can be much more interesting to the audience.

> **OVER-THE-SHOULDER:** Close up of one character, shot from behind another character in the scene; OTS.

> **TIP:** *An over-the-shoulder shot can use a stand-in, or double, for a subject who's unavailable. When you shoot over the double's shoulder, only a portion of the back of his head will appear in the frame—eliminating the need for close physical resemblance with the original subject. You can dub in the subject's dialogue later without having to sync it because viewers can't see the double's lips move. However, if the shot is done badly—if the angle is wrong or if the double's motions appear unmotivated—the audience will become aware that the double is just standing there bobbing her head rather than speaking lines.*

Reverse Angle

In a pair of shots, if the second shot appears to view the scene from a direction more or less opposite to the first shot, it's a reverse angle. In most cases, the reverse shouldn't be *exactly* reverse—a 180-degree reverse would cross the stage line between the actors. Instead, a reverse is any complementary shot from a nearly opposite direction that doesn't cross the stage line. So, if the first shot were a CU on Amanda shooting over Adam's right shoulder, the matching reverse would be a CU on Adam, looking over Amanda's *left* shoulder. (Shooting over her right shoulder would commit the error of crossing the stage line.)

> **INTERCUT:** Insert one shot into another; also, cutting back and forth repeatedly from one shot to another.

In choosing camera angles for reverse angles—as well as for *intercut* closeups in general—be guided by the eye line between the actors. If you shoot Amanda, a tall actor, looking down at Adam in one shot, the camera in the reverse angle should be lower—near Adam's eye level—so he's looking up at Amanda. The camera should also be just to one side of the eye line, so the actors appear to be looking into each other's eyes, not into the camera lens. (An exception to this rule: a matching pair of ECU shots with the actors looking directly into the lens, as if at each other, is a technique directors like Steven Soderbergh have used to heighten the emotional intensity of a confrontation scene.)

REALITY CHECK: *The correct focus of attention in an OTS shot is just a few inches to one side of the camera lens. Rookie actors sometimes make the mistake of looking directly into the camera, but the director or anyone watching the monitor will catch it. A subtler problem all but the most experienced actors can have is breaking attention and glancing away, however briefly, or blinking during a take. (Blinking is particularly hard to see on the set.) The effect on the audience is a jarring break in concentration, making the actor come across as weak or indecisive. For more information on the subject of actors' sight lines, see Michael Caine's book and companion video,* Acting in Film.

> **SINGLE:** Shot that frames one actor; or "clean single."

A reverse that follows a CU on one character and shows the CU of the other, is a matching closeup, or matching *single*.

Single

A single shows just one actor in the frame, usually (but not necessarily) in closeup.

In a variation on the single—the so-called *dirty single*—a small portion of the listener's body can appear. This might be a hand, or the side of the face, but not quite as much as you'd see in a conventional over-the-shoulder shot. The dirty single has become common in the small-screen television era because it lets you take a closer look, to see some physical interaction between actors. You might use a dirty single if the listener's hand motion is significant to the story—picking up a knife, say, as the other actor threatens her.

To distinguish it from the dirty variation, a single is sometimes called a *clean single*.

 REALITY CHECK: *From a practical standpoint, it can be tempting to shoot a clean single without the other actor being present at all—which might conserve the offscreen actor's labor hours but leaves the on-camera actor delivering lines to a stand-in, crew member, or empty space—none of which are likely to motivate an interesting performance.*

Insert

The *insert* is a shot that's briefly intercut with a longer scene to show an object or some other meaningful detail. Traditionally it's a CU or ECU. An example would be a CU of a newspaper headline inserted into a dialogue scene in which two characters are discussing the news.

> **INSERT:** Shot briefly intercut with a longer scene, usually showing some meaningful detail.

REALITY CHECK: *Tight inserts don't show surroundings of a particular location or set. Wise production managers take advantage of this and often schedule all inserts at the end of a production or at some other convenient time, usually done by a separate, less senior crew called the* second unit. *Studios sometimes shoot all their inserts on separate, smaller sound stages called* insert stages.

SECOND UNIT: Often used on large-scale movie productions; auxiliary director and location crew that may shoot concurrently with the main production to save time and expense by capturing establishing shots, backgrounds, inserts, and so on.

INSERT STAGE: Small sound stage on a movie lot used primarily to shoot inserts, or tight closeups of props or gestures; small stage in television studio used for remote interviews and field reporting, typically with the local cityscape added electronically in the background.

CUTAWAY: Any shot that interrupts or follows a scene, relieves its tension, or comments on it.

Cutaway

A *cutaway* is any shot that takes the audience out of a scene, usually to add information. For example, we see a man hurry offscreen and then cut away to his wife in another location glancing anxiously at her watch. Or during a shot of two characters walking on the beach you might cut away to a shot of a seagull floating over the waves. Although using a cutaway is ultimately an editing decision, you won't have the clips to work with if you don't plan the shots in advance.

 REALITY CHECK: *Stock footage, or clips from a film or video archive, can be an economical source of cutaways, particularly if the duration of the shot is so short the audience doesn't have a chance to study it for details that might not match.*

POV

A *point-of-view (POV)* shot shows us what one character sees and helps the audience identify with him. In most other types of shots, the actors must stay focused on each other, not at the camera. But in the matching reverse of a POV, the other actor must look straight into

POV (POINT OF VIEW): Shot showing what one character is seeing.

the lens. One use of the POV is a horror-movie stereotype—to show the concealed monster's view of the unwitting victim. (At screenings, cinema buffs have been known to yell, "Watch out! There's a camera operator in the bushes!")

Reaction

A *reaction shot* shows an actor's response to something he's just heard or seen. Like the cutaway, the juxtaposition of a reaction shot is an editing choice, but if your coverage only includes talking heads, you won't have the option.

> **REACTION SHOT:** A shot that shows an actor's facial expression or body language in response to some speech or action.

 REALITY CHECK: *When shooting closeups for an emotional dialogue scene, directors should pay particular attention to the performance the actor is giving in the spaces* between *the lines—when listening to the offscreen actor. These reactions are often more important to the emotional truth of a character than the lines of dialogue, and these reaction shots can be used in the edit to heighten the scene's impact. For more information on getting good reaction shots, see "Working with Actors" in Chapter 9.*

Blocking the Action

Blocking is a term inherited from live theater to describe an actor's movements on stage. Your ideas about blocking a scene will have a big impact on camera placement and other elements of your shot plan.

> **BLOCKING:** An actor's movements within a scene.

Naturally, you want to limit the actors' movements so they won't stray beyond the boundaries of the set or move into areas that would be out of focus or poorly lit. At the same time, effective blocking is every bit as important—sometimes more so—than dialogue in conveying information and emotion to the audience.

 REALITY CHECK: *Screenwriting instructors talk about the notion of "character" as the totality of a person's actions. In a theatrical sense, blocking defines action within a playing area, or set. Yes, dialogue contributes to character. However, as in life, audiences are convinced more by what people actually do than by what they say they're going to do.*

Blocking should be repeatable from one take to another, or your shots may fail to maintain continuity when you cut them together. Also, if there's too much variation in blocking, you will never know if you have captured the scene the way you visualized it in your storyboard and shot plan. Improvisational directors who permit spontaneous variations in actors' blocking must be prepared to spend more time in the edit finding ways to preserve continuity in the assembled takes.

> **Input from the Rehearsal Process**
>
> *Filmmakers who favor improvisational methods often criticize structured shootists for a lack of spontaneity due to blocking that's worked out in advance.*
>
> *Improvisational directors trust their actors to figure out where their bodies want to go in the heat of the moment. The resulting action may well be more realistic, more inventive, and more interesting to watch than the preconceived idea in a script or storyboard.*
>
> *But waiting until you get on the set to figure out the blocking is risky. Some directors get away with it, but it takes a fair amount of experience (and luck) to set camera and lights if you don't know exactly where the actors are going to be.*
>
> *A good compromise is to allow plenty of time for rehearsals. Hold preproduction sessions to read through the scene with actors. Let them play it out, and watch how they naturally want to move. Then, after rehearsal (but well before shoot day), you can design your shots and draw up your shot plan with its blocking informed by the rehearsal process.*

DRAWING SHOT PLANS

All the elements we've discussed in this chapter culminate in a shot plan—a document that diagrams your camera setups, blocking of actors, and shots for every scene (**Figure 5.19**).

One important reason to draw up a shot plan for every scene is to make sure you will actually get the coverage you need. And the purpose of coverage, as noted earlier, is to assure that you have enough material to assemble the scene in the editing room without gaps in the action or breaks in the continuity. Remember, when you're working film style, you'll be shooting out of sequence. In the frenzy of production, you'll be concerned with getting all the shots on your list before the light is gone or your location becomes unavailable. So—unless you have a really sharp script supervisor—if a shot isn't on your list, it won't make it into the can.

As shown in Figure 5.19, the traditional approach to covering a scene assumes dialogue between two actors. The scene in the example is a sequence of two conversations: First Josh talks to his boss, Atwater, who exits; then coworker Phil enters, crosses to speak with Josh, and exits.

 The Josh-Atwater-Phil scene is Scene 3 from the short When Harried Met Sally. *You'll find both the finished video and the script on the disc.*

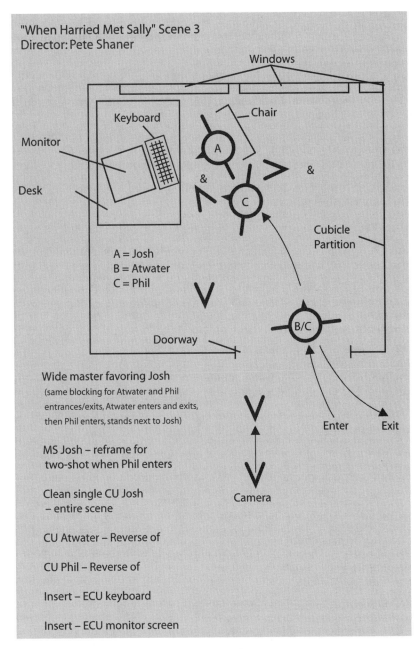

"When Harried Met Sally" Scene 3
Director: Pete Shaner

Windows

Keyboard

Monitor

Chair

A

Desk

&

&

C

A = Josh
B = Atwater
C = Phil

Cubicle
Partition

Doorway

B/C

Enter Exit

Wide master favoring Josh
(same blocking for Atwater and Phil
entrances/exits, Atwater enters and exits,
then Phil enters, stands next to Josh)

MS Josh – reframe for
two-shot when Phil enters

Clean single CU Josh
– entire scene

Camera

CU Atwater – Reverse of

CU Phil – Reverse of

Insert – ECU keyboard

Insert – ECU monitor screen

Figure 5.19 Here's a shot plan for Scene 3 of *When Harried Met Sally*. Do one shot plan for each short scene. For longer scenes, draw a plan for every two or three setups on the same set. Your plan won't include lighting at this point: Concern yourself with translating your shot designs into the physical reality of actors talking and moving in the physical space.

Among the numbered camera setups, the first one captures the entire scene in a master shot. Arrows indicate the actors' blocking, and text written below the diagram describes the action.

The second setup doesn't require moving the camera. Instead, it calls for reframing from MS on Josh to a two-shot when Phil enters. (Reframing might also involve pushing in or pulling out.)

The third setup calls for getting a clean single on Josh for the duration of the entire scene. Since Josh is the main character of the story, the audience will presumably be interested in his reactions. The editor will have the option of cutting back to this CU at any point rather than going to the wide-shot master.

The fourth and fifth camera setups capture reverse CUs of Atwater and Phil, in turn. As with the master shot, you have the option of pushing in from these positions to get ECUs. Depending on the length of the actors' speeches, you might not need to shoot the whole scene each time. However, remember that reaction shots can be extremely useful in the editing room for telling a story, so it's a bad plan to shoot an actor only when she's talking.

Setups six and seven get in very close on Josh's keyboard and monitor to show his hands typing and the document he's editing on the screen.

When developing your shot plans, think about how the scene will cut together. In a master-scene approach like this one, the editor will probably intercut the CUs and ECUs to come progressively closer to the subjects as the scene unfolds—pulling viewers into the scene. Cutting back to the master shot would have the opposite effect—relieving tension and giving the audience a chance to reflect.

It's possible that you won't use the master shot at all when you do your edit. You may cut from the previous scene directly to a CU, or even an ECU of the speaker to tell the story with more impact. You might not need to use the master to orient the audience to the setting, especially if they were expecting to return there or if the emotional content of the speech is more important. But think of the master shot as protection in case your closeups won't cut together for some reason.

> **TIP:** Cutting back to the master can cover breaks in continuity between closeups. For example, if cutting from one closeup to another crosses the stage line, the effect will be less jarring if you cut to the master first, then to the second closeup on the "wrong" side of the line.

A good shot plan follows through on the visual concepts in the script and storyboard, and it anchors your shot designs within the real constraints of a particular set.

EXTRACTING THE SHOT LIST

Now, working from your shot plan, make a list of the shots you intend to get, in the order you intend to get them. (Refer again to **Figure 5.3**.) If you're working from a storyboard and didn't do a shot plan to accompany it, you'll have to give some thought to the order of setups and shooting.

Start by listing the shots in story sequence, then sort them by master shot, and finally by increasing degrees of closeup. For example:

1. Master two shot: Josh and Phil at the desk

2. All Josh's CUs

3. All Josh's ECUs

4. All Phil's CUs

5. All Phil's ECUs

6. All inserts

7. Next master shot: reverses on Atwater and Phil at door

As your production planning evolves, you'll probably re-sort the list several times, grouping shots by location, interior or exterior, day or night, scene, setup, and shooting day. For example, it's wise to shoot exteriors before interiors, regardless of their sequence in the story. That way, if it rains and you can't shoot the exteriors, you'll still have shots you can get indoors.

You can then use the shot plan and shot list to open discussions with the DP and crew about the details of camera setups and lighting. (For more information on lighting your setups for DV, see "Three-Point Lighting" in Chapter 6.)

MAKING IT VISUAL

Shot design is where good screenwriting and visualization intersect. The inspiration for a compelling image may come from the writer in her shot description or from the director as he develops a storyboard. But the visual concept has to be in the design of the shot or the editor will be short of usable material.

A classic example of expert visualization is a scene in *The Merry Widow*, a romantic comedy directed by Ernst Lubitsch in 1934. The plot requires that the King find out the Queen has taken a lover. If this were a television soap opera—a notorious instance of radio-with-pictures—a trusted servant might tell the King the disturbing news. That's the obvious choice, and it's not a particularly interesting one.

But here's how Lubitsch, a consummate master of subtle screen sexuality, and his screenwriter, Samson Raphaelson, get the idea across—with no dialogue at all:

On leaving his marriage bed in the morning, the King dresses hastily, takes leave of the Queen, and hurries down the long circular stairway of the castle. Halfway down he pats his middle and realizes he's forgotten something. He returns to the bedroom, grabs a sword belt from the bedpost, makes another fond farewell, and takes leave of his wife once more. On his way down the stairs he tries to buckle the belt around his ample belly—only to find it's too small for him.

Now, *that's* telling a story with pictures.

CHAPTER SIX
Lighting for DV

With one exception—video's relatively narrow contrast range—lighting for DV is very much like lighting for any other film or video shoot, posing similar technical challenges and offering similar creative opportunities. Good digital videographers employ the same time-tested techniques of lighting that served master cinematographers James Wong Howe and Rudolph Maté. Of course if you're shooting news style, you'll have to use the resources at hand, but you'll still get better results if you keep these film-style lighting principles in mind.

PAINTING WITH LIGHT

Film (and film-style) lighting is both a craft and an art. The practical purpose of lighting is simply to make sure that the subject and its surroundings will be visible on screen by achieving the correct exposure for film or CCD. At the same time, the cinematographer's art of painting with light is a visual storytelling tool: It shows the audience where to look. Lighting technicians achieve both these goals by selecting and placing lights, reflectors, and other light sources on a location or set.

Lighting also establishes and reinforces a mood. For instance, TV sitcoms are always brightly lit and cheery, priming the audience for laughter. Horror films usually transpire in dark interiors with mysterious shadows, carefully designed to inspire anxiety and reinforce a scary story.

Video, both analog and digital, has a bad reputation for flat, boring lighting. Part of that reputation is deserved—and is rooted in historical necessity. Live broadcasts on early television used multicamera setups, which required the set to be lit more or less equally from all angles. In fact, many types of TV shows are still lit that way, including newscasts, game shows, and soap operas. When video ventured outdoors to cover news and sports, artful lighting was rarely possible; it was hard enough to follow the fast-breaking action.

But that's an old story. Today's DV camcorders are small and portable, with excellent low-light sensitivity. That means you have an opportunity to tell your story or convey your message by painting with light, just as the great cinematographers always have. And we're not talking about art for art's sake. Creative lighting not only adds aesthetic interest to your productions, it allows you to direct your audience's attention to elements within the images you want to emphasize.

 REALITY CHECK: *One of the few television soaps to use artistic, directional lighting instead of notoriously flat studio lighting style is* The Young and the Restless. *It also happens to be shot digitally—on HD.*

MEET YOUR LIGHTING CREW

Lighting a set is a complex activity that's very difficult to do by yourself. To light film style you need crew members to place lights, rig them, and move them around between takes. (For techniques on lighting news-style shoots, see "Three-Point Lighting, News Style" later in this chapter.)

In professional film and video production, job descriptions for lighting technicians have become quite specialized. Feature-film production crews have a strict division of labor—and union rules to enforce it. Even if your production is small, someone will need to perform these functions, and your lighting crew members will probably end up wearing more than one hat.

Director

As a visual storyteller, the director is a painter who never wields a brush. Her job is *not* to tell the crew how to light a scene but to let them know if she's pleased with the way they've lit it. She will decide on the action in a scene, as well as the setting and mood she wants to surround it. Then, she may (or may not) communicate those decisions to the director of photography (DP). Either way, the DP and the lighting technicians will find ways to achieve the director's intended results.

In evaluating the lighting of a scene, the director draws on both experience and artistic taste. Experience allows her to predict how highlights and shadows on the set will appear on the screen. Artistic taste will determine if she prefers hot (bright) lighting, atmospheric shadows, or some other aesthetic effect.

For the director, lighting is not a technical issue at all. It's about creating an impression in the minds of the audience—a game for which there are no rules.

Director of Photography

Whether the medium is film or videotape, the person in charge of both lighting and camera operations is the director of photography—the person who, in effect, selects the paints and uses the brush.

The DP's job is both artistic and technical. From an artistic standpoint, a DP must understand the results the director wants to achieve. To deliver those results the DP must, among other technical decisions, select and coordinate camera settings for variables such as depth of field and color, choose lenses and filters, and pick lighting elements.

The DP directs the activities of the lighting and electrical crews, specifies which lights to use and where to place them, and supervises the rigging and adjustment of lights to achieve correct exposure and color rendition. Once the lights are in place and rigged, the DP measures the light intensity and specifies f-stops and other settings for the camera operator to use.

Above all, a DP must be a master lighting technician. Like the director, only more so, the DP must know how technical decisions will show up on the screen. Experience with different film stocks and video media under a variety of lighting conditions is the best teacher.

Good DPs are highly paid, and work consistently.

Although the DP may also operate the camera, that's not always the case on a set with a full crew. And while some directors got their start as DPs, it's rare for a director on a film-style shoot to serve as DP. (Of course, on low-budget productions, all bets are off.)

Grips

A *grip* is a crew member with the authority, strength, and skill to get a "grip" on something and move it. In effect, grips deal primarily with the equipment that doesn't plug in. Common grip duties include laying dolly tracks, erecting scaffolding, implementing various rigging, and pushing the dolly.

The *key grip* is the head grip. He may also serve as a construction coordinator. He works closely with the gaffer and the DP, and he or any of the other grips in his department will help hang lights, make adjustments to lighting, and so on. The key grip's assistant is the second grip, or *best boy* (so named whether the person is male or female).

> **GRIP:** A crew member who deals primarily with the equipment that doesn't plug in.
>
> **KEY GRIP:** The head grip on a crew.
>
> **BEST BOY:** The second grip, or assistant to the key grip.

Gaffers

The *lead gaffer* is the head lighting technician, and is responsible for the design and execution of the lighting according to the instructions of the DP. The lead's second in command is the best boy gaffer. Big productions may have a half-dozen or more gaffers. Union crews observe a strict separation between gaffers and grips; on low-budget, nonunion productions, the same crew members often do both jobs.

Other job specialties within the gaffers' group include *rigging gaffers* (who fit lights with various accessories to control their effect), *generator operators* (who operate gasoline-fueled power sources), *lamp operators* (who replace burned-out lighting units), and *set wiremen* (who rig electrical lines).

> **NOTE:** *Grips and gaffers are unionized job specialties. In the film industry, experienced lighting technicians and electricians typically belong to IATSE (International Alliance of Theatrical Stage Employees). In broadcasting, crew members may be covered by IBEW (International Brotherhood of Electrical Workers) or NABET (National Association of Broadcast Employees and Technicians).*

GAFFER: A lighting technician on a movie or video set.

LEAD GAFFER: The chief lighting technician, or simply "the gaffer."

RIGGING GAFFER: The electrician on a set responsible for stringing, connecting, and securing power lines to lights.

GENERATOR OPERATOR: Gaffer who operates a gasoline-fueled electrical power source on a set.

LAMP: The bulb or light-producing device within a light.

LAMP OPERATOR: Gaffer who replaces burned out bulbs or other lighting elements.

SET WIREMAN: A gaffer who specializes in bringing electrical power to the set.

Line Producer

The line producer doesn't work with lights on the set but still has a very important role in lighting operations and is also ultimately responsible for compliance with union rules and safety regulations, including local codes regarding electrical wiring and fire prevention. He or she is in charge of budgeting, scheduling, contracting, and paying for all equipment and crews.

Whether your project has a line producer or not, *someone* has to be concerned with these issues. Particularly on low-budget productions, the task may fall to the director by default, possibly because no one thought about it ahead of time. Having the director also handle traditional line producing functions is not a good idea – it's too much for one person to do.

Of course, the line producer is closely involved with all phases of production, as well as project administration. We mention this essential person now because this stage of production planning is when you must think ahead about work practices and safety. Simply put, whoever is handling line-producer responsibilities must hire enough crew people or conditions on set will quickly become unsafe. For more information on safety when handling lighting equipment, see the sidebar "Safety First" later in this chapter.

Using Three-Point Lighting

Effective film and video lighting almost always follows a three-point plan (**Figure 6.1**). This basic technique works for all types of projects, shooting styles, and lighting situations, whether indoors or out.

Three-point lighting doesn't depend on the type of light source. Your sources can be sunlight, movie lights, table lamps, even car headlights. In your planning, you must also consider indirect lighting—reflections from direct lights, which you can often use as controlled, supplementary sources of illumination.

The objectives of three-point lighting aren't just to put enough light on the subject for correct exposure but also to separate the subject from the background (**Figure 6.2**). Typically, lighting for correct exposure involves a light source on either side of the subject. Lighting from a third point, usually from behind the subject, can give the impression of depth. And giving depth to your images is the best way to overcome the typical flat look of video.

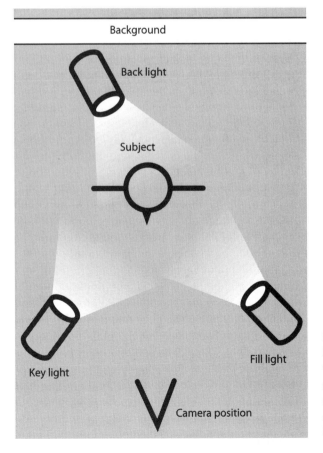

Figure 6.1 In an ideal three-point lighting plan, key light accentuates the subject, fill light reduces its shadow areas, and back light creates depth and heightens interest by drawing the subject away from the background, toward the audience.

Figure 6.2 The purpose of three-point lighting is to create the illusion of depth in a two-dimensional image by lighting the subject not only from the sides but also from the back. The desired effect is to pull her forward in space.

Key, Fill, and Back Light

The three light-source points in an ideal lighting plan are:

- Key light
- Fill light
- Back light

Key Light

The *key light* is the primary light source in a scene, the light that draws the viewer's attention to the subject.

The location of the key light should be about 45° from the line of sight between the camera and subject—usually at a midpoint between the camera and the subject. The classic approach to setting a key light is to place it

> **KEY LIGHT:** Central point of a classic, three-point lighting plan; "Rembrandt" lighting.

above the actor's head, just to one side (**Figure 6.3**). From the viewpoint of the camera, with the actor facing the lens, if you're lighting the actor's right side, place the light in the 10 o'clock position; if you're lighting the actor's left, place the light in the 2 o'clock position.

When you're working with actors or interview subjects, it's traditional to place the key light so the shadow of the tip of the person's nose touches the corner of the mouth. Because this painter of portraits used it so consistently, key light is also called *Rembrandt lighting*.

HIGH KEY: In a three-point lighting plan, a bright primary light on the subject, suitable for comedy.

LOW KEY: In a three-point lighting plan, a subdued primary light on the subject, suitable for drama.

Key light is the controlling factor in the overall lighting intensity—and mood—of a scene. Bright key light, called *high key*, is usually the right choice for comedy. *Low key* is more suitable for drama. From a technical viewpoint, if you need to adjust the overall intensity of a scene to try a different camera exposure, always adjust the key light first, then all the others.

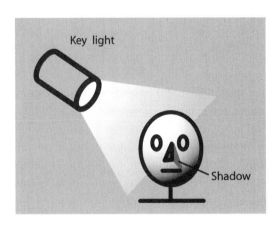

Figure 6.3 The classic approach to placing a key light, shown here in an actor's closeup, creates a shadow from the tip of the nose to the corner of the mouth.

Fill Light

You can use *fill light* to soften and fill in the shadows created by the key light (refer again to **Figure 6.1**). The source of fill light should be on the opposite side of the subject from the key light. It should also be more diffuse, less intense, and less focused.

FILL LIGHT: In a three-point lighting plan, the light that softens and fills in the shadows created by a key light.

The main purpose of fill light is to reduce contrast within the key-lighted areas. Because of video's relatively narrow contrast range (as compared to film), the artful and carefully controlled use of fill lighting is a necessity.

For example, if you were shooting video outside on a bright, sunny day, you might use the sun itself as the key light. But if that were the only source of illumination, setting the camcorder exposure to capture shadow areas would overexpose the brighter ones, a condition videographers call *blown-out whites*. However, exposing for the light areas risks losing detail in the dark areas, which might go totally black. The solution is to use artificial light, or a reflector, to create fill lighting that will decrease the difference in brightness between sunlit and shadowed areas.

> **AMBIENT LIGHT:** Naturally occurring light.

Both key light and fill light can be *ambient* (naturally occurring) or artificial (from lights). If your key light isn't too bright, ambient light—from ceiling lights in an office, for example—may provide sufficient fill. Both sources could be ambient if the second is a reflection of the first but comes from a different angle.

Back Light

The third lighting point falls on the subject from behind, and is called *back light* (refer again to **Figure 6.1**). Back light can be either narrowly focused or diffuse, depending on the effect you want.

> **BACK LIGHT:** In a three-point lighting plan, light that falls on the subject from behind and separates it from the background.

Back light can be flattering—giving that special sheen to an actor's hair, for example—and it also makes the subject "pop," pulling it forward in space, toward the audience and away from the background.

Using Practicals

Lighting fixtures that appear in a shot, such as table lamps that actually work but aren't necessarily primary light sources, are called *practical* lights, or simply *practicals*. They make perfect motivators for off-camera light sources. (For more information on *motivating* light sources, see "Motivate the Key Light" later in this chapter.)

> **PRACTICAL:** A working light source visible in the scene; any working appliance on a set that must have electrical power.
>
> **MOTIVATING A LIGHT SOURCE:** Convincing the audience that your light source mimics real-world lighting.

Using Hard and Soft Light

Once the lights are set, grips can fit them with various accessories to control the quality of light—making the light *hard* or *soft*. Hard light casts dark shadows with sharp edges. Soft light creates vaguer shadows, or no shadows at all.

> **HARD LIGHT:** Bright illumination emanating from a point source, such as a single, bare lamp; causes sharp shadows.
>
> **SOFT LIGHT:** Diffuse illumination coming from a large, bright area like a reflector.

For instance, on a cloudless day the sun is a hard light. On an overcast day, sunlight is diffused by the clouds, creating a soft light.

DPs love soft light because it "wraps around" the subject in a pleasing way, softening or eliminating shadows. Soft light requires less fill to achieve correct exposure, especially given the narrow contrast range of video. (For more information on shooting DV with soft light, see "Bounce Your Fill Light" later in this chapter.)

Other Types of Highlighting

Once three-point lights are set, a DP may consider additional types of highlights to add creative effects and interest to a scene.

Eyelight

Eyelight, a narrowly focused spotlight aimed at an actor's eyes, is often used in the movies. DPs typically mount an eyelight on the camera itself, directly above the lens, so the reflection will be centered in the subject's eyes. The effect adds sparkle, interest, and personality (**Figure 6.4**). Notice the striking difference between a closeup with no eyelight (**Figure 6.5**) and the sparkle and personality it adds (**Figure 6.6**). Villains are usually lit without eyelight, giving them a dead, soulless look that emphasizes their evil nature. Even without a black hat, the audience knows right away this stranger is not to be trusted.

> **EYELIGHT:** A narrowly focused spotlight aimed at an actor's eyes for the purpose of adding sparkle, interest, and personality.

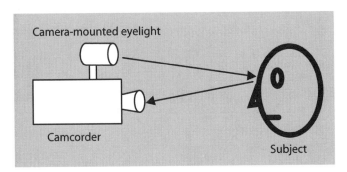

Figure 6.4 A camera-mounted eyelight can be aimed to create a reflection in the subject's eyes that will be directed back into the camera lens. An eyelight might provide just the right extra touch if you are shooting a spokesperson's pitch or a CEO's address to stockholders. (A standard lighting plan will also include key and fill.)

Figure 6.5 In a closeup with no eyelight, the subject seems to lack personality.

Figure 6.6 Adding eyelight perks up the subject and draws the audience into her look.

Rim Light

A kind of back light that adds a pleasing glow to an object's outline, and emphasizes its edges, is called *a rim light*. It's particularly useful for *beauty shots* of products in commercials (**Figure 6.7**). (Some lighting technicians use the terms back light and rim light to mean the same thing.) Depending on the light intensity, the effect on the scene can create a glow around the subject (**Figure 6.8**).

> **RIM LIGHT:** Back light that adds a pleasing glow to an object's outline.
>
> **BEAUTY SHOT:** Highly flattering, meticulously lit closeup of a star in a movie, or a product in a commercial.

Spotlights

Spotlights are intense beams that can be trained on objects or areas in a scene that aren't already being illuminated by the key light. Spots can give the impression of light spilling from another room, bright reflections, or accents on objects (**Figure 6.9**). Light spilling from a doorway into a darkened hall can impart a sense of mystery (**Figure 6.10**).

Kickers

Kickers are spotlights placed on the fill side of a subject to emphasize its contours. Often a back light can double as a kicker if you move it slightly to the left or right while keeping it aimed at your subject. Kickers can add emphasis to jaw lines or cheekbones; they are traditionally used to make a leading character appear more heroic (**Figure 6.11**). The effect can be downright glamorous (**Figure 6.12**).

> **SPOTLIGHT:** Intense beam, a very hard light, on a specific object or area in a scene; also called a "spot."
>
> **KICK:** In lighting terminology, any bright reflection off an object.
>
> **KICKER:** Spotlight placed on the fill side of a subject to emphasize its contours.

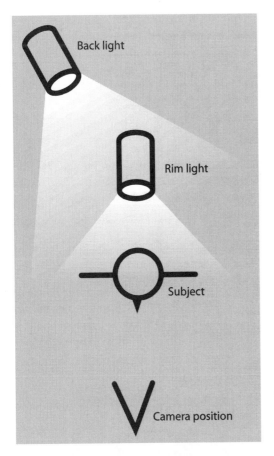

Figure 6.7 Although back light and rim light often mean the same thing (lighting the subject from behind), you might add an extra small rim light to emphasize the outline of a particular character or object. (A standard lighting plan will also include key and fill.)

Figure 6.8 The glow of a rim light can be angelic or menacing, depending on the look of the character and the dramatic situation.

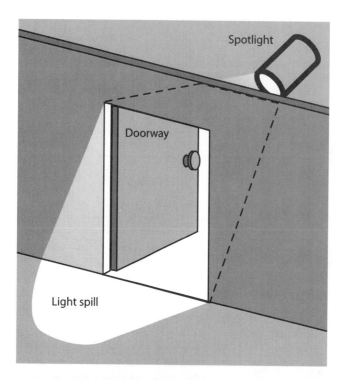

Figure 6.9 Locating a spotlight on the other side of a wall can create a pool of bright, hard light that spills through the doorway and onto the floor.

Figure 6.10 The spotlight here makes the warmth of the brightly lit interior contrast sharply with the gloom of the darkened hall, creating a sense of danger and anxiety.

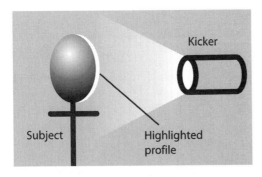

Figure 6.11 Positioning a kicker light to the side of the subject will highlight and emphasize its profile. (A standard lighting plan will also include key and fill.)

Figure 6.12 A kicker can make the subject appear more lovely. Here the highlight adds luster to her hair.

Background Lighting

Unlike back light, which is focused on your subject, *background lighting* illuminates the setting (or background) that surrounds your subject. Use background lighting when necessary to reduce overall contrast within a scene or to make objects in the scene more visible,

> **BACKGROUND LIGHTING:** General illumination of a set, particularly the back wall, rather than specific objects or players in it.

such as a wallpaper pattern on a dark wall (**Figure 6.13**). Without back light, the audience might not even notice a picture on the wall (**Figure 6.14**). With back light added, the picture and detail of the wall become interesting details in the scene (**Figure 6.15**).

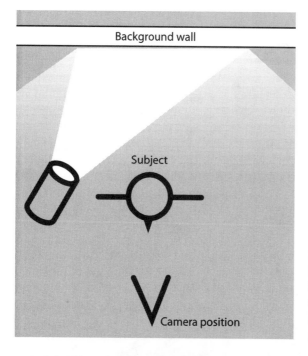

Figure 6.13 Bouncing a background light off a wall behind the subject can increase the overall lighting intensity of the scene and bring up any significant details on the wall. (A standard lighting plan will also include key and fill.)

Figure 6.14 Without background light, details on the wall will probably go unnoticed by the audience.

Figure 6.15 Adding background light not only brings up detail there but also makes the environment more interesting.

CONTROLLING COLOR TEMPERATURE

"White" light sources actually have distinct tints, or *color temperatures*, which lighting technicians measure in degrees Kelvin (°K).

> **COLOR TEMPERATURE:** Tint of white light, measured in degrees on the Kelvin scale (°K).

Using a combination of light sources, all with different tints, is called *mixed lighting*. This is typical of most real-world shooting, which is why it's a challenge to achieve *color balance*— adjusting the tints of the various light sources so colors look natural and pleasing.

In everyday life we ignore minor differences of color temperature because the human eye compensates for them. But film and CCDs don't compensate as well as our eyes, and the recorded results can be noticeable and unattractive.

For example, sunlight is at the blue end of the spectrum, while *incandescent* lights like table lamps tend to be orange. If you are shooting in a room with sunlight coming through a window, you must use movie lights with daylight color temperature (about 5500°K) or tint the windows to match *tungsten* movie lights, which give off about 3200°K.

> **MIXED LIGHTING:** Lighting setup containing light sources of varying color characteristics.
>
> **COLOR BALANCE:** Compensation for different color temperatures within a lighting setup to achieve pleasing overall color rendition.
>
> **INCANDESCENT:** Any lamp whose light comes from a glowing wire or filament.
>
> **TUNGSTEN:** Particular type of incandescent light with filament made from this metal; European crews may call it "wolfram."

Another way to deal with color temperature is to adjust the overall color response of the camera. In photography, you can choose between film stocks that have emulsions balanced either for outdoors (daylight) or for indoor incandescent (tungsten) lighting. DPs also place tinted filters over the lens to adjust the color characteristics of cameras, whether film or video.

Since camcorders don't use film, you can't adjust for color temperature by using different film stocks. Instead, camcorders rely on a continuously variable white-balance feature, which takes a white sample area in the scene as a reference for setting maximum RGB pixel values. White balance should *always* be set manually; automatic white balance features are unreliable, even on expensive camcorders. (For more information on using white-balance camcorder controls, see "The Importance of White Balance" later in this chapter.)

SELECTING PROFESSIONAL LIGHTS

A complete survey of lighting gear would make a thick catalog, but here are some guidelines on the main types of light sources and how to apply them to achieve your technical and creative goals.

While there's no type of lighting that's specially designed for DV, or even for video, DV's greater sensitivity to light at low levels makes it possible to use lower-powered lights— especially if you're shooting indoors.

On the other hand, when you're shooting outdoors, particularly in bright sunlight, you may actually need bigger, brighter lights than a film crew would. The sun can create such hot key light that you might need high-powered lights to create sufficient fill to come within an acceptable contrast range for DV. An inexpensive way to achieve more balanced lighting outdoors is to use reflectors.

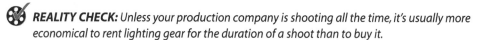 **REALITY CHECK:** *Unless your production company is shooting all the time, it's usually more economical to rent lighting gear for the duration of a shoot than to buy it.*

Basic Characteristics of Movie Lights

When it comes to selecting lights, the essential differences among them come down to:

- Color temperature
- Intensity
- Beam angle
- Throw
- Portability

Color Temperature

Professional movie lights are categorized by color temperature—tungsten (indoor, orange color balance) or daylight (outdoor, blue color balance).

Unlike shooting with available light or practicals, a major advantage of using professional movie lights is the precision and reliability of their color-temperature ratings. All lights of a given type from a particular manufacturer will have pretty much the same color temperature. (However, the color temperature of a light can change with the age of the lamp.)

Intensity

The absolute measure of the brightness of a light source is its *intensity*. In practical terms, the effective intensity of a movie light depends on its lamp type, its electrical *wattage*, its distance from the subject, and the effect of any diffusing techniques you use to soften its beam.

> **INTENSITY:** Absolute measure of the brightness of a light source.
>
> **WATTAGE:** Measure of electrical power consumption.

Wattage, however, is only useful for comparing lamps of the same type. If two lights use different lamp technologies, comparing their wattage won't be helpful at all. For example, a 40-watt household light bulb isn't as bright as a 75-watt bulb. But a 40-watt *fluorescent* tube is brighter than either of them (because fluorescents convert electricity to light more efficiently than incandescent bulbs).

> **FLOURESCENT:** Tube-style light with no filament, filled with a gaseous metal that glows when electricity passes through it; in professional terminology, a "Kino Flo," named for one manufacturer.

How much overall intensity you'll need to light a scene depends on the size of the room or set, and the mood you want to establish (bright, dark, or something in between). For a small- to medium-sized room and a moderate, overall lighting level, three relatively small halogen-type movie lights of 300 watts each might be enough. To illuminate the same scene for a brighter effect would require higher-powered 650-watt lights of the same type.

Beam Angle

Beam angle describes the number of degrees through which illumination remains bright enough to be useful. For example, lights with a narrow beam angle are suitable as key lights or spotlights; those with wide beam angle are better for fill.

> **BEAM ANGLE:** A light's area of coverage, measured in degrees within which intensity is at least half of the light's rating. For example, a narrowly focused spotlight might have a beam angle of 20 degrees.
>
> **OPEN FACE:** Movie light fixture with no focusing lens.

Beam angle is determined by the design of the light. One factor may be the shape of the light's reflector, the shiny surface behind the light source. Some lights also use adjustable lenses to concentrate their beams; these are called focused lights. Lights with reflectors but no lenses are called *open face* (**Figure 6.16**).

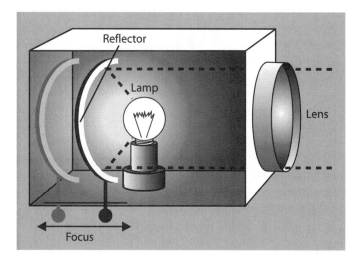

Figure 6.16 Two aspects of movie light design that concentrate the lamp's beam are the shape of the reflector and the focusing characteristics of an optional lens. Focusing is achieved by changing the position of the reflector, not the lens.

It's also possible to control the beam with various lighting accessories. (For more information, see "Tools for Controlling Light" later in this chapter.)

Throw

A light's *throw* is the distance its beam can cover without fading to the point of inutility.

> **THROW:** Distance a beam can cover before becoming too faint for lighting purposes.

Throw is a function of both a light's power and its beam angle. The larger your set or location area, the greater throw you'll need from your lights.

Portability

Some lighting technologies are more compact, and therefore more portable, than others. Portability can be a factor in selecting lights because it will affect crew size, transportation costs, and ultimately how many setups you can fit into a day's shooting.

In general, lights with lenses are considerably heavier than open-face lights, because their housings must be stronger and more durable to hold the lens and withstand the heat it absorbs. All of which means you will need a heavier and stronger adjustable stand on which to mount it.

More powerful lights tend to be bigger and heavier due to the greater size of all the elements—lamp, lens, housing, stands, and so on. For example, a big 10K light is about the diameter of an office trash can and is almost too heavy for one gaffer to handle.

Lamp Technologies

Lighting manufacturers tend to specialize in different lamp technologies, and technicians sometimes refer to movie lights by the name of their manufacturer. Types of lamps, each with characteristic color-temperature ranges, include the following.

Tungsten Lights

Most lights used for indoor videography are tungsten lights. Tungsten lights use lamps with filaments, much like the glowing wires that illuminate household light bulbs. However, unlike ordinary light bulbs, lamps in professional tungsten movie lights are usually filled with a gas, such as halogen, that glows brightly when heated by the filament. They fall at the orange end of the spectrum.

> **HALOGEN-QUARTZ:** Incandescent lamp with tungsten filament and filled with a mixture of halogen gas and vaporized quartz. The gas glows brightly and helps prevent the filament from combining with oxygen so as not to burn up at high temperatures.

MINI: Mid-range in power but compact in size and therefore highly portable, an open-face halogen-quartz movie light; in smaller sizes, "teenie weenies" or "betweenies;" in larger sizes, "redheads," "Mickeys," "blondes," or "mighties."

BARN DOORS: Hinged panels on the front of movie light housings that can be adjusted to control the beam angle of the light.

GEL: Transparent optical material that changes the color of light passing through it.

(Most tungsten movie lights are of the *halogen-quartz* type, a lamp that can withstand the high heat it generates.)

Typical tungsten designs include the following:

Minis are one of the most popular lights for indoor videography; these small, open-face halogen units are typically found in 300- or 650-watt versions (**Figure 6.17**).

Because of its adjustable features (*barn doors* and beam control), you can use a mini for key light as well as for fill, provided you can position it within a few feet of the subject.

Lighting technicians call minis *teenie-weenies* or *betweenies*. Similar open-faced halogen lights in higher wattages (800–1000 watts) are often called *redheads* (or *Mickeys);* even larger versions (2000 watts) are called *blondes* (or *mighties)*. You'd select the higher wattages to cover larger indoor areas.

Beam control

Holder

Barn doors

Figure 6.17 This halogen-quartz movie light made by Mole-Richardson has a lightweight, open-face design that includes a set of barn doors for adjusting the beam and a holder for inserting scrims and *gels*. A knob at the back of the housing lets you adjust focus by moving the lamp in relation to the reflector.

Fresnel lights are named for the inventor of the lens used on this type of focused tungsten light (**Figure 6.18**). Halogen-based Fresnels are available from several manufacturers and their primary use is as key lights and spotlights. They tend to be heavy, due to the weight of the heat-resistant glass of their lenses and their heavy-duty housings. They are far less portable than open-face minis, but they provide unmatched precision in your ability to focus them by adjusting the distance of the lamp from the lens. Most of the big lights you see on movie sound stages are Fresnels.

> **FRESNEL:** Halogen movie light equipped a with glass lens for focusing the beam; sizes from small to large include: "pepper," "inkie," "betweenie," "tweenie," "baby-baby," "junior," "senior," and "tenner." Pronounced "frehnel."

Fresnels come in a wide range of wattages, starting smaller than 250 watts and going all the way up to 10,000 watts. They go by various colorful names, in ascending order of wattage:

- Pepper (tiny)
- Inkie
- Betweenie
- Tweenie
- Baby-baby
- Baby
- Junior
- Senior
- Tenner (huge)

Lowel is a manufacturer of halogen-based open-face lights. Lowels are quite popular for fill and background lighting, thanks to their wide beam angles and long throws (**Figure 6.19**).

Fluorescents

Fluorescent tubes are very well suited for low-light conditions, especially when a softer quality is desired. Fluorescents are filled with a gaseous metal that glows when electricity passes through it; no hot tungsten filament is required.

> **BALLAST:** Starter/regulator for fluorescent lights.

Fluorescents consume less electrical power than tungsten lights for the light they produce, so they can be less expensive to operate. However, although the tubes themselves are lightweight, they require bulky *ballasts*, or regulating devices, which limit their portability.

Conventional fluorescents of the type you'll find in office ceiling fixtures aren't good sources of illumination for film or video, as their characteristic green cast gives people's faces a sickly look.

Fluorescent tubes designed for movie lighting have more precisely controlled color temperatures, as well as special ballasts that eliminate a tendency to flicker. Although the output of household fluorescents is usually in the tungsten range (orange, but mixed with green), tubes can be manufactured to produce almost any desired color temperature, ranging from 2950°K (yellow-orange, like tungsten) to 6500°K (blue, daylight). Typically, professional movie-style fluorescents are either 3200°K tungsten equivalents or 5600°K daylight models.

Kino Flo is well known in the industry for making flicker-free ballasts and color-controlled fluorescents for movie lighting. Many lighting technicians refer to all fluorescents as *Kino Flos.*

Figure 6.18 Augustin-Jean Fresnel invented a lens with a set of molded concentric glass rings. This design, combined with a special grade of glass, resists cracking even at the high heat generated by tungsten lamps. Gaffers focus Fresnel lights by moving a knob that slides the lamp back and forth in the housing, varying the distance between the lamp and the lens.

Figure 6.19 This open-face halogen-quartz movie light made by Lowel has a dish-shaped reflector that casts a powerful beam over a wide area, making it a good, lightweight choice for fill and background lighting.

HMI Lights

HMI (hydrargyrum medium-arc iodine) tungsten-gas lights are balanced for daylight shooting and are many times brighter than halogen lights of the same wattage. This fact, combined with their characteristic blue color temperature, makes them perfect for shooting outdoors. HMI lights aren't heavy, but they require ballasts, which makes them bulkier than tungsten lights to transport and move.

> **HMI LIGHTS:** Daylight-balanced, incandescent lamps with tungsten filaments and filled with hydrargyrum medium-arc iodine gas, which glows brighter than the halogen-quartz type.

Other Light Sources

If you're on a budget or need to improvise, here are some other lighting sources you might consider:

Photofloods. These are cone-shaped tungsten light bulbs, often used for amateur photography. They have a reflective coating inside, which creates a spotlight effect, and range in wattage from 75 watts to 1 kilowatt, with color temperatures of either 2800°K or 3200°K, depending on the brand and model. Special *daylight blue* photofloods are intended for outdoor use, but their color temperature is about 4800°K, not quite up to the 5600°K considered standard for daylight shooting. Photofloods burn less brightly than halogens and have a shorter throw. You can buy or rent movie-style fixtures to hold them, which feature barn doors and *gel*-frame holders, but if you're going to go to the expense and trouble of renting these fixtures, you'd be better off choosing halogen minis instead of photofloods in the first place.

> **PHOTOFLOOD:** Cone-shaped tungsten light with built-in reflector used to provide area lighting for photography.
>
> **DAYLIGHT BLUE:** A light source color-balanced for use outdoors, to supplement or simulate sunlight.

Lanterns and balloons. For years, Chinese lanterns made out of paper have been a trade trick used by DPs to achieve soft lighting of large areas for fill and background. The source inside the lantern can be an incandescent bulb or a coiled string of low-wattage ornamental lights. However, if the wattage is too great, or you're tempted to use hot-burning halogen bulbs, you may set the paper lantern on fire. A professional variation on this idea is a translucent, helium-filled balloon with a halogen light inside. These fixtures (available from vendors like Airstar Space Lighting) range in size from small globes the size of Chinese lanterns to huge, radio-controlled airships.

Practicals. It's tempting to use ordinary household lights as sources of illumination, especially if they're in the shot already. This can be tricky. Practicals like table lamps typically throw too much light on the subject, blowing out its highlights, or don't light it enough, creating deep shadows. A more controlled approach would be to place low-wattage bulbs in practicals to motivate more powerful off-camera lights.

Available light. Sources you can use—and often can't avoid—are sunlight and overhead lights inside buildings. You can make good use of sunlight, particularly if it's diffused by cloud overcast, or if you can find a way to reflect it back on the subject as the second source of a three-point plan. Overhead lighting can be a source of area lighting, increasing the overall illumination of a scene, but it's best to avoid including the source itself in the shot. (For more information on using available light, see "Three-Point Lighting, News Style" later in this chapter.)

Safety First

Hazards of working with high-temperature movie lights include fire, electrocution, and physical injury. So be careful!

- *When rigging lights, follow local fire and electrical codes.*

- *Fingerprints on lamps cause them to heat unevenly and burn out rapidly—or explode. So use gloves and eye protection when handling and replacing lamps, and make sure they are firmly seated in their sockets before switching them on.*

- *Avoid putting any flammable material, such as cardboard, paper, or cloth, close to a lamp, even if it's a low-wattage household bulb.*

- *Take the time to tape electrical lines to the floor. Tripping over cables is a major cause of accidents on the set.*

- *Rig silks, flags, and other gear on C-stands to distribute weight as evenly as possible. Weight the legs with sandbags to prevent tipping.*

- *Use grip clamps, C-47s, or heat-resistant gloves to adjust barn doors and other hot lighting components.*

- *All high-intensity light sources can be hazardous, but HMI lighting equipment is particularly dangerous. These lamps have a nasty tendency to explode, most often when they are switched on. Gaffers should warn cast members and crew before they switch on an HMI unit, and make sure no one is standing directly in front of it. Also, since part of their spectrum extends into the ultraviolet range, HMIs can cause sunburn. Keep HMI lights at least several feet away from actors or interview subjects. Gaffers who work closely with these lights should use sunblock.*

- *As a general rule, no matter what kind of lights you're using, warn actors, interview subjects, and crew before you turn on those lights, and ask them to move away from the lamps. Let lights warm up for several minutes before shooting, and keep them on to stabilize color temperature—but turn them off promptly after the last take.*

- *Let hot lights cool down before moving them. Never attempt to break down hot lights or put them in packing cases.*

- *Even though DV-style shooting encourages rapid shooting schedules, be deliberate and careful in setting and moving lights. Hurrying will cause carelessness and accidents.*

Lighting Kits for DV

Minis are a good, all-around choice for shooting DV. They are lightweight, highly portable, and come in both open-face and Fresnel fixtures. A kit of three minis, just what you'd need for lighting a small room using the three-point approach, fits in a single trunk-sized case that one crew member can carry. A three-light kit typically comes with either 300-watt open-face, or 650-watt fresnel lights. It sells for around $2,000, and rents for about $60 per day.

Two such kits, comprising six minis, is a good all-around set of gear for most small-scale indoor shoots. A lower-cost alternative is a *combo kit* with two 650-watt and two 300-watt lights, for about $3,000 or $75 per day rental.

TOOLS FOR CONTROLLING LIGHT

Your basic lighting procedure will go something like this:

1. Select lights for color temperature and wattage.

2. Place them to achieve a three-point plan.

3. Adjust the camcorder for white balance and correct exposure.

However, in real-world shooting situations these steps don't give you enough control. You'll also need a variety of accessories to further control and distribute the output of lighting sources.

C-Stands and Other Grip Equipment

The *C-stand* is the grip's multipurpose holder for all kinds of devices that diffuse, filter, mask, or reflect light (**Figure 6.20**). It's an adjustable metal stand with a folding tripod base, equipped with two circular clamps, one on the stand and one on a movable arm. The height and angle of the arm are adjustable, and the clamps hold accessories securely.

> **C-STAND:** Movie grip's adjustable metal stand, a multipurpose holder for devices that diffuse, filter, mask, or reflect light.

C-stands weigh about 20 pounds each, which provides strength and stability, but even with the tripod legs folded the stand is cumbersome to handle. It can be difficult for a grip to carry more than two at a time for any distance.

An essential accessory for C-stands and stands used to hold light fixtures is the sandbag. Once lights and C-stands are in place, grips drape sandbags over the legs of the stands to prevent the stands from tipping over (**Figure 6.21**).

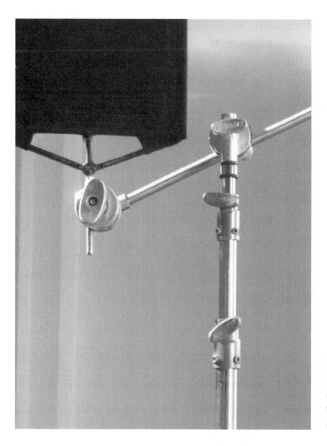

Figure 6.20 Knobs on the C-stand (called knuckles) let you adjust its arms to various heights and angles; vise-like clamps hold a variety of grip gear—a flag, in this case.

Figure 6.21 A safety procedure used by grips is to drape the legs of movie lights and C-stands with sandbags. The sandbag helps balance the weight of fixtures and accessories, providing stability so the stands are less prone to tip over. Since it's all too common for actors and crew members to stumble over a stand, the added weight of the sandbags can prevent an accidental tip-over that could cause a lamp to explode.

Gaffer's tape. No lighting kit would be complete without a roll of gaffer's tape, which resembles household duct tape but is less sticky for easier removal. As you might guess, it gets its name from the gaffer who uses this tape to, among other things, fasten electric cables to the floor so people don't trip over them. But gaffer's tape is also an all-purpose fastening tool that can be used by any crew member to fasten or fix an accessory in a hurry. Gaffer's tape can also be used for securing props to a table, mending rips in costumes, and other purposes too varied to mention.

GRIP CLIP: Spring-loaded hand vise used by grips to fasten accessories such as flags to C-stands or to each other.

C-47: Movie-grip term for a common clothespin.

Grip clips and C-47s. Another all-purpose tool is a spring-loaded hand vise called a *grip clip,* often used for fastening accessories to C-stands or to each other (**Figure 6.22**). Smaller than a grip clip, but serving much the same purpose, is the mysteriously named C-47, which is nothing more nor less than a common, spring-loaded, wooden clothespin. (Grip lore has it that C-47 was the military requisition number for clothespins during WWII.) Gaffers use C-47s to clip gels and diffusion materials to barn doors, or sometimes as handles for adjusting the barn doors themselves—which get quite hot after the lights have been on awhile.

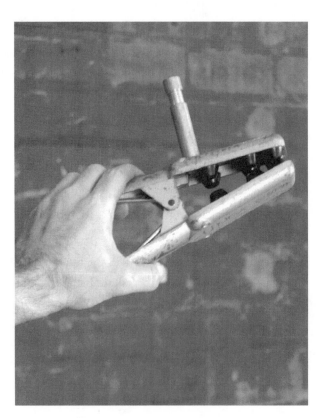

Figure 6.22 This alligator is a fancy variation on the grip clip. It has a set of rubber teeth and a metal extension called a *spud* for insertion into the clamp of a C-stand.

TIP: Simple and non-technical as C-47s are, there's one big caution about them: always use the wooden kind. The plastic ones will melt onto barn doors, resulting in a bill from the rental house for a replacement set.

Filters and Gels

Filters and gels are made of colored/transparent optical material that changes the hue of the light passing through them. Filters attach to camera lenses, while gels (colored gelatin sheets) fit into holders that mount in front of light fixtures.

> **DAY FOR NIGHT:** Practice of shooting night scenes during the day by placing a dark blue filter over the camera lens.

Using a lens filter changes the overall color balance of a scene, so it's a poor tool for correcting color-temperature discrepancies among multiple light sources. For this, you may have to gel the lights individually. DPs use lens filters more often for creative effects: enhancing a sunny or a gloomy mood, or making a daylight scene look like it was shot at night. (This last effect is called *day for night.* For more information, see "Shoot Day for Night" later in this chapter.)

Gels come in sheets and rolls, which must be cut by hand and sandwiched in metal frames for insertion into the light fixture. The gels deteriorate rapidly from the heat of the light and must be replaced several times a day. Grips also tape large sheets of gel in front of windows to balance daylight with indoor tungsten lighting. Rolls of color-corrective gels are available from equipment rental houses and photo supply stores.

Types of colored gel and their uses are listed in **Table 6.1**.

Here's an example of how you'd use a gel: If you're shooting indoors and you white balance a camcorder under tungsten light, any sunlight coming through a window will cast an undesirable, cold blue tint. To prevent this, cover the window area with a sheet of CTO gel. The gel's orange color compensates for its opposite primary color, blue, balancing the color temperature of the interior scene.

Table 6.1 Color-Corrective Uses of Different Lighting Gels

Gel Type	Effect
ND (neutral density)	Reduces overall light intensity
CTO (color temperature orange)	Changes daylight to tungsten
CTB (color temperature blue)	Changes tungsten to daylight
Plus green	Changes daylight or tungsten to fluorescent
Minus green	Changes fluorescent to daylight or tungsten

Reflectors and Bounce Boards

The purpose of reflectors and bounce boards is to direct light, usually sunlight, toward the subject. As a rule, reflectors have shiny, silvery surfaces while bounce boards are matte white. A useful lighting accessory is a piece of foam core (two cardboard layers separated by a sheet of Styrofoam) having a shiny reflective surface on one side and a matte white surface on the other.

Reflectors and bounce boards can be clamped to C-stands with grip clips, or can be secured to walls or furniture with gaffer's tape.

Professional reflectors are available from supply and rental houses as collapsible units with their own folding stands. A line of these reflectors is available from manufacturer Flexfill in white, silver, gold, translucent, silk, black absorbent, and black mesh. (These different colors produce different creative effects for selected areas in a scene—much as you might use color filters on a lens.)

Black Wrap, Scrims, Silks, and Flags

All the following gear is used for blocking or masking light.

Black Wrap

Just as the name implies, this is a dull, black foil that can be wrapped around barn doors or fixture housings and secured with C-47s. It masks light leaks at the sides, effectively narrowing the beam angle of the light.

Scrims

A *scrim* is a saucer-sized disk of wire mesh that gaffers insert in a gel holder on a fixture to reduce the intensity of a light. Scrims come in single- and double-mesh density, and you can increase their effect by inserting as many scrims as will fit in the holder.

> **SCRIM:** Saucer-sized disk of wire mesh that reduces the intensity of a light.

Silks

As you might imagine, *silks* are panels of translucent cloth with handles designed to fit in C-stands (**Figure 6.23**). Silks diffuse light, reducing its intensity and creating a softer look.

Silks are just one type of diffusion material, a category that includes many types of cloth used to scatter light. Diffusion material comes in sheets and large rolls for covering windows.

> **SILK:** Panel of translucent cloth stretched on a frame that can be mounted on a C-stand for the purpose of diffusing light.

Flags

Flags look just like silks and also have handles for attaching them to C-stands. The difference is that flags are opaque and are used to mask light from the subject.

> **FLAG:** Opaque cloth panel stretched on a frame that can be mounted on a C-stand for the purpose of masking light.

Figure 6.23 This silk, mounted on a C-stand, diffuses light from two minis. Sometimes doubling up on smaller lights is a flexible alternative to bringing another big light, especially if you can diffuse and soften their output to achieve area or background lighting.

Cukies

A *cukie* (pronounced "cookie,") is a sheet of opaque material, usually metal or wood, with a pattern of holes cut in it. It mounts on a C-stand in front of a spotlight and casts a pattern of light on the set, usually against a wall. For example, cukies are often used to create the effect of light coming through venetian blinds, a familiar effect in film-noir movies. However, the spotlight must be both intense and focused, or the cukie will simply diffuse the light.

> **CUKIE:** Sheet of opaque material such as metal or wood with a pattern of holes cut into it so that light casts a pattern when projected through it. Movie lore has it that cukie is short for "Cucalorus," name of the gaffer who invented it.

Dimmers

Just as they do in households, dimmers vary the electrical voltage that feeds a studio lamp, allowing you to fine-tune its brightness. The professional dimmers gaffers use with movie lights are heavy duty, since they need to handle hundreds, even thousands of watts. Dimmers are used mainly with tungsten lights. Putting a dimmer on a fluorescent will create a bad flicker, or may not work at all.

It's usually just as effective, and cheaper, to move a light back rather than adjusting a dimmer to reduce intensity. You might use a dimmer to change lighting levels during a take for some special effect.

Another handy use for dimmers is to control the output of practicals. Since the light output of practicals is inconsistent and difficult to estimate until you've actually lit the set, placing dimmers on them gives you some control. Be aware that when you dim a light, its color temperature will drop, or become more orange.

Other Tools

Expensive lighting gear is all very well, but a creative DP can often do wonders with some cardboard and a roll of gaffer's tape. Aluminum foil often comes in handy, either secured to cardboard as a substitute for a reflector, or as an alternative to black wrap (if you're careful about reflections).

Cloth of various kinds can be a diffusing material. Felt is particularly good for blocking light. In a pinch, you can rearrange furniture and props to block light selectively. There are even some good tricks for working outdoors with available light; we'll list them later in this chapter.

Fire safety is a key issue when you make creative substitutions for professional materials. Movie lights are hot! And most professional materials are fire retardant, designed for routine use around high-powered lights. Experienced gaffers know how to minimize risks, but cardboard and cloth are highly flammable, so putting them anywhere near hot lights can be dangerous.

If you use alternative types of masking and diffusion, such as cardboard and cloth, fluorescent sources may be your safest bet. You can buy the "warm white" kind, which are close to tungsten in color temperature, and use "daylight" or "design white" to balance sunlight. You'll have to shoot some test scenes to see whether flicker is noticeable in your recordings.

LIGHTING TECHNIQUES

Volumes have been written on movie lighting methodology, but here are some techniques that are particularly useful when you are shooting DV.

Light for Narrow Contrast Range

The single most important thing to remember about lighting for DV is that, like all video, it has a much narrower contrast range than film. As we noted in Chapter 1, film has a working contrast range of about 100:1, while video has only 30:1.

Keep It Within Five F-Stops

DPs recommend keeping the contrast range of a video scene within five f-stops on the camera.

 REALITY CHECK: *The easiest way to work within DV's narrow contrast range is to soften your light sources by adding diffusion, or bouncing them off walls or reflectors. This tends to keep the dark areas from getting too dark and the bright ones from getting too bright.*

One way to measure contrast is to zoom into the darkest area of the scene so it fills the frame. Adjust the f-stop for proper exposure. Then do the same for the brightest area. If you have to turn the aperture ring on the lens (or turn the aperture dial on the camcorder) more than five f-stops, re-light the scene—you'll either blow out the highlights or lose shadow detail. If you are within five f-stops, the correct overall exposure for the scene will be somewhere between those low and high f-stops.

A more precise method requires using an *incident light meter* to measure the dark and bright areas in the scene after the lights are set (**Figure 6.24**). To do this, you must first set the meter to the equivalent film speed of CCDs—between 325 and 500 *ISO/ASA*.

Stand in the brightest area of the scene to be measured and point the photocell back toward the lens of the camera. The meter will indicate the corresponding f-stop value. Then take a reading in the darkest area of the scene. If the readings differ by more than five f-stops, relight the scene to reduce contrast.

> **INCIDENT LIGHT METER:** A photocell device that measures the intensity of light falling on the subject, rather than the overall level of light reflected into the camera lens.
>
> **ISO/ASA:** In photography, a numeric index of film speed, or sensitivity to light.

It doesn't make a difference whether the overall intensity level of the scene is bright or dark—as long as you maintain the recommended f-stop interval. (For more information, see "Reduce Light Here Rather Than Adding It There" later in this chapter.)

Figure 6.24 An incident light meter has a white translucent bubble over its photocell. On meters like this one you have to slide the bubble into place over the photocell before you can take an incident reading. If you are shooting NTSC, you might have to set shutter speed at 1/30 second on a photographic meter rather than having the option of selecting 30 fps on the dial.

TIP: When you're using a light meter indoors, take an incident reading at the subject's face. When shooting outdoors, take two reflected readings with the meter pointed at the subject: one from the camera position and one from two feet in front of his face. Don't include too much sky or you'll underexpose the shot. If the two readings differ, split the difference—but finesse a bit closer to the "face" reading.

Shoot in the Shade

The narrow contrast range of video can work to your advantage when you're shooting indoors. Since there can't be much variation in intensity, you can often make do with lower overall lighting levels than you'd use for film. That translates into relatively inexpensive, low-powered, portable lights—like a kit of mini halogens.

Unfortunately, when you are shooting outdoors the opposite can be true. If you find yourself shooting in full sunlight, you'll need relatively high-powered lights (which can require special rigging and generators for operation outdoors) to fill in the deep shadows. For videographers on a modest budget, the solution is to set your action in shaded areas—or shoot mornings, evenings, or on overcast days.

Use Smaller Crews

One reason DV has earned its reputation for economy is that it allows you to shoot using fewer, lower-powered lights, with lower overall lighting intensities. Lightweight halogens require fewer crew members to transport, set up, and rig—which translates to smaller crews and modest labor cost. Moreover, a small crew with lightweight equipment is faster on its feet, and can move more quickly from one setup and location to another. This pace makes it feasible to shoot six, or even eight, script pages per day, rather than the two to four more typical of film production.

Motivate the Key Light

Convincing the audience that your primary light source mimics real-world lighting is called *motivating* the key light. Even though your key light is probably artificial—a movie light set by the crew—the audience should believe it's coming from a natural source, such as a window, table lamp, or bright reflection from a nearby object, like a light-colored wall or mirror.

Ideally, the DP will approach lighting a scene by first determining the motivation—and thereby the source and location—of the key light. Only then will she consider the other two points of the three-point scheme. Occasional exceptions involve strong sources of available light that must be dealt with before you can set the key. For example, if you are shooting indoors, you would color correct, or mask, the bright light coming through a window before setting any other lights. If you use sunlight in your plan—even if you supplement it with a movie light—it should motivate the key because, for the audience, the window is the obvious natural source.

Bounce Your Fill Light

Remember that soft light is not only pleasing to the eye, it's also an effective way to stay within the five f-stop range. The quickest and cheapest way to soften your lighting is to bounce fill light off a ceiling or light-colored wall. The ceiling is a particularly good choice because it's motivated—the audience will think the illumination is coming from overhead lights.

When you bounce the fill off a wall, the soft light can mimic any off-camera source, such as light spilling through a window or doorway (**Figure 6.25**). If the wall is too dark to cast a reflection, tape a bounce board to it, or mount the board on a C-stand.

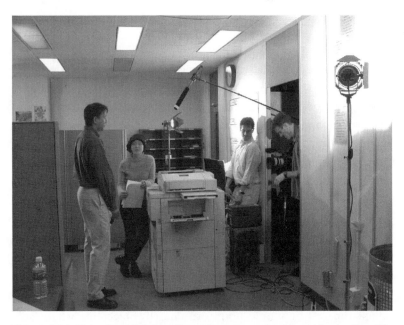

Figure 6.25 Bouncing fill light off a wall creates soft, almost shadowless fill. It can also mimic ambient light from doorways. This setup uses two diffusion techniques: wall bounce and silks on C-stands. Bounced light from the wall comes from two movie lights, creating both the key light and fill on the actors' faces. The bounced light is diffuse and soft, much like the overhead lighting in the office.

Keep Colors Balanced

When you are shooting indoors, use one of the following strategies for best color balance:

- Gel the window shades with CTO, or mask them entirely. Use tungsten lights all of the same type, and mask, turn off, or at least dim the overhead lighting.

- Leave the windows open. Use artificial sources color balanced for daylight, and mask or turn off overhead lights.

- If the scene takes place in low light (indoors at night, for example) mask the windows, turn off the overheads, and try using practicals with dimmers. You may need to use some diffuse artificial sources for fill to avoid losing shadow detail.

It's tricky to mix artificial sources, such as different types of tungsten, if their color temperatures differ widely. You can gel one set of lights selectively to match the other, possibly using multiple layers of gel to increase the effect. Even then, it's best to shoot a short test, play it back, and see whether the overall color looks right.

The Importance of White Balance

All the color-temperature correction you do on location won't matter much if the camcorder's white balance is improperly set, causing the entire scene to take on an undesirable tint. You may be able to fix this in post (DV has some advantages over film in this area), but life will be simpler if you get the scene in the can properly white balanced to begin with.

White Balance Every Setup Manually

It's strongly advised that you turn off the automatic white balance (AWB) control on your camcorder. If you don't, the camcorder will use the brightest area in a scene as its definition of white—even if it happens to be tinted. The result can throw all the other colors off. Instead, use the manual white-balance control every time you change camera setups, or when you move or adjust lights.

It's a straightforward procedure: Place a white object, such as a bounce board, in the scene. Zoom in on it until it fills the frame, and set the white balance. On many camcorders, that's as easy as pressing a button (**Figure 6.26**).

Figure 6.26 Setting white balance on a camcorder is a quick and easy manual procedure, provided you get in the habit of doing it for every setup. When you are shooting news style outdoors, as this crew is, a bounce board can double as a white-balance target and sun reflector for creating fill light.

Three-Point Lighting, News Style

Even if you're shooting outdoors, news style, with little or no equipment or crew, you must still observe the rules for three-point lighting and acceptable contrast ranges. Just follow these steps:

- Move your camera position so the sun is behind the subject.

- Use one daylight-type source as your key light. If you must shoot alone, it can be a camera-mounted photoflood. Better yet, take along one crew member to carry and operate an HMI light.

- Use a reflector or bounce board to reflect the sun back toward the subject to create fill.

You'll improve the odds of getting good shots by doing whatever you can to reduce the overall contrast range of the scene—moving into the shade or shooting mornings, evenings, or on overcast days.

Figure Out the Film-Speed Equivalence of Your Camcorder

To properly control the contrast range in a scene, you have to measure dark and light areas as precisely as possible using an incident light meter. The secret to doing this right is to determine the actual film-speed equivalence of your camcorder. It may well be in the manufacturer's specs, and you can set your meter accordingly. But if it isn't, follow these steps.

1. If your camcorder can display zebra bars, set them for 100 IRE. (On prosumer and professional camcorders, zebra bars appear in the viewfinder within hot areas of a scene to indicate overexposure. For more information on IRE settings and zebra bars, see "Use the Zebra Pattern" in Chapter 3.)

2. Focus the lens on a white card until it fills the frame, as you would when setting white balance.

3. Adjust the f-stop on your camcorder until zebra bars appear in the viewfinder, or until you can't see a pencil mark on the card (indicating blown-out white). Note the f-stop reading.

4. Set your incident light meter to 1/30 second (if you're shooting 30 fps NTSC), or 1/25 (if you're shooting 25 fps PAL), and film speed of 100 ISO/ASA.

5. Take an incident reading at the card and note the f-stop reading on the meter.

6. Adjust the ISO/ASA dial on the meter until the meter's pointer shows the same f-stop reading as the lens. This ISO/ASA index is the effective film speed of your camcorder.

7. Use this ISO/ASA setting on your incident meter when you check the light and dark areas in your setups.

Match Lighting to Content and Mood

When you're limited to five f-stops as the total variation between light sources, you must rely on the overall lighting level to convey emotional overtones and subtexts.

If you want brilliant highlights or deep blacks, you have the creative option of permitting them to be blown out or black; in other words, you *can* break the five f-stop guideline as long as you do it on purpose. However, it's best to make sure those out-of-range areas are relatively small in relation to the other objects in the frame—so the audience won't miss any important details.

Use Color to Direct the Eye

The concept of painting with light began in black and white films, but now that color is the norm, you can use *it* to direct the audience's eyes to specific people or actions. Brightly colored clothing, props, or settings can supplement key lighting and won't cost you anything in terms of lighting levels or contrast range. For instance, put your subject in colorful clothes and shoot him or her against neutral-colored surroundings. Or, direct the action so your actor walks from a dull-colored area into a colorful one at a critical moment in the story.

Reduce Light Here Rather Than Adding it There

If the f-stop range exceeds five stops, you have the option of adding light to the dark areas or taking it away from the light areas.

In fact, it will almost always be cheaper and easier to take light away from a hot area in a scene—and perhaps open the aperture—than to add light to the dark areas. Since the contrast range of video is so narrow, you won't see much benefit from adding light unless you add it almost everywhere. The exception is when you shoot in bright sunlight. Then your options are either using big fill lights and/or reflectors, or not adding lights, which means losing details in the shadows. The quickest way to reduce the intensity of a light is simply to move it back, away from the subject. Intensity of light that falls on a subject from a single light follows the inverse square law: Moving a light twice as far from the subject will decrease its intensity by one-fourth of what it was before.

Here are some other techniques for reducing light:

- Turn off, or mask, available light, including windows and overhead lights.

- Add scrims, flags, or diffusion to reduce the output of movie lights.

- Use dimmers on practicals and tungsten lights that can't be diffused, or on any lights that must fade up or down during a scene.

Compensate for Overhead Light Sources and Reflections

Fluorescent ceiling lights can vary widely in color temperature, depending on the type of tube. It's best to identify their type when scouting locations; if you know whether they're closer to daylight or tungsten, you can choose your movie lights accordingly. But you may arrive at the location without advance information.

It might look unnatural for your scene if you shut off all the overhead lights in an office. But if you must leave them on, and you haven't determined their color temperature in advance, be prepared to cover them with sheets of gel, or gel your lights individually. Also, keep the overheads out of the frame if at all possible.

Another complication that's difficult to assess ahead of time is unwanted reflections in windows and pictures on the wall. One way to eliminate reflections is to apply dulling spray, available from photo supply houses. The spray won't damage surfaces and wipes off. (In a pinch, you can use hair spray, but it *does* damage surfaces, and you'll need soap and water or household cleaner to get it off.)

Dim Lighting on Areas Behind the Subject

Reducing light on background areas—by using silks and flags on lights, bouncing lights instead of using direct lighting, moving lights back, or turning down a dimmer—can lower the overall lighting level of the scene and make it possible to use what lights you have to your advantage. Otherwise, you may need most of your fill lights simply to compensate for the bright background.

Use Rim Light for Depth

Rim lighting is especially important in video because, as we mentioned earlier, video has greater depth of field than film: Almost every part of a video shot will be in sharp focus. Film cameras allow you to choose your plane of focus with greater precision. For instance, a good DP can keep objects 15 to 20 feet from the lens in focus, while everything else blurs out.

One counter-intuitive effect of video's deep focus is that you lose the sense of three-dimensionality a filmmaker can achieve by using shallow focus. In order to re-create that sense of depth on video, sometimes your only option is lighting. Creative use of back light and rim lighting will often do the trick.

Use Flat Lighting for Things That Move

When shooting moving subjects such as vehicles or athletes on video, the safest choice is to light the scene as flat as possible, even at a sacrifice of visual interest.

A gaffer can keep a movable spotlight (or follow spot) trained on the subject, but the effect will look phony to the audience unless there are some motivating sources in the scene, such as car headlights.

If you are shooting outdoors, you can follow the techniques described earlier for news-style shooting. Try to keep the sun behind the subject, and use a camera-mounted photoflood, and one or more reflectors. This is one instance in which news-style shooting might actually look better than a film-style setup.

Plan Ahead for Digital Mattes

You can do all kinds of compositing with digital post-production tools, but you'll have trouble achieving some of these special effects if you don't actually plan for them beforehand. Among the effects you have to prepare for are *digital mattes*, the equivalent of film double-exposures.

DIGITAL MATTE: Special effect achieved by compositing two scenes, such as superimposing a real subject over a fantasy background.

In traditional filmmaking a *matte* is a device placed over the camera lens to mask a portion of the scene from being exposed. The purpose is usually to permit a double exposure—adding another image later in the masked area. In the days before CGI, the second image was usually a *matte painting* that an artist had done on a glass plate. (If you ever saw an old movie with a brief shot of a castle on a hill, chances are it was a masterful matte painting.)

MATTE: In filmmaking, a cardboard or metal cutout placed over the lens of a motion picture camera to mask part of the frame from exposure.

MATTE PAINTING: In traditional filmmaking, a fake background done as a painting on glass to be double-exposed with a live scene.

Understanding the Keying Process

In both analog and digital video, matte shots are achieved by a compositing process called *keying*. In postproduction, the editor can select a specific color in the scene for which a second scene will be substituted. If the color is pure black or pure white, the process is called *luminance keying*. If the color is green or blue, the process is called *chroma keying*.

KEYING: In video postproduction, compositing process that substitutes portions of a second scene for every instance of a value (luminance key) or color (chroma key) in the first scene.

STATIONARY MATTE: Static composited scene in which the subject and background don't move, or move only slightly in relation to one another.

Luminance keying was the first type of video matte, developed in the analog era for doing *stationary mattes*, or static scenes, such as adding titles or graphics. However, if you're dealing with a moving subject, luminance keying is messy, since it's hard to control all the changing highlights and reflections that might be mistakenly interpreted as part of the matte.

TRAVELING MATTE: In filmmaking, a double-exposure matte that moves along with its subject; travel matte. In video, a keying process involving a moving subject.

The process of keying a moving subject is called a *traveling matte*, or *travel matte*, and the most reliable way to create it is with a chroma key color of green or blue. (In theory, keying can be done with any color, but the reason to use green or blue is because they don't normally show up in your subject's skin tones.)

The most common type of traveling matte shot is to use the chroma key color as the background. So, by compositing the shot, your subject can appear to be transported to another place, such as a remote location or a fantasy set. In fact, placing TV meteorologists in front of weather maps was one of the first applications of chroma keying.

 REALITY CHECK: *With the advent of digital postproduction, the opposite situation is possible: Paint a prop or clothe the subject in a primary-colored body stocking onto which a synthetic creation can be keyed. The actor who played* Golem *in* Lord of the Rings: The Two Towers *wore a bright blue body stocking, and a grotesque CGI character was keyed over it.*

How to Light for Effective Keying

As you might expect, the reason for mentioning chroma keying here is because it places particular requirements on lighting. The main problem is keeping the chroma-key color from showing up where you don't want it—especially in the subject. This causes the second scene to "bleed through" the first when composited. In particular, the subject's outline—its edges that border the background—can be troublesome.

Here are some lighting procedures that should help you achieve cleaner and more realistic matte shots in postproduction:

1. Choose your key color, selecting either green or blue, depending on the color least likely to appear in the rest of the shot. For example, if you're only masking part of a scene that has some foliage in it, pick blue. If it's essential that the character's costume be blue, pick green.

2. Determine how you will dress the set with the key color. You can buy special chroma-key-colored fabric and paint at photo supply outlets. One handy accessory is a small, folding chroma-key screen that resembles those sun visors you can buy for the windshield of your car. It can therefore be transported more easily than a larger board or screen, and when unfolded it provides enough area for the background of an interview subject's headshot (**Figure 6.27**).

Figure 6.27 A folding cloth green screen stretched between two C-stands became the backdrop for chroma-key inserts in, *Ten Ways to Make DV Look Like Film*. Hollywood tyro Allen Smithee was later composited with amateur footage so he could make astute wisecracks about how it should have been shot.

3. Avoid a sharp edge where the background meets the ground or floor, if it will be framed in the shot. In the studio, walls used for mattes have a *cove* base, or curved bottom, to soften the corner. Allowing a sheet of heavy chroma-key paper to curve gradually near the floor will achieve the same thing.

> **COVE:** On a studio set, curved boundary between a background wall and the floor, for purposes of eliminating shadows that would be created by a hard corner.

4. Light the chroma-key background as evenly as possible. Avoid highlights and shadows that might not be included in the matte.

5. Try setting the background at an angle with respect to the lights and the camera lens. Check the viewfinder or monitor to make sure you're not getting any kick off the background.

6. Use back light and rim light to heighten the subject's edges and separate it from the background. Some cinematographers recommend using a gel of the opposite color

from the chroma key on these highlights. If the chroma key is blue, use a straw (pale yellow) gel; if green, minus-green (magenta).

7. Since crisp edges are essential to the matte process, don't use soft focus or autofocus on your subject, and check manual focus carefully.

8. Avoid costumes, makeup, or clothing accessories on your subject that contain the chroma-key color.

9. Don't stand the subject too close to the chroma-key background, where reflections of the key color could show up in the face or on edges.

10. Especially if the effect is a major part of your story or presentation, shoot some tests and take them through the postproduction process. Watch for some of the problems mentioned here. For example, if you're in doubt about whether wardrobe might contain or reflect the key color, include it in your testing.

If you don't follow these steps, or if you're not entirely successful overcoming their challenges, it doesn't mean you can't attempt compositing in postproduction. But if the key color spills onto the actor's forehead, for example, expect to see the background bleed through in that spot. There are various techniques for correcting this problem in the edit, but all of them are apt to be more tedious than lighting the scene correctly in the first place. For more information on this type of compositing, see "Combining Imagery" in Chapter 11.

Should You Try Luminance Keying?

Even though chroma keying is the accepted way to go, you may be able to achieve some impressive effects by using luminance keying. Besides solid-color chroma keying, some non-linear editing systems permit you to use pure white or black as a key. That means you could try to add a synthetic background to any outdoor scene if you let the sky blow out, or become pure white. This could be particularly useful when you're keeping the sun behind the actors and using a bounce board to fill the faces. In such a situation, you could matte in a gorgeous sky, such as a sunset, later.

> **TIP:** If you take this suggestion and decide to matte in the sky later, set the camcorder zebra to 100 IRE and make sure the background is really fully blown out. Then get some matching shots of the sky with the clouds both in and out of focus. Use the soft shots with your closeups to effectively reduce the appearance of depth of field, giving the composited scene a more filmic look. Keep your key light soft to avoid bright kicks on edges, and make sure there's no white, such as a shirt collar or even a pocket handkerchief, in your actors' wardrobe.

Shoot Day for Night

It's actually quite a challenge to shoot night scenes at night—although people do it. In DV, shooting scenes in low light usually means increasing the gain on the CCDs, making the dark areas noisy (filmmakers would say "grainy"). Of course you can always use the noisy texture as a creative effect, but that might not fit with the mood of your story.

One approach to shooting night scenes is inherited from motion-picture conventions and is called *day-for-night*. You shoot during the day, underexposing and keeping contrast low, and perhaps using a dark-blue filter. You can also use a strong rim light to simulate the moon. Realistically, the effect doesn't much resemble nighttime, but audiences have come to accept it.

Experienced DPs use some day-for-night tricks you might find useful:

• Unless the subjects are walking past a building with a lighted window, or some other available source, the motivation for the key light should be the moon. Therefore, since the moon is supposed to be behind the camera, be careful that it doesn't accidentally appear in the shot. Also, as DPs know—and horror-film fans will attest—the imaginary moon in day-for-night scenes is always full.

• Since the motivation for the key light is the moon, gel your movie lights a heavy blue, even though there's also a blue filter on the camcorder.

• All the other guidelines for shooting DV outdoors apply. To control contrast range, shoot on overcast days, or move into the shade. Use daylight-balanced movie lights, if necessary, to provide rim or fill.

Or—Night for Day?

When you think about it, movie crews shoot night for day all the time, they just don't necessarily call it that. The situation arises when you're shooting an interior—whether on location or on a sound stage—and you don't rely on ambient daylight coming through the windows. The standard approach is to place a sheet of diffusion outside the window, then point a big light at it from behind. The effect will be to nearly blow out the exposure of the window—creating convincing artificial sunlight and conveniently eliminating the need to show any details of the scene outside.

In addition to letting you shoot daytime interiors at night, this approach has some other distinct advantages:

- On location, because the diffusion completely covers the windows, bystanders won't be able to look into the set.

- You'll have tighter control over color temperature, more nearly matching tungsten interior lighting without having to gel the window.

- You won't have to worry about the passage of time or the angle of the sun—it will always appear to be the same time of day on the set, unless you adjust the intensity of the artificial sunlight.

PAINTERLY ART

It takes technical study and lots of practice to become proficient in selecting and position-ing lights, matching color temperature, and rigging lamps for correct exposure, but once you get it, it's fun. However, as with many other aspects of moviemaking, no matter how seductive the technical details of the lighting technician's craft may be, they will take you only so far.

Then the challenges become artistic.

In fact, of all the moviemaker's storytelling tools, lighting is potentially the most powerful—because it's so *painterly*. Dialogue, performance, story, and subtext all play to our conscious minds—but images, painted in light, come in under our intellectual radar and can be unfor-gettable in literally wordless ways.

CHAPTER SEVEN

Sound on the Set

Many people think of film and video as visual media, but moviemakers understand that the soundtrack is incredibly important, too. Images carry much of the story's emotion and power, but dialogue imparts a presentation's information, while the music and sound effects enrich the whole experience.

Consider what happens when you mute the sound on a television program. You might see the characters in heated disagreement, but you'd have no idea what caused their tempers to flare or what's at stake.

Now turn the sound back on and walk into the next room. If you can still hear the dialogue, you'll understand most of what's going on. Even if the program is highly graphic—a battle scene, for example—dialogue gives you key facts, sound effects pull you in deeper, and music enhances emotional texture.

PLANNING FOR PROFESSIONAL SOUND

A soundtrack consists of dialogue, music, and sound effects (which sound editors refer to in shorthand, as *D, M, and E*). Music and most effects will be added during postproduction, which means your audio goal on the set is to record clean, clear dialogue. Digital video doesn't provide any special tools to help you do this, nor does it include any magic solutions for unscrambling garbled speech or fixing bad dialogue tracks in post. While it's true that sound editors can do amazing things with digital editing systems like ProTools, no amount of expertise will be as effective as capturing good sound in the first place.

D, M, E: Abbreviations for dialogue, music, and (sound) effects.

If you don't have a quality soundtrack, you don't have a quality project. And if the audience can't understand the dialogue, you won't have much of a story either. Poorly recorded dialogue is probably the single most common mistake made by first-time moviemakers, whether they are working in film or in video.

> **NOTE:** *From a technical viewpoint, much of getting good sound is about preserving high-frequency information. That's where the consonants and plosives of human speech occur—the sounds of p, k, st, and ch, for example. Without plosives, dialogue is almost impossible to understand. Preserving high-frequency sound during your shoot is like trying to keep lettuce crisp—there are lots of ways to spoil it, and if you do, there's no way to bring it back.*

> **PLOSIVE:** Sound made in human speech by expelling a small blast of air.

CAPTURING REALISTIC SOUND ON THE SET

In most respects, recording audio for digital video is much like recording audio for film: It takes careful planning and close attention during the shoot.

Prime Directives

The three prime directives for recording audio are:

- Capture clean dialogue.
- Make sure *audio perspective* matches the action.
- Avoid extraneous background noise.

> **AUDIO PERSPECTIVE:** Apparent direction, volume, and distance of an audio source in relation to screen action. Also includes the distinctive *spatial quality* of a particular room or space.

Capture Clean Dialogue

Record speech as a distortion-free *monophonic* track. You'll add sound effects, music, and stereo effects in post.

No doubt you've heard of *ADR (automated dialogue replacement)*, the practice of re-recording and dubbing actors' voices in postproduction. Yes, it's a commonly used technique, but it's difficult to do well and can be very expensive and time-consuming. Don't plan on it or assume that it's a viable alternative to capturing clean dialogue on the set.

> **SPATIAL QUALITY:** Amount of echo, or apparent depth, and other noise characteristics of a room or space.
>
> **MONOPHONIC:** Single-channel audio track: left (L) or right (R) channel of a stereo track.
>
> **AUTOMATED DIALOGUE REPLACEMENT (ADR):** Re-recording sync-sound dialogue in postproduction; dubbing.

You *must* get a good, clear, clean recording of the dialogue. It's absolutely crucial to the success of your project.

TIP: *By all means, attempt to capture sound effects that are unique to the action while you're on the set—but it won't be a disaster if you don't. Oddly enough, live effects often don't sound "real." The contrived, artificially constructed sounds you build in post may well be far more convincing to an audience. Make sure, if you do record effects on location, that you capture them "clean," by themselves, apart from dialogue. This is known as* wild sound *or* wild track.

> **WILD SOUND:** An audio-only take of sound on the set, with no corresponding picture; the sound of a slap, for example; wild track.

Make Sure Audio Perspective Matches the Action

Position your microphones so the audio perspective matches the visual perspective of the shot. For instance, if you're shooting a closeup, the mic should be very close to the actor (it's called being *close-mic'd*). If you're shooting a long shot, the microphone should be farther away from the actor. The distance between the actor and the mic is called *air*. For a long shot, you'll want more air.

> **CLOSE-MIC:** Placing microphone near the subject, appropriate for a closeup shot.
>
> **AIR:** Distance between a subject and the microphone.

In practice, mic placement often takes care of itself. If you're shooting a long shot, the microphone has to be farther away from the actor in order to stay out of the shot. But you can get in trouble on a long shot by getting the wrong audio perspective if you're only using a *lavalier mic* worn on the actor's body. It's advisable to have a second mic recording ambience, which can be mixed with the sound coming from the lavalier in order to give it more air. (For more information, see "Adding Audio Perspective to Lavs" later in this chapter.)

> **LAVALIER MICROPHONE:** Small mic worn by the subject, clipped to a tie or pocket, or concealed in clothing or hair; lav.

Avoid Extraneous Background Noise

Dialogue should never be obscured by extraneous sounds. If a bus roars by or a plane flies overhead while you're shooting, call for another take. Also, watch out for sounds that occur while an actor is speaking a line. For example, if an actor slams a car door during a speech, the sound of the door slamming may obscure some of the dialogue. Call for another take, directing the actor to say the line, and *then* close the door.

One of the most important functions for the sound crew is to monitor the recording during a take and warn the director of any noise that might be difficult to remove in post. Ultimately, it's the director's responsibility to decide whether to do another take or attempt to repair the glitch later.

No MOS!

Some veteran sound technicians have this slogan emblazoned on their caps and t-shirts—and into their professional attitudes. It means never shoot silent (*MOS*, or "mit out sound"). Always record sync sound—the live sound made by whatever the camera is seeing. Granted, you might not use the track later, but you will have it if you need it. Even if you replace the original recording with a synthetic effect in post, the sync sound can serve as a *guide track* for building the effect and inserting it into your edit.

> **MOS (MIT OUT SOUND):** Hollywood term for shooting picture without recording sound, derived from a German émigré director who yelled: "Ve zhoot it mit out sound!"
>
> **GUIDE TRACK:** Sync sound track that serves as a template for a synthetic replacement track built during postproduction.

Meet Your Sound Crew

Members of a sound crew on a movie set have highly specialized jobs, and union rules to define them. If you need to cut corners on crew expense, don't do it in the sound department. If you think holding a microphone is the perfect job for a nonprofessional, think again! Use inexperienced volunteers for heavy lifting or coffee runs, but keep them away from the mics and sound gear.

Some soundtrack artists don't go to work until you get to postproduction: ADR supervisors, Foley artists, musicians, composers, voice-over talent, and so on. We'll discuss them in postproduction chapters. (For more information on postproduction sound, see "Replacing Dialogue" in Chapter 11.)

Sound Recordist

If recording is done entirely in-camera (*single-system sound*), audio recording will probably be the responsibility of the camera operator. However, on shoots using *dual-system sound*, where audio also goes to an external tape recorder, a technician designated as *sound recordist* will operate the recorder. (Sometimes this is an additional responsibility of the sound mixer.)

> **SINGLE-SYSTEM SOUND:** Recording sync sound entirely with the camcorder.
>
> **DUAL-SYSTEM SOUND:** Simultaneously recording sync sound on an external tape recorder and the camcorder.
>
> **SOUND RECORDIST:** On the set, an audio technician who operates a tape recorder external to the camcorder.

Sound Mixer

The person who controls the audio input level is the *sound mixer*—which is also the name of the piece of equipment he uses to combine inputs from multiple audio sources. On small crews, the boom operator may have sound mixing equipment clipped to his belt, or attached to a shoulder strap, so he can do the sound mixing himself.

Boom Operator

For most shots the mic is attached to a microphone boom, or *boom pole*, a device that looks like a long fishing pole. This way of rigging and holding a mic is the best all-around method for capturing realistic sound, indoors or out. The person who holds the boom pole is called the *boom operator*. It's a tedious job that requires considerable practice and skill to do properly. (For more information on correct boom technique, see "Rigging and Handling a Boom" later in this chapter.)

Second Assistant Camera Operator (Clapper/Loader)

On a movie set, the camera crew's second assistant usually operates the *clapper* on the *slate* to mark the beginning of each take. Although not strictly a member of the sound crew, whoever operates the clapper serves a very important function for recording reliable sync sound. In Britain, this person goes by the name of *clapper/loader* because her other main responsibility is reloading film magazines for the lead camera operator. (For more information, see "Using a Clapper Board and Timecode" later in this chapter.)

SOUND MIXER: Audio technician responsible for monitoring sound levels and operating mixer equipment on the set.

MIXER: Audio module for connecting multiple sources (channels) and controlling their volume levels; also, the person who operates it.

BOOM POLE: A long pole to which the microphone is attached; microphone boom.

BOOM OPERATOR: On the set, the audio technician responsible for holding and positioning the boom pole and its attached microphone. On low-budget crews, the junior person on the crew roster often gets stuck holding the boom, which can yield very disappointing results.

CLAPPER: The hinged part of a slate that makes a clapping sound when snapped shut; image and sound of clapping provide easily identified simultaneous events so the editor can sync the picture and soundtrack.

SLATE: Hand-held chalk or marker board—nowadays often a digital LED device—for recording the scene and take number, held in front of the lens to mark the beginning of a take for the editor and clapped to establish sync; clapper board.

CLAPPER/LOADER: British term for second assistant camera operator.

Interviewer

On a news-style shoot, the interviewer may be either the on-camera talent or an off-screen questioner—but if she's holding the mic, she's a member of the sound crew. Make sure she knows good mic technique. (For more information, see "Doing Interviews with a Lav and/or a Short Mic" later in this chapter.)

SELECTING PROFESSIONAL MICROPHONES

The microphone is the sound technician's "camera." If the mic's audio quality is poor, or if it's the wrong type for the job, someone will have a horrible time trying to repair your soundtrack in post. Often, no repair is possible. So choose both the operator and the equipment carefully.

Microphone Characteristics

Characteristics of professional mics, and considerations for choosing them, include the following.

- Pickup pattern

- In the shot or not

- Dynamic or condenser

- Connectors and cables

- Line level

Pickup Pattern

A mic's *pickup pattern* is the geometric locus within which it is most sensitive to sound (**Figure 7.1**). It's by far the most important characteristic of a microphone. *Off-axis sound* (sound from outside the mic's pickup pattern) will be tinny and hollow compared to on-axis sound.

Typical pickup patterns include the following.

Omnidirectional: As the term suggests, an *omnidirectional* mic picks up sound equally well in all directions; the pickup pattern is spherical. Omnidirectional mics are generally poor choices on the set. They pick up the

> **PICKUP PATTERN:** Locus within which a microphone is most sensitive to sound.
>
> **AXIS:** Imaginary line through mic defining the core of its pickup pattern.
>
> **OFF-AXIS SOUND:** Weak audio signals emanating from outside a mic's pickup pattern.
>
> **OMNIDIRECTIONAL:** Type of microphone that picks up sound equally well from all directions.

rumble of passing trucks and people coughing behind the camera just as readily as the actors' lines. An omnidirectional mic would be a good choice to record the ambient noise of a street fair or the crowd at a concert.

Cardioid: Named for its heart-shaped pickup pattern, a *cardioid* mic is optimized to pick up sound directly in front of it, with some sensitivity to either side. A cardioid mic is a good choice for recording singers and performers, as well as for mounting on a stationary stand, especially if a technician isn't available to aim it during a take. A variation on the cardioid type is the *supercardioid*, which has a narrower pickup pattern and is mainly sensitive to sounds directly in front of it.

Hypercardioid/Shotgun: This pickup pattern is narrower still. In fact, it's so directionally sensitive that it requires a technician to keep it aimed at a specific sound source. *Hypercardioid* mics are also called *shotgun* mics because of their relatively long barrels. A shotgun mic, controlled by a boom operator, is the mainstay of movie production because it records only what you point it at and rejects or minimizes noise from other sources.

> **CARDIOID:** Typically short style of microphone that is sensitive mainly to the sound directly in front of it, often used by singers and interviewers.
>
> **SUPERCARDIOID:** A type of microphone that is more narrowly sensitive to sounds directly in front of it than the cardioid type.
>
> **HYPERCARDIOID:** Type of microphone with an extremely narrow axis and long focal distance; shotgun; a typical boom mic.
>
> **SHOTGUN:** Hypercardioid microphone with characteristically long barrel, often used as a boom mic.

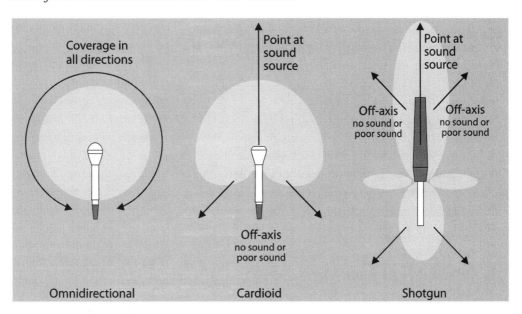

Figure 7.1 A mic's pickup pattern defines the area in which it will capture the loudest and clearest sound with the greatest fidelity and widest frequency response. The pickup pattern determines how the operator must aim the mic for best effect.

In the Shot or Not

Mics come in a variety of shapes and sizes, from tiny pickups the size of a pencil eraser to large shotguns used in TV studios that require light-duty cranes to hold and operate them. To decide what kind of microphone you need for a given shot, and where to place it, consider the following questions:

Can a mic be carried or worn by the subject? Placing a mic on or near the subject means you won't need a boom operator, and you'll get clear audio no matter where the subject is in relation to the camera.

> **TIP:** If you're shooting a dramatic scene in which a mic is visible (such as an actor standing behind a podium), it's generally best to record the sound using a standard boom mic instead of putting a working mic on the podium. The boom mic puts control in the hands of the boom operator so the actor can turn her head without worrying if she's off-mic. And the boom gives you better sound quality. Effects such as reverb and feedback—common problems of podium mics, which provide realism—can be added in post.

> **OFF-MIC:** Referring to a speaker who is off the axis of the microphone.
>
> **REVERB:** Echo effect; short for "reverberation."
>
> **FEEDBACK:** Undesirable whine in an audio circuit, usually caused by locating a mic too close to a loudspeaker.

Will the mic be visible in the shot? A concealed mic must be small enough to be tucked into the subject's clothing or hair.

Will audio cables interfere with the movement of actors or subjects? If so, you'll need a wireless setup that connects one or more actors with body mics to mixers and recorders via radio-frequency links.

Is the mic sensitive enough? If you prefer to position the mic somewhere outside the frame, it must be sensitive and directional enough to pick up the subject clearly from a distance.

Dynamic or Condenser

Dynamic microphones are inexpensive and easy to use. *Condenser* mics offer superior sound reproduction, but they are pricey and require connection to a source of electrical power.

Most professional mics used on movie sets are the condenser type. Sometimes they're battery powered; other times they take their electric power from the sound mixer via outputs called *phantom power.* The voltage of these phantom outputs can vary; you must be careful to match the voltage to the mic's requirements or you could damage the mic.

> **DYNAMIC:** Type of microphone that senses sound by the movement of a diaphragm within an electrical coil.
>
> **CONDENSER:** Type of microphone that senses sound by the compression of a material such as crystal.
>
> **PHANTOM POWER:** External electrical voltage supplied to a microphone for the purpose of powering its condenser circuit.

Connectors and Cables

Professional microphones use three-prong XLR connectors. Consumer gear commonly uses ⅛-inch mini connectors, but you'll also see RCA-type and ¼-inch connectors (**Figure 7.2**).

> **TIP:** *Corroded metal contacts on audio connectors can hurt sound performance. Some audio plugs have gold-plated surfaces, which resist corrosion; if you can afford it, they're worth the extra cost. Either way, a spray can of electrical contact cleaner is good to have on the set; you can use it to clean audio contacts if you're hearing static on the line.*

XLR connectors are designed to terminate shielded audio cables that resist signal loss and noise over relatively long distances, even runs of up to 100 feet (**Figure 7.3**). In technical language, these are balanced, *differential* audio lines.

DIFFERENTIAL: Referring to an electrical circuit that relies on differences in parameters between two different signals.

PHASE: Timing of the continuous cycling of alternating current (AC) electricity.

In XLR circuits, one of the wires carries a copy of the primary audio signal that's 180 degrees out of *phase*, which helps cancel 60 Hz hum. When you use an adapter to connect an XLR cable to a mini plug, you use just two of the lines—bypassing this feature and its noise-canceling benefits. Consumer cables, even if shielded, don't operate the same way, and you shouldn't use them anywhere on the input side of the recorder, or for runs of more than 10 feet.

Figure 7.2 Headphones, which are on the output side and don't provide input to the recorder, generally use ¼-inch connectors.

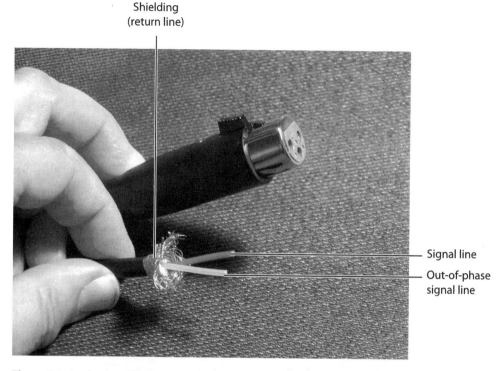

Figure 7.3 Professional audio cable has two insulated wires surrounded by wire-mesh shielding. The shielding is the third conductor and helps protect the two signal lines from interference.

There's no substitute for XLR connectors and cables. Remember that one of the drawbacks of minis is their poor handling of high-frequency signals—just the part of the audio spectrum you need to preserve clear, intelligible dialogue.

> **TIP:** If you need to resolve incompatibilities among connectors, avoid using adapters except for non-recorded outputs, such as headphones. If possible, make all connections at the mixer, where you will find a variety of input and output connectors.

Line Levels

It's a bad idea to intermix professional and consumer mics and gear, but if you do so you must do it very carefully. The main problem is *line level*: the voltage level of audio output signals. Professional mics, and any audio equipment that uses XLR connectors, operate at higher voltage levels than consumer gear. This helps assure a

LINE LEVEL: Voltage level of audio output signals, measured in decibels (dB).

SIGNAL-TO-NOISE (S/N) RATIO: Strength of the information-carrying signal in an audio line in relation to the amount of noise; the higher the ratio, the better the quality of the audio signal.

higher *signal-to-noise (S/N) ratio* and delivers an audio signal that's stronger and more noise resistant.

Line level is generally rated as either +4 dB (professional) or –10 dB (consumer). So if you plug a consumer mic into a professional mixer, you'll have to turn up the audio gain 14 dB (quite a lot) to match the other inputs. Using that much gain amplifies noise as well, and since the consumer signal has a lower S/N ratio to begin with, you may end up with a very noisy soundtrack.

You'll run into even more serious problems if you plug a professional mic into consumer mixing or recording equipment—or the input jack of your camcorder. The professional voltage is too high for consumer-grade circuitry, and you can damage the equipment.

> **ATTENUATOR:** Variable-gain junction box for connecting audio cables that can also compensate for electrical mismatch in the lines; pad.

The solution is to insert an *attenuator*, or *pad*—a variable-gain junction box for matching line levels—between the XLR plug on pro microphones and the mini-style input jack on your camcorder. The pad has a knob you can use to reduce the gain to match professional output to consumer gear input.

Types of Mics

There are four main types of mics used in videography: short, boom, lavalier, and plant.

Short

A short mic, or *shortie*, is a cardioid dynamic type used for on-camera interviews and sometimes held by singers (**Figure 7.4**). Being dynamic, a shortie doesn't need external power, and since it's usually visible in the shot, the cable to the camcorder can be relatively short.

> **SHORTIE:** Cardioid dynamic microphone popular with singers and interviewers.

Figure 7.4 Much favored by newscasters, a shortie mic is a cardioid dynamic type, which requires no external power. It's the right choice when you're up close and personal with the subject.

Since you don't have to worry about long cable runs, it's better to use a consumer-grade mic (one rated at –10 dB output) if you'll be plugging it directly into a camcorder that has mini-style or RCA audio input jacks.

Boom

A boom mic is a shotgun condenser type with a directional supercardioid or hypercardioid pickup pattern (**Figure 7.5**). Most require phantom (external) power and an operator to hold it just out of frame and aim it at the subject.

Lavalier

These mics are designed to be worn by the subject, clipped to a tie or pocket, or concealed in clothing or hair. Today's lavalier mics, or lavs, are very tiny—about the size of a pencil eraser. Some lavs are even flesh-colored (in a variety of skin tones) for easier concealment.

Lavaliers use a special type of condenser, which means they require external power, usually provided by a watch battery encased in the cable. The pickup pattern can be omnidirectional or cardioid, but the pattern doesn't matter too much because the sound source will be just inches away.

In a typical situation, you might clip a lav to an interview subject when you are a video crew of one, with no interviewer and no boom operator. Or you might put one on an actor in a fast-moving action scene where it will be tough to follow action with a boom.

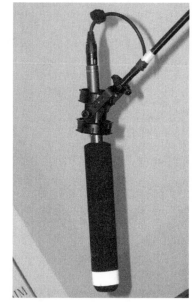

Figure 7.5 This boom mic is covered with a foam windscreen, which reduces wind noise when you're shooting outdoors on a breezy day. It can be mounted at the end of a boom pole, as shown here, or hand-held.

Plant

A *plant mic* is generally a cardioid or hypercardioid unit with a *pickup head* that can swivel through 90 degrees. The name derives from planting such mics somewhere out of sight to capture sound in shots where boom or lavalier mics would be impractical. For example, in a long shot in

> **PLANT MIC:** Cardioid or hyper-cardioid microphone with swivel pickup head that can be hidden, or planted, in or near an object.

> **PICKUP HEAD:** Portion of a mic containing its audio sensing component.

a crowded restaurant, you might hide a plant mic in the centerpiece on the table and aim it at the speaking characters. It may be either dynamic- or condenser-type.

TOOLS FOR CONTROLLING AND CAPTURING SOUND

Besides mics, the basic tools of the sound technician are a mixer (to control audio levels and combine inputs) and a recorder (which can be the camcorder itself), plus the connectors, cables, and line pads needed to hook them all together.

Even today, most of this gear, except for the recorder, is analog. The audio inputs of your camcorder are analog, after all. Unless you're using a sophisticated dual-system sound rig or working in a recording studio, audio doesn't become digital until it's in the recorder.

Sound Mixers and Boards

A mixer gets its name from its ability to combine multiple inputs, but you'll need one even if you're only using a single mic, since a mixer is the best way to control audio levels. Even if you're recording sound in-camera, it's much easier to work the controls on a mixer than to try to adjust the level controls on the body of the camcorder.

A portable sound mixer often used by DV crews is the Shure FP33, which is small and light enough to be worn on a shoulder strap by a boom operator (**Figure 7.6**). It operates either on AC power or its own internal 9V batteries, so you can take it anywhere. And it has phantom power output for condenser mics.

Figure 7.6 This lightweight field mixer is specifically designed for ENG crews, but it's an excellent choice for any DV setup that involves no more than three stereo inputs. (Photo © 2002 Shure Incorporated. Used by permission.)

A *sound board* is a bulkier piece of gear—generally briefcase-sized or larger—that does much the same thing as a sound mixer but gives more control over more channels, including *equalization* (frequency-response adjustment). You'll need a sound board if you're shooting a concert or a complicated action sequence that requires multiple mics.

> **SOUND BOARD:** A type of audio mixer that can control both levels and equalization for many audio lines.
>
> **EQUALIZATION:** Adjusting frequency response of audio lines in relation to one another.

Controls and meters on mixers and sound boards include:

- Audio gain

- Pan/balance

- Master level

- VU meter

- Equalization

Audio Gain

The front of the mixer will have a set of knobs or slider switches for varying the audio level of each input. The FP33 has input jacks for three mics, or two mics and an electric guitar pickup, or any combination of three sound sources.

Pan/Balance

Panning controls and balance controls do the same thing. They adjust the mixture of L and R signals in the corresponding channel to make a given sound seem to swing right, left, or center. There's a separate knob for each input channel, and one for the output channel. The input knobs are labeled "Pan" and the output knob, "Balance."

> **PANNING:** In audio terminology, mixing Left and Right stereo signals; adjusting audio balance.

Inputs are stereo, with L and R channels, even though you'll probably be recording in mono. You may need this control because some mics have stereo output, and you'll want to favor one side or the other. Or, you can treat the L and R channels as entirely separate tracks; they don't have to come from the same sound source.

Master Level

The mixer's master level output control is a knob or slider for adjusting the overall audio level of the combined mixer output; this is the signal you'll be feeding to the recorder.

VU Meter

A meter with a needle indicator, or LCD bar graph, shows the gain in *volume units (VU)* from the master-level output control. It's actually no different from a dB scale.

> **VU METER:** Audio level indicator marked off in a range of volume units (VU), which is equivalent to the dB scale.

Equalization

While sound boards typically feature equalization controls, and mixers don't, the more expensive sound boards break equalization down into multiple ranges. On a lower-priced sound board, typical equalization ranges would be High, Medium, and Low—three settings for one knob. On the more expensive boards, more ranges and more knobs permit fine-tuning of frequency response.

Audio Recorders

You have the choice of recording sync sound on the camcorder, using an external recorder, or both. We recommend using both. (For more information, see "DV Camcorder Audio Recording Modes" in Chapter 3 and "Should You Record Separate Sound?" below.)

Currently, your choices in digital external recorders come down to *DAT (digital audiotape)* and *MD (MiniDisc)*. Also, professional MP3 recorders, which make recordings on electronic memory chips, are just starting to come on the market.

These days, most professional sound technicians use DAT. A DAT cassette is slightly larger than a Mini DV and uses a similar helical recording method. DAT recording is the preferred method for capturing dual-system sound on DV shoots because the format gives excellent audio quality and the gear is reliable. For a handy alternative to renting a DAT recorder, see the accompanying sidebar, "Use Your Laptop as a DAT."

> **DAT:** Digital audiotape; a cassette tape format.
>
> **MD:** MiniDisc, a small magnetic disk for digital audio recording.
>
> **JAM SYNC:** Multiple-device time-code synchronization technique by which one device serves as the master timecode generator and all linked devices serve as slaves. If the master signal becomes unstable for any reason, the slave uses its internal timecode, then resynchronizes with the master when the signal is restored.

One of the key features of professional DATs is that they accept external timecode signals, which lock the recording to the camcorder through a process called *jam sync*. (For more information, see "Using a Clapper Board and Timecode" later in this chapter.)

> **Use Your Laptop as a DAT**
>
> *With installation of sound recording software, any laptop with a sound card can serve as a high-quality digital audio recorder. Shareware programs for sound recording include PolderbitS Sound Recorder and Editor for Windows, and Sound Sculptor II for Macs (both are available for download at www.tucows.com). You can set the software to capture WAV or AIFF files at 48 Kbps on your hard drive—the highest quality DV can handle. Just be sure to take along an adapter (and possibly also an attenuator) to convert any XLR feed to the stereo mini jack on your laptop marked "Audio In."*

Should You Record Separate Sound?

Short answer: yes. Shooting separate (or dual-system) sound is generally a good idea, especially if you're shooting film-style and can afford the extra crew and equipment.

You'll end up with two recordings of the same take—a primary (on DAT) and a backup (on Mini DV). Besides providing protection against data loss, having two versions of the soundtrack is a very good idea for technical reasons.

When to Use Dual-System Sound

Like meticulous lighting, dual-system audio is a film-style technique, and the only reason *not* to do it is that it involves additional time and expense—luxuries you may not have on a news-style shoot.

Low-Quality In-Camera Audio Circuits

Even though consumer and professional DV recording formats are identical, lower-priced consumer and prosumer units suffer from notoriously poor (and sometimes even downright noisy) audio circuitry. In comparison, professional camcorders have higher-quality audio because they are designed for single-person ENG crews that must rely on in-camera recording for broadcast.

How can you tell whether a camcorder has pro-style audio? Look at the audio input jacks. If they are XLR plugs, it's a pro unit. If not, it may be a lower quality audio machine—and you have that much more reason to shoot dual system.

Troublesome or Unyielding Audio AGC

Some consumer camcorders won't let you turn off Automatic Gain Control. As we've already discussed, this can ruin your soundtrack, often producing a very undesirable effect called *pumping*. (For more information, see "Audio Level Controls" in Chapter 4.)

If you're stuck with such a camcorder and can't go dual-system, try routing the mic input through a mixer, then through a pad, and into *both* L and R channels of the camcorder, turning the gain to near maximum on the mixer and near minimum on the pad.

> **PUMPING:** Erroneous operation of automatic audio gain control in which the circuit keeps adjusting the level up and down as it seeks to compensate for sudden conditions of loudness or quiet.

Sometimes this will force the AGC to stay at low gain because the voltage of the professional mixer is so much higher than the consumer audio input level. (You may have to experiment and do a few test recordings to get the levels right.) However, if the audio circuits of the camcorder tend to be noisy anyway, this workaround could just make the problem worse.

A better solution by far is simply to go dual-system to get a high-quality soundtrack.

Complex Setups

The more complex your sound setup, the more reason to do dual-system recording. If you're using multiple sound sources and mics (a wireless lav on each actor, for example) a DV camcorder that only records two tracks at a time won't allow you to keep sound sources and tracks separate until you get to postproduction. For that, you'll need a multi-track DAT recorder.

 REALITY CHECK: *It's rare to use a separate track for each actor, even today when multi-track recorders offer this capability. In the days of analog sound recording, the maximum number of tracks you could record was two. Combining the inputs from multiple mics in a single scene was done at the mixer, where the operator would make sure all the input levels were compatible. The composite audio signal would then be recorded on a single track. This practice is still widely used.*

Recommended Dual-System Setup

Our recommended setup for recording film-style audio for digital video uses a boom mic to capture dialogue, a mixer to control audio levels, and dual-system audio to record on an external DAT and the camcorder at the same time (**Figure 7.7**).

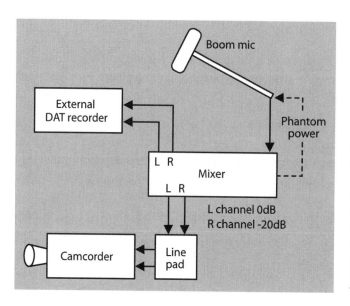

Figure 7.7 Our recommended dual-system setup uses a boom mic, a mixer, and redundant dual-system recording. If the camcorder audio input is a mini or RCA plug (indicating a consumer-grade line voltage level), insert a line pad to reduce the input voltage and avoid damage to the camcorder circuit.

If the mic output is mono, connect it to either the L or the R jack of any available mixer input channel. Then connect both L and R channels of the mixer's master output to the recorder. And be sure phantom power is available from the mixer to any powered mics.

Make sure all components—mics, mixer, and recorder—are rated at the same line level, or insert line pads to correct any mismatches. Adjust levels, keeping an eye on the VU meters on mixer *and* recorder, and by listening through headphones. Adjust until you get 0 dB and –20 dB—as shown on the recorder's VU meter—for L and R input recording levels. (See the section, "Hedging Your Bets on Audio Levels," later in this chapter for more details about why and how to protect yourself by recording mono dialogue at two distinct levels.) Don't worry about setting different levels for L and R. Remember that your production dialogue track need only be monophonic. You can (and should) add stereo dimension in postproduction.

For cable runs longer than 10 feet, use XLR connectors and shielded audio cables to preserve signal quality and minimize power-line hum. (It's also good practice to route audio cables some distance from electrical power cords on the set.) As an added precaution, if

> **ROLL OFF:** Audio engineer's term for turning equalization control down, filtering out lower frequencies.

your mixer or sound board permits you to adjust equalization, *roll off* (filter out) frequencies below 90 Hz. This will reject power-line (60 Hz) or heavy electrical machinery hum. It will also reduce the effect of any low-pitched noises such as rumble from trucks and buses.

TIP: Even though your mixer may allow you to adjust equalization, it's generally best to avoid altering the sound too much on location. Any changes you make while recording can limit your creative options in postproduction. Your goal on set should be to record the cleanest, strongest signal possible. Remember, if you roll off frequencies on the set, you can't get them back in post.

When to Use Single-System Sound

The main reason to employ single-system sound is if you're in a news-style situation where you don't have crew, equipment, or time to rig external mixing and recording.

Many run-and-gun videographers insist that in-camera recording is "good enough." Further, they argue that matching, or syncing, externally recorded soundtracks to video in post is time-consuming. Well, that may have been true years ago, but with current NLE software, syncing tracks to clips is as quick and easy as cut-and-paste by using the sync sound from the camcorder as a guide track for positioning the externally recorded one. (For more information on sound editing, see "Using Software Tools to Repair and Enhance Soundtracks" in Chapter 11.)

SOUND TECHNIQUES

Here are some experience-tested procedures for rigging and monitoring audio in a variety of production situations. For details of wireless setup, and particularly for tips on eliminating RF interference, we recommend befriending the support technician at the rental house.

TIP: On a fully crewed set, sound technicians typically rig their own equipment; gaffers don't get involved except to run power cords. Even if you're a one-man show, use good gaffer practice in rigging lines and C-stands. Tape cables to the floor, and sandbag the stands to prevent them from toppling over. Make sure actors or interview subjects are aware how their cabling might limit their movements.

Avoiding the Built-in Microphone

Don't use the built-in camcorder mic. It's impossible to say "never," because you might have to grab your camcorder and shoot in the middle of an earthquake. And, in certain situations, it might come in handy for capturing a guide track.

It's not that the audio quality is necessarily poor, although it might be on cheaper camcorders. There are two even better reasons to avoid using an internal mic:

- Built-in mics pick up the machine noise of the camcorder motor. Since the motor has a distinctive whine, you might be able to digitally subtract it from the track in post—but why create such grief in the first place?

- A mic located at the camera will give the wrong audio perspective: It isn't nearly close enough to the subject for anything but an extreme closeup.

On a news-style shoot, use a shortie (if hand-held), or clip a lav to the subject. If you can take along just one more person on a news-style shoot, she can probably manage two crucial tasks that will improve production quality: Holding both an external microphone and a bounce board to provide some fill light. If you want to take one more step to improve sound quality, have her operate a small, wearable field mixer.

Obviously, on a film-style shoot, using the built-in mic isn't a good option, except as a backup or as a guide track.

Doing Interviews with a Lav and/or a Short Mic

On news-style shoots (particularly if your interviewer is on-camera talent rather than a sound-crew veteran), be sure to coach him on basic mic technique.

- He should hold a short cardioid mic at chest level, pointing it at about a 45° angle toward the speaker's mouth. The chest reverberates the bass and mid-range tones of speech, and the mouth supplies the plosives. Properly aimed, the cardioid mic will pick up both.

- He should slip a foam-rubber windscreen on the shortie and leave it there. It will prevent noise from breezes as well as minimize the distortion effect of a speaker's overdone plosive (called a *popped p* in the trade).

> **POPPED P:** A speaker's overdone plosive, which causes distortion in the audio recording.

> **TIP:** *The most common type of windscreen looks like a hollowed-out foam-rubber ball—which is just what you can use if you don't have one handy. Wrapping a handkerchief or other cloth around the mic won't work if there's much of a breeze; the mic will pick up the rustling of the cloth.*

- The interviewer should always point the mic at the person speaking. This sounds simple, but when interviews become fast-paced, novice interviewers seem to think that waving the mic rapidly back and forth between themselves and the subject looks silly. (But it's not half as silly as not being able to hear what one or the other of them is saying.)

- If you use lavs for interviews, remind both interviewer and subject that their mics are on all the time, not just when they're talking. Muttered comments, clothing noises from fishing around in a pocket for a stick of gum, chuckles, and snorts—if people aren't careful, you'll have it all for posterity.

If the interviewer doesn't follow your instructions, call for retakes—politely but insistently—until you get clean sound.

Rigging and Handling a Boom

The boom mic should be a shotgun, hypercardioid type such as the Sennheiser 416. Audio Technica also makes them, but many audio engineers think the output from the Sennheiser has a richer sound.

> **BLIMP:** Canister-like windscreen that fits around a microphone.
>
> **STRAIN RELIEF:** Rigging technique in which cables are looped or taped in place to prevent connectors from separating if someone trips or tugs on the cable.

Encase the shotgun in a windscreen, or *blimp*, and mount it on an adjustable-length boom pole. The pole should extend 8–12 feet. Professional boom poles have shock mounts that suspend the mic in a mesh of broad rubber bands, cushioning it from the operator's handling of the pole.

Run an XLR cable from the input side of the mixer to the pole. Fix the cable to the end of the pole with gaffer's tape, coiling it first for *strain relief*.

A portable, wearable sound mixer can make it possible for the boom operator to do both jobs, especially if the boom is the only mic on the set. Handling both the boom and the mixer controls won't be physically impossible unless the operator tries to ride gain during a take—something she shouldn't be doing anyway.

> **TIP:** In a pinch, you can make a boom pole from a broomstick, suspending the mic from it with gaffer's tape to provide a shock mount. But pro models aren't expensive to rent and are well worth the expenditure for their light weight, adjustability, and durability. A handy T-shaped type boom pole fits into a socket on the operator's belt and eases the muscle strain of holding the mic aloft during long takes.

Give the boom operator a pair of headphones connected to the output side of the mixer. Listening to the dialogue through the headphones will be the best way for her to assure that she's pointing the mic on-axis, and getting the loudest, clearest sound possible. (The director should wear headphones, as well, but he should be paying attention to nuances of dialogue, not so much to technical quality.)

Some mixers feature a *talk-back circuit*—jacks for headsets with earphones and mics worn by the mixer and the boom operator that allow them to remain in two-way communication. This encourages the boom operator to report problems out of earshot of cast and crew (between takes, of course).

> **TALK-BACK CIRCUIT:** On some sound mixers, output jacks for headsets with earphones and mics to be worn by the mixer and boom operator so they can communicate.

Holding the boom may look easy, but it's an acquired skill. Here's the best way to do it:

Hold the pole over your head with your hands spread about three feet apart (**Figure 7.8**). This overhead position works best for holding the mic steady throughout an entire take, which may last several minutes. As an actor begins to speak, twist the pole to rotate the mic in his direction. Aim the mic at the person's chin, where you'll pick up sound from the lips, throat, and chest. Rotate and re-point the mic each time another person starts speaking, and follow that person as she moves around the set.

Figure 7.8 The ideal boom-pole position is horizontal, held over the operator's head. Not only is this position easier for the operator to maintain for long takes, it's also better than angled positions in which the boom pole may accidentally slant into the shot.

TIP: Operating the boom? Take any rings off your fingers. Boom poles have foam rubber grips but not along the entire length. Rings will click against the pole, and the mic will pick up the noise.

Keep re-pointing the mic at each actor for best output, even if the action is fast-paced. If it's just too fast to follow, pick a compromise overhead position where the level from each actor is about equal. Establish this position during rehearsal, and advise the director if an actor strays so far off-mic that his level is noticeably lower than the others'.

The ideal position for the boom mic is just outside the frame—usually no more than a foot or so from the top of the actor's head. Just before a take, dip the mic into the shot and back it out slowly until the camera operator tells you it's no longer visible. Back it out a few inches more to allow for some sagging as your arms get tired. That's your position; try to keep the mic there during the take.

A boom mic that slips into the shot is one of the most common undetected errors on the set. The camera operator should be watching carefully to see whether the boom mic dips into the frame. Even so, if it enters for just a second, it's easy to miss. If you think its position wavered during a take and no one noticed, wait until the shot is over and notify the camera operator. (Playing back the take on the set in hopes of spotting the error on the monitor risks breaking the timecode. Let the camera operator and director make that decision. For more information, see "Preventing and Troubleshooting Common Problems" in Chapter 9.)

The boom operator should be part of the rehearsal process—both to work with the sound mixer in setting levels, and to anticipate the actors' blocking, or movement, on the set. A good boom operator knows the dialogue in the script and the actors' blocking, so he can anticipate when to move the mic from one actor to another.

TIP: Think of a shotgun mic as a telephoto lens for sound—it magnifies sounds that are far away (provided they're on-axis). A shotgun also compresses distance in the same way a telephoto lens does. For example, if a source of noise like a busy freeway is beyond the subject but in line with the extended axis of the microphone, it will sound as if the subject is standing in the middle of traffic. Always know where the extended axis of the mic is pointing and, if necessary, reposition either the subject or the mic. A shotgun mic tends to reject sound coming from the rear, so position it pointing away from any sound you want to minimize.

Attaching and Rigging Lavalier Mics

Always place a lav within 10 inches of the subject's mouth.

After physical location, the most important single checklist item for a lav is whether it has a fresh battery—typically a silver-disk, watch-type battery housed in a small case in the lav cord. Your sound technician should carry a battery tester (an inexpensive digital multimeter will do) and a supply of spares.

Concealing a lav in an actor's wardrobe takes some inventiveness. You want the face of the mic—where the holes are—to be in the clear, not buried in clothing or hair. It can peek out of a pocket, emerge from a neckline, appear under the brim of a hat, or deck the edge of a headband or scarf.

An ideal location for a flesh-colored lav is right at the hairline, with a thin cord threaded through the hair, down the back of the head, and taped at the neck. (Perhaps your bald actors should wear hats?)

Another technique is to use surgical tape to fix a lav directly to the skin. Use astringent on a cotton ball to cleanse oil from the area first. On shoots that last several days, actors should apply a coating of tincture of benzoin to the skin, let it dry, then apply the tape. This coating is a clear cosmetic base, available at drug counters. It dries tacky and minimizes skin irritation from repeatedly applying and removing the tape.

Don't affix lavs on the set. Have it done in a dressing room or some other private area. Ideally, coach the technician who is responsible for the person's wardrobe and hair so she can place the lav correctly.

If the lavs are professional models, their thin cords will terminate in bulky XLR jacks. Coil the connection to the audio cable for strain relief and use gaffer's tape to secure it out of sight, perhaps under clothing. Affixing the connection to the back of a belt often works. Or run the cable down the back of the leg and tape the connector at mid-thigh or calf. The location and fastening must allow the person to disconnect himself whenever he must leave the set. (It's also a good idea to supervise any disconnection, if you can.)

Multicamera Guerrilla Technique

Co-author Pete Shaner shot multi-camera like a guerrilla when he attended the Edinburgh International Festival, where he coached an actor friend's one-person show and videotaped the performance. He took along only as much gear as he could fit in a small suitcase but ended up achieving what amounts to a guerilla-style multi-camera shoot—with a crew of one!

He took two palm-sized Canon ZR-series camcorders, setting up one on a tripod near his seat in the theater balcony and using the other handheld to cover the actor's movements in closeup. (Since any shakiness of the camera is magnified in such a telephoto shot, he broke one of our cherished rules left auto image stabilization on.) He was able to use an audio feed from the actor's lav mic, connected through the theater's sound board, into has laptop—using it as a DAT recorder. By also breaking our rule about not using on-camera mics, he also had the recordings from the two ZRs. The lav gave very close perspective on the actor, and by picking up the theater loudspeakers, the on-camera mics gave the audience perspective and room tone from the distance of the balcony. By varying the mixing of these three tracks in post, he was able to control the audio perspective precisely, giving a nice balance between intelligible speech (close-mic'd) and the rich ambience of the theater (balcony perspective).

Adding Audio Perspective to Lavs

Remember that lavs usually fail to capture much in the way of spatial quality, since a) they're very close to the subject, and b) there's no change in audio perspective as the subject moves around. You can enrich the sound of a lav by mixing its output in post with that of a boom mic or even a stationary mic held on a C-stand—any source of room presence for the scene. To give you the greatest flexibility in post, use a multi-track recorder and put each mic input on a separate track.

Rigging and Adjusting Wireless Mics

Don't use wireless rigs unless you have to. They're expensive to rent, complicated to set up, and tricky to operate—especially when you need multiple mics and channels. In most situations, you'd be wiser to use a boom instead.

The most common application of wireless audio on the set is to link multiple lavs worn by individual actors—a situation in which audio cables would be both cumbersome and unsightly. Since the lavs lack audio perspective, you have to wonder whether the results are worth the extra expense and effort. But for that chase scene through the streets of Chinatown or a live rock video, wireless gives your subjects relative freedom of movement while assuring they can't run off-mic.

Some shortie mics have built-in transmitters, and lavs can be plugged into a palm-sized transmitter box worn by the subject–usually fastened at the back of the belt, or taped to the skin beneath clothing.

Wireless is line-of-sight technology. It won't work well if people or objects are blocking the path between transmitter and receiver. For this reason, sound technicians generally place wireless receivers up high at the back of a set where they're less likely to be blocked.

Wireless Checklist

Once you're on the set, here's a basic checklist for making sure all the gear is working:

1. Put fresh batteries in every transmitter every morning. The best wireless system will be useless if the transmitters are weak. If you're using rechargeable batteries, the rule of thumb for camera packs applies: You should have three sets—one in the gear, one set of fresh spares, and one set in the charger.

2. Position wireless receivers behind the set where moving actors are less likely to block the line of sight to the transmitters. A typical setup uses one receiver for each transmitter, each transmitting on a different frequency. Run tests to verify that each receiver

is getting a strong signal from its transmitter by checking the RF level indicator on the receiver. Remember that, for each separate track you want to lay down on tape, you'll need a separate recording channel on a multi-track recorder.

3. Check each line through the headphones to be sure it sounds clear and that no interference is present. Especially with multi-channel setups, dealing with interference can be very tricky. A sensible first step is to determine whether the source of interference is one of the other wireless transmitters, or the electrical power lines on the set. Listen to the master output at the mixer, and shut off transmitters one at a time. If you still get interference, the source is in the electrical system. From there, it's another complex process of elimination.

4. Have one technician (or the subject herself) walk the wireless mic through the set to all positions required by the scene while another technician monitors the RF level on the receiver. If the level falls off at any location, reposition the receiver until all locations are covered equally well.

5. When actors are on the set, run tests of the equipment when they are speaking their loudest and adjust the transmitter gain. When gain is set correctly, the meter on the receiver, typically a glowing LED, should flash only briefly at voice peaks. If the indicator flashes too frequently, reduce transmitter gain. If it hardly flashes at all, increase it or move the receiver closer to the transmitter to boost reception.

6. Once transmitter gain is set, adjust the receiver and mixer gain so that the master level of recorder input never peaks above 0 dB. Don't allow positive dB readings during peaks, and don't adjust levels during a take.

Using a Clapper Board and Timecode

The familiar filmmaker's slate, or *clapper board*, is a valuable tool for establishing sync between audio and video (**Figure 7.9**). (If you don't have a slate, you can have a crew member clap his hands in front of the lens before a take.) Whether it's a handclap, or the clapping of the slate, you can then sync the resulting spike in the soundtrack to the image of the hands or clapper board coming together when you're editing. (Picture and sound for each clip come across FireWire in sync; however, you'll need the clap if you move tracks around or want to sync up a dual-system recording.)

> **CLAPPER BOARD:** Another term for a filmmaker's slate.
>
> **SMART SLATE:** Electronic clapper board, or slate, with numeric LED display of timecode.

Modern clapper boards—so-called *smart slates*—are electronic, with internal clock circuits and an LED display for timecode. When you clap them, the running timecode display freezes so the camera can capture it.

Figure 7.9 This smart slate has a mechanical-style clapper and an internal electronic clock circuit that generates timecode for the LED display and jam sync output. (Photo courtesy Denecke, Inc.)

Smart slates also have an output jack for the timecode signals they generate. Connecting that output to the external sync jack of your camcorders and external recorders is one way of achieving jam sync—so multiple camcorders, recorders, and the slate all remain in perfect sync using the same timecode. Of course, you won't be able to use the jam sync feature unless all your camcorders and the external recorder have an input jack for externally generated timecode.

Hedging Your Bets on Audio Levels

In conventional analog recording, you can permit levels to peak above 0 dB—but you can't work that way in digital. The maximum recording level you can use without danger of audio distortion is 0 dB. Any signal above 0 dB can cause distortion and may simply be clipped, or cut off at a certain frequency, by the recorder.

To protect yourself, split the microphone output—using a *splitter*, or Y-connector—and send it to both L and R channels of the mixer input. Set the L channel gain at the mixer to 0 dB. Set the R channel to –20 dB. If there are loud noises during a take, and levels *do* go higher than 0 dB, that portion of the L track

> **SPLITTER:** Electrical connector that branches one input to form two output lines; Y-connector.

will be distorted and unusable. But since the R track is recorded at a safer, lower level, you have it to fall back on. You can increase the gain on the R track in post, inserting it in place of the damaged L track.

> **TIP:** You can use this dual-level scheme even if you are recording in-camera without a mixer. Feed mic inputs into both channels—using a splitter—and using the camcorder's audio level controls, adjust the L gain to 0 and R gain to –20 (or somewhere between the 7 and 9 o'clock positions on the dial, if it isn't marked in dB). You'll have the same protection in case of loud noises during a take, even if the AGC is on. Don't use a splitter to go the other way—to combine two outputs to form one input. You won't be able to control the level or quality of the result. Use a mixer instead.

Monitoring Audio

Everyone needs to listen to the audio during a take. The boom operator, sound mixer, sound recordist (if you're using one), and director should all wear headphones connected to the master output from the mixer. In a professional setup, headphones are typically connected to small wireless receivers that slip into your pocket, or clip onto your belt.

> **TIP:** Audio levels in headphones can be high enough to damage hearing. It should be part of the sound mixer's job to check levels in the headphones before other people put them on. He should turn the master level down before putting his own headphones on, then bring it up gradually.

If the director doesn't want to wear headphones, it's the sound mixer's job to notify her if there's a problem with the sound. An actor might be off-mic, the boom might be aimed badly, there could be interference in the line, or a loud, ill-timed bus might have passed by outside.

The director should establish some ground rules about when and how she wants to be notified. Most directors don't want a take interrupted until they call "Cut!" no matter what. After all, some things *can* be fixed in post, and there are other reasons for letting the take run through to completion. A good compromise might be for the mixer to signal silently to the director—raise his hand, say—if he hears a noise on the track. The director can then decide whether to keep the camera rolling.

| RIDING GAIN: Adjusting audio levels at the mixer on a set while a take is in progress. |

Only an experienced sound mixer should attempt to adjust levels, or *ride gain*, during a take. Generally, it's best to set levels carefully during rehearsals or run-throughs—using the real actors or subjects, not stand-ins—and then leave them alone.

Recording Room Tone

If you want to keep your editor happy, remember to record at least one minute of silence, or *room tone*, for every camera setup. Standard practice for film crews is to record room tone as the last take before moving to the next setup.

> **ROOM TONE:** Audio recording of a "silent" set or studio, to be used during the edit for putting in pauses or covering sound holes; also called "presence."

The purpose of room tone is to help you match the sound quality of audio edits in post, especially when you're adding sound effects or dialogue that weren't recorded on the actual set. Each room or location has its own distinctive tone—and dead silence without room tone on a soundtrack insert will be very disturbing to the audience. You therefore need enough room tone so you can cut, paste, and mix it to your heart's content during the editing process.

When you are recording room tone, anyone remaining in the area must be absolutely quiet. In post, if you need a longer segment of presence, you can paste several copies of the room-tone take together. But when you do this, even the slightest noise will show up— usually as repetitive clicks. You can use digital audio tools to subtract the noises, but it's an extra step you can easily avoid.

AVOIDING NASTY SURPRISES IN POST

The purpose of capturing the cleanest possible dialogue on-set is to avoid nasty surprises in postproduction. Here are a few pointers to help you anticipate the challenges you'll face in dealing with audio post.

Consider Recording Separate Tracks

Remember that your primary objective in capturing audio on the set is to keep dialogue clean. Ideally, if there are ambient sound effects or even live music in the action, you'll want to segregate the dialogue on its own track. When there's any kind of extraneous noise, mic the actors closely, or use a highly focused mic that will reject off-axis noise. You can use a second mic set off at a distance and record it on a separate track, which you'll mix with the first in post to add perspective.

The same holds true when you're using multiple mics, such as a separate lav on each actor. Despite the fact it's movie industry practice to mix multiple mics down to a single track on the set, you needn't follow this rule. Working instead as musicians do, you might consider recording multiple mics on separate tracks, which will give you more flexibility in the mix. Since a DV camcorder can only record two tracks during a take, you'll need an external multi-track recorder if you need more than two channels.

Always Roll Audio

Every time the camera shoots something, record a matching audio track. And vice versa: If you record wild sound effects, shoot the action that accompanies them. Use a clapper board at the beginning of every take, or just clap your hands in front of the lens.

Provide Footage for Transitions

One advantage to working with a fully detailed script is that you'll know where you plan to insert musical transitions, or other extended transitions using dissolves or special effects. When you're shooting those scenes, be sure to let the camera run long enough to provide footage for these transitions.

> *TIP:* You can often find creative solutions to sound problems. Some videomakers were shooting an unrepeatable action sequence when, to their horror, a marching band began to practice nearby, leaking music onto the soundtrack. Their clever solution: Incorporate the band music in the scene. They recorded more of the band on a separate track to mix with other scenes and provide continuity.

THE MARK OF PROFESSIONAL VIDEO

Recording a professional soundtrack with impeccable vocal quality and the right audio perspective for each take is a complex process. You must select a mic with the right pickup pattern, position it correctly for a good recording (while hiding it or keeping it out of frame), avoid interference and distortion, and make sure sound levels don't peak over 0 dB.

But it's well worth the trouble to get it right. To an audience, one of the most noticeable differences between an amateurish home video and a professional presentation will be the quality of the soundtrack.

A good soundtrack won't necessarily make your movie, but a bad one will surely ruin it.

CHAPTER EIGHT
Preproduction

Forget that you're an inspired artist. Forget that you're a brilliant video technician. In the preproduction phase of your project you must become a military planner. Your mission is to lay out, in meticulous detail, a tactical battle plan for exactly how your project can be achieved in the real world of time and money. As every great leader knows, the way to achieve a complex undertaking is to break it down into simple, achievable steps. Your weapons are organization, scheduling, and budgeting.

CHOOSING A PRODUCTION STYLE

Careful preproduction planning is contrary to running and gunning, so (with a few exceptions) the main focus of this chapter will be on film-style shooting.

Use Your Script As a Tool

In preproduction planning, the script is a key organizational tool—a way of describing and documenting the work to be done and a template for discussions with your production team. Writing a script forces you to describe what will happen in front of the camera in specific detail. Locations, characters, time of day, actions, *props*—these are the kinds of details a script allows you to specify in advance of shooting. Understanding your project at this level will help you organize the labor and equipment you'll need for each scene, schedule the work, and estimate what it will cost.

> **PROP:** Object used by an actor in some on-camera action.

If you don't use a script, then a storyboard, shot plan, or shot list can function in the same way. The important thing is to be able to describe the production requirements for your project, on paper, as far in advance as possible.

Recall from Chapter 2 that if your project demands impromptu, news-style production, you'll get more predictable results if you can take the time to develop a script—or at least an outline—as a planning tool. As with the time-tested principles of good lighting and sound, you should know how film-style planning is done and apply it wherever possible to your news-style projects.

Prepare for News-Style Interviews and Documentaries

Consider writing a "script" for interviews and documentaries even if you don't stick to it. You can then apply film-style preproduction techniques, such as breaking down your scenes, which we'll describe shortly.

For example, if you can gain access to an interview subject in advance, try conducting a preliminary interview. Knowing some of your subject's responses will help you put your questions in a more logical order, sharpen them, and suggest good shooting locations and interesting follow-up questions.

Even more important, these preliminary responses can fill in the "dialogue" of your pro forma script, and guide your thinking about what shots will be most effective in visualizing your message. Even if the presentation will be mostly talking heads, picturing those heads in a specific environment will generate visual ideas.

Also, drawing up a shot plan for the locations in an interview or documentary will help you decide how to use the space, its furniture, and its props. You should try to formulate answers to questions like: Will I want an establishing shot of the building entrance? How important will ECU (extreme closeup) inserts of products or hand demonstrations be? Do I need reaction shots of questioners or audience members? (For more information, see "Drawing Shot Plans" in Chapter 5.)

Remember, even news-style shooting requires getting the coverage you need to assemble a visually interesting story or presentation in the editing room. Concepts and ideas expressed in dialogue can be abstract, but when you're designing a shot plan you can't think in terms of generalities. Everything the camera sees is specific and concrete.

As we cover the steps in film-style preproduction planning in this chapter, you'll see how learning to think in terms of visual detail will greatly improve your ability to organize, schedule, and budget even a news-style project.

HOW MUCH STRUCTURE?

Chapter 5 contrasts the structured approaches of Hitchcock and Spielberg with the improvisational approaches of Coppola and Altman. Early in your project, you'll have to decide between structured and improvisational production styles. Aesthetic issues aside, a structured approach will allow you to create far more accurate schedules and budgets.

How Much Coverage?

Choosing whether to shoot in a structured or in an improvised mode impacts a crucial trade-off, one that involves every aspect of scheduling and budgeting: how much coverage you'll need to shoot. If you don't have a shot plan or storyboard, you won't know how the sequence will cut together—which means you'll have to spend lots of time and money shooting coverage so when you *do* get to the editing room, you'll have all the angles you need. On the other hand, if you have a detailed shot plan—including designing shots in advance—you'll know exactly what shots you need, and you can stop shooting when you get them.

Structured Production Style

You've heard the cliché, "There's no business like show business." But in fact, there's no business *less* businesslike than show business. Ever since the silent era, filmmakers have wrestled with the challenges of producing great art, albeit on schedule and on budget. The artistic aspects of moviemaking sometimes defy all the rules about how to turn ideas into pictures. It's a paradox: You're trying to impose structure on creativity.

Still, imposing a structure on your production offers these advantages:

* Shooting is fast and efficient; you know what you want.

* Shooting is economical; you need fewer shots. This has far less impact on video production, since you won't be paying for raw stock, processing, or transfer costs—but you *will* be paying crew time and equipment rental.

* Editing is straightforward and fast; you don't have as many choices.

Structure also has its disadvantages:

* Structured shooting is predictable; it lacks spontaneity. Happy accidents are less likely to occur.

* If something goes wrong on the set (and it often does), an inflexible shot plan may prevent you from seeing creative alternatives.

Cutting In-Camera

Carried to its furthest (and least desirable) extreme, a structured production style may lead to *cutting in-camera,* meaning you plan to get only one good take of the shots you know you'll need, or that you shoot only the portions of scenes from a given setup you expect to actually appear on the screen. Editing is reduced to simple assembly.

> **CUTTING IN-CAMERA:** Shooting just one good take of every shot you need; shooting only the portions of scenes from a given setup you expect to use in the edit (*e.g.,* not shooting a master all the way through if you'll cut to closeups instead).

Cutting in-camera is a very bad idea, since you'll have no choice but to use almost all of your footage, and the actors will only get one attempt at each scene. Also, a shooting plan that includes little or no additional coverage closes off your range of creative choices in the editing room. And of course, if you find that you need a work-around for a shooting mistake, you'll be out of luck.

Improvisational Production Style

As you'd expect, the advantages of improvisation are mostly the *disadvantages* of structured shooting:

- Improvisational shooting encourages pleasant surprises and is more likely to create an atmosphere in which spontaneity can occur.

- If something goes wrong, you'll be more likely to find a creative solution, since you're already prepared for anything.

- If you're shooting DV, you don't have to worry about raw stock, processing, or transfers. You can shoot as many takes as you like (until the sun goes down or they ask you to leave the building).

Disadvantages of improvisation include:

- Shooting schedules will be less predictable and should be padded with extra days, incurring extra expense.

- Many storytelling decisions will be shifted to the editor, who must sift through lots of takes (some of which might not follow the script at all) to build the story.

The Dump-Truck Director

At the furthest (and least desirable) extreme of improvisational production, you will find the *dump-truck director,* who habitually overshoots coverage for every needed shot

> **DUMP-TRUCK DIRECTOR:** Perjorative term for a director who overshoots and lets the editor deal with the consequences.

and dumps it all on a bewildered editor, who will face a huge challenge just to watch and make sense of it all.

While the dump-truck approach won't necessarily result in a bad product, your shooting and editing expenses will be much greater than if you planned your shots more deliberately.

Multicamera Styles for Live Events

Covering a wedding, a concert, or a sporting event imposes special challenges in preproduction. Although some of these assignments can be shot using a simple, straightforward news-style approach, weddings, concerts, and ballgames generally follow predictable formats—so you *can* approach them as structured, film-style shoots. For most intents and purposes, they are scripted events.

Still, no two of these events are ever the same—their novelty and delight involve the elements of spontaneity and surprise. Since you'll want to capture those unique moments on tape, you can't avoid some improvisational shooting. However, spontaneous shots are tough to plan for.

If you can afford it, the best way to cover a live event involves a multicamera setup. Use two or more stationary camcorders to cover prearranged angles on the stage or playing area where the "rehearsed" action will take place. Then deploy one or more roving camcorders in the audience, backstage, or on the sidelines to seek out the surprises—the fast breaks and reaction shots.

Scout the Location

Be sure to look over the location in advance. (See "Scouting Locations," later in this chapter.) Attend rehearsals or practice sessions, if possible.

Bond with the Manager

Meet with the manager of the venue well in advance of the event, and nail down a specific agreement on when your crew can gain access for setup and shooting. Unlike other types of production, your video shoot isn't the main event, and if you don't make arrangements, no one else will.

Make Sure Camcorders Match

All stationary camcorders should be the same make and model to assure that the resolution and color balance of your shots will match. You can use the same make and model for the roving camcorders as well, but if you prefer smaller, lighter units such as Sony's

DSR-PD1, make sure their video outputs match the stationary units as closely as possible (**Figure 8.1**). Shoot tests in advance and compare the outputs. For example, if the stationary camcorders have professional 4:2:2 color space, don't use roving consumer-level units with 4:1:1 color.

Figure 8.1 Sony's DSR-PD1 is a palm-sized DVCAM unit specifically designed as a roving camcorder for multicamera shoots. Its resolution and color balance match the video output of the larger DSR-series camcorders you're likely to use as your stationary units. (Photo courtesy Sony Electronics Inc.)

Avoid Multiple Microphones

Try to simplify the sound setup as much as possible. Given the complexity of a multicamera shoot, it's tempting to plan for multiple microphones as well, even wireless ones. This can become a big problem. Multiple mics mean lots of extra cabling and generally require a multi-track DAT and mixer as well. Wireless setups are always problematic, and multichannel wireless can be a nightmare. (For more information, see "Rigging and Adjusting Wireless Mics" in Chapter 7.)

Don't plan on using the audio from built-in camera mics. Regard tracks you record this way as backups. You can always go back to them later if your primary audio is flawed. Use one boom mic, and run it into a mixer and the DAT recorder. If you absolutely must add an additional mic, such as a lavalier, bring it into the mixer and mix down to a mono track that you feed to the DAT. Unless the DAT is a multi-track unit, you'll be recording in stereo, but we recommend that you mix both sources down to mono, recording the signal at different levels on L and R tracks. (For more information, see "When to Use Dual-System Sound" in Chapter 7. For those situations when you might want to consider multi-track recording, see "Complex Setups" and "Adding Audio Perspective to Lavs" in the same chapter.)

Use Jam Sync

The more camcorders and audio recording channels you use, the more essential timecode sync becomes in post. To assure accurate timecode, rent camcorders and DATs that have jam sync input. (For more information on jam sync, see "Using a Clapper Board and Timecode" in Chapter 7.)

Reach Out and Touch Someone

With all those camcorder operators running around, you'll need some way to tell the roving units where to go and how to stay out of each other's shots. All camcorder operators need headsets linked to the director or to the lead camera operator via walkie-talkies. (The sound mixer and boom operator can communicate over the mixer's talk-back circuit.)

SCOUTING LOCATIONS

It's essential to inspect the places you intend to shoot before the day you arrive with a full cast and crew. On big-budget movies, a production staffer called a *location scout* checks out the sites in person, then makes recommendations to the director and DP, possibly showing them stills taken to match the views in the storyboard frames.

> **LOCATION SCOUT:** Movie professional who identifies and travels to prospective locations to judge and report back to director and producers on their suitability.

> *NOTE: The location scout might be either a location manager or a production assistant who reports to the location manager. (See "Meet Your Crew," later in this chapter.)*

Transportation and Logistics

Questions you (or your location scout) should ask:

- Does the location require a permit, either from the building owner or an agency of city government, before you can shoot? What fees will be involved? (Typically, shooting on city streets and sidewalks, and inside parks and public facilities such as schools and courthouses, requires a permit, as does shooting moving vehicles or shooting from inside a moving vehicle.)

- Will you be required to hire security personnel or police? What fees will be involved?

- What's the route? What's the travel time to the location from studio/network equipment storage? From truck rental agency to movie equipment rental house to location? From cast/crew homes to location? What factors (rush-hour traffic, narrow alleys) might cause delays on shoot day?

- Where will the crew unload and load? Is there access to a loading dock? A freight elevator? Are permits, passes, or keys required to gain access?

- Are there any physical restrictions—such as steep stairways or narrow doorways—that will present barriers to moving equipment?

- Where will cast and crew park? Are prior arrangements required? Fees?

- Where will the cast dress? If you plan to use trailers or mobile homes for dressing rooms, where will they be parked? Where are public restrooms, and are they unlocked or keyed?

- Will food services be required? If so, where will they set up? Where will they serve?

- What public activities will be taking place at the location on shoot day? What is your plan for making sure these activities are disrupted as little as possible? Will shooting attract a crowd? What crowd-control measures might be necessary? Who will provide them? What will this service cost?

- Is it possible, or desirable, to use the location on a weekend, on a holiday, or after hours? If so, what special arrangements must be made, especially for access or services not normally available during these times?

- Are waste disposal and recycling bins available? (Your cast and crew will inevitably fill several trash bags, especially from food services.)

Lighting Considerations

Review the lighting requirements listed in Chapter 6. Then make sure you and your DP go through these questions on-site:

- Are the available light, color of the walls, and decor in the room appropriate for the mood of the scene? Is the location dark and gloomy? Bright and cheery?

- Is there enough electrical power to run movie lights? (If you're not working with experienced gaffers, the equipment rental house can advise you on the recommended amperage of electrical circuits for the lights you're using.) Where are the outlets and breaker boxes? Can extension cords be run to outlets on separate circuits to avoid overloads?

- How do local electrical and fire codes apply to this location?

- What's the drill if your lights overload a circuit and blow a breaker? Will the crew have access to the breaker panel, or must a building maintenance person be available?

- If local power isn't sufficient, you'll need to rent a portable gasoline or diesel generator; this can be a significant expense. Where can you place the generator so its power lines will reach the set but its noise won't interfere with shooting? Where can you bring the lines into the location? (The best movie generators are so quiet they can be placed almost anywhere.)

- How many windows does the set include? If you plan to use tungsten movie lights indoors, will it be practical to gel or mask the windows to achieve color balance? If so, how many square feet of CTO gel or masking will you need, and how much time and labor expense will be involved in putting it up and taking it down?

- Can ceiling lights and other available light sources be turned on and off? Masked? Can any of them provide motivation for movie lighting?

- If you're shooting outside, is there a shaded area where you can shoot to avoid having to use high-powered fill lights or reflectors? Where will the sun be at various times on shoot day? How will having to deal with bright sunlight affect your lighting plan?

Sound Considerations

Review the audio requirements listed in Chapter 7. Then go to the location and ask yourself:

- Do the acoustics of the room match your expectations about the quality of sound in the scene? For instance, does it have an echo?

- What type of heating, ventilation, and air conditioning does the location have? How noisy is it? Can it be turned off during a take? Can you gain access to the controls?

- Is any heavy machinery, such as a compressor or a refrigerator, located near the set? Can it be turned off during a take? Can you gain access to the controls?

- Is the set near a busy city street where trucks and buses travel? Is the location on the approach pattern of an airport? Is it near a hospital or fire station where sirens might blare? Is it near a parking structure with frequent car alarms?

- What ambient noise can you detect in the room? What other sources of noise would you expect to hear on shoot day?

SHOOTING OFFSHORE—OR OUT OF STATE

Your choice of shooting locale may have financial as well as aesthetic implications. Many municipalities, states, and even foreign governments offer inducements to encourage you to shoot—and spend money—on their turf.

U.S. tax law once provided incentives for investment in movies, but these provisions were eliminated years ago. However, government subsidies for film investment still exist in other countries.

Incentives for offshore production often take the form of direct subsidies paid to production units rather than investors. Much of the time, the subsidy is tied to moving some or all of your production to the country in question and contributing to local employment. For example, producers may apply for credits on sales taxes for meals and lodging, payroll taxes on wages paid to local workers, or even a percentage of the production's expenditures within the country.

Additional savings may result from the fact that while specialists such as DPs, set designers, and set construction crews in foreign film production centers like Rome and Prague are highly skilled, they don't command Hollywood rates. Additional financial benefits show up as savings on equipment rentals and local labor rates.

The tradeoff is the significant travel and subsistence expenses for flying your cast and crew to a remote location.

U.S. film workers aren't pleased about such "runaway productions," particularly those shooting in Vancouver, Canada, which has excellent production facilities, a skilled local work force, and generous government-sponsored incentives. California's legislators continue to talk with the industry about trying to prevent productions from leaving the state, but the issue probably won't be resolved any time soon.

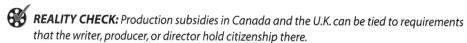 **REALITY CHECK:** *Production subsidies in Canada and the U.K. can be tied to requirements that the writer, producer, or director hold citizenship there.*

State film commissions may send photos and other helpful information on suitable places to shoot, clarify local labor laws and electrical codes, obtain police cooperation, make it easier to shoot in public facilities, coordinate (and possibly waive) location fees, and provide tax subsidies or rebates.

Another reason producers like to shoot in remote locations is to avoid the strong union cultures in major production centers like Los Angeles and New York. Although experienced union workers often have the know-how to work quickly, efficiently, and safely, combining union and non-union people on the same crew to save money can be a challenge in places where the unions have strong influence. For example, do your drivers need to be Teamsters?

Bottom line: You can save plenty of money if you do some research before committing to a location. There's lots of information available on the Web and from filmmakers' organizations such as the Independent Feature Project (*www.ifp.org*).

MEET YOUR CREW

Previous chapters have introduced you to many of the technicians in the departments of Electrical Operations, Camera Operations, and Sound Operations. On a full-scale film-style production, there are lots more skilled people on a set. Here are some of their job descriptions and reporting relationships:

- **First assistant director (AD)** is the director's primary assistant, responsible for supervising operations on the set. She has control over the shooting schedule and is responsible for keeping to it. At any point, if the crew isn't shooting, the AD's job is to know exactly what it's waiting for and how long it will take.

- **Second AD** assists the First AD. He is usually responsible for some kinds of record keeping and for getting cast members to and from the set.

- **Production manager** reports to a line producer and oversees the budget, hires crew, and approves payments. Although production manager responsibilities are often assumed by producers, this job is considered a below-the-line function. (See "Above the Line, Below the Line" later in this chapter.)

- **Location manager** is responsible for securing locations as well as supervising the set construction. Location manager is usually a studio job, and even then a producer often does it. Or she may report to the producer or line producer. Although location manager responsibilities are often assumed by producers, this job is considered a below-the-line function.

- **Set construction crew** reports to the line producer or production manager. Specific job categories may include supervisor, builder, and painter. The team that actually assembles a set is called the *swing gang,* not because of the timing of their shift but presumably because they flail away with hammers.

> **SWING GANG:** Team within a set construction crew that assembles a set.

- **Production designer** works with the DP and designers in other creative departments. He's primarily responsible for the look of the movie. Sometimes known as art director.

- **Set decorator/designer and dressers** are responsible for the interior decorating that makes a set look real. Their department reports to the production designer.

- **Costume designer/dressers** belong to another creative department that reports to the production designer.

- **Makeup and hair** is a creative department that reports to the production designer.

- **Special effects crew** reports to the director or to the DP and devises and rigs all kinds of cinematic tricks done on the set, such as knife-throwing scenes and exploding *squibs* of red dye to simulate bullet wounds.

- **Production assistant (PA)** is an all-around assistant (or *go-fer*) to various production crew members. Often an intern or apprentice.

- **Prop master** is responsible for all props or objects used in on-screen actions. She reports to the production designer.

- **Prop technicians** bring props to and from the set, rig them, and instruct actors in their use. They report to the prop master.

- **Transportation crew** must be members of the Teamsters union, at least on a union set. These drivers handle anything with an engine and wheels: cars, vans, and limos for actors and crew; trucks for equipment; actors' trailers (mobile dressing rooms); portable restroom vehicles (called *honey wagons*), crane trucks, and trailers that carry electrical generators.

> **SQUIB:** Small explosive charge worn by an actor; when fired by remote control, simulates a gunshot wound.
>
> **HONEY WAGON:** Rolling portable toilet facility for use on movie locations.

STAFFING REQUIREMENTS

Staffing a film-style production poses many of the same challenges whether you're shooting a Hollywood feature or an inexpensive training video. The only significant difference between big-budget studio productions and low-budget indies is how many hats you ask people to wear.

Above the Line, Below the Line

For purposes of planning and budgeting, salaries on movie projects are traditionally divided into two categories.

Above-the-Line Salaries

These expenses include "high-profile" (and often high-priced) personnel like directors, writers, producers, and leading actors. Although their minimum compensation may be set by unions and craft guilds, what you actually end up paying will usually be a matter of negotiation based on the perceived value of a person's creative contribution and level of experience. Above-the-line salaries are often based on a percentage of the overall budget or sometimes a percentage of the profits in addition to a set fee. Nonprincipal actors and stunt people will usually receive no-more-than-minimum salaries based on standard union rates.

> **FALL:** Single performance of any type of stunt, even if it doesn't involve falling.

> **NOTE:** *Stunt people get paid per fall. Fees depend on the degree of difficulty and danger involved.*

Typical percentages used in the motion-picture industry for estimating above-the-line salaries are shown in **Table 8.1**.

Table 8.1 Typical Above-the-Line Salaries as Percent of Budget

Director	5%
Producer	5%
Writer	2.5%
Actors	28%

Above-the-line artists often receive salaries based on percentages of the overall budget as negotiated by their agents and managers. As well, above-the-line credits typically (but not always) appear at the head of the movie, below-the-line at the tail.

Below-the-Line Salaries

Expenses in this category include all the "other" people who work on a set or provide transportation. By convention, salaries for editors and assistant editors are also shown below the line.

Factors that affect below-the-line crew selection and budgeting include:

Technical requirements. Make your decisions about how many on-set technicians to hire based on how many lights, microphones, and audio channels they will have to rig as well as the relative complexity of camera rigs and movement. (For more information on technical requirements for lighting and sound, see "Lighting Techniques" in Chapter 6 and

"Sound Techniques" in Chapter 7.) If your plans include wireless audio, covering large window areas with CTO gel, doing crane shots, rigging stunts, or running a portable electrical generator, you'll need to budget for additional labor expenses.

> **CATERING:** Meals served to cast and crew on the set.
>
> **CRAFT SERVICES:** Snacks and beverages made available to cast and crew on the set.

Support services for larger productions. As the complexity of your production increases, so will your need for transportation, *catering* (meals), and *craft services* (snacks) to support additional crew members. As the size of the cast increases, you'll need more people working in wardrobe, makeup, and hairdressing. As the size of your total crew increases, you'll need more administrative and secretarial support, roles typically filled by production assistants.

Budgetary level and union jurisdiction. Your overall budget will determine the experience, skill, and degree of specialization of the people you can afford to hire. Experienced people tend to be union members, so specific jurisdictions and work rules apply to professional productions with big budgets.

In setting rules and pay scales, the various craft unions and guilds follow budgetary divisions established by the above-the-line guilds—the Directors Guild of America (DGA), Writers Guild of America (WGA), and Screen Actors Guild (SAG). Television actors are usually covered by the American Federation of Television and Radio Artists—AFTRA.

 REALITY CHECK: *For decades now, actors' unions SAG and AFTRA have made attempts at merging. Since many professional actors belong to both organizations and pay dues to both, proponents argue that a combined union would be more powerful and efficient. The issue is far from being resolved, however. From your standpoint as a production planner, be aware that different unions sometimes claim jurisdiction over the same or similar functions.*

For example, all the above-the-line guilds agree on two basic pay scales for feature production: High Budget (above $2 million total) and Low Budget (less than $2 million). In practice, however, budget categories for features break down as follows:

* High-budget union production: Total budget $10 million or above. Typical of motion pictures produced by major studios and intended for theatrical release.

    > **NOTE:** *Signing a major star might cost an additional $10 million in salary, and the decision will have a ripple effect on the below-the-line budget as well. You can't ask a star to dress in the restroom, so there's the cost of a trailer and its driver. You'll also have to add additional costs such as private auto transportation, dresser, assistant, makeup, hair, and so on. Furthermore, a star will often demand a specific co-star, writer, director, or DP, whose salaries might be well above what you've budgeted. We've even heard of a star requesting his own sound technician to make sure the quality of his voice recording was just right.*

- High-budget nonunion production: Total budget $2-10 million. Typical of movies produced for television, cable, or direct-to-video release by independent producers who hold contracts with distributors.

- Low-budget union or nonunion: Total budget under $2 million. Typical of independent features produced for future sale or license without prior guarantees of distribution. Note that SAG, WGA, and DGA all have "Low Budget" contracts. However, the terms and conditions of these contracts may vary from one guild to another. Be sure to check with each guild to see how its guidelines apply to the specific circumstances of your project.

- Ultra-low budget and experimental: Total budget under $500,000, which includes most independent DV features. To make it possible for low-budget producers to use union actors, SAG has a special Experimental Film Agreement. Under this agreement, actors' salaries may be deferred if the total budget (non-deferred) is $75,000 or less and the entire production is shot in the United States. (Other rules apply as well.) Although crew members usually won't work for deferred pay, they tend to respect the sanction of other unions. For example, you may have some negotiating flexibility on below-the-line labor rates if your production is sanctioned as a SAG Experimental project. The DGA also has an Experimental contract, but it's intended primarily for sanctioning directors making sample reels not intended for commercial distribution. Here's another instance where the name of the contract and budgetary category is the same but the terms and conditions differ between the guilds.

 REALITY CHECK: For a project to be sanctioned by SAG in the Experimental category, you must submit your shooting script and budget to the union for review. Don't do this without adequate preparation, because you generally get one chance to get it right. The union is understandably suspicious of producers who might claim low-budget status with the intention of avoiding the usual working rules.

> **STRIKE:** To take down a set and pack up equipment in preparation for moving to another location.

Time constraints. If you have access to a location for only a limited time, you may need to increase crew size so you can get the work done in the time allowed. (If the police are blocking off a city street for you, be prepared to move fast.) Staffing up on gaffers, grips, PAs, and set dressers can save setup and *strike* (take-down) time. However, no matter how you double up on work roles, you can't do much to compress the time required to transport equipment or to dress actors, and you can't make shooting go faster unless you're willing to shoot fewer takes.

How to Employ a Name Writer on Deferred Pay

Responding to the explosion of indie feature productions, in 2003 the WGA instituted the Independent Writers Caucus. Its purpose is to sanction and promote involvement of WGA writers in low-budget productions, permitting producers to defer payment of some or all screenwriting fees until the movie has made money or is in distribution. (In some cases, at somewhat higher budgets, a portion of the fee will be due upon the first day of principal photography.) These deals are implemented by a union contract called "The WGA Low Budget Agreement," which covers the purchase of an existing script and one rewrite. If a producer intends to purchase such a script, the writer must apply to the Guild for coverage under this contract.

Be aware that the Guild minimum fees are no different under this contract than for studio projects—the agreement only affects the timing of the payments. (For more information, visit www.wga.org.)

A producer can't use this agreement to hire a WGA writer to develop a new script from scratch. It only applies to independently written scripts. And under any circumstances, WGA writers are prohibited from writing scripts on speculation ("on spec"), meaning that a producer can't ask them to write a script from scratch with payment being conditional—based on whether the producer or backers like the script, the project gets financed, a star becomes interested, and so on.

ON SPECULATION: Practice of working (usually writing) for a producer with payment conditional on some future event or decision; writing a spec script; on spec.

However, the Guild does not prevent its members from initiating or developing scripts on their own initiative and on their own time. Every screenwriter, whether he's commercially successful or not, has his own stories and pet projects. It's the sale of these scripts as indie projects that the Low Budget Agreement covers.

So, if you can find a talented writer who has a script on the shelf, the WGA has made it possible for you to hire that writer and defer the fee with its blessing. You can find finished scripts online, including synopses and full manuscripts by both new and established writers, at www.inktip.com. You'll have to register at the site and prove your status as a bona fide producer to gain access. InkTip also has a listing of scripts for shorts, which are not covered by the WGA. Fees for shorts are open and negotiable with the individual writers.

Crew Roster for a Full-Scale Film-Style Shoot

Shown in **Table 8.2** are the job titles on a movie set, grouped by department. The second and third columns suggest how to scale down crews for lower-budget productions.

Depending on the scaling factors we've just described, there can easily be a hundred people on the crew. Big crews have multiple gaffers, grips, sound technicians, wardrobe and hair technicians, set builders, painters, production assistants, caterers, craft service people, and drivers. In general, there will only be one DP and one first assistant director, unless the production uses a second unit to capture supplementary footage.

Table 8.2 Below-the-Line Crew

Full-Scale	Low-Budget	Ultra-Low Budget
Production Staff		
First Assistant Director (AD)	✓	(Director fills in)
Second AD	(PA fills in)	(PA fills in)
Script Supervisor	✓	(Director fills in)
Production Manager	(Producer fills in)	(Producer fills in)
Location Manager	(Producer fills in)	(Producer fills in)
Production Designer	(Creative dept. heads fill in)	(Not used)
Catering	✓ (or PAs fill in)	(PAs fill in)
Craft Services	(PAs fill in)	(PAs fill in)
Production Assistants (PAs)	✓	✓
Set Construction		
Construction Supervisor	(AD fills in)	(Use real location)
Builders	(PAs fill in)	(Use real location)
Painters	(PAs fill in)	(Use location as is)
Special Effects		
Effects Supervisor	(No special effects)	(No special effects)
Technicians	(No special effects)	(No special effects)
Set Dressing		
Decorator/Designer	(Director fills in)	(Director fills in)
Set Dressers	(PAs fill in)	(Use location as is, or PAs)
Property		
Prop Master	(AD fills in)	(PA fills in)
Prop Technicians	(PAs fill in)	(PAs or actors fill in)
Wardrobe		
Costume Designer	(Director fills in)	(Director and actors fill in)
Dressers	(PAs fill in)	(Actors fill in)

Table 8.2 Below-the-Line Crew *(continued)*

Makeup and Hairdressing

Lead Makeup Artist	(Not used)	(Not used)
Makeup/Hair Technicians	✓	(Actors fill in)

Electrical Operations

Key Grip	✓	(DP/Director/PA fills in)
Lead Gaffer	✓	(DP supervises PAs)
Best Boy/First Assistant	✓	(PA fills in)
Rigging Gaffers	(Lead gaffer/grips/PAs fill in)	(PAs fill in)
Generator Operator	(Not used)	(Not used)
Lamp Operators	(Grips fill in)	(Not used)
Set Wiremen	(Grips fill in)	(PAs fill in)
Grips	✓	(PAs fill in)

Camera Operations

Director of Photography (DP)	✓	(Director fills in)
Camera Operator	(DP fills in)	(Director fills in)
First Asst. Camera Operator	✓	(optional; PA fills in)
Second Asst. Camera Operator	(PA fills in)	(PA fills in)
Dolly Grip	✓	(PA fills in)

Sound Operations

Sound Mixer	✓	(Boom operator fills in)
Sound Recordist	(Mixer fills in)	(In-camera)
Boom Operator	✓	✓
Rigging Technicians	(Grips or PAs fill in)	(PAs fill in)

Transportation

Transportation Coordinator	(AD schedules)	(Producer fills in)
Driver Captain	(Not used)	(Not used)
Drivers	✓ (or PAs fill in)	(PAs fill in)

The special-effects people listed in the table are technicians who rig stunts and visual effects on the set, but they are grouped in the same budget category as the people who create synthetic effects in post.

> **SET DRESSING:** Furnishings and decorations on a movie set.

There's a strict distinction between *set dressing* and props. Set dressing covers furnishings and decorations. A prop is an object that an actor holds or manipulates in the action. This distinction becomes important both for job descriptions and for breaking down your script.

Crew Roster for a Low-Budget Film-Style Shoot

The second column of **Table 8.2** notes the personnel you'll need to hire for a low-budget production.

One key difference between high- and low-budget operations is the size of the camera crew. Normally, on a full-scale production, the camera crew has at least five members. In low-budget operations, the DP often doubles as camera operator; you still need a focus puller, but you can use PAs as second assistants and dolly grips.

Although the table shows two people in the low-budget sound department, you may be able to shoot with just one skilled sound technician if you have the boom operator wear a lightweight portable mixer.

On low-budget productions, it's common for production assistants and interns to work as gaffers, but for safety's sake they should be supervised by an experienced electrician.

As a rule of thumb, figure that even a low-budget feature might have as many as 25 people on the set, including cast and crew. Keep that figure in mind when you plan meals and transportation.

Crew Roster for Ultra-Low-Budget Shoots

As the third column of **Table 8.2** shows, you can get by with a very small crew, provided you keep sets and setups simple. In fact, you can do bare-bones film-style shooting with just three people:

- DP/camera operator
- Boom operator/mixer
- Production assistant

If you want to minimize equipment, transportation, and labor expenses, use available light and have the production assistant carry a bounce board. (For more information on lighting run-and-gun shoots, see "Three-Point Lighting, News Style" in Chapter 6.) If you can afford to add a fourth person to your economy-class crew, make him a focus puller and use cinema-style lenses with markings.

If you're trying to motivate people to join an ultra-low-budget shoot, an effective strategy is to offer them a position somewhat above their experience level. For example, promote a PA to a second camera assistant, a second AD to first AD, and so on. Bear in mind that it may take the person some time to get up to speed.

> **TIP:** *The more hats you ask people to wear, the longer shooting will take. There's a financial trade-off between adding extra people and paying for additional shooting days and equipment rental.*

Do You Need Specialists?

Some jobs relate directly to the type of project you're shooting and its content. Here are a few examples:

- *Product technical specialists for commercials, to advise on correct or safe use of products and rigging of demonstrations*
- *Hand models or people with special skills for demonstrations*
- *Pyrotechnical experts for creating fires and explosions*
- *Firearms experts, effects riggers, and handlers*
- *Technical advisors for historical or scientific content*
- *Musicians to advise actors who must appear to be playing musical instruments*
- *Police for crowd and vehicle control in public areas; private security guards for audience control on shooting stages and protection of actors when shooting in dark or dangerous urban areas*
- *Standby medical team*
- *Technicians to create weather effects—rain, snow, wind, or fog*
- *Stunt actors and stunt coordinators*
- *Teleprompter operators*
- *Standby painters (unlike construction painters, must be on-call to fix scenery between takes)*
- *Dialect coaches and interpreters*
- *Production photographer*
- *Body doubles for actors*
- *Greensmen (bring trees and shrubs)*
- *Specialty drivers for shooting exotic vehicles or chase scenes*
- *Helicopter pilots for aerial shots*
- *Martial arts advisors/choreographers for combat scenes*
- *Instructors and caregivers for child actors*
- *Animal wranglers*

Calculate Crew Salaries

Crew salaries vary widely by specialty, union affiliation, industry segment (commercial, interactive video, and so on), and metropolitan area. Daily and weekly rates depend on whether a crew member is a grip or a gaffer, a member of IATSE or NABET (and seniority level), works in television, film or industrials, and the production is shooting in Los Angeles, Chicago, New York, or Atlanta. For example, an experienced DP might make as much as $25,000 for a five-day week on a big-budget movie; the same week on a low-budget shoot might pay just $3,000.

 REALITY CHECK: *IATSE and NABET are another example of unions with potentially overlapping jurisdictions. In fact, besides all kinds of below-the-line crew, IATSE has traditionally represented animators. More recently, WGA claimed representation for writers of animation. One jurisdictional dispute erupted in mid-2003 when producer Dreamworks asserted that the animator/writers on a particular project were covered by IATSE rather than WGA.*

Rates for other below-the-line jobs don't vary quite so much. According to currently prevailing rates in Los Angeles, the average crew member makes $2,000 to $3,000 per week on a high-budget movie, $500 to $2,000 on a low-budget movie, and between zip and $500 on an experimental film. A production assistant on a low-budget project might make $25-75 per day (or nothing more than mileage expense and lunch if he's an intern).

Different rates and working rules apply to different segments of the media industry. Currently, SAG has specific producer agreements for the following segments:

- Theatrical/television
- Commercials
- Industrial/educational
- Interactive media
- Low-budget (the under-$2-million category described above)
- Experimental
- Performances by extras
- Internet presentations

Overtime and holiday rates apply, but unions have different rules about calculating them.

PENSION AND HEALTH (P&H): Fringe benefits stipulated by union contracts for actors and crew.

For any union member you hire, add approximately 14 percent of her salary to the budget to cover *pension and health (P&H)* benefits. Actual rates vary by union. Even if the union allows you to defer salary, the P&H contribution may have to be paid concurrently with the work.

Budgeting Resources

Many industry unions post labor rates on their web sites, with the caveat that rates are subject to their working rules (which can be complex).

Before you get too far in your budgeting, check the latest labor rates that apply to the jobs you need to assign. *EP Paymaster Rate Guide* is available in either book or Adobe Reader (PDF) format from Entertainment Partners (*www.entertainmentpartners.com*). This updated resource replaces a previous CD version called *Movie Magic Labor Rates,* a set of tables for use with Movie Magic Budgeting software. The *Industry Labor Guide* includes separate sets of tables covering major metropolitan areas in the United States. (For more information, visit *www.scriptdude.com*.)

Jeffords' Rules and Regulations is a pamphlet that lists labor information for many specialties. It's particularly useful if you're planning a union production that's not covered by special low-budget contracts or waivers. Compiled by the late Bob Jeffords, highly respected production manager on *Murphy Brown* and other major shows, it's available on request from the Directors Guild, but only for DGA members.

WHAT TO RENT, WHAT TO BUY

For a typical three-week DV shoot, it's generally more economical to rent camcorders, audio gear, and lights than to buy them. Furthermore, you can rent better equipment than you can buy for the same amount of money.

> **FOVEON CHIP TECHNOLOGY:** Single-chip digital-camera image sensing that relies on the optical principle that red, green, and blue light penetrate the chip's silicon layers at different depths—possibly emulating the behavior of conventional film stock better than three-chip CCD designs.

A possible exception is camcorders. Every camera operator wants her own camcorder and grows to love (or hate) the way it handles and responds. But when you think about how fast DV technology is changing—especially with the advent of prosumer 24P and the prospects of *Foveon chip technology*—anyone but a career videographer should think carefully before investing several thousand dollars in a camera that won't be the latest and greatest for very long.

The figures in **Table 8.3** compare rental versus purchase prices for three major categories of production equipment.

> **TIP:** Some videomakers like to buy nice new gear for a shoot and then resell it when the production wraps.

These figures show that you can rent high-quality professional gear for about the same amount of money you'd need to purchase prosumer gear. Similarly, you can rent prosumer gear for nearly the purchase price of low-end gear. (Prices compiled by Bruce R. Cook from outlets and rental houses in the Los Angeles area.)

Table 8.3 Purchase Price vs. Three-Week Rental

Purchase	High-End (Pro Level)	Mid-Range (Prosumer Level)	Low-End
Camcorder, tripod, lenses, accessories	$ 6,000	$ 4,000	$ 2,000
Audio mixer, boom mic, accessories	$ 3,000	$ 1,300	$ 600
Lighting kit, accessories	$ 1,800	$ 900	$ 0*
Total Purchase	**$ 10,800**	**$ 6,200**	**$ 2,600**
Rent (3 weeks)			
Camcorder, tripod, lenses, accessories	$ 3,000	$ 1,500	$ 1,000
Audio mixer, boom mic, accessories	$ 2,100	$ 600	$ 500
Lighting kit, accessories	$ 900	$ 600	$ 0*
Total Rental	**$ 6,000**	**$ 2,700**	**$ 1,500**

* Use available light

Dealing with Rental Houses

Here are some pointers on dealing with equipment rental houses. They are designed to help you get what you need and keep the rental staffers on your side for this production—and the next.

Secure a Business Line of Credit

Depending on the rental agency's policy, you will probably have to apply for a credit account and provide evidence of insurance well in advance of walking out the door with your stuff—or secure your rental with a credit card. A far more cost-effective alternative to using a retail credit card is to apply for a business line of credit with a third-party lender, such as a bank or finance company. The commercial interest rate could be easily half the cost of retail credit.

 REALITY CHECK: Financing your production with credit cards may seem attractive, especially with low promotional interest rates. Beware of exceptionally low rates, however, and read the fine print. Typically, if you miss a payment or are late for any reason (including being busy on location), the lender can raise the rate significantly higher, without further notice.

Rent the Right Stuff and Be Sure You Know How to Use It

Make sure you book the right equipment for the job. If you're in doubt, ask the tech support staff. Don't be shy about asking for training from the rental house or manufacturer either. It's a huge waste of time and money to rent expensive gear you or the crew doesn't know how to operate.

Always Horse Trade

Rental houses publish daily rates, but those rates are generally negotiable, especially for longer terms. Don't be afraid to haggle or ask for a better deal. Equipment sitting on the shelf isn't earning the rental agency any money. Furthermore, it's probably more profitable for the agency to let you keep the gear for another week at a slightly cheaper rate than to log the equipment back into inventory, inspect and recondition it, and turn it around.

As a rule of thumb, you should be able to get a weekly rental rate (five shooting days) at two to four times the daily rate. A monthly deal should run no more than 8 to 12 times the daily rate. Slow times in the industry are great opportunities for you to get bargain rates.

Always Get Spares

Be sure to include spares and consumables in your rental deal: extra halogen lamps, mic batteries, gels, black wrap, gaffer's tape, and so on. Even if the rental agency's prices are slightly higher than those of a supply house, it won't be worth your additional time, labor, and fuel expense to make separate runs just to save a few pennies on those items.

BREAKING DOWN THE SCRIPT

Breaking down your script is the first step in preparing a schedule and calculating a budget. The breakdown lists every element (cast, crew, equipment, materials, and so on) you'll need for each scene in your production (**Figure 8.2**). You can do a breakdown manually, or use a computer application like Movie Magic Scheduling.

> **SCRIPT BREAKDOWN SHEET:** List of production items and budgetary elements specified in a script for one scene.

If you're doing a manual breakdown, you'll start by annotating various elements in your script with color-coded markers. (See **Table 8.4** for standard color-coding conventions.) Then you'll list the elements by category on a *script breakdown sheet,* one sheet for each scene in the script.

Script Breakdown Sheet

Date: 08/01/XX

Production Company: Peachpit Press
Production Title: "When Harried Met Sally"
Breakdown Page No.: 3
Scene No.: 3
Scene Name: Josh's Office – Atwater/Phil
Int/Ext.: INT
Day or Night: DAY
Page Count: 3

Cast:	Stunts:	Extras/Atmosphere:
Josh Atwater Phil	None	None

Special Effects:	Extras/Silent Bits:	Vehicles/Animals:
None	None	None

Wardrobe:	Props:	Sound Effects/Music:
Nothing special	Headset for Josh Computer monitor (practical) Computer (practical) Keyboard (practical)	Record wild keyboard FX

Special Equipment:
None

Makeup/Hair:
Nothing special

Production Notes:
Phil mentions
Hackey Sack –
need prop?

Figure 8.2 Here's the script breakdown for Scene 3 of *When Harried Met Sally*. In addition to listing the usual scene heading information and cast members, the only notable breakdown items are props, a sound effect, and production notes.

Table 8.4 Script Breakdown Categories and Coding Conventions

Script Element	Description	Color or Mark
Scene number	Sequential number in the script	List in sheet heading
Scene name	Usually the name of the set, *e.g.*, "Josh's Office"	List in sheet heading
Breakdown page number	Sequential number of breakdown page, not the scene number; stays the same as you rearrange shooting days	List in sheet heading
Interior or exterior, day or night	Day Exterior Night Exterior Day Interior Night Interior	Write in heading; yellow Write in heading; green Write in heading; white Write in heading; blue
Page count	Number of script pages in the scene; helps estimate number of shooting days needed	Write in heading; show fractional pages as eighths ($\frac{1}{2}$ page = $\frac{4}{8}$)
Cast	Principal actors who must be on set for the scene	Red
Stunts	Events and actions, not names of actors or stunt technicians	Orange
Extras/silent bits	Nonspeaking actors who have specific actions to perform on camera	Yellow
Extras/atmosphere	Nonspeaking actors who have no specific actions to perform on camera	Green
Special effects	Created wholly or partially on the set, not just in post	Blue
Props	An object an actor needs for a specific action on camera	Violet
Vehicles/animals	Specifically called for in the action; not background or atmosphere	Pink
Wardrobe	Unusual or exceptional items; *e.g.*, duplicate items of clothing that must be on hand if original will be soiled or torn in the action	Circle the item in the script
Makeup/hair	Anything unusual	Place an asterisk beside the character name/ action in the script
Sound effects/music	Performed on the set, not added in post; *e.g.*, live musicians or audio playback	Brown
Special equipment	Crane, fog machine, etc.	Draw box around the action in the script
Production notes	Possible problems; reminders; questions about details for director; body doubles or stand-ins	Summarize on breakdown sheet

Each element has a standard color or mark, and although scheduling software is supposed to eliminate the need for color marking, it still follows motion-picture industry color-coding conventions. One main reason for doing this is to enable the creation of a *manual production board* (also called a *strip board*), which shows the sequence of production days and required elements on color-coded strips. Many producers who are quite expert with computer-assisted scheduling still use a color printer to output strips for a manual production board to be used by the production manager and First AD on the set.

> **MANUAL PRODUCTION BOARD:** Color-coded production schedule in which each vertical paper strip holds the information for one scene, and scenes are arranged in the calendar order in which they will be shot; first AD or second AD has custody of the board on the set; strip board.

A script breakdown deconstructs your movie into the specific elements you need to get each scene on the screen. When marking up your script, you don't have to use the industry-standard coding conventions shown in the third column, but experienced directors and production managers will expect to see production boards with the elements color-coded in standard style.

Once you've finished your breakdown sheets, make lists of like-coded items and determine the crew specialties and production resources required to put them on the set under normal working conditions. Related labor activities may include procurement, transportation, construction, rigging, operations, and striking. For more information on how your breakdown sheets become inputs to the scheduling process, see "Sort Elements to Produce a Schedule" later in this chapter.

CASTING AND IMPROVISATION FOR DV

The high cost of film discourages directors and producers from shooting repeated takes and extra coverage. Improvisation is often equated with irresponsibility. However, compared to the cost of film stock and processing, shooting DV tape is so cheap you might as well think of it as free.

In the world of DV, it costs you nothing to record as many takes as you like within the limited time of the shooting day. Hence, there's much less pressure to follow a structured approach. Improvisational styles don't come at such financial premium, especially if you get results. This can have a big impact on casting actors.

In turn, your approach to casting and rehearsal impacts not only how you plan to work on the set but also how many days you allow for production.

The Casting Process

When you're casting a DV production, you don't necessarily need actors who can repeat a take exactly the same way each time; you can encourage variety in their interpretations. Look for actors who are spontaneous and directable.

Many DV productions are low budget. In fact, they probably wouldn't exist as projects at all if the gear weren't so cheap. A corollary is that when you're casting this type of production, you may find yourself forced to work with actors who are either inexperienced or who have no formal training.

Although you want the most skilled actors you can find, lack of experience needn't be a show-stopper *if* you know what to look for when you're casting and how to work with your actors.

DV Auditions

Evaluate all actors—regardless of experience level—using a structured audition process:

HEADSHOT: Actor's publicity photo, typically with a resume printed on the back or stapled to it; photo and resume (P&R).

When you hold auditions, start off by trying to put the actor at ease. Even a pro can be tense and anxious in these situations. As the actor enters and presents you with his *headshot*, chat a while to let him know it's okay to relax.

Choose scenes that require reacting as much as speaking. You want actors who are expressive when they're listening—artists who can re-create a rich inner emotional life and let it play on their faces. Keep the camera trained on the actor throughout the session, while another actor or PA reads the other character's lines off-camera.

Videotape three readings. Politely decline to give the actor any information or coaching before the first reading; encourage her to give her own interpretation the first time out. You want to observe her instincts.

The second time, give the actor some direction—nudging her toward the performance you want. If the actor is directable, you'll observe a change from the first reading.

On the third reading, coach the actor to go in the opposite direction—comic instead of dramatic, confident instead of frightened. Again, watch for any change. The most interesting differences may be in her reactions. Study the reactions when you play back the tape later.

Inexperienced actors may have trouble incorporating your suggestions and will give you the same, uninspired performance each time. These actors are neither spontaneous nor directable.

Other actors with more experience might have preconceived notions about the character. The first reading might be brilliant—but you'll see it over and over. Unless this interpretation is exactly what you're looking for, you don't want to cast these actors, either.

The kind of actor you want will give a fresh, spontaneous reading each time. On the set, her performance will be different on each take—changing in response to suggestions you give. If you insist on 35 takes, even the last one will be different.

You may discover that actors who have learned improvisational techniques, or who have television or film experience, are better suited to DV productions than actors with traditional theatrical training, which often concentrates on polished, repeatable performances.

> **NOTE:** On higher-budget productions, hire a casting director to assist you with this process. He can screen hundreds of submissions and present you with a few promising ones. He will also have access to the agents and personal managers of name talent, as well as be aware of which co-stars have worked well together or might be looking for opportunities to work together. Some very successful actors are approachable about working in indie productions, and the casting director should know who they are.

If you're taping real people for interviews and documentaries, you won't be grilling them this thoroughly. But you should still keep in mind the qualities of freshness and spontaneity that you want on the screen. If you have a choice, pick people who are comfortable in front of the camera and who are expressive and animated in their speech and gestures.

Work with Actors During Casting and Rehearsals

Although techniques for working with actors are properly part of the shooting process, you'll need them as soon as you start casting and holding auditions. (For more information, see "Working with Actors" in Chapter 9.)

For starters, any director who coaches actors by telling them the desired result is using the wrong mindset.

Give actors suggestions as actions to perform, not as qualities for them to be.

For example, don't say, "You need to be on the other side of the room." Say, "You forgot your keys. Go back for them."

Don't say, "Be sexy." Say, "Seduce him."

Cast for Special Skills

If you're shooting a training presentation or commercial that involves some kind of demonstration or instruction, the subjects' special skills will figure strongly in your choices.

Teachers, politicians, trial lawyers, seminar leaders, and salespeople are used to public speaking and probably won't be shy about expressing themselves in front of a camera. Go for people who already know how to interact with an audience and think on their feet.

Here are some other characteristics to look for:

- Trained speakers can look straight into the camera and deliver an entire speech without averting their eyes or blinking. This makes the audience see them as persuasive and effective.

- Don't pick someone for a product demonstration based solely on his technical knowledge. Make sure he speaks clearly and has the manual dexterity and know-how to operate the product on camera. In general, salespeople give better demonstrations than engineers because it's their job to understand their prospects' expectations.

- Shoot tests of potential subjects. Many articulate and charming people freeze up when the movie lights come on.

REHEARSALS, BRIEFINGS, RUN-THROUGHS

It might seem like a contradiction, but you won't be successful with an improvisational production unless you and your cast plan for it very carefully.

For a feature-length production, whether structured or improvised, budget the time and money for one or two weeks of extended rehearsals in advance of shooting. Even interviews and documentaries can benefit from preliminary meetings. Make the subjects comfortable. Tell them what situations you'll be putting them in. Give them a list of questions to think about. Do a fake interview.

If you're rehearsing dramatic material, let the actors become familiar with their roles, lines, and actions. Encourage them to do their own research into dress and mannerisms and to ask questions. Let actors, trainers, product demo people, and interview subjects handle any props they must manipulate on camera, try on costumes, and see the set designs.

Be sure to let on-screen talent know how much improvisation you'll allow on the set and where they should set the boundaries of their experimentation.

Know when to stop rehearsing. Once the actors know their lines and you've all agreed on the action, it's time to move on, even if you haven't seen the flash of brilliance you're expecting. That flash may happen only once, and you want it to be on the set, in front of a rolling camera.

SCHEDULING AND BUDGETING FOR DIGITAL VIDEO PRODUCTION

Scheduling and budgeting for DV production are highly complex activities—and hard-won professional skills. We can't possibly cover the whole process here. A pair of software packages can help you do the job: Movie Magic Scheduling and its companion, Movie Magic Budgeting. Or you can do your scheduling the manual way, using color-coded markers and breakdown sheets as described in the bible of production managers: *Film Scheduling,* by Ralph S. Singleton. But whichever approach to scheduling you choose, you can automate much of your budget preparation by using spreadsheet software.

> **NOTE:** *There are at least two software alternatives for the budgeting process. For production companies with ongoing projects such as TV series and computer-based accounting systems, Entertainment Partners has developed EP Budgeting. This program can import Movie Magic Budgeting files and also integrates with the company's EP Vista accounting and payroll system. For budgeters on a more modest budget, consider Easy Budget (www.scriptdude.com), which works with your own spreadsheet software.*

Scheduling

As previously noted, many full-scale film features have six-week (or longer) shooting schedules. Low-budget productions, including DV features, often shoot either three six-day weeks or two consecutive seven-day weeks.

The 14-day schedule is more feasible if you can use a second unit—perhaps not even shooting concurrently—to capture establishing shots, inserts, and actors in non-speaking roles. If you're borrowing nonprofessional or deferred-pay actors from their day jobs, these people can probably arrange two-week vacations without jeopardizing their employment.

How Many Setups Can You Do in a Day?

DV productions, which are often fast and light on their feet due to smaller crews and lighter equipment, have been known to shoot as many as eight script pages per day. It's easier to hit this mark if you shoot mostly interiors in smaller rooms and minimize the number of setups. For instance, if you're planning an ultra-low-budget production, try setting most of the action in the same house.

Another way to save time is to plan for less time to light. Achieving balanced light levels when shooting interiors often goes faster in DV than film because, with the relatively narrow contrast range and low-light sensitivity of video, it's usually just as effective to take away light as it is to add it. You can use modest-sized light kits, which require fewer grips and gaffers and less transportation and setup time.

Working at the same location (especially if you don't need to build sets), you can usually shoot two or three master scenes in a day, each with several setups. Remember, each time you move the camera to a new position, it can take anywhere from 15 to 45 minutes to relight. (For more information, including the challenges of shooting exteriors, see "Lighting Techniques" in Chapter 6.)

In preparing your schedule, remember that moving to another location usually requires starting there the next day. Transporting, unloading, and setting up at a new location can easily take several hours. However, if you've got the crew members and equipment to spare, you can pick up speed by dispatching a separate crew to the new location to start getting set up while you're wrapping the shoot at the current location.

Some related factors to consider:

Setting up. Remember that setting up requires rigging lights and sound, set dressing, cast preparations, color balancing, and sound checks. Budget time for gaffers to take safety precautions, such as sandbagging stands and taping electrical lines to the floor.

Striking the set and transportation. It can take just as long to strike a set as it did to put it up in the first place. It's not just a matter of ripping everything down; you have a responsibility to return the facility to its original condition. And don't underestimate how long it takes to get equipment down to the loading dock, onto the truck, tied down, and driven across town.

Sort Elements to Produce a Schedule

Returning to your script breakdown sheets (each one devoted to a separate scene), the scheduling process is essentially a matter of shuffling and sorting those scenes to group them so that needed resources (a fog machine, a leading actor) can be used as much as possible on continuous shooting days.

Try to sort your scenes using the following ordering system, each successive step being a finer degree of detail:

1. Locations you use the most

2. Different sets within the location

3. Exteriors before interiors (save interiors as contingency for rain days)

4. Days before nights (everyone will lose less sleep this way)

5. Continuous scheduling of principal actors

6. Continuous scheduling of special equipment, vehicles/animals, stunts, and effects

For example, you'd normally want to shoot all the scenes at a given location on successive days. But access to a location and the costs of moving locations aren't the only factors to consider. Even though your principal actors will probably be scheduled nearly every day of the shoot, it can be cost-effective to hire supporting players by the week (see "Actors' Schedules," later in this chapter). Therefore, it might be a better plan to sort all scenes involving those actors into the first week, even if it means an extra location move, then drop them from the payroll and return to the first location to get scenes involving only the principals in week two.

When you factor in other requirements, such as hiring special-effects crews for particular scenes, the scheduling process can grow quite complex. That's where scheduling software pays for itself; it lets you try different what-if scenarios to see where you can save time, money, or both. (For more information, see "Scheduling Software" later in this chapter.)

Constraints on Scheduling

Don't forget to factor the following constraints into your schedule.

Location Availability

One big limitation on your scheduling will be the hours during the day (or night) when a facility is available to you. Unless you're shooting on a sound stage, this will be largely beyond your control. You'll have to match up the day and night requirements in the script with the actual times of day the location is available.

Night Time Is the Right Time

Thanks to lighting technicalities, as well as the comfort of cast and crew, it's usually more practical to shoot day-for-night than actually shooting night scenes at night. That said, only way to capture an authentic after-dark look is to shoot after dark.

However, there's a catch: If you schedule 12 hours of nighttime shooting (say, 6 p.m. to 6 a.m.) be prepared to get only as much footage as a nine-hour daytime shoot. For some reason, crews work slower at night, even when they're well rested.

Actors' Schedules

Another big constraint on your schedule will be actors' availability, which is subject to SAG (or AFTRA) rules and industry practice. Even if you're shooting under the Experimental Agreement, you must adhere to these rules and keep accurate time records.

Your options for booking and scheduling actors are:

RUN OF SHOW: Type of employment contract extending for the duration of a shoot, requiring the worker to be on call every day.

DAY PLAYER: Actor whose services are hired for one specific shooting day.

PER DIEM: Daily pay rate; also, daily allowance for personal expenses such as meals and parking.

Run of show: Actor will be available and on call for the duration of the shooting schedule; used mainly for principal roles.

Weekly: Producer can drop actors from the payroll and pick them up later if the unpaid interval is at least 10 days; not used much on low-budget shooting because schedules aren't long enough to apply this rule.

Day player: Actor is scheduled for specific days; *per-diem* fee.

Children: Time-honored showbiz wisdom states, "Never work with children or animals." The advice was originally aimed at stars, who feared being upstaged by a cute rival, but it's still good advice for videomakers trying to prepare a reasonable schedule and budget. Labor regulations vary, but many states limit the number of hours a child can work on the set. For example, current law in California limits a child actor's workday during the school year to nine hours—five working, three being tutored at the producer's expense, one for rest and relaxation. You'll need to hire instructors and social workers as well.

Animals: Even highly trained animals are unpredictable. Do yourself a favor and write them out of the script (or use an actor in a bear suit).

Scheduling Software

We've touched on scheduling software several times already, but if you're new to production planning, we recommend that you do it manually the first time. There's something about marking a script, sorting the pages, and arranging strips on a production board that anchors the concepts and grounds you in the process.

Still, since most of us have co-dependent relationships with our computers, that suggestion may seem a bit outdated.

Basically, the computerized scheduling process for input to Movie Magic Scheduling works like this: First, you write your script using a word-processing application with the proper page layout. Then, you format your script text file as a Script Export (.SEX) file; Movie Magic Screenwriter and Final Draft scriptwriting programs can do this automatically. Then you import it into Movie Magic Scheduling, which extracts the slug lines of each scene (flagging whether they are Interior or Exterior, Day or Night), and lists cast members based on the character names it finds in the text.

How to Think Like an Experienced Production Scheduler

The real power and labor savings of production scheduling software is the ability to play "what if" games with the schedule. For those familiar with database software, it's a process of setting up queries—searching and sorting according to different criteria, often in combination. For example, you might search for INTERIOR NIGHT locations involving the CASTLE and both the actors LADY GUENIVERE and SIR LANCELOT but not KING ARTHUR. Your objective might be to schedule the love scenes, which you expect will take lots of time, and you don't want the poor king (your expensive senior actor) just standing around.

If database query seems like a foreign language, here's a way to get some grounding in its concepts. Transfer your breakdown sheets to colored index cards in four colors, one each for Interior/Day, Exterior/Day, Interior/Night, and Exterior Night. (Remember that Day and Night refer only to production shifts. An exterior scene shot at dawn or a twilight would normally be scheduled as an Exterior/ Day because it will be shot on a day shift in at least partial sunlight.)

It will probably feel more natural to shuffle cards than to rearrange strips on a stripboard. Try shuffling and arranging them in a preliminary schedule. Sort them by location, shooting day, and other criteria—one stack for each day, spread out on a large tabletop.

At the very least, taking this manual approach to scheduling will help you visualize the query process. But if your project is the least bit complex, it will motivate you all the more to conquer the learning curve of scheduling software, which will enable you to see many more possibilities with much less tedium.

TIP: Movie Magic Scheduling doesn't work well unless you're absolutely consistent about the names you give locations and settings in the slug lines of your script. For example, it will interpret EXT. HOSPITAL DRIVEWAY and EXT. HOSPITAL CIRCULAR DRIVE as two different locations.

Movie Magic Scheduling can save you time, but it can't do the thinking of an experienced production manager. For instance, it can't parse action paragraphs to extract props, effects, and so on. Nor can it interpret how an action description like "Mary jumps into the shower" might affect makeup and hair. So, once the program extracts as much scheduling information as it can from the script, you'll probably have to identify additional elements and enter their descriptions into the electronic breakdown sheets.

When you finally have all the data entered, scheduling software becomes a joy to use. You can sort and re-sort scenes and shooting days on your electronic production board any number of ways, using multiple priorities. You'll see ways to slice and dice the elements and days that might not otherwise have occurred to you.

Plan Ahead, Safety First!

Many accidents on the set are caused by the person responsible for creating the shooting schedule. If the schedule doesn't allow enough time for transportation, setup, and striking the set, your crew may be tempted to skip good practices and abbreviate safety procedures in their haste.

DEVELOPING A BUDGET

The budget for your project will combine labor rates for cast and crew, purchase and/or rental of equipment, cost of construction materials and props, and support services such as transportation and meals. The price of each resource will be multiplied by the number of days you'll need it.

By movie industry convention, each of the breakdown items in **Table 8.4** is associated with a specific budget category for accounting purposes. Accounting schemes vary, but in our sample budget Cast, Day Players, and Stunts are grouped under account number 1400; Special Effects goes into account 2600; all lighting equipment and gaffer services are listed in Electrical Rig, Operations, and Strike under account 3200, and so on.

TIP: Make sure your budget doesn't skimp on meals. Budget for catering and craft services, and have the staff prepare nutritious meals and serve them on schedule. Snacks are equally important: Cast and crew need to maintain their water intake, blood-sugar levels, and energy through long mornings and afternoons on the set.

You can import the data generated by Movie Magic Scheduling, which groups breakdown items by budget account, into budgeting programs. Or, many producers prefer to set up their own spreadsheets in a program like Microsoft Excel, listing account categories, costs, days, and subtotals.

Case Study: *Falling Like This*

Let's look at a sample budget. This one is for *Falling Like This,* an ultra-low-budget feature shot and edited on DV by Dani Minnick (director), Alessandro Zezza (DP/editor), John Diehl (actor/producer), and Lulu Zezza (producer). The film received a lot of attention in the indie production community because it was ambitious in scope—including fast action and even car chases—but was produced for a relatively small amount of cash.

> **NOTE:** Falling Like This *was released in the U.S. and Canada on VHS and DVD in November of 2003 by Vanguard Cinema. So, you can judge for yourself the challenges they faced shooting moving vehicles on the busy streets of Los Angeles.*

The budget summary, or *top sheet* for *Falling Like This* is shown in **Table 8.5.** In your *line-item budget*, you'll show lines of detail for each cost item within the accounts. The summary simply gives subtotals by account.

The estimated cash outlay to produce this DV feature was only $67,648, comfortably beneath the $75,000 ceiling for a SAG Experimental project, which it was.

> **TOP SHEET:** Summary budget page showing subtotals for each department and major budget category.
>
> **LINE-ITEM BUDGET:** Detailed budget that supports the summary page.

We can't go into great detail here—that would require an extensive breakdown of this project to see the line items in each budget sub-account category. But this summary will give you a sense of how these moviemakers translated their vision into a practical reality—and how you can do the same.

Alongside the account number and description, the budget table shows the estimated final cost for each item, the amount that was originally budgeted by the producers, and the amount each category was over- or under-budget.

A few notes based on the moviemakers' comments to an interviewer from *Filmmaker* magazine will explain the costs in some key budget categories.

Table 8.5 *Falling Like This*—Budget Summary

Budget Category	Description	Estimated Final Cost	Total Budget Amount	Over/Under Budget
Above-the-Line Expenses				
1300	Direction and supervision	$ 34	$ 300	$ 266
1400	Cast, day players, stunts	$ 2,610	$ 2,850	$ 240
Subtotal Above-the-Line Expenses		**$ 2,644**	**$ 3,150**	**$ 506**
Production Expenses				
2000	Production staff	$ 124	$ 1,280	$ 1,156
2100	Extra talent	$ 1,535	$ 2,900	$ 1,365
2300	Set construction	$ 169	$ 2,800	$ 2,631
2600	Special effects	$ 0	$ 200	$ 200
2700	Set dressing, operations, and strike	$ 3,269	$ 1,500	($ 1,769)
2800	Property, operations and strike	$ 2,274	$ 1,900	($ 374)
2900	Wardrobe	$ 1,924	$ 2,250	$ 326
3100	Makeup and hairdressing	$ 238	$ 600	$ 362
3200	Electrical, rig, operations, and strike	$ 2,963	$ 3,750	$ 787
3300	Camera operations	($ 830)	$ 3,500	$ 4,330
3400	Sound operations	$ 3,130	$ 2,649	($ 481)
3500	Transportation	$ 15,719	$ 16,150	$ 431
3600	Location	$ 29,348	$ 23,655	($ 5,693)
3700	Production film and laboratory	$ 483	$ 2,520	$ 2,037
Subtotal Production Expenses		**$ 60,346**	**$ 65,654**	**$ 5,308**
Postproduction Expenses				
4500	Editing	$ 699	$ 2,290	$ 1,591
Subtotal Postproduction Expenses		**$ 699**	**$ 2,290**	**$ 1,591**
Other Expenses				
6700	Insurance	$ 3,901	$ 2,200	($ 1,701)
7500	Fees and charges	$ 58	$ 105	$ 47
Subtotal Other Expenses		**$ 3,959**	**$ 2,305**	**($ 1,654)**
Totals		**$ 67,648**	**$ 73,399**	**$ 5,751**

Table © *Filmmaker: The Magazine of Independent Film*. Reprinted with permission of the publisher.

Camera Operations

The team bought a Canon XL1 camcorder, then resold it at the end of the shoot. They made a small profit on the sale, hence the negative cost in this category.

Sound Operations

They recorded single-system audio in-camera. They admit they didn't spend enough on sound, and they didn't budget enough for shooting tests.

Location Fees

The script called for shooting on Los Angeles city streets, parks, and in public buildings; hence the production had to pay over $19,000 in permits. (If you're pals with the mayor of a small town, shoot there!)

Catering and Craft Services

The producers spent over $10,000 on food for cast and crew, and don't regret it.

Deferred Fees and Expenses

As with most ultra-low-budget projects, the surprisingly low out-of-pocket expense was achieved by deferring salaries. The moviemakers' estimates of the deferred amounts are shown in **Table 8.6**. The videomakers hadn't yet paid themselves for writing, directing, and producing the movie, so there's a question mark for above-the-line expenses. Also, as of this acounting, certain postproduction services had not yet been paid.

The makers of *Falling Like This* estimated their break-even point is actually somewhere north of $1 million once they include deferred compensation and marketing costs.

Table 8.6 Deferred Expenses

Budget Category	Deferred Item	Amount Deferred
1300	Direction and supervision	?
1400	Actors' salaries and fringe benefits	$ 112,000
2000–3400	Crew salaries	$ 340,000
3400	Additional sound work	$ 45,000
4500	Music licenses	$ 36,000
4500	Color correction and dubbing	$ 50,000
Total deferred		**$ 583,000+**

DEALING WITH LEGAL ISSUES

Don't even think about starting a major DV production project without a competent attorney on your team, especially one who specializes in entertainment law. Your friendly family lawyer isn't up to the job in this highly specialized area. If you're working in a business environment, seek the cooperation and support of your organization's corporate counsel. There's no substitute for professional legal advice. Here are some issues to run by the experts.

Incorporate and Insure the Production Entity

Producing a video as an individual is dangerous. You need to protect yourself and your colleagues as much as possible from liability. Accidents can happen on the set. Movies often lose money. Sponsors might feel their product has been misrepresented. Subjects or holders of real-life story rights might decide they've been portrayed incorrectly. Investors' moods shift every time there's a dip in the stock market. Hence, a common practice of media production companies is to incorporate a special entity just for the duration of a project.

Once you've created such an entity, in whatever form you decide to incorporate it, make sure it's insured. For instance, most equipment rental contracts require you to carry at least $1 million coverage, including personal injury due to accidents on the set. (Movie lights get hot, and lamps can explode.) If you're making the video for a company, or are an employee of that company, make sure your production is covered under its insurance policy, including not only general liability but also "errors and omissions," a type of coverage that can give some protection against claims of copyright infringement.

> **SIGNATORY:** Producer who signs an agreement to abide by a union's working rules.

If you want to employ union workers, an officer of your production entity must sign working agreements, making the entity a "*signatory* producer," bound to follow the union's rules and regulations.

Location Permits and Fees

Shooting in metropolitan areas often involves significant fees paid to government agencies. If you try to skirt the requirement, a police citation can be costly—and may even bar you from using the location at all. One strategy is to keep your lawyer's phone number handy. Another is to relocate your production to someplace where fees might be waived as an incentive to bring employment to local workers. (For more information, see "Shooting Offshore—Or Out of State" earlier in this chapter.)

Deal Memos

A hiring letter that agrees to employ a member of the cast or crew is called a *deal memo*. Typically, producers have formal contracts on file with unions covering all employees in a given category. The deal memo employs one individual, incorporating and perhaps modifying the terms of the union contract. It usually specifies job description, pay rate, deferral terms (if any), duration of the shoot (and whether the assignment will be for specific days, weeks, or run-of-show), tentative screen credit (sometimes subject to union rulings), and other important details. Be sure to document any hire with a deal memo, even if the work is deferred or unpaid.

> **DEAL MEMO:** Letter of agreement used to hire members of the cast and crew.

Actors' Releases

Whether or not you pay an actor, be sure to get a written release from her, including permission to use and exploit her likeness. In the case of professional actors, the employment contract or deal memo should always contain such a release clause. Your attorney or a production accountant should keep these documents on file and make sure you have a signature from everyone in the cast. You will also need such releases from subjects of interviews and documentaries. However, for documentary and news, there's an exception for people who are in a public place or attending a public event where they know there is a likelihood they will be recorded.

 You'll find sample production documents, such as a deal memo and an actor's release, in the Forms folder.

Actors' Working Rules

If you produce a movie under the SAG Experimental Agreement, deferred salaries become due (and your production reverts to the terms of the SAG Low-Budget Agreement) if and when your show is placed in commercial distribution. Even if you're deferring compensation, you must keep accurate time records according to the union's working rules.

To gain some types of distribution, your production may have to be "grandfathered"—authorized by the union retroactively. Your distributor will want proof that you've complied with SAG and other craft union regulations, and you'll need to submit paperwork to the unions. Part of your responsibility includes accounting for and paying P&H, as well as workers' compensation as required by the laws of your state.

Plan for Success

Do yourself a big favor and make written agreements, in advance, between yourself and your associates defining arrangements for deferred payments to yourselves. One of the worst nightmares imaginable is to suddenly find that your video is the hottest ticket at Sundance only to fall out with your colleagues about how to divide the potential profits. Profit-participation formulas in the entertainment industry are quite tricky; your entertainment attorney can help you draft these agreements.

Preparing to Shoot

Now that you've developed a schedule, set a budget, booked your equipment, and hired your cast and crew, it's time to shift your attention from business to creative affairs, and start shooting. But here are some things you need to do first.

Plan Test Shots

Chapter 4 encourages you to take your camcorder out of the box and do some test shots before production day. As you finish your preproduction planning, you should have a much better idea of what technical challenges you'll face on the set. Try to simulate these potential problems in your tests so you'll know how to deal with them under the pressure of production.

Even if you're sure you know exactly what you're doing, don't skip testing. Everyone, even pros (such as the authors) can make mistakes. Our personal list would include:

- Dead battery! (Where's the indicator?)

- We rented tungsten lights and we're shooting *outside*?

- No tape in the thing! Did you remember to bring more?

- I taped over a good take! You said, "Start the tape," so I pressed Start!

- Wrong mic connector. What do we do now?

- This mic needs external power. Did you hook it up before the take?

- Everything on the tape has a greenish cast. Did you check white balance? (Or, I thought I told you to switch off the ceiling lights.)

Get some practice with your gear before you start production, and hopefully you'll have fewer horror stories to share at cocktail parties.

Plan for Compositing

It might seem elementary, but you can't achieve most special effects in postproduction if you don't plan for them during the shooting. In particular, to do mattes and other types of composites, you must storyboard them meticulously, discuss them in detail with your creative and technical teams, and make sure you get all required elements in the can.

And, unless you're experienced with these techniques, include them in your preproduction test shots.

For example, if you intend to achieve a matte shot through luminance keying, you must make absolutely sure that, when the time comes to do the shot, its white areas will be fully blown out (100 IRE). This requires both selecting a camcorder with the zebra-pattern feature and constructing the set, selecting backdrops, or framing the sky to provide the white area. If you're doing chroma keying instead, more logistics will be involved in acquiring, setting up, and lighting a special blue or green backdrop. In either case, you must select wardrobe and set dressings carefully to make sure that the key color doesn't show up in unwanted places.

For more information on technical requirements for composites, see "Plan Ahead for Digital Mattes" in Chapter 6.

Secret Weapons for Shoot Day

It's the night before D Day. You won't sleep any worse if you were going to scale Mt. Everest in the morning. However, perhaps you'll sleep a little better knowing you've remembered to pack the following items:

Interchangeable lenses come with a variety of essential accessories, including filters, lens hoods, matte boxes, protective carrying cases, and so on. Be sure to bring a circular polarizing filter (reduces glare), an ultraviolet filter (UV, cuts daylight glare), a neutral density filter (ND, reduces light intensity similar to stopping down), a diffusion filter (softens detail), and a set of various color-correcting filters. (For more information on using filters for color correction, see "Color Temperature" in Chapter 6.)

If your camcorder comes with a nonremovable lens, or if you're using a smaller unit for handheld work, buy a lens adapter. These are supplementary lenses that fit over your existing lens to change its focal length. You may not be able to fully compensate for the limited focal length of a built-in lens simply by using an inexpensive telephoto adapter, but it might be better than sacrificing resolution by resorting to the camcorder's digital zoom. (Availability of lens adapters is an excellent reason to favor one model palmcorder over another that doesn't offer them.)

Bring a padded case for the camcorder to protect it from the rigors of transportation. These essential accessories cost between $150 and $350; look for brands like Kangaroo, Kata, and Porta-Brace. Some of these manufacturers also make "raincoats" for cameras, but if you don't want the extra expense, you can do the same job with a plastic painters' drop cloth.

> **TIP:** If you can't afford a camera case, that's no excuse to leave home without one. Slip the original packing material—box and Styrofoam inserts—into a canvas shoulder bag.

Cinematic Survival Kit

Some of the most important video tools don't come from a camera store.

For instance, don't leave home without headphones, a small flashlight (for inspecting camcorder settings when daylight begins to fade), a multiblade screwdriver and knife, any audio connector adapters you might need (especially mini-to-XLR and vice versa), and an extra handheld microphone.

EATING THE ELEPHANT

An old adage goes, "How do you eat an elephant? One bite at a time."

In preproduction, you share the same challenges that face project managers the world over, whether they're planning missions to Mars or developing recipes for a new fast-food product. Perhaps it's not as creative as writing a script or drawing a storyboard, but preproduction planning is the only way you'll ever get to make your video happen.

Planners get to shoot their movies. Dreamers don't.

CHAPTER NINE

On the Set

This is the moment. Now is the time.

Most of this chapter will be devoted to film-style shooting on a set (or a carefully prepared location), using work methods inherited from the old studio system. But even the run-and-gun soldier of fortune who sets out before dawn with just a camcorder, a few accessories, and a bag of trail mix needs to prepare for his news-style shoot with much of the same mental and technical discipline.

RUNNING AND GUNNING

Up to now we've mostly talked about *getting ready* to run and gun. But when you're out there on your own, doing it, here's some advice on how to cope.

Capturing the Fast Breaks

Although you'd be well advised to shut off all automatic camcorder controls, sometimes you just can't. When it's only you and the camcorder, and the story is breaking fast, by the time you adjust this control and check that setting, the action might be over and you missed it.

In a tough spot, consider judiciously using *some* automatic camcorder settings to capture fast-breaking action. For instance:

- If you use a camera-mounted floodlight, turn on the camcorder's spotlight mode, if it has one. If you expect to shoot with a flood often, buy a camcorder with a spotlight mode—as well as a hot shoe for mounting the light itself. In spotlight mode, the camcorder's image processing circuitry reduces the video gain at the center of the picture where the highlights on your subjects' faces might otherwise get blown out by the intensity of your single light source. (For more information on news-style lighting, see "Three-Point Lighting, News Style" in Chapter 6.)

- Turn auto-focus off. With a little practice, you should be able to work the focus ring on the lens manually, even when you're in a hurry. This will help you keep the real subject—and not simply whatever happens to be in the center of the frame—in focus as you follow the action.

- Turn auto-exposure on. If the action is fast-paced, you probably won't have time to adjust the f-stop settings manually, especially as you operate focus and zoom.

- If the aperture is wide open and your shots are still underexposed, go ahead and switch on low-light sensitivity (if it doesn't come on automatically), or activate the automatic video gain control. Even if the picture is a bit noisy in the dim light, you'll have fulfilled your assignment by getting the best possible result under challenging conditions. However, try to avoid panning across bright spots in this mode, or you'll blow out the image.

Using the Built-In Mic (If You Must)

Clipping a lav to the subject or using a handheld mic is always preferable to using the built-in camcorder mic, which picks up motor noise and gives the wrong audio perspective.

But sometimes, if you're going to get the shot at all, you have no choice. If you find yourself compelled to use the built-in mic, try this:

- To use the signal from the on-board mic, check the audio input switch on the camcorder and set it to use internal rather than external input. On some camcorders, like the XL1S, you set the switch to Audio 1. On others, including many consumer models, simply inserting a mini plug into an External Audio jack will turn *off* the on-board mic, which is on by default, so make sure nothing is plugged in.

- Turn off audio AGC by switching the audio recording level to Manual. The only reason to use audio AGC is if you expect the range of audio levels to be wide and unpredictable—sudden variations from whispers to shouts. When audio AGC is on, the camcorder will crank up the gain all the way whenever things grow quiet, causing pumping if it happens repeatedly.

- Select video recording mode.

- Record someone speaking loudly nearby. (Record your own voice if you have no alternative.)

- Increase the manual sound level (or audio gain) control as much as you can without causing distortion. On most prosumer, and all professional models, use the camcorder's audio level meter to set the level. Remember, anything above 0 dB will be distorted or clipped. On less expensive camcorders without audio meters, you'll have to listen through the headphones for the distortion.

Powering Your Camcorder

Do you remember Willy Loman, the tragic hero of *Death of a Salesman*, who was out there riding on "a shoeshine and a smile?" Well, when *you're* out there alone, you're riding on your batteries. For starters, remember the three-battery rule: Always have three sets of rechargeable batteries—one in the camera, one in your backpack, and one in a charger at the closest outlet you can find.

Here are several other survival tips to make sure your video doesn't turn into a tragedy when you run out of juice.

Check the Specs

All rechargeable batteries suffer from the dreaded *memory effect*, which means they run down more quickly if you recharge them before they are totally exhausted. (Manufacturers claim lithium-ion batteries don't behave this way, but in our experience, they do.) Theoretically, this means you're supposed to run down batteries all the way before you recharge them—but of course this risks running out of power in the middle of a critical take. (Camcorder battery monitoring circuits aren't always accurate, either.)

> **MEMORY EFFECT:** Tendency of rechargeable batteries to recharge only to the same degree they've been discharged.

So what can you do? When choosing rechargeable batteries, pay attention to the rated battery life between charges *and* the recharge time. Nickel metal hydride (NiMH) and lithium-ion (LiIon) batteries may not be perfect or free from memory effect, but they are more reliable and last longer between charges than older-style nickel-cadmium (NiCad) batteries.

Buy a Battery Pack That Accepts Drugstore Batteries

Some adapter packs accept a handful of ordinary alkaline batteries from the nearest drugstore. This option can save the day in a pinch. But don't store the batteries in the pack or camcorder between shoots; eventually they'll leak, which can ruin your equipment.

Belt Up

If you do a lot of news-style location work, buy a battery belt. It surrounds your midsection and carries enough rechargeable batteries to last most of a shooting day.

Interview Techniques

Impromptu sidewalk interviews will work out better if you follow a few simple rules.

Ask the Subject to Repeat Every Question

If you're doing your own interviewing while you operate the camcorder, ask the interview subject to repeat each question you ask before answering it. Once you edit out your off-mic mumbles, the audience will think that the interview subject was speaking from his or her own agenda, leading to a logical flow of topics. Also, if you change the order of questions and responses in editing, having the question precede the answer makes it easier for the audience to follow the interview.

Keep Rolling

Always keep the tape rolling, even *between* questions— with your subject's permission. The offhand remarks, gestures, and comments you capture in these moments will give you additional choices in the editing room and can add spontaneity, even touches of humor, to your show. (This is just as good an idea for film-style shooting, by the way.)

THE CALL SHEET

Now that the run-and-gunners are out covering the news, let's look over the shoulder of the director on a full-scale, film-style shoot.

Your shooting schedule officially begins on the first day of principal photography. (And yes, it's called photography even if you're doing it with a camcorder.) It doesn't matter if the second unit has already started shooting inserts or establishing shots; principal photography begins the day the first unit starts shooting.

Thanks to the planning and scheduling process, the first assistant director will have specific assignments for each member of the cast and crew, which he'll compile into a *call sheet*. This document, duplicated and distributed just before the end of each day's shoot, tells every member of the cast and crew when and where to report for the next day's shooting (**Figure 9.1**).

Call Sheet

Production:	*When Harried Met Sally*		Shooting Day:	**1 OF 2**
Producer/PM:	G. Jones		Date:	**Saturday, August 10, 20XX**
Director:	P. Shaner		Crew Call:	**6:00 AM**
AD:	R. Knerr		Shooting Call:	**7:30 AM**

SET	SCENES	PAGES	CAST NO.	LOCATION
Josh cubicle	1, 3, 10	3 4/8	1, 2, 4, 3	4th Floor South
Phil office	4	6/8	1, 3	4th Floor South
Sally cubicle	2, 11	1 4/8	1, 4	4th Floor South
Reception desk	9	6/8	1, 5	4th Floor South
Copier room	5, 6, 8	4	1, 6, 7	4th Floor North
Park bench	7	4/8	4	Courtyard

NO.	CAST MEMBER	PART OF	MAKE-UP	SET CALL	REMARKS
1	Josh			7:30 AM	
2	Atwater			7:30 AM	
3	Phil			6:00 AM	Setup crew
4	Sally			8:30 AM	
5	Richard			O/C	Cell no 888 555-1234
6	Ann			O/C	Cell no 877 555-4321
7	Ric			O/C	Cell no 877 555-1303

ATMOSPHERE / EXTRAS	PROPS	SPECIAL INSTRUCTIONS
"Squeaky" OS scene 3	Phone headset - Josh Computer/keyboard	Need doc file for computer to match report for screen shot and Insert

OTHER CALL TIMES:			VEHICLES & OTHER:
Director	6:30 AM	Camera	Van - load on wrap for transport
First A.D.		Sound	to Sunday AM location TBD
Second A.D.		Grips	
PA		Electric	
Craft Services	10:00 AM	Art Dept.	
Script Super		Make-up	
DP	6:30 AM	Wardrobe	

NOTES AND CHANGES:

Arrive having had breakfast. Buffet lunch from craft services table.

Walkaway dinner 1 hour.

Count on OT--We will shoot until building security goes home at 9 PM. Strike must

be done and all equipment secured in closet or van before that time.

Actors responsible for own makeup, hair, and wardrobe. See PA for personal props.

Cast members in scenes not shot today are O/C for Sunday.

Figure 9.1 This call sheet (found in the Forms folder on the DVD) shows the first day of shooting for *When Harried Met Sally*. Because large-scale productions require lots of information for each day's shoot, studio call sheets are typically printed in tiny type on both sides of legal-sized paper. The first side is laid out much like this sample, but with many more details. The back shows individual crew assignments and special call times by department.

The call sheet always lists at least two separate times: *crew call* and *shooting call*. The crew call applies to everyone, cast included, who doesn't have a separately scheduled, individual call time. If a cast member requires special makeup and wardrobe, her call will be earlier than the general crew call, and a specific time will be shown opposite her name on the call sheet. Cast or crew members who are assigned to work for the day, but have no set call times, must remain *on call* (shown on the sheet as O/C) by phone or walkie-talkie. The shooting time is when the first AD expects the camera to roll for the first take. All setup, preparation, and on-set rehearsals must be done by shooting time.

> **CALL SHEET:** List of cast and crew assignments and reporting times, as well as equipment requirements, instructions, and contact numbers for the next shooting day.
>
> **CREW CALL:** Call time for anyone who doesn't have a separately specified reporting time on the call sheet.
>
> **SHOOTING CALL:** Approximate time the first AD expects the camera to roll for the first take.
>
> **ON CALL (O/C):** Cast or crew member assigned to work for the day, but with no set call time.

Notice how closely the call sheet resembles the script breakdown page (refer back to Figure 8.2). In fact, much of the data is the same, showing required elements, grouped by department, for one or more scenes to be shot on a given day.

> **TIP:** *A call sheet is derived from the same database as the schedule, and Movie Magic Scheduling is capable of printing it out automatically.*

In effect, the call sheet is the first AD's master plan for the day's work. Besides scheduling everyone, it gives details and production notes on setups, meals and breaks, props and effects, contact phone numbers and/or walkie-talkie channels for department heads, on-call people, and the nearest hospital emergency room.

When in doubt about anything involving logistics, setup, or call times, the first place cast and crew should look is the call sheet. And if the AD and production manager are on top of things, most of the answers will be there.

TRANSPORTING AND MANAGING EQUIPMENT

You may be tempted to save money by picking up all your gear from the rental house on the morning of the first shooting day. Don't.

Even on small-scale projects, your first shooting day should start bright and early, with everyone (and all needed equipment) on the set. Otherwise, you may not get around to shooting your first take until mid-afternoon, putting you behind schedule from day one.

An ideal plan is to rent a truck and pick up your lights, mics, cables, and all the rest of your gear two days in advance (D-Day −2). (You might want the camcorder even earlier, for shooting tests.) Check everything out the next day (D-Day –1), and start shooting on D-Day. (For more information on planning your equipment rental, see "Dealing with Rental Houses" in Chapter 8.)

Even if you're rushed, you should allow at least half a day to thoroughly check out any camcorder you rent. There can be defects in CCD chips, recording heads, or circuitry. So shoot some tape and play it back, making sure there are no dropouts in video or audio. Also, exercise the controls you'll be using. For example, try the zoom control to make sure the motion is smooth. This is functional camera testing. We're not talking about test footage or broadcast-color or film-transfer tests, which you should have done much earlier to help you make creative decisions.

Renting a truck from a third-party agency is often less economical than renting a specially equipped truck from a movie equipment rental house. The truck-and-equipment package not only saves you time—you pick it up already loaded— but it also has customized racks, shelves, and drawers in the cargo area so keeping track of gear is quick and easy.

Here are a few more tips on picking up equipment and getting it safely to the location.

Bring Crew

Pick up your gear promptly on the appointed date and time, and bring along enough crew to handle loading.

Get a Count

Make sure you count everything you pick up by checking off all items on the rental agreement before you leave their lot. And keep a detailed inventory updated throughout the shooting day. Unfortunately it's way too common to drive away from the rental house with, say, five identical light kits, only to find four packing cases in the truck at the end of the first day—and not know where the other one went.

Open the Cases

Check all equipment against your inventory sheet before accepting delivery. The rental house won't be trying to cheat you, but mistakes can happen.

Get Spares

Make sure you have enough spares, such as mic batteries and halogen lamps.

Bring it Back the Way You Picked it Up

Pay attention to how the gear was packed, and plan to return it the same way—with cables coiled and tied, and stowed in the same cases.

Pack for the Move

Always pack your gear completely and neatly when making a move between locations. For example, light fixtures and mics should be returned to their snug, foam-cushioned cases, not still attached to stands or piled in the truck bed.

Tie it Down

Secure equipment so it doesn't slide, roll, or shift around in the cargo area during transit. It's doubly important to tie down loads if you're using a pickup truck. An unsecured load could bounce out, especially at high speed, not only damaging the equipment but also possibly causing a road hazard and drawing a traffic citation.

SETTING UP FOR A SCENE

Setup happens before every scene—and generally follows a five-step program inherited from the Hollywood studio system.

The Setup Drill

Even if you're working on a smaller-scale production with less formal procedures, you should know how the drill goes on a studio lot.

1. As preparation begins for a new scene (which may or may not be on a new set), the director *claims*, or assumes authority over, the set. He sends the technicians on a break so they can make personal calls, grab a snack at the craft services table, or gossip. He dismisses the crew so he can discuss the scene with the actors and give them his full attention, without being distracted by technical questions. *Stand-ins* observe.

2. The actors run through the scene once or twice, working with the director. Although the principals have probably rehearsed the scene previously, this may be the first time they've been on the set together. It may also be the first time supporting players have met the principals. The actors have the opportunity to ask questions and work out kinks in the scene. The director may ask for

walk-throughs, in which actors literally walk through their blocking, saying their lines but not really performing. During a walk-through actors concentrate on use of props (when to put down a cup), *business* with wardrobe (when to take off a coat), and changes to the blocking (deciding to push in a chair when getting up from a table).

> **CLAIMING THE SET:** Assuming authority over operations on the set at a particular time; during shooting, this responsibility is alternately held by the director and the first AD.
>
> **STAND-IN:** Substitute for an actor who has the same build and wears similar clothes. Stand-ins walk through a scene to assist the DP in setting lights.
>
> **WALK-THROUGH:** Informal rehearsal on the set in which actors say (but don't perform) their lines and go through their blocking with the director.
>
> **BUSINESS:** Physical action by an actor.
>
> **REHEARSAL FOR THE KEYS:** Run-through for department heads.
>
> **SPIKE:** Mark an actor's final position with tape on the floor of the set.
>
> **TECH REHEARSAL:** Last run-through before the first take.

3. The director recalls all his department heads for a *rehearsal for the keys*. Keys, in this context, means key personnel—the department heads. The head of wardrobe might be thinking, "If he's going to remove that jacket, I'll have to put him in a different shirt." The prop master notes, "She puts that cup down so forcefully, it might break. Do we have any spares?" The DP is thinking through her lighting plan, which can't be finalized until she sees the positions of the camera and the actors in the space. At the same time, the first AD—who is always thinking about the day's schedule—is estimating how long it will actually take to shoot the scene and how he can prepare for the next setup. Also during this time, the director, the DP, and the first AD make a final decision on the sequence of shots (making sure, for example, to first get all the shots involving a particular day player or special effect).

4. These matters having been resolved, the second AD takes the actors to makeup and wardrobe. The director turns the set over to the first AD and leaves to do administrative tasks and individual conferences. Stand-ins walk through the scene as the DP tells the grips how to set the lights. Meanwhile, the first assistant camera ("AC" for short) moves in to *spike*, or mark, actors' positions. (For more information, see "Reinventing Your Shot Plan" following this section.)

5. The first AD calls for the actors, the second AD delivers them, and the director reclaims the set. In a final *tech rehearsal* the DP makes sure the lights are set properly, the AC checks his focus marks, the property master makes sure props are in place and actors are handling them correctly, and the other creative and tech heads make sure everything is ready.

PLACES: Request for actors to assume their starting positions in a scene.

Having completed the five steps, and being satisfied that everything is indeed ready, the director (or first AD) calls "*Places!* Roll camera! Action."

NOTE: *On a film set, after the camera operator starts the camera (and before the director calls action), the camera operator calls "Rolling!" and the sound recordist calls "Speed!" to let the director know that camera and audio recorder have both reached full operating speed. In DV, both camcorder and DAT will be at speed before the director can take a breath. However, this formality is still observed—partly to confirm that recording is actually underway, and partly because it's a tradition.*

Reinventing Your Shot Plan

If you're working on location (as opposed to a sound stage), the first day of principal photography will probably be the first time you get to see the fully dressed set with all the crew and equipment in it. And despite your carefully drawn shot plans, it's a sure bet that something won't fit as planned.

For example, the camera's line of sight might include a larger portion of a doorway or window than you'd planned—with a view of another room or exterior building that doesn't fit the scene. You'll have to rework the angles in your shot plan. The natural light from a window may be brighter at this time of day than you expected, so you'll need to move the camera or reframe the shot. Or, the room may be too small and the furniture too big to provide clearance for actors to move comfortably and naturally, as required by your blocking plan.

Here are some tips on adjusting your shot plan without wasting a lot of time:

- If you need to rearrange furniture, try to avoid moving any practical lights that appear in the shot. Otherwise, you'll have to relight to make the motivation look correct.

- If the space looks too small and cramped, try using a wide-angle lens to make it appear larger.

- To make an overlarge space appear foreshortened and closed-in, use a telephoto lens.

- Sometimes, when you're actually in the space, you may discover that for one reason or another the angles you planned don't work. This is a common problem with location shooting. You may not have time to redraw the shot plan, so while it's certainly no guarantee of success, you might simply try flipping the plan to see if it works that way. (People and furniture now on the right go to the left, and vice versa.) If you do this, think about the effects on continuity of seeing actors on opposite sides of the screen. Continuity will be particularly important if the editor must match cuts to any other setups in the same scene.

Spike Actors' Positions

In shots where lighting must be just so, it's customary to spike the actor's position. The mark is a *T* on the floor made from two strips of tape (**Figure 9.2**). Structured film-style production, which requires precise blocking, makes extensive use of marks. Improvisational-style directors only rely on them for critical closeups.

Figure 9.2 The correct way for an actor to hit a mark is with one foot on either side of the T. Hitting a mark on the run is difficult; hitting marks as you deliver emotionally charged lines is an advanced, hard-to-acquire skill of the experienced actor.

Shooting Plain-Vanilla

When setting camcorder controls for a shot, experienced DPs never make choices in-camera that can be left until postproduction.

For example, suppose you're considering having a sequence appear in sepia (monochrome). If your camcorder gives you an option to *shoot* in monochrome instead of full color, you might be tempted to use it. However, that would be a bad decision.

If you shoot in monochrome mode, and later your producers or your clients decide they don't like the sepia effect and want to go back to full color, you've hit a wall: you'll have to tell them it's impossible unless someone pays (maybe you) to reshoot. You can always achieve the look you want later, in postproduction, by using a color-correction step.

For the same reason, it's wise to avoid in-camera effects such as fades and dissolves that you can and should do in the edit. Also, aside from watching the color temperature of your lights and the white balance of the camcorder, don't be overly concerned about doing color correction in-camera. All that can be done later, in post.

Monitoring Video Quality

If the camcorder has a black-and-white viewfinder, that's the most accurate way for you to evaluate focus. (Technically, a b&w viewfinder uses the signal from the green CCD, which has more edge information than the other two colors.) However, it's easier to judge composition and framing on the big screen of a color monitor. Filmmakers have been using field monitors for years to look at instant video replay on the set.

Don't use a conventional TV as your field monitor if you can avoid it. Television sets have built-in color-correction circuits that won't show exactly what you're getting. Use a real monitor, designed for this purpose, and connect it to the camcorder's Video Out (or Monitor) jack. Use the S-Video or Y/C jack, if available, for the best possible picture.

The most accurate way to judge picture quality is to use a waveform monitor, a type of oscilloscope that shows voltages of various video parameters on a graphic display. If you're skilled at reading it, a waveform monitor can be a very precise way of measuring and monitoring exposure levels and RGB color. Although it's rare for a traditional filmmaker to know how to use one, waveform monitors will become increasingly prevalent on the set as digital video tools replace film.

Artful Composition

Storyboards and shot plans represent an idealized notion of what you want to capture in every shot. But when you're on the set, the dreaming stops. You can only shoot what's in front of you, with the tools at hand. Unless you're Alfred Hitchcock, you'll rarely be able to capture a shot that duplicates your original sketch perfectly. But that's OK. Sometimes, when working on the set, you can compose a shot that's better than anything in your sketches.

Composing a video shot uses many familiar principles of graphic design. In fact, the arrangement of people and objects in a visual frame, as well as the framing of the shot itself, both follow some basic rules of graphic composition.

> **NOTE:** Like screenwriting, graphic design is a subject so huge we can't deal with it adequately here. For more information on composing your shots with artistry, see Bruce Block's book, The Visual Story: Seeing the Structure of Film, TV, and New Media.

As you begin to frame your shots, here are two important compositional techniques for making them more effective on the screen.

Rule of Thirds

The composition of your shots will be more visually pleasing, and probably more effective for an audience, if you follow the well-known *rule of thirds* (**Figure 9.3**).

The rule of thirds divides a frame into three equal-sized horizontal slices and three equal-sized vertical slices.

> **RULE OF THIRDS:** Guideline for visual composition that divides a frame into horizontal and vertical thirds.

Intersections of the guidelines indicate the most interesting points in the frame. For example, you could use the horizontal guidelines for composing a landscape shot. To show more sky, giving the audience a feeling of openness and freedom, locate the horizon line at the lower guideline so the sky takes up two-thirds of the frame and the land takes up one-third. To show more land, giving the audience an impression of endless rolling acres, locate the horizon line at the upper guideline so the sky takes up one-third of the frame and the land takes up two-thirds.

When you're shooting a closeup, put the actor's eyes on the top horizontal guideline. One of the reasons the rule of thirds works so well is that human faces are composed roughly in thirds:

- From the chin to the mouth
- From the mouth to the eyes
- From the eyes to the top of the head

Generally, use the vertical guidelines for positioning actors in favor of centering them in the frame.

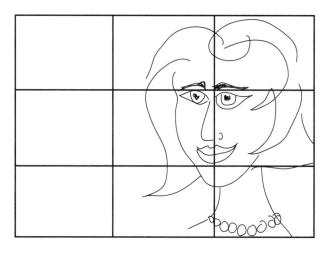

Figure 9.3 The rule of thirds gives you compositional guidelines for relative proportions, positioning, and framing of shots.

Positive and Negative Space

A related rule is to maximize *positive space*—a compositional technique that defines the apparent amount of space in front of an actor as positive and the space in back of the actor as negative. For example, in a closeup, the area in front of the subject's head—in the direction of his gaze—is positive; the area in back of his head is negative. So, if he's looking *frame left* in the shot, put his face on the right vertical guideline. This puts the positive space on the viewers' left side of the screen and makes it larger than the negative space on the right.

> **POSITIVE/NEGATIVE SPACE:** The amount of space in front of (positive) or in back of (negative) an actor in a frame.
>
> **FRAME LEFT/FRAME RIGHT:** Screen direction based on the viewpoint of the audience.

TIP: *To audiences that live in Western countries, the left side of the frame—as well as leftward motion—give a negative feeling; the right side, and rightward motion, feel more positive. That's because we read from left to right and associate motion toward the right with progress. People in cultures that read from right to left or from the top downwards have different perceptions.*

KEEPING TRACK OF YOUR TAKES

Slate every take! The slate should show the scene number, take number, and beginning timecode. If you are shooting dual-system sound, use a clapper board. (For more information on smart slates and dual-system sound, see "Using a Clapper Board and Timecode" in Chapter 7.)

If you fail to slate a shot at the beginning, shoot the slate at the end of the take, but hold it upside down. Reasons to skip the front-slate might include wanting to start the camcorder quickly to capture an actor's sudden burst of emotion or shooting an ECU so tight that the slate won't fit. All experienced editors will recognize this industry practice of *tail-slating* a take.

> **TAIL-SLATING:** Shooting an upside-down slate at the end of a take.

When you start a new DV cassette, set the timecode. You will recall that timecode follows the format HH:MM:SS:FF (hour, minute, second, frame). On many prosumer and most professional camcorders, you can set the first two digits of the timecode manually. Although the default timecode begins with "00," experienced camera operators learn to set the hour digits to "01" on the first tape they use, "02" for the second tape, and so on, incrementing the hour code for each additional tape. That way, each shot on each tape has a distinct timecode—and no two frames in the clips will have the same timecode. (This is immensely helpful to an editor.)

CAMERA LOG: A written record of what's been recorded on each reel (DV cassette) and track (DAT cassette), with corresponding timecodes for each take. Also camera and sound log; daily editor's log.

A traditional method for keeping track of takes, held over from film production, is the *camera log,* also known as a *camera and sound log,* or a *daily editor's log* (**Figure 9.4**). The original purpose of the camera log was to make it easy for the editor to match up a film clip with its corresponding audio track (which was on a separate roll of magnetic tape). If you're recording audio in-camera (single-system sound), a camera log isn't necessary—at least not for that purpose—because the audio track is already in sync with the picture on the tape. However, your editor will want to know which scenes are on which tape, so it's a good idea to keep a log of starting and ending timecode indexes for each take—even if it's just annotations in a script. Follow the numbering scheme just described.

Camera & Sound Log

Date: 08/01/XX Title: "When Boy Meets Alien"
Work Day: Mon Director: P. Shaner
A.D.: R. Knerr

Cam Roll	Snd Roll	Set	Scene	Take No.	Start	Finish	Description
01	01	Snack Bar	45	1	01000000	01000213	NG
				2	01000216	01000301	OK
				3	01000306	01000518	OK
				4	01000520	01000735	Noise?
01	01	Base Camp	43	1	01000749	01001702	OK
				2	01001710	01002820	OK
				3	01002859	01003934	NG
				4	01004001	01005314	OK
02	02	Base Camp	47	1	02000000	02000103	OK
				2	02000125	02000245	OK
				3	02000259	02000321	NG
				4	02000354	02000443	NG
				5	02000458	02000522	OK
02	02	Base Camp	49	1	02000541	02000803	Noise
				2	02000812	02001102	OK
				3	02001123	02001435	OK

Wild Tracks		Remarks					
None		45-4 Bus rumble -- low level					
		49-1 Car alarm					

Script Supervisor

Figure 9.4 A camera and sound log for a dual-system DV/DAT shoot shows reel (cassette) numbers, and beginning and ending timecode for each take.

If you're shooting dual-system sound, your editor will need the camera log so she can match up DV cassettes with corresponding DATs.

On the set, the second assistant camera is responsible for keeping the camera log, recording information reported by the camera operator, and labeling tapes. If you don't have a second assistant on your crew, give this job to whoever slates the takes.

> **TIP:** In Chapter 7, we recommended clapping your hands in front of the camera if you're shooting dual system and don't have a clapper board. Single-system videographers use a different technique: They simply wave their fingers rapidly in front of the lens at the beginning of a take. It's an easy action for editors to spot when running clips in fast forward or rewind.

CALLING FOR QUIET BETWEEN TAKES

Sometimes the material you get *between* takes can be very useful, particularly for reaction shots, which is why you'd be wise to keep the camera rolling after you say, "Cut." After all, tape is cheap.

For example, you might get footage of an actor shifting his weight from one foot to the other, with an impatient expression on his face as he waits for the director to call the next take. But cut this footage into the scene of an argument with his wife, and the same offhand gesture becomes a powerful reaction, conveying disapproval and disgust. What's more, since the expression is natural and understated, it may work better than any of the actor's "acting."

To maximize the possibility of using such between-the-shots footage, it's best if the cast and crew avoid shouting their enthusiasm (or dismay) the minute the director calls, "Cut." Such outbreaks are a perfectly natural release of tension, but they will spoil the soundtrack that accompanies that impromptu reaction shot.

Let the cast and crew know the set is *hot* all the time. (Of course you'll want to call a break eventually, shut off the camcorder, and give everyone a chance to relax.)

> **HOT SET:** Set where camera and sound are rolling. Also, any idle set that's not to be disturbed because it will be used later.

In any case, don't be in a rush to call, "Cut." Even if you don't keep the camera rolling through several takes, continuing to roll for a few seconds after a take is good practice for several reasons:

- Often an actor's most interesting work and most powerful reactions occur just after the scripted part ends.

- Sounds won't be clipped and will fade away naturally.

- It gives the editor some extra footage if she decides to do a fade or dissolve.

WORKING WITH ACTORS

Continuing a discussion started in Chapter 8, here are some fine points for directing actors on the set. You may find some of these techniques equally useful when you're working with subjects of interviews and documentaries.

The Illusion of the First Time

The famous acting theorist and teacher Constantin Stanislavsky, advised actors to create "the illusion of the first time." That is, the actor should deliver a line as though he just thought of it. This is even more important on screen than it is on the stage, when the image of an actor's face may be so large you can practically see him think.

It can be very difficult for an actor to give this impression when he's memorized his lines and repeated them many times over during rehearsals and takes. Giving the audience the impression of spontaneous thought and feeling is an advanced magician's trick, the height of the actor's art.

In the theatrical tradition that preceded Stanislavsky's work in the early 1900s, actors relied on "technique"—vocal tricks and rehearsed mannerisms—to be convincing. A slight hesitation, a clearing of the throat, or even a stammer at the beginning of a speech could make a line seem fresh. The term has a pejorative connotation today, as when an actor who has run out of emotional steam talks about "falling back on technique." At its worst, technical acting may turn into "chewing the scenery," a derogatory term for egregious overacting.

The evolution of film art, and particularly its reliance on the closeup, has encouraged actors to adopt Stanislavsky's approach—particularly his advice to *re-create the emotion* that might give rise to a required speech and action.

Today's audiences expect to see this intimate level of emotional reality on the screen, and they lose interest if they don't get it. So be on the lookout for actors who repeat vocal inflections, gestures, and mannerisms. You're watching technique, not believable film acting.

The Perils of Indication

Another term actors use to describe a results-oriented performance that isn't motivated by emotion is *indication*. When an actor is indicating, he is so concerned about what the director or the audience wants to see that he simply mimics it. The performance is mechanical and unsatisfying.

> **INDICATION:** A performance intended to please the director or audience by producing a particular result or impression.

The perils of indication are that:

- It's all too easy for actors to do.

- It produces a mediocre result.

- It can lead to chronic overacting.

If you give actors direction by describing the result you want to achieve (for example, "Be more judgmental."), you are encouraging indication. You'll get much better performances if you describe the actions you want them to take and let them discover the feelings that motivate those actions.

Actor Jack Lemmon had a successful career on the Broadway stage before he came to Hollywood. His stock in trade was comedic technique, a polite way of saying he hammed it up a lot.

Lemmon's first film role was for director George Cukor. After the first take, the director quietly asked Lemmon to give less next time.

They did another take, and Lemmon reined in his enthusiasm.

Cukor was still not satisfied. Take after take, Cukor insisted he wanted less and less.

Finally, an exasperated Lemmon complained, "George, if I give you any less I won't be acting."

Cukor said that was the idea.

Late in his career, Lemmon said it was the best coaching he ever got.

Lose the Battle, Win the War

The actor is always right. This isn't to say that the actor will always deliver a perfect performance, or even the desired result. But if the actor is experiencing the emotions of the moment, trust her instincts, because they are genuine.

Put another way, if an actor disagrees with you about subjective issues like motivation, feelings, or intentions, it's best not to contradict her. In these situations, the director must become a diplomat. In effect, you bargain with the actor.

Let the actor do the take her way. Then announce that the shot is in the can but you want to try an experiment. Give direction, and do another take. Having gotten her way the first time, it will be the rare actor who won't make a sincere attempt to follow your suggestion on another take.

Trust vs. Trickery

The underlying relationship between a director and an actor is one of trust. The actor is in emotional free fall and needs to know the director has a firm grip on the safety net.

When some directors don't get the results they want, they resort to trickery. Going for a reaction shot showing panic, the director has a PA sneak up in back of an actor and startle him. Or, coaching a fight scene and going for anger, the director draws one of the actors aside and tells her to really connect (hopefully, not too hard) with the next blow.

This kind of coaching sacrifices trust, and it's generally a bad idea. You might get one good shot but at a loss of morale and the spirit of creative collaboration.

Admittedly, this is one of those gray areas. If the trickery is subtle and no harm is done, isn't that okay?

Consider what happened on the set of *Glory,* a Civil War picture directed by Ed Zwick. In one scene, Denzel Washington's character is being whipped by an army officer. In the closeup, Zwick wanted a tear from Washington, but the actor wouldn't do it, feeling that the character would be too proud to give his torturer the satisfaction.

Zwick took the actor playing the army officer aside and told him to keep whipping however long the camera rolled. (The whip is wet felt and doesn't hurt the actor.)

On the next take, Washington expected the whipping to stop after the agreed-upon number of lashes. But the lashes kept coming and the camera kept rolling.

Zwick walked to an off-camera position where he could look Washington in the eye. And the lashes kept coming.

Perhaps out of sheer frustration, perhaps out of fury with Zwick, perhaps dredging up an emotion to satisfy the moment and get on with his life, Washington produced the tear.

We don't know whether Zwick was right to trick his star, nor do we know how well the rest of the shoot went with trust between Washington and Zwick possibly compromised. But it's a memorable shot, and a stunning performance.

It's always the director's call.

When Actors Don't Know Their Lines

Sometimes actors don't have their lines memorized, which is normally unforgivable. They might receive new script pages the day of the shoot—professionals still get their lines down in time for shooting. But an actor might fall ill and you'll have to make a last-minute substitution. Or, you're working with non-professionals who need help. What to do?

Television shoots use an electronic teleprompter, which displays the lines on a monitor or LCD mounted directly above the camera lens. That's a fine solution if you're budgeted for this special equipment and you can afford a skilled teleprompter operator.

> **TIP:** *Teleprompter operator is not a job for a PA. Skill and experience are required to match the scrolling of the dialogue text on the display with the actor's pacing. Miss the beats by even a little bit, and you'll make an already nervous actor's job that much more difficult.*

Here are some less expensive ways to solve the problem when actors must be prompted:

- If it's plausible for the actor to be reading a book or magazine in the scene, paste the script page there.

- Write the lines in bold marker on a sheet of poster board or foam core. Have a PA hold the board off-camera and as close as possible to the actor's sight line.

- For a matching single, tape a page with the lines printed in bold to the off-camera actor's shirt.

- The audience will notice if the actor breaks eye contact to read. So have the actor read the lines before the take and then repeat them as the camera rolls, maintaining eye contact through the take.

- Keep takes short; most actors can remember two or three lines they've just seen. Or have a PA read the lines to the actor just before the take, and roll camera as she parrots them back. (The only problem with this method is that actors tend to mimic the PA's line readings rather than giving you a fresh interpretation.)

Get What You Need

Whatever is or isn't on the screen is ultimately the director's responsibility—and the director must do whatever is necessary to get the desired result. Where you draw the line is up to you, your conscience, and your sponsors.

Of course, it works both ways. If you're walking the walk, you have the right to talk the talk. Feel free to act as though everything in the movie is the result of a deliberate choice.

For example, suppose a critic asks, "What about that bumpy camera move?" Give him your best director's smile and ask, "Did you like that?"

WHAT IS A SENSIBLE SHOOTING RATIO?

The shooting ratio is the average number of takes you require for each shot. If a director records only one take of each shot, and uses every one of those takes in the final edit with no wasted footage, the ratio would be 1:1. A practitioner of the dump-truck style might shoot 30:1, running each scene 30 times in various angles so the editor can assemble one final scene.

A sensible shooting ratio for most projects is somewhere between 4:1 and 10:1. Any less and you risk not getting the coverage you need; any more and you're wasting time and money.

Yes, DV tape is cheap and there are no direct cost penalties for shooting more takes. But keep in mind that you also need to conserve the energy, enthusiasm, and momentum of your cast and crew. A perfectionist who insists on take after take can run his crew into the ground. Certainly, there are directors who seem to enjoy their reputations as intimidating and even unreasonable as a matter of personal style, but don't adopt them as role models.

MOVING THE CAMERA DURING A SHOT

Along with techniques such as a 24 fps frame rate and a grainy look, intentional camera moves during a shot is another way to achieve a film look.

You can spend a lot of money on gear to help you do camera movement, but guerilla film-makers know there are several low-cost alternatives. Here's a list of things you can do on the set to move the camera and make shots more interesting. The options range from simple and inexpensive to complex, requiring special gear and considerable advance planning.

Ideally, you've already provided for camera moves in your shot plan, but if you pick a technique that doesn't require a lot of gear, you can improvise on the set.

Here are some of your options:

- Camera lens and tripod mount
- Handheld shooting
- Portable camera stabilization rigs
- Improvised dollies
- Movie dolly and track
- Crane

Camera Lens and Tripod Mount

Among the most basic types of camera moves are zooming with the camera lens, and panning or tilting the camera on the head of the tripod. For more information on designing shots that include camera moves, see "Moving the Camera" in Chapter 5. For best results, choose a tripod with the *fluid head* feature, and match the sturdiness of the tripod to the weight of the camera. (Service technicians at the rental house can advise you on this choice. DPs who shoot with cinema-style HD cameras may prefer more complex gear-driven heads with hand cranks.)

FLUID HEAD: Swivel mount on a camera tripod that contains hydraulic fluid to dampen jarring and assure smooth movement.

Handheld Shooting

Carrying the camera in your hands as you follow the action is a staple among news crews and guerilla moviemakers. Here's how to do it so the result doesn't look like a home movie:

- **Despite our usual advice to the contrary, turn the camera's image stabilization feature on, if it has one.** If you plan to shoot handheld much of the time, or even just for key sequences, choose a camera with optical image stabilization rather than the digital kind. For more information on why this is important, see "The Price You Pay for Image Processing" in Chapter 3.

- **Cradle the camera in your hands in front of you and away from your body, with your elbows tucked in.** This posture will help you steady the camera as you walk.

- **If the camera has a flip-out LCD screen, use that instead of the viewfinder to frame the shot.** If it doesn't, hold the eyecup of the viewfinder an inch or so from your eye. Otherwise, the bobbing of your head as you walk will jiggle the camera. Either way, being able to use your peripheral vision to spot subjects as they enter and exit the frame will help you follow the action more closely.

- **To minimize jiggle, use the widest possible angle for the shot.** By contrast, telephoto angles greatly exaggerate any vibration and therefore are almost impossible to do handheld. Remember, however, that a wide-angle shot will be the least flattering for actor closeups.

Portable Camera Stabilization Rigs

Camera operator Garrett Brown invented a body-mounted camera-stabilization rig in the 1970s that allowed for smooth, gyro-controlled, handheld camera movement. Cinema Products bought the rights and named it Steadicam; the device revolutionized mainstream cinematography. But the early Steadicams were designed for relatively heavy film cameras. You don't need a rig that bulky or complicated to shoot the equivalent of Steadicam in DV.

The Steadicam Jr. is designed specifically for camcorders. Competitors such as Glidecam, VariZoom, and others also make lightweight handheld models. Some of them are available in different configurations that achieve additional support from mounts on the body or forearm.

> **GIMBAL:** Mechanical device that allows a camera to remain level even if its mount is tipped.
>
> **GYRO:** Continually spinning, weighted mechanical disc assembly that resists movement perpendicular to its axis of spin. With a gyro-equipped camera stabilizer pole, the operator must exert some effort to tip the camera; short for gyrostabilizer.

The basic principle of the lightweight image stabilization rigs commonly used for DV is a camera-mount pole. The operator grasps the pole in the middle and holds it vertically. The top end has a *gimbal* mount that minimizes any jarring of the pole being transferred to the camera. The bottom end has a counterweight that balances the camera like a dumbbell, as well as a *gyro* to steady the operator's movements. Movie equipment rental houses usually have a selection of these rigs.

As with other types of handheld shots, minimize jiggle by turning on image stabilization and favor wider angles.

If the camera operator must run to follow the action, use one of the stabilizer rigs that are supported by the hand or forearm. Or, use a body-supported model if the operator must carry the camera for extended periods.

Improvised Dollies

Classic Hollywood-style dolly shots can be gorgeous on the screen, but they require careful advance planning, lots of setup time with special gear, and meticulous execution. But just about anything with wheels can serve as an improvised dolly, and indie filmmakers have tried them all—wheelchairs, shopping carts, child's wagons, even skateboards. There isn't much setup time, and the only additional expense is a PA to push or pull the thing as the camera operator rides it.

> *TIP: If you insist on acting like a skateboarder, wear a helmet. Come to think of it, that's a good safety precaution, with elbow and knee pads, for any of these vehicles prone to tipping over.*

The main disadvantage of improvised dollies is that you must deal with all the challenges of shooting handheld: All the cautions about stabilization and camera angle apply. If the ground surface isn't smooth, an improvised dolly is susceptible to every bump and pebble in the road, and your PA probably won't steer it exactly the same way twice.

If you're shooting interiors on a slick floor, like the hallway of a building, the operator can sit on a blanket, and the PA can tug a rolled-up edge to slide it along.

Movie Dolly and Track

For shots that must be smooth as silk, consider renting a movie dolly and going to the effort of laying track. In fact, using one of these rigs is the only reliable way to get smooth camera movement in a telephoto shot.

> **DOORWAY DOLLY:** Rolling platform that accepts a camera tripod and rides along sectional, tubular track.

A modestly priced rig, available from most movie equipment rental houses, is called a *doorway dolly* (**Figure 9.5**). As its name suggests, the traditional use of this type of dolly was to follow actors into and out of doorways, but in practice you can use one anywhere—even outdoors if the ground is fairly level.

A typical doorway dolly is a carpeted plywood platform mounted on four tires. The camera is mounted on a conventional tripod that's been secured to the platform.

The tires have semi-circular grooves that ride along stainless-steel tubular track. The track comes in interlocking, collapsible sections —curved or straight—much like old electric train sets.

> **SHIM:** Wooden wedge used to level dolly track.

The main caution about laying dolly track is to make sure it's as level as possible. Even slight variations in a floor's surface can cause dips that will show up in the camera movement. To correct this, grips use *shims,* or wooden wedges, beneath track sections to shore up the dips.

> *TIP:* Another caution about laying dolly track is not to get your fingers caught in the interlocking levers that join track sections. To make a tight connection, they snap shut with some force.

Some more expensive dollies have seats for the operator and a built-in mount for the camera. Others are equipped with boom arms for doing low-level crane shots. For more information, see "Crane" in Chapter 5.

Figure 9.5 A doorway dolly is essentially a rolling platform that runs along sectional track. Note the tie-down chain that secures the tripod to the platform to prevent a tip-over accident. The crew member on the right is the dolly grip, who has his hands on a T-bar by which he can push the dolly along the track.

Cranes

A studio crane is mounted on a truck and looks much like a skewed playground teeter-totter, with one end much longer than the other. The long end is levered aloft with the camera and its operator. The short end has huge counterbalancing weights so that it doesn't take a lot of physical strength to execute a move.

Realistically, you can't hope to use a crane without a skilled crane operator. Those folks are usually union crew, and you hire crane, operator, truck, and driver as a package.

Low-budget alternatives to renting a crane might be various types of hydraulic lifts used on loading docks and in warehouses. Most agencies that rent industrial equipment have this type of gear. But you'll still need a flatbed truck and a driver licensed for commercial vehicles to transport it to the location (unless you actually happen to be shooting in a warehouse.)

TIP: If you're going to use a makeshift device as a crane, make sure you have a safe and reliable way to secure the operator and camera to the lift. But the most important caution about doing a crane shot is to be careful not to make contact with overhead electrical power lines. Don't even operate close to them. The risk isn't worth it. Even skilled utility workers have been electrocuted in accidents involving cranes.

RECORD KEEPING

Record keeping on movie sets involves practices inherited from the old studio system, but even modest-sized video productions need to follow them. Each of the following reports has its own purpose.

Production Board

We've already mentioned the first AD's production board, or strip board, which shows the entire shooting schedule as a sequence of vertical paper strips, one strip for each scene (**Figure 9.6**). Whether you schedule your board manually or with the aid of a computer, eventually you'll want to sort and arrange the scene strips in shooting sequence. (For more information, see "Breaking Down the Script," in Chapter 8.)

During production, the first AD meets with the director every night to discuss how the results of the day's work will affect the next day's schedule. Any scenes that were missed must be rescheduled, revising the call sheet for the next day, if necessary.

Camera and Sound Logs

When shooting is complete for the day, the second AC turns her logs over to the assistant editor, along with all DV and DAT cassettes. The assistant editor is responsible for uploading the clips into the NLE system, after which the editor can use the logs to search for specific takes. (A separate sound log might simply keep track of DATs and timecodes.)

NOTE: On a film shoot, the need to get the exposed stock to the lab every day imposes a regular schedule on submission of dailies to the editor. But particularly on low-budget DV shoots, an Editor might not even be hired until shooting wraps, in which case the schedule for reviewing dailies will be entirely up to the director and AD. Nonetheless, it's a good idea to involve an editor in reviewing your dailies while shooting is underway so he can point out things you missed while you can still do something about them.

"When Boy Meets Alien"

	S1	S2	S3	S4	S5	S6	S7	S8	S9	S10	S11
Location No.	1	1	1	1	1	1	1	1	1	1	1
Breakdown Sheet No.	19	18	18	18	11	11	13	14	10	3	6
Day or Night	D	D	D	D	D	D	D	N	D	D	N
Script Pages	1 6/8	2 3/8	1	1	4	2 1/8	2/8	4 6/8	2 2/8	2 1/8	2
Scene No.	#45	#43	#47	#49	#60	#39	#41	#34	#53	#61	#58
	EXT SNACK BAR	EXT BASE CAMP	EXT BASE CAMP	EXT BASE CAMP	EXT MOON RANCH	EXT MOON RANCH	EXT HANGAR	EXT HANGAR	EXT LAUNCH PAD	EXT LAUNCH PAD	EXT LAUNCH PAD

Character Name:

#	Name		S1	S2	S3	S4	S5	S6	S7	S8	S9	S10	S11
1	Herk	1	1	1		1	1	1	1	1	1	1	
2	Prebble	2			2						2	2	2
3	Melon	3	3	3	3	3	3	3					
4	Kenny G	4									4		
5	Urson	5			5						5		
6	Lady #1	6	6		6	6							

Figure 9.6 Each scene on a strip board is represented by a single, vertical paper strip. The AD arranges the strips in shooting sequence from left to right. Scenes grouped together will be shot on the same day. Numbers in a strip show which actors need to be called for that scene. Strips are colored according to these codes: Day/Ext.=Yellow, Night/Ext.=Green, Day/Int.=White, Night/Int.=Blue.

Script Notes

One of the primary duties of the script supervisor is to keep track of continuity. Although some script supervisors keep their own shot logs, the most common approach is simply to make notes on the script. When shooting wraps for the day, she gives her notes to the editor.

Timekeeping and Day-Out-of-Days Reports

Part of the second AD's responsibilities is to keep track of the cast. He records attendance of each cast member on each shoot day on the *Day-Out-of-Days Report*, updating it at the end of each shooting day. This report

DAY-OUT-OF-DAYS REPORT:
During a shoot, the second AD's record of cast scheduling and actor time and attendance.

has two parts: 1) scheduling of actors to show work assignments for specific shooting days (**Figure 9.7**), and 2) summary of days worked (**Figure 9.8**). The work summary details *drops* and *pickups* of daily and weekly players, and is useful for rescheduling.

TIP: *You can also use Day-Out-of-Days Reports to schedule other limited-availability elements, such as vehicles, special effects crews, costumes, or props.*

DROP: Release of an actor (usually a weekly player) from the shooting schedule and from the payroll.

PICKUP: Restoration of an actor (usually a weekly player) to the shooting schedule and to the payroll after having been dropped.

"When Boy Meets Alien"	Report date: 08/05/XX							Page 1
Month: August	**Day of Month:**	**5**	**6**	**7**	**8**	**9**	**10**	**11**
	Day of Week:	**Mon**	**Tues**	**Wed**	**Thu**	**Fri**	**Sat**	**Sun**
Character Name:	**Shooting Day:**	**1**	**2**	**3**	**4**	**5**	**6**	**7**
1 Herk			SW	W	W	W	WF	
2 Prebble					SW	W	WF	
3 Melon			SW	WF				
4 Kenny G		S				W		
5 Urson				SW	H	WF		
6 Lady #1			SW					

Figure 9.7 The Day-Out-of-Days Report uses the following codes to show actor assignments for each shooting day: S=Start, W=Work, F=Finish, H=Hold, T=Travel, R=Rehearse. A Hold indicates the actor isn't working that day but remains on the payroll, a Finish is a drop, and a pickup is a new Start.

"When Boy Meets Alien"	Report date: 08/05/XX								Page 2
Month: August	**Day of Month:**	**9**							
	Day of Week:	**Fri**	**R**	**T**	**W**	**H**	**S**	**F**	**Total**
Character Name:	**Shooting Days:**	**5**							
1 Herk		WF			5		08/01/XX	08/05/XX	5
2 Prebble		WF			3		08/03/XX	08/05/XX	3
3 Melon					2		08/01/XX	08/02/XX	2
4 Kenny G		1					08/04/XX	08/04/XX	1
5 Urson					3	1	08/02/XX	08/04/XX	4
6 Lady #1					1		08/01/XX	08/01/XX	1

Figure 9.8 The second part of the Day-Out-of-Days Report shows how many days each actor has worked to date, whether any drops or pickups have occurred, and start/end dates.

Daily Progress Report

Prepared by the script supervisor in consultation with the first AD, the *Daily Progress Report* recaps the day's shooting, giving the number of scenes, pages, minutes, and setups done that day (**Figure 9.9**). It also records the number of script pages added or deleted. The main purpose of this report is to communicate progress to the *front office*—producers who don't visit the set.

> **DAILY PROGRESS REPORT:** During a shoot, the first AD's statistics on what was accomplished that day.
>
> **FRONT OFFICE:** In the studio system, the executive suite on the lot.

PREVENTING AND TROUBLESHOOTING COMMON PROBLEMS

We've covered some of these problems already, but here's a handy checklist of what can go wrong on the set— and what to do about it:

- Don't schedule scenes that are technically or emotionally challenging on the first few days. Give your cast and crew a chance to become a team before you start shooting the tough scenes. Save the longest and most difficult scenes for late in your schedule, if possible. Scheduling software ought to take this sort of thing into account—but it doesn't, so you'll have to.

- Don't expect to shoot as many pages per day in the first couple of days as you will later on. If the schedule calls for shooting an average of six pages per day, plan to shoot four on day one.

- To maintain production speed and economy, when setting lights and attempting to control contrast range, try taking light away from highlight areas before you start adding it to shadows.

- Slate each take with timecode. Avoid replaying takes on the set since this can cause a break in the camcorder timecode—a disaster after which timecode restarts from all zeros. If a break occurs, fast-forward past the end of the take and, to be safe, reset the timecode on the camcorder to about five minutes later than your best estimate of the correct index. (Whenever you insert a new tape, manually setting the hour digits to match the tape number will also help prevent the editing chore of dealing with timecode breaks. If your numbering scheme begins with "01" and for any reason the camera resets the code to "00," you won't have any duplicate timecodes unless you experience a second break.)

Daily Progress Report

Shoot Call	8:00 AM		8/1/XX
1st Shot	8:14 AM	**Work Day**	Monday
Lunch	11:45 AM	**A.D.**	R. Knerr
1st Shot	12:50 PM	**Title**	When Boy Meets Alien
Dinner	6:30 PM	**Director**	P. Shaner
1st Shot	7:23 PM		
Cam Wrap	9:46 PM		
Snd Wrap	9:50 PM		

	Scenes	Pages	Minutes	Setups
Total Script	60	112	120	202
Added	0	0	0	0
Deleted	0	0	0	0
New Total	60	112	120	202
Shot Prior	0	0	0	0
Shot Today	4	5 1/8	7	8
To Date	4	5 1/8	7	8
To Do	56	106 7/8	113	194

Scenes Covered	Wild Tracks	Retakes	Remarks
Ext. Snack Bar #45	None	None	
Ext Base Camp #43			
Ext. Base Camp #47			
Ext. Base Camp #49			

Script Supervisor

Figure 9.9 The Daily Progress Report is a kind of box score of production progress, based on the number of pages and scenes shot each day. Experienced producers can study these statistics and judge whether a production is keeping pace with its schedule.

- Make sure sound levels don't peak above 0 dB. If you expect sound levels to vary widely during a take, split the signal and record the L track at 0 dB and the R track at –20 dB for protection.

- Designate a PA to watch the field monitor and make sure the boom doesn't dip into the frame during a take. If the boom operator's arms are growing tired, it's time for a break—or a fresh operator.

- If your camcorder is NTSC or PAL, shoot everything in 4:3 aspect ratio, even if you expect to edit and master in 16:9. If you're shooting with an HD camcorder, shoot everything in 16:9 even if you will eventually go to 4:3. This assures the highest resolution, and you can change those aspect ratios in postproduction.

- When shooting outside, work in the shade if at all possible. If it rains, shoot interiors that day and rework your production board and shooting schedule that night.

- Shut off air conditioning during a take to reduce noise levels, but leave it on between takes to keep cast and crew comfortable.

- If a noisy piece of heavy equipment such as a refrigerator is running near the set, shut it off—but put a driver's car keys inside so you don't forget to turn the unit back on before you leave. (Thawed or spoiled food is a particularly nasty calling card to leave your hosts.)

- If ambient noise ruins a shot, get some wild takes of the effect on the chance you can incorporate it into the soundtrack of surrounding scenes in the edit.

- Break for hot meals at lunch and dinner. Don't force a steady diet of junk food on your team. Keep a variety of snacks and beverages handy at all times, and make sure the crew has at least five minutes off every hour. (They'll be happier and you'll get more work done.)

- Be sure to record 60 seconds of room tone at the end of each setup.

- Sit down whenever you can.

Making Changes

Projects can get thrown off track when unexpected changes occur. If you're producing your own movie, the responsibility for deciding when and if to make a change is largely yours, within the constraints of available time, money, and resources. But if you're working in a corporate environment and have to answer to project sponsors or clients, requests for changes may come from influential people outside the project who have control over what you do.

> **PROJECT CHANGE NOTICE (PCN):**
> Documented request for change
> to a project; requires signed
> authorization before the change
> can be implemented.

Our advice in these situations is to do what professional project managers do: establish a mechanism for managing change. Whenever you receive a request for changes that will impact your schedule and/or your budget, write it up as a *Project Change Notice (PCN)* before you implement it. Describe the change on a piece of paper, along with its impact in additional production days and expense. Include the name of the person making the request and the date she did so. And provide a place for your sponsor to sign off.

If you don't get authorization, don't make the change. That way, your sponsors will have to assume responsibility for making the decision and setting aside funds to cover additional costs, if necessary. The PCN is an effective means of communication that keeps everyone informed about project status. It also protects you against accusations that you blew the schedule or budget, and you'll live to shoot another day.

> **TIP:** *It can be a challenge to keep track of script changes. In the movie industry, the accepted practice is to issue each new version of script pages on a different color paper. By the time you reach the set, the updated scripts are usually multicolored explosions of page colors.*

STRIKING THE SET

After the last setup of the day, follow the steps below to finish the job professionally. Your goal should be to leave the space in better condition than you found it. That way, you and other crews may have the opportunity to shoot there again.

Strike

Take down the set (or any location decorations) and your equipment as carefully as you put it up. Don't invite an accident by rushing.

Pack

Stow light fixtures and equipment in their proper cases. Coil cables and cords.

Clean Up

Bag all the trash, and carry it to receptacles and recycling bins. Wipe down the snack tables, mop the floors, and vacuum the rugs.

Restore

Put furniture, potted plants, and wall hangings back where you found them.

Touch Up

If your gaffer's tape took paint off the wall, touch it up. Leave no damage, or make specific arrangements to repair it later.

Inspect

Take one last tour through the space to make sure it's clean, and check to see that you haven't left any equipment or personal belongings behind.

Sign Off

Turn the space over to its custodian, security guard, or other responsible party, and make sure someone is prepared to lock up after you leave.

ABBY SINGER AND THE MARTINI

According to Hollywood lore, the *martini* is the last shot of the day—because the shot after that will probably be in a chilled glass at the closest bar.

> **MARTINI SHOT:** Last shot of the day.

Calling for the martini is the director's prerogative, since it's often necessary to keep everyone on the set until the day's shooting is in the can. Days that last 10–12 hours are routine. And even when the cast and crew pack up, the director and AD will be planning to meet after a break to go over the reports and review the schedule. (You won't get much sleep during this time, so make sure you're in good physical shape.)

As the hours stretch on, crew members yearn for the next shot to be the martini.

In the studio system of the late 20th century, a legendary First AD named Abby Singer had a habit of calling for the martini even though the director wanted to keep shooting. Named in honor of the man who couldn't wait to call it a day, the second-to-last shot is now called the *Abby Singer.*

> **ABBY SINGER:** The second-to-last shot of the day.

CHAPTER TEN

In the Cutting Room

A familiar Hollywood truism tells us that a movie is "written" three times: once by the writer, once by the director, and once by the editor. In some ways, the last of these "writes" is the most important. Editors are primarily storytellers, and the digital video revolution hasn't changed that part of the job one bit.

Editing is a heady experience. When all the footage is put together, the editor's version of a scene might be very different from its original description on the page, or even its performance on the set. With little more than a mouse click or a keystroke, the editor can put a fire truck in the middle of a scene where no fire truck existed before. Or, she can delete a scene that cost $250,000 and took a week to shoot, as if it never happened. An editor can make a tragic scene play like comedy, and vice versa. She can find a story to tell where only incoherent scenes existed before.

In one sense, editing is easier than ever before. In the film world, cutting a picture used to be tedious, complicated, and time-consuming. Even today, once you cut the negative, it's expensive and impractical to go back and make changes. In contrast, digital nonlinear editing (NLE) is like word processing: Making changes can be so fluid and easy that some editors (and directors) find it hard to stop.

At the same time, the DV revolution has made it so much easier for directors to shoot take after take that an editor can be deluged with material. Not only that, the editor's job has become a lot more technical. Today's editor must be a digital wiz, dealing with all the show's technical requirements from the pixel level on up.

You don't necessarily need a huge body of technical knowledge and experience to assemble a video presentation. It's much like using a camcorder. You can point, shoot, and get results without ever cracking the manual. But if you want a polished, professional look for that presentation, it takes study and practice to develop the necessary skills. That's just as true for editing as it is for shooting.

We don't plan to give you a full tutorial on video editing techniques, although we'll tell you how to get one. What we *will* do is step through the kinds of decisions you'll need to make as you approach the editing process: Should you retain the services of a professional editor with his own equipment and software? Should you assemble your own editing system and learn to use it? And if you decide to tackle the edit yourself, how should you select and configure the best NLE system for your project? We'll also survey NLE basics and share some tips and techniques that you won't find in many instructional books or courses.

THE EDITING PROCESS

In the film world, once shooting is complete it's customary for the director to confer with the editor, then return weeks or perhaps months later to view a *rough cut*—the editor's first draft of the picture. However, in video production, many directors prefer to supervise the editor directly as she works. (There's no practical reason for this difference, except that film and video are separate cultures.)

The editor's first assembly of clips into a story sequence is called a *string-out*. Starting from there, she will go through several versions, each more polished, before arriving at the rough cut.

Working closely with the director, the editor will go through several more refined, intermediate cuts. When the director is reasonably satisfied, that version of the show becomes the *first cut*. On a typical studio production, once the first cut is complete, the editor gets a new boss—the producer, who usually has authority over the *final cut*. Sometime during these early stages temporary music and effects may be added.

> **ROUGH CUT:** Editor's first version of a show, usually without special effects or music.
>
> **STRING-OUT:** Editor's preliminary assembly of clips.
>
> **FIRST CUT:** Director's approved edit of a show.
>
> **FINAL CUT:** Producer's approved edit of a show.
>
> **FINE CUT:** Any late version of an edit in progress.
>
> **LOCKED:** Approved, edited version of a show, to which no further picture changes are made.

A final cut isn't necessarily final, especially if you're dealing with a corporate-owned movie studio. Studios do so much test marketing that there are often many different versions of the final cut based on audience responses to sneak previews, opinion polls, and focus groups. Any version of the movie at this late stage may be called a *fine cut*. At some point, one of the fine cuts will be judged absolutely final and the picture will be *locked*. Only after the picture is locked will the finished music and sound effects be added, and a sound mix done.

MEET YOUR EDITING CREW

Initially, film editors and video editors used very different techniques in their respective industries. Film editors literally cut strips of film and spliced them together; video editors sat at consoles and copied scenes from one tape to another.

NEGATIVE CUTTER: Laboratory technician who literally cuts, or conforms, the original camera film negative according to the editor's detailed instructions.

NEGATIVE CONFORMING: Process of matching physical cuts in a film negative to the editor's instructions.

Once NLE technology was introduced, video and film editing converged rapidly—as did the job descriptions of film and video editors. Within the last 20 years it has become routine for film dailies to be transferred to video for editing in an all-digital environment. Work doesn't resume on the film itself until *negative cutters,* working with lint-free gloves, cut and assemble the negative for striking release prints, *negative conforming* from the edited video version.

Editing a digital video production employs exactly the same NLE techniques, hardware, and software as film-to-digital editing; the only difference is that the footage starts out in digital video format, and no film transfers are required unless the video is going to be released on film.

Even though almost all film and video postproduction today is digital, the job titles come mainly from the film industry. Here are the traditional roles.

Editor

The editor is sometimes called a *picture editor* to distinguish her from other editorial specialties, such as sound editor, effects editor, or music editor. Her main task is to assemble clips to tell a story in a way that pleases (initially) the director, and (ultimately) the producer. Working from the script, the storyboard, and the outline—and referring to pertinent

PICTURE EDITOR: Lead editor, primarily responsible for assembly of a movie; cutter.

production notes—the editor starts by building sequences of shots into scenes, then assembles sequences of scenes into a complete movie or video presentation.

Supervising Editor

In situations with an abundance of footage and a tight deadline, multiple picture editors might be hired to work simultaneously on different sections or scenes. The person in charge of managing an editorial team is the supervising editor, usually a veteran cutter.

Assistant Editor

The assistant editor's job is to prepare video and audio material for assembly by the editor. During production on major projects the assistant editor functions as liaison between the script supervisor, the first AC, the sound mixer, and the editor. In postproduction, the assistant editor provides systems and organizational backup for the editor; concerning himself with digital sampling quality, system storage capacity, picture and audio quality, and so on—all the technical details that free the editor to concentrate on being an artist, or at least a storyteller. Assistant editor is the first step on the career path to picture editor, so if you aspire to be an artist/editor you'll need to begin as an apprentice, sweating the bits and bytes.

Dialogue Editor

The dialogue editor works entirely with production sound, especially the actors' dialogue recorded on the set. She selects the cleanest audio takes, removes as much noise as possible, adds room tone to cover cuts where necessary, and identifies dialogue that needs to be rerecorded in ADR. She also makes sure the dialogue track syncs with the picture.

Music Editor

This editor works with the director to create a list of music cues—places where music needs to be inserted in the movie. Then he lays in temporary tracks to give the impression of the finished music while the project is being edited. Once the picture is locked he creates a *click track,* or rhythmic guide, and prepares a list of precise scene and shot timings to help the composer score the picture.

> **CLICK TRACK:** Music guide track for use by composers and/or performers that marks tempo as a series of audible clicks.

Sound Effects Editor

The sound effects editor lays in effects recorded live during the shoot, created afterwards, or synthesized. She also works with the Foley artists who create effects like footsteps, rustling of clothes, and so on.

Visual Effects Editor

The visual effects editor creates or supervises video compositing, such as titling and CGI, and incorporates these effects into the edit.

THINKING ABOUT YOUR DIGITAL EDITING SYSTEM

We're going to start by trying to talk you *out* of building a sophisticated digital video editing system—unless you have some experience with the editing process. Even if you yearn to get hands-on and do the edit yourself, you don't need to load up with thousands of dollars of high-performance computer gear right away. At least read through the rest of this chapter before you decide. Then, if your heart is still set on that shiny new gear, see Appendix B: Selecting and Building an NLE System.

Do You Really Need to Buy One?

If this is your first production, and you have commercial aspirations for it, we'll be blunt: *Don't do the edit yourself.*

Video trade magazines, indie film journals, and film websites are full of ads and posts offering the services of trained, talented video editors, available at reasonable hourly rates; most of them even have their own desktop systems. Make some calls, ask for demo reels, do some interviews, and chances are you'll find someone who has his own ideas, yet will listen respectfully to yours—and who will make a sincere effort to help you realize your vision.

If you insist on doing the edit yourself, you run the risk of getting caught up in the technicalities of postproduction and losing sight of what's important in your story or message. And if that happens, who will follow through on your vision?

If you hire a veteran editor, you can deliver your material, have a chat, go away, and try to relax while she assembles the rough cut. That's not a bad way to work. The editor can be objective about the material, and after you've spent some time away from it, you'll be able to give the rough cut a fresh look.

> **Editing ACEs**
>
> When movie credits roll, you may see the abbreviation ACE after the editor's name. It stands for American Cinema Editors, Inc. Unlike the DGA for directors, WGA for writers, or SAG for actors, ACE is a professional society, not a craft union or guild. The organization has no jurisdiction over labor rates or working conditions. The ACE designation indicates a level of professional achievement requiring at least 60 months of industry experience, sponsorship by two ACE members, and approval by a board of directors.
>
> Editors can also be union members. Typically they'll belong to IATSE if they work in motion pictures, or NABET if they work at a television station or network.

But unless you picked an editor with a weird attitude, you don't have to let him go it alone. As a matter of fact, looking over the shoulder of an experienced editor is an excellent way to learn how to edit. A good editor will involve you in editorial decisions—you'll be able to review and approve takes, cut points, effects, and so on. You'll learn what the key decisions are, but you won't have to sweat the technical details of how to make them happen. You can put your attention where it should be—on building the story.

Of course if it's *not* your first production, or you're an experienced editor, or you're determined to wear the editor's hat, or you can't afford to hire an editor, or you simply have NLE Fever—there's probably no stopping you (an admirable quality in a videomaker).

How Does NLE Work?

One of the main reasons film and analog video editing used to be so time-consuming is their inescapably linear nature. For instance, to add a shot at the end of a scene, you first have to find the scene, roll through to the end, roll to the beginning of the insert, and either splice the film together or record a new version to tape. A lot of wasted time in the editing suite was spent waiting for the tape (or the film) to shuttle back and forth.

Disk-Based Editing

NLE spares you this grief by storing your digital clips on a computer hard drive. Making an editing selection is virtually instantaneous; you can go directly to any shot on the disk. Better yet, digital editing is *nondestructive* because you can always undo your changes; in fact, you can always go right back to the original version of the clip.

> **NONDESTRUCTIVE EDITING:** Editing a clip without affecting the source material.

There's only one catch: NLE software is one of the greediest applications imaginable in terms of computer disk storage and processing speed. You need a fairly powerful (and relatively expensive) computer to make it work efficiently.

 REALITY CHECK: *Yes, the price of entry-level computers has been coming down, but the speed and capacity of all computers continues to increase. The net effect seems to be that the price for a serious machine stays about the same: $2,000 – 3,000.*

The Timeline Concept

NLE's primal metaphor is the *timeline*—a graphic representation of the emerging structure of your show as seen on the computer screen, just as if you were looking at

> **TIMELINE:** Graphic representation of the edited sequence of video and audio tracks.

physical strips of tape or film. The timeline represents the edited sequence of video and audio tracks, starting from the left and flowing to the right (**Figure 10.1**).

The timeline grows in length as you continue to insert clips. But you can select any time-code location in your show quickly and easily if you want to work on it simply by clicking on its corresponding location in the timeline.

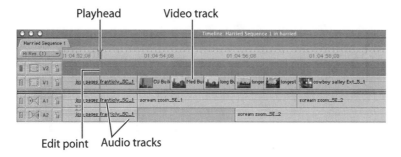

Figure 10.1 The timeline is a graphic representation of the tracks you're assembling. Time flows from left to right. The timeline of the assembled show has its own continuous timecode. For each clip, the program keeps track of both the original camcorder timecode and the inserted timecode in the presentation sequence.

Rendering and Playback

Although every vendor would like you to believe that its application is overwhelmingly superior to its competitors, the fact is that all NLE packages are pretty much the same, at least in terms of core editing functions. (We'll point out a few important differences presently.) The main distinction between NLE systems (software and hardware in combination) is how quickly they can generate a result (a process called *rendering*), and how pretty and smooth that playback appears on the screen.

> **RENDERING:** Mathematical calculations required to display digital imagery on a computer screen; playback of your movie, with effects, in NLE software.

 REALITY CHECK: *The NLE marketplace is rapidly sorting itself into graduated levels of price and performance. To capture the attention and loyalty of beginners, software manufacturers have been in a race to offer new, low-priced, versions—with a limited set of features. These products offer some useful functionality but force you to upgrade when you take on a more complex project. As a result of competition, these low-priced versions now offer more real utility, becoming useful production systems rather than demonstrators.*

Accurate playback is absolutely crucial to the video editor. Whether you're judging the timing of a cut or the pacing of a fade to black, there's no way to tell whether you've achieved the effect you want unless you can see it just the way the audience will.

Why Is Rendering So Hard?

When you edit, the computer records your choices as a series of events (insertions, transitions, and so on) that occur at specific timecodes. This detailed list of events and timecodes is called an edit decision list (EDL).

When you want to play back the edit, the computer processes the EDL and generates all the required video frames. If you didn't make any changes to the images the camera captured, playback is straightforward and should look fine. But if you applied color correction, used a dissolve, or supered a title, the NLE has to generate a lot of images that didn't exist previously. And it has to create and play them back at full video frame rate or the preview will look jerky.

For example, in the case of a simple dissolve, the computer must merge two scenes by increments, generating new pixel values for hundreds of frames in a transition that will take just a few seconds.

This is why rendering takes every bit of image processing power your computer can muster.

EDIT DECISION LIST (EDL): Text file identifying all clip files, sequences, and transitions in an edited show, including instructions for assembling the finished presentation.

Basic NLE Functions

Whether you're assembling a home movie on your laptop or cutting a television special in a network editing suite, NLE systems don't differ much in terms of basic editing operations. Essential functions include the ability to:

- Upload clips from a camcorder or deck to create computer files on a hard drive

- Name video clips

- Organize video clips in folders

- Insert clips into a timeline to build scenes and sequences of scenes

- *Trim* clips (marking *in and out points*) either as you upload them, just prior to inserting them on the timeline, or after they are in place on the timeline

- Display multiple video and audio tracks on the timeline

- Add transition effects, such as *dissolves*, between edited clips

TRIM: Mark the in (starting) and out (ending) timecodes of a clip.

IN AND OUT POINTS: Pointers that mark the beginning and end of that part of the clip you'll use in the final sequence.

DISSOLVE: Gradual transition from one image to another by momentarily blending the images. Also called "cross dissolve" or "cross-fade."

- Adjust the properties of transition effects (such as the length of a dissolve)

- Import music and sound effects as clip files

- Adjust the level of audio tracks at any point on the timeline

- Edit, replace, or add audio tracks for a particular video clip

- Add titles

- Use mouse selections, keyboard shortcuts, or a combination of both to make edits

- Play back clips and assembled sequences on the screen

- Generate finished video output in a variety of formats, including NTSC, PAL, MPEG-2 for DVD, and streaming video files for the Web

Advanced NLE Features

Not every NLE package includes the following capabilities, but many do. If your NLE doesn't support an advanced feature you need, you may be able to buy a *plug-in,* a supplementary software module that appears as a menu selection within your NLE and delivers the desired function.

> **PLUG-IN:** Software module that runs inside another application to extend its capabilities; add-in.

Autocapture

This handy feature—available in most mid-range NLE systems—is also called *DV scene detection.* It simply means that, as you're uploading a recording from your camcorder, the program will detect stops and starts on the tape and automatically save them as separate clips. Doing it the old way, you'd have to mark and select the clips you want and upload them all in a batch, or start and stop the camcorder manually as you identify and upload each clip one by one.

> **AUTOCAPTURE:** Ability to identify and segregate clips automatically during a DV upload; DV scene detection.

Multiple Levels of Undo

Selecting Undo lets you cancel a mistake by reverting to a previous version of the edit. Multiple levels of Undo make it possible to roll back many versions.

Large Number of Stacked Tracks

You must have at least three tracks on a timeline—one for video and two for audio (stereo L and R). You won't need multiple video tracks unless you're doing compositing. However, multiple-level soundtracks are very common. Even a low-budget production might have as many as eight audio tracks, and a sophisticated production could require as many as 100 audio tracks in the same scene. Most entry-level products can't handle that many. Needing more tracks is one of the compelling reasons to upgrade to a more feature-rich, professional version.

EDL Import/Export Capability

You'll recall that the EDL is a text file that includes all the instructions for assembling the finished presentation. If you're using an NLE system to edit a film, negative cutters will use a printout of the EDL as a guide for conforming the negative to your video edit.

In the world of video editing, the EDL becomes important mainly when you're moving projects between dissimilar NLE systems. For instance, you might export an EDL from your Premiere Pro system, and then import it (along with copies of your clips) into a colleague's Vegas system.

The ability to export an EDL as a guide for film cutting and to edit 24P video go hand in hand—both require a picture rate of 24 fps, a feature offered only in professional software versions.

Animated Titles

Most NLE packages allow you to superimpose a title, but if you want scrolling titles or titles that include effects, you'll need an NLE that provides these types of animation. Or you can add a more sophisticated plug-in for this purpose, such as Inscriber Technology TitleMotion.

Editable Effects

One of the most powerful advanced features of NLE systems is *keyframing,* or *in-betweening*, by which you can create custom transitions and effects by transforming existing ones. To do this, you make a change to the first frame in the transformation (distorting a shape, for example) and the last one, and the computer fills in, or *interpolates*, all the frames in between.

> **KEYFRAMING:** Creating transformation within a video sequence by changing the starting and ending frames; in-betweening; interpolation process.

Compositing

Sophisticated NLE systems will include built-in compositing functions, such as 3D effects, graphic objects, animation, and *texturing* (adding variegated surfaces) of objects. It's not uncommon to find compositing available as a plug-in—Boris Red for titles, for instance.

> **TEXTURING:** Adding a synthetic surface to a 3D graphic object.

Color Correction Controls

Fine touches you might want to add just before generating your final output include color correction to meet broadcast standards, matching flesh tones, or compensating for poor lighting during the shoot.

Compatibility with High-End NLE Systems

EDLs don't necessarily have the same parameters from one brand of system to the next, so transferring your project from a desktop system to a high-end editing suite can be a challenge unless this portability is built into your NLE. A system such as Avid Xpress DV is designed to assure compatibility with its high-end product family; other desktop NLEs may not transfer so well.

Compatibility can also involve machine-control functions so instructions in the EDL can work directly with studio switchers and decks. If your NLE is deficient in this department, try an add-in like Automatic Duck.

Ability to Customize the User Interface

This feature lets you reprogram keyboard shortcuts and buttons on menus to suit yourself—or to set up one work station like other consoles in an editing suite.

TV Monitor Output

To view video output on a monitor, you'll need a composite or S-Video output card in the computer and NLE software that's fast enough to generate the analog video stream in real time. Presenting real-time digital display on a computer monitor may only require some compression, unless effects or transitions are complex. Software-based desktop systems do this just fine, most of the time. But analog playback requires conversion of every frame from digital to analog—a huge computing task and a major reason for the special-purpose hardware you'll find in expensive editing suites.

Support for Multiple Processors

Dual-processor desktop computers make fast editing systems, but some NLE software can take better advantage of the extra power than others. The results are reduced rendering time and smoother playback, particularly if transitions or effects are complex.

> **DUAL PROCESSOR:** Computer with two processors working in tandem.

NONLINEAR EDITING BASICS

As we said in the chapter introduction, we don't propose to give you a tutorial on video editing techniques. Experienced media professionals won't need one, and beginners will require far more than one section of one chapter.

But if you're new to this game, here's a quick overview, an introductory survey like those "appreciation courses" they give to nonmajors in college. Rather than teaching you which button to press or which command to use, we'll concentrate on what you can do—not how to do it. And we'll include a few basic tips to help you get started.

There's very little difference between the way the various desktop systems perform basic NLE techniques, but since the authors used the Final Cut Pro program to edit *When Harried Met Sally* and the other videos on the DVD, we'll use that application as we step through the basics.

Finding Your Way Around the Desktop

When you start Final Cut Pro, you'll see four distinct windows, or workspaces: the *browser*, the timeline, the *viewer*, and the *canvas*. You can arrange these windows on the screen to suit yourself. On single-monitor systems, the windows will be arranged patchwork-fashion. An example of a dual-monitor arrangement is shown in **Figure 10.2**.

> **BROWSER:** In Final Cut Pro, a window that displays a directory of captured clips.
>
> **VIEWER:** Window showing the clip you're working with.
>
> **CANVAS:** Window showing the frame at the current position of the playhead in the timeline; also displays playback of sequence.

You build a sequence by locating clips in the browser, editing their in and out points in the viewer, inserting them into the timeline (and possibly adding a transition effect between them), and playing back the sequence in the canvas.

Browser

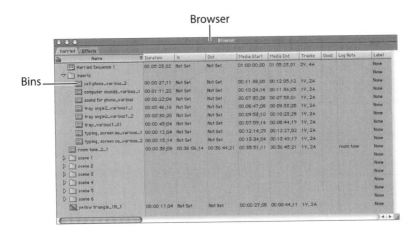

Bins

Viewer   Current clip   Edited sequence   Canvas

Viewer
playback
controls

Viewer
playhead

Timeline
playhead

Edit point

Timeline

Figure 10.2 Here's a typical dual-screen setup for Final Cut Pro. The page is too narrow to show both screens side by side, so we've moved the left-hand screen on top. Although Final Cut Pro only runs on the Mac platform, as a general rule you can set up a dual-screen desktop with either Mac or Windows NLE applications as long as your computer has two video outputs. When you move the mouse in the display, it will track seamlessly from one screen to the other, as if the two screens were a single, wide desktop.

Browser

Final Cut Pro uses the term *browser* to describe the window that displays a directory of captured clips for a project. Initially, the browser is empty. When you open an existing project, or upload clips for a new one, the browser will show a list of those clips. You can create a text description for each clip you upload.

> **BIN:** A folder used to group and store DV clips; trim bin.

Seen in the upper image of Figure 10.2, the browser layout is very much like a computer disk directory, and you can create and use folders for storing your clips in groups. Each folder is called a *bin*, analogous to the film-editors' term *trim bin*, which refers to a physical container used to hold film clips.

Timeline

As noted earlier in this chapter, the timeline (seen in the lower portion of the screen in Figure 10.2), is a graphic representation of the edited sequence of video and audio tracks, starting from the left and flowing to the right. The playback head, or *playhead*, is a special cursor that marks your current position on the timeline. Any insertion you make into the timeline will occur at this position, also called the *edit point*.

> **PLAYHEAD:** A cursor that marks the position on the timeline of the video frame currently being displayed in the canvas.
>
> **EDIT POINT:** Position in the timeline at which the next edit will occur.

Viewer

Seen at the top left of the lower portion of the screen in Figure 10.2, the viewer window displays the clip you're currently working with and allows you to mark and adjust its in and out points. The viewer has its own playback controls and playhead, so you can run the clip without affecting the canvas or the timeline; if you're not running the clip, the viewer displays a still video frame. You select a clip for viewing by highlighting it on the timeline.

Canvas

Seen at the top right of the lower portion of the screen in Figure 10.2, the canvas window lets you play back and view the sequence you're building. If you're not running the clip, the canvas displays the video frame at the playhead location on the timeline. If you have a TV monitor connected to the system, it will normally display whatever you're seeing in the canvas window.

Selecting and Uploading Clips

Uploading clips from your camcorder to the editing system (and identifying and labeling them) is one of the most tedious steps in making a video—and one of the most critically important. If you do this job well, you'll save your editor countless hours of frustration looking for (and possibly not finding) a clip she absolutely must have.

To begin, select File > Log and Capture from the program menu; the Log and Capture window will open (**Figure 10.3**). Now you can identify and label the next clip you will upload.

Part of capturing a clip involves marking its in and out points, corresponding with its starting and ending timecodes. The quickest way to do this is to run the clip in the viewer, type "I" to mark in and "O" to mark out. The program will insert the correct timecodes for the clip automatically.

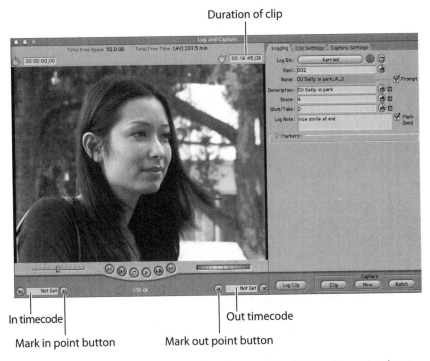

Figure 10.3 The Log and Capture window lets you identify the clip you're about to upload and mark its in and out points. You can upload your clips one by one, or log all your clips and then capture them in a batch operation.

If your camcorder or deck is connected to your computer via FireWire, and it's supported by the program, you don't even have to press the Play button on the camcorder to start the upload. Click the Capture Now button in the Log and Capture window, and the upload will start at the "in" timecode you marked. When the upload is complete, the clip's label will appear in the browser listing, and its first video frame will appear in the viewer.

Using Descriptive Labels

The more descriptive and accurate you label your clips, the easier it will be to find just the take you want later. Make use of the OK / NG marker in the Log and Capture window to rate each clip; you can search on these tags later. Include anything that was distinctive about the take in your description. Select Log Clip to enter descriptions of the clip. For example, "Good expression, but her hair was mussed."

Digitizing Analog Sources: Video and Audio

You may occasionally need to upload analog video footage or analog music clips from tape or LP.

If you're working in a fully equipped editing suite, you'll probably be able to use a special deck for this purpose (**Figure 10.4**). These decks contain the required A/D (analog-to-digital) conversion circuitry.

However, if you're not working in an editing studio, there's a quick, reliable way to do the same trick without a special deck.

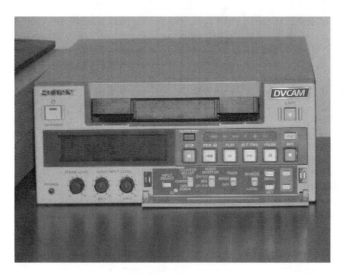

Figure 10.4 You can use a DV deck for uploading camcorder recordings or for encoding signals from external analog sources such as VHS videotapes and audio cassettes. This deck reads Mini DV, Standard DV, and DVCAM digital cassettes.

For starters, if you can, make sure the clip didn't originate in digital format. (For instance, you might see some digital signature like mosquito noise—a particular type of video artifact that appears around the edges of moving objects and looks like a swarm of flying insects.) Resampling an analog version of a digital recording can generate noticeable errors. If you believe the analog clip you're about to work with originated as a digital clip, stop and try to get a copy of the digital original.

Otherwise, assuming you've got a genuine analog clip, you'll need an analog player (such as an audio cassette deck, a turntable, or a VCR) and a DV camcorder with a mini jack labeled something like "A/V In/Out" (**Figure 10.5**). This jack connects to a built-in analog I/O circuit.

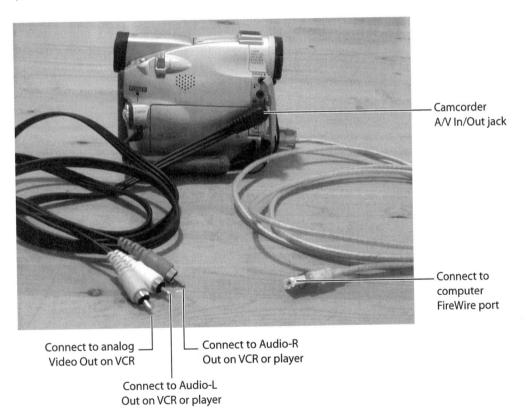

Camcorder
A/V In/Out jack

Connect to
computer
FireWire port

Connect to analog
Video Out on VCR

Connect to Audio-R
Out on VCR or player

Connect to Audio-L
Out on VCR or player

Figure 10.5 A quick way to handle an analog-to-digital conversion is to run the analog signal into a DV camcorder via its A/V In/Out jack, and send the digital output via the FireWire cable into your computer. A low-cost camcorder will do the job just as nicely as an expensive one—as long as it has a jack for analog inputs. (Be sure to turn camera power on.)

Use a hookup cable with three RCA plugs for connecting the Video, Audio-L, and Audio-R jacks on your analog player to the matching inputs at the camcorder's A/V In/Out jack. Use your regular FireWire cable to connect with the computer's IEEE 1394 port.

Turn on the camcorder and press Play on the source deck. The camcorder will handle the A/D conversion, and the output up the FireWire will be a perfectly acceptable DV signal. You can then upload the clip through the Log and Capture window.

If you have neither a camcorder nor a DV deck, you'll need to digitize the signal via an analog video capture card in the computer. (If it's audio only, you can input it to the computer's sound card.) However, here's why we prefer the camcorder method:

- The digital output of your analog capture card must match the DV spec; some older models don't.

- On input, the device driver for the capture card may prompt you to set encoding options. If you choose the wrong ones, or if the card simply isn't fast enough, you'll get frame dropouts or other technical problems in the DV recording.

> **TIP:** *If you want to incorporate a film clip into your DV edit, take the clip to a film lab that offers "telecine transfer." Typically, the output of a telecine will either be analog videotape or Digibeta. You may have to pay an additional charge to have the lab downconvert the clip to DV.*

Trimming Clips

Experienced editors have learned the hard way that it's dangerous to trim shots too tightly when you're capturing clips. In building scenes, it's best to leave some wiggle room for making decisions. If you trim a clip too tight, you won't be able to start it any earlier, or end it any later, or dissolve it in and out, without going back and recapturing from the original tape.

When you're working with a clip in the viewer, it's a different story. One of your first editing decisions should be to trim it more closely by adjusting its in and out points. To do that, simply drag the outer edges of the slider at the bottom of the viewer to the right or left, which corresponds to timecode points along the clip's timeline (**Figure 10.6**). The left edge is the in point, the right edge the out point.

> **TIP:** *The time-honored editor's advice for trimming clips is the same as that for attending a Hollywood party: Arrive late and leave early. To hold the audience, cut into a scene when it's already in progress, and cut away the instant you've established the plot point or delivered new information—in short, get out before it gets boring.*

Organizing Clips

You'll find that the better you organize your clips in the browser window, the better (and faster) your editing will go. You can rearrange clip descriptions in the listing (by dragging clip names around in the display), create and name folders to hold similar clips, even nest folders within folders.

As with logging and capturing, taking time to organize your clips in the browser will pay dividends. We suggest setting up a folder scheme that corresponds to your shot plan. For example, each folder might be a separate scene, such as "Josh's Office." Within that folder you can create several subfolders to hold the shots from each setup, named, for instance:

- Josh-Phil two-shot master

- Josh singles

- Josh ECU

- Phil singles

- Phil ECU

This structure follows the logic of the script and the shot plan, and helps you visualize the flow of the story line and the shots you'll need to build it. For example, in the organization just listed, if you don't have any clips in the "Phil ECU" folder and you can't find any on your original tapes, you know you don't have any good reaction shots of Phil from this scene and may have to borrow some from other takes.

Inserting or Overwriting Clips on the Timeline

Once you've selected and organized your usable clips, you're ready to start building the story. You do this by inserting clips on the timeline one after the other—a process that's analogous to splicing film clips together.

All NLE tools provide several equally effective ways to cut clips together. The method you choose will simply be a matter of personal work style.

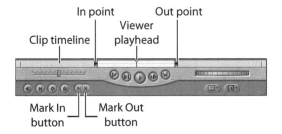

Figure 10.6 Drag the edges of the timeline in the viewer to adjust your clip's in and out points; or play back the clip and mark the desired points by typing "I" or "O" on the keyboard or by clicking the Mark In or Mark Out buttons.

One way to insert a clip on the timeline is to drag it from the viewer window and drop it on the canvas window. As you drag, a menu of options will appear on the right of the screen (**Figure 10.7**). By dropping your clip onto one of the options, you can select whether the clip will overwrite the current clip on the timeline (indicated by the edit point) or be appended to it. You can also specify a transition effect, such as a dissolve, or (if you don't specify one) use a straight cut. (You can always go back and add an effect later. For more information, see "Adding Dissolves and Transitions" later in this chapter.)

Building and Editing Sequences

As you insert clips, the timeline shows the sequence of the scene you're building. Each layer on the timeline is a separate audio track. When you shoot sync sound (as you always do in DV unless you're deliberately shooting MOS), the audio track drops into the timeline in perfect sync with the picture, indicated as a separate track below the video.

As you add music and effects, the video tracks will probably end up with several audio tracks below them on the timeline.

Syncing Sound

When you shoot dual-system sound, you'll upload your DAT clips using the log and capture procedure, just as you would with any other clip. They'll appear in the browser along with all the other clips and can be treated as any other.

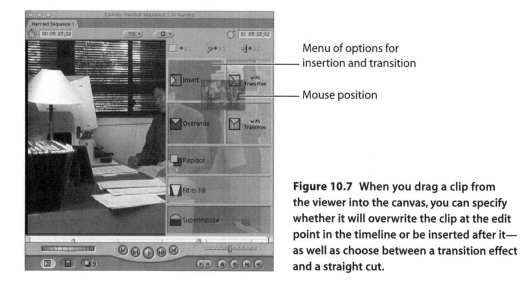

Menu of options for insertion and transition

Mouse position

Figure 10.7 When you drag a clip from the viewer into the canvas, you can specify whether it will overwrite the clip at the edit point in the timeline or be inserted after it—as well as choose between a transition effect and a straight cut.

If you used jam sync, the DAT tape will have the same timecode as the camcorder recording, and the NLE program will match the timecodes automatically. As long as the timecode is unbroken, you won't have to worry about sync at all.

If you shot dual-system sound without jam sync, you'll have to sync up picture and sound manually, but that's not a big deal in NLE. For starters, mark approximately the same in and out points when you are previewing (listening to) and capturing the clips. Then drop the DAT clip onto the timeline beneath the video track of the clip to which it belongs. Line up the ends for a rough sync.

Make sure your audio tracks are displayed as waveforms in the timeline. Click on the DAT track and slide it back and forth on the timeline to change its position. The DAT track will be in sync with the video when its peaks and shape match and line up vertically with those of the camcorder track (**Figure 10.8**).

> **TIP:** To make sure two audio tracks are in sync, select both in the timeline and play them back simultaneously. If you hear what sounds like an echo or reverb, they're not in perfect sync.

Once the DAT track is in sync, you can delete the camcorder guide track.

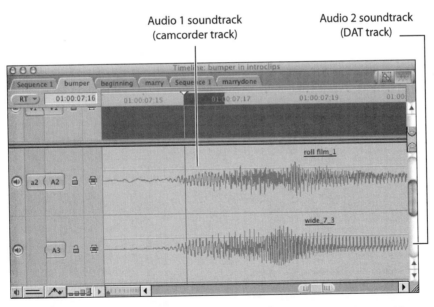

Audio 1 soundtrack (camcorder track)

Audio 2 soundtrack (DAT track)

Figure 10.8 Soundtracks displayed on the timeline can be shown as graphical representations of sound waves. Two identical tracks are in sync when the peaks line up. For reference purposes, the black vertical bar is exactly one video frame wide.

Adding Dissolves and Transitions

Creating a transition effect, like a dissolve, where only a cut exists is quite easy: Click the cut in the timeline, select Effects > Video Transition from the menu, and select the name of the effect you want, such as a Dip to Color Dissolve, from the list that appears.

> **NOTE:** In Final Cut Pro terminology, a dissolve is called a cross dissolve. Its variations include dither (ant-like), ripple (pond-effect), and dip to color (fade in/fade out, or FIFO).

When you double-click an existing effect in the timeline, the Transition Editor window will open, and you can adjust its properties (**Figure 10.9**). For example, you can make it faster or slower by adjusting the Start or End sliders.

NLE programs provide hundreds of built-in transition effects, and by changing their properties you can create many more. But you needn't stop there. You can use plug-ins like Boris Red to create or enhance transitions with spinning animations and all manner of artistic wizardry. You've seen many of them, especially in commercials, and can probably visualize them just from their names: explode and implode, page peel, slide, zoom, stretch, checkerboard, Venetian blinds, and zigzag.

Dissolve

Editors use dissolves to indicate a time lapse between one scene and the next. A similar effect that merges the brightness of two scenes, creating a flash at the midpoint, is an "additive dissolve." Variations include "non-additive," "dither," and "ripple" dissolves.

In film terminology, prolonging the effect is called a *lap dissolve,* which has a languid, dreamy quality.

> **LAP DISSOLVE:** Prolonged dissolve.

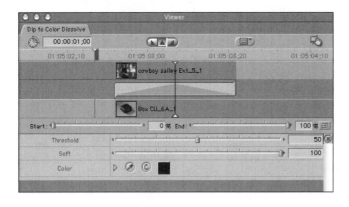

Figure 10.9 The Transition Editor shows properties of a Dip to Color Dissolve at the edit point. Changing the Soft property, for example, will blur the pixels as the two scenes merge, softening the effect.

Fade In, Fade Out

The dimming of a scene to black is a "fade out;" brightening from black is called a "fade in." Fading out on one scene and then fading in on the next is a kind of full stop: One chapter ends and another begins.

In cinema terminology, a dissolve is nothing more than a double-exposed, overlapping set of fades, sometimes called a "cross-fade."

But Final Cut Pro has its own set of definitions. A fade-out followed by a fade-in is called a "dip to color dissolve." The traditional effect fades to black, but you can select another color if you like. If the effect fades only to black, the Final Cut Pro editor calls it a "fade in fade out (FIFO) dissolve."

Wipe

A *wipe* gradually reveals the next scene as the current scene is wiped off the screen—it's like sliding one sheet of paper over another. In cinematic language, a wipe usually means "meanwhile," and is generally used to intercut concurrent actions in different places. But some directors (like Akira Kurosawa, for instance) have used it as a way of moving from one scene to the next. A common version is the *clock wipe*, or *radial wipe*, which looks like the rotating hand of a clock.

> **WIPE:** Transition effect that gradually reveals the next scene as the current scene is wiped off the screen.
>
> **CLOCK WIPE:** Spiraling wipe transition effect; radial wipe.

Iris

A technique inherited from silent movies (and seldom used these days), an *iris in* spirals down like the closing of a lens aperture; an *iris out* opens in reverse fashion. Irising out usually suggests "in the beginning," while irising in implies a conclusion or ending. In old movies, an iris in was also used to highlight a detail within the frame—for example, a cowboy gripping the handle of his pistol.

> **IRIS:** A traditional spiraling transition effect.

In Final Cut Pro, something like the traditional effect is called an "oval iris." You can also select other shapes, including cross, diamond, point, rectangle, and star.

Don't Overdo It

Traditionally, any transition effect (other than a cut) signaled to the audience that they were about to be transported to another place or time. Today's audiences don't need such visual hints: They are accustomed to seeing stories told almost entirely with straight cuts, even if some of those cuts bridge abrupt jumps of time and place. A cut advances the story as quickly as possible, and that's the pacing a modern audience expects.

Experimenting with transition effects can be fun. Just don't overdo them in your finished presentation. Effects can be visually impressive, but they aren't the stars of the show. Overuse of transition effects is a sure sign of a novice.

The Magical Split Edit

When you're editing dialogue, it's often far more interesting to watch the person who's listening than the one who's talking. The audience wants to see how the listener reacts—which is precisely why we've emphasized capturing *reactions* when you're shooting.

> **SPLIT EDIT:** Transition in which the picture of the incoming scene precedes the sound cut (L-cut), or the sound of the incoming scene precedes the picture cut (J-cut).

One way editors keep the audience focused on those all-important reactions is an old film editing trick called the *split edit*. At the transition point between two shots, a split edit lets you change the audio before or after the picture changes, or not at all.

For example, we cut away to Amanda's face while Adam is still speaking (picture cut before sound cut), then cut the audio to her line as she starts to speak in reply. Alternately, we hold on a shot of Adam while we bring in Amanda's next line on the track (sound cut before picture). Only after we see Adam reacting to that line do we cut to Amanda's face as she continues her dialogue.

Split edits keep the audience emotionally involved in a scene and let you tighten the pace. They also help you make cuts so smooth most viewers won't notice them.

We mention split edits here because while they can be tedious to do when cutting film, they're a snap in NLE. Basically, you start out making a simultaneous cut—then you grab either the picture or audio cut and drag it forward or back. Couldn't be easier.

> *TIP: L and J cuts get their names from the way they look when sound and film tracks run by on a console film editing machine—with the sound and image cuts offset. They have a similar appearance on an NLE timeline.*

Fixing Common Sound Problems

We'll survey advanced sound-polishing techniques in the next chapter, but here are some basic fixes you'll probably want to make when you're assembling your rough cut.

Kill That Dog Bark

If there's an unwanted noise, such as a dog bark, on the soundtrack, you'll see it as a spike when you look at the track in the viewer. If the sound is in the clear (with no dialogue over it), you can get rid of it easily by fading down the level of the audio track for the duration of the unwanted noise. However, when you play the scene back, the soundtrack will go dead for a moment—which will sound awful. But that's not a problem: This is why you recorded room tone on the set. Grab a clip of the room tone just long enough to cover the gap and drop it onto the timeline as a separate audio layer.

Make More Room Tone

If you don't have enough room tone, you can drop in several copies of what you've got to make a longer clip. If you forgot to get room tone at all, you'll have to search for short periods of silence in the various takes and cut them together. (If you go back to the location to rerecord the room tone, chances are it won't be the same—but people do it as a last resort.)

Find and Fix Distorted Audio

If the track is distorted because the audio was recorded too hot, you need to replace it. Here's where the backup track you recorded at –20 dB comes in handy. If you captured it in the camcorder using our recommended procedure, it will be on the right stereo track and already in sync. (For more information on shooting dual-system sound, see "Recommended Dual-System Setup" in Chapter 7.) If the production audio track is on DAT, sync it up as previously described. Adjust the level to match the preceding and following clips.

Punch Up Audio That's Too Soft

Repairing an audio track that was recorded at too low a level is a bit tricky, since simply increasing the level can cause distortion. To get around this problem, insert multiple copies of the audio segment, one beneath the other, on the timeline; just make sure they're in perfect sync. The net effect will be a louder track.

Finesse an Unwanted Sound

If an unwanted sound effect, such as a police siren, is ruining your scene, and overlapping dialogue (or some other problem) makes it impossible to simply remove it, try incorporating it into the ambience. Sneak some other street noises, maybe even another siren, into the earlier parts of the scene. As the audience comes to accept the background effects as part of the environment, by the time the annoying noise comes along they'll probably ignore it.

Pacing, Pacing, Pacing

Officially, the editor's job involves building clips into a logical sequence that tells a story, but her unofficial job is pacing—which is a quick way of describing the manipulation of the *illusion* of the flow of time as the audience experiences it. As a general rule, pacing should be brisk, but you may want to slow it down occasionally to emphasize a feeling, or to allow a plot complication to unravel in satisfying detail.

One telltale sign of a novice videomaker is pacing that's too slow or erratic. Much of the excitement of a well-edited movie (even a training demonstration) comes from its artful compression of time; a realistic recording of real life at its real pace is far too boring to watch.

Even if you're not aware of it, you probably have a fairly good sense of cinematic pacing picked up from all the movies you've watched. Learn to trust it. You know, for example, that movie stories tend to avoid "shoe-leather" scenes—showing the actor in transition from one place to another. Such scenes are usually a waste of precious screen time and slow down the pacing.

The true start of a scene is called the *point of attack*—and it should always come just a breath before some interesting development occurs: Don't cut into an explosion, cut into the burning fuse. For the same reasons, a wise editor cuts away the instant a transaction is complete. You'll rarely see a screen character say "good-bye" to end a phone conversation. He'll simply hang up the phone, often without any polite formalities.

> **POINT OF ATTACK:** Point at which the audience is introduced to a new scene.
>
> **BEAT:** In writing, acting, or editing, a change of an actor's mood or intention in a scene; also, a momentary pause in pacing.

In terms of working hours spent in the editing room, most editors take relatively little time to assemble a show—and then put in endless hours cutting and recutting it until the pacing is right. For instance, you start by cutting out all the pauses between speeches so one line follows quickly on another. Then you play back the scene, looking for the emotional *beats*, the changes of mood or intention. *That's* where the pauses go, to give the audience a chance to breathe.

Pacing is exquisitely subtle, like the rhythm of a poem or the groove of a piece of music. It has a lilt all its own, and if the ebb and flow are just right, the audience won't notice your manipulations.

NO NEED FOR PERFECTION

One of the biggest pitfalls of digital editing is not knowing when to stop. NLE technology makes it so easy to arrange and rearrange your clips that you could grow old trying them all. And once you get caught up enhancing your soundtracks and adding special effects, several festival submission deadlines could come and go before you think you're ready.

We know student filmmakers who are still working on their short subjects a year after the footage was in the can. They've burned through their budgets and are maxing out their credit cards to buy time at the post house, or making up for lack of money with hours of unpaid time at their own PCs, seeking perfection.

AIR DATE: Scheduled broadcast date for a television or cable show.

Of course if you're working in a commercial environment, you'll probably be working against a hard deadline, or even an *air date*, and sooner or later you'll be forced to submit the work. But even after it's in commercial release, you'll lie awake nights thinking of ways you could have improved it.

There is no need for perfection, nor is there enough time in this life to achieve it.

If your story works, if your video communicates... it's time to stop. Everything else is "finishing," which can be more sophisticated or less sophisticated, but is basically icing on the cake.

SHOW IT TO SOMEONE BEFORE IT'S TOO LATE

One last word of advice: During the editing process it's almost impossible to avoid getting too close to the material. This is why directors hire editors rather than doing the job themselves. As the edit nears completion, nobody will have much objectivity left. This is one reason movie studios use test screenings to refine their final cuts.

If you're working outside the studio system, you should arrange for your own test screenings. At the very least, find some people to watch your proposed final cut with you—preferably people who aren't in the business. Even if your invited audience doesn't give you notes, simply watching the presentation with them will change your perspective and highlight things you need to fix.

STORING YOUR PROJECT FILES FOR POSSIBLE RE-EDIT

It may feel like this edit will never end, but it will—and you'll need to think about how to store your work materials when you're done. Even professional systems with their huge hard drives don't have enough disk storage to hold more than one big project at a time. When you remove a project from your computer to get ready for the next one, you want to make sure you'll be able to resume the edit later, if necessary—even at another editing facility, on a different NLE system, or with a different editor.

As you prepare to take a project off your system, follow these guidelines:

- Keep the original camcorder and DAT cassettes. Don't reuse them. Store them in a separate location from your other backup media, along with the logs and an exported copy of the EDL file (which will usually be small enough to fit on a diskette).

- Since most NLE systems do nondestructive editing, they don't actually trim your captured clip files. So be sure to back up all video data folders in the NLE system. The clips will still be there as you captured them initially. Use uncompressed recordable DVDs, or data DAT tape, as backup media.

- If you don't back up all your NLE system data, including the captured clips, at least save a copy of the *project file*, which (in Final Cut Pro) contains all the data in your browser. If you want to resume editing later, and you still have your project file and your camcorder cassettes, you can upload only the clips you used, and you won't have to log them (since all that data is in the project file).

> **PROJECT FILE:** In Final Cut Pro, a document that contains all the data in the browser, which you can use to reconstruct a project from the original camcorder tapes.

- Make complete backup copies of any source material you used, such as music cuts and sound effects. The clips you actually selected will be saved in the files you back up from the computer, but you might eventually want to use one of the other tracks from a borrowed CD.

- Make a printout of the exported EDL and save it with the backup media.

- Label all media clearly and store them in a secure, cool, dry place.

LEARNING TO USE YOUR EDITING SYSTEM BETTER

Instructors who teach NLE for a living estimate it takes about 40 hours of hands-on experience to learn the basics, and another 40 hours before you are proficient enough to edit a show without consulting a training book or manual.

Here are some useful training options.

Trade School or University Extension Courses

We strongly recommend taking a semester-long university course to get up to speed on your NLE system. It's usually far less expensive than a three-day training seminar, and you'll get much more practice during a course that meets, say, once a week for eight or ten weeks.

Professional Training Seminars

Sponsored by software dealers, or staged at manufacturer-certified training centers, these seminars can be excellent opportunities for gaining hands-on training—but they tend to be costly and a bit too concentrated. How much can you really absorb during a three-day session? And once the seminar is over, you'll be left to practicing on your own.

Online Tutorials

If you're comfortable with interactive media and don't mind working by yourself, try the online approach. It has the advantages of being the least expensive and letting you fit your training time into a busy schedule.

Resources

You'll find full listings of training options at these Web sites:

- Avid: *www.avid.com/training/index.html*
- Apple: *www.apple.com/software/pro/training/*
- Adobe: *www.adobe.com/products/premiere/training.html*
- Sony Pictures Digital Vegas (third party): Sundance Media Group (*www.sundancemediagroup.com*)

CHAPTER ELEVEN

Polishing Sound and Images

When futurist Arthur C. Clarke observed, "Any sufficiently advanced technology is indistinguishable from magic," he could have been talking about movie postproduction. Movie magic would be much less compelling without synthetic sound and imagery—effects so artfully artificial, and so invisible, as to create a "realism" that's totally fake.

There's a long tradition of such wizardry in film, but less so in video: Most broadcast TV runs on tight deadlines that don't allow much time for postproduction polish. But television series and movies-of-the-week are produced film style, which allows their soundtracks and imagery to be more sophisticated.

As production goes digital, the demand for special effects and the ability to deliver them are increasing. Why? Because audiences demand ever more dazzling entertainment, and technological advances are making this dream world easier and cheaper to produce.

Today, even low-budget training videos and local cable commercials can feature narration in multiple languages on separate tracks, digital music that sounds like a full orchestra, and stunning 3D titles. So studying the film-style postproduction techniques of big-time filmmakers will help you improve the quality and effectiveness of your show.

POST TOOLS

There are hundreds of video postproduction applications on the market. They are designed to work with (or sometimes right inside) your NLE application and provide advanced features and capabilities such as titling and animation. We'll give you an overview of what you can achieve with sound editing and image-finishing tools in this chapter. DVD authoring is covered in Chapter 12.

The software marketplace is chock full of specific programs for very specific tasks. An example is Digital Anarchy's Aurora Sky, which generates astoundingly beautiful synthetic sunsets and cloud banks. But before you go shopping for such specialized tools, consider this emerging standard—"plays well with others."

Can We Upgrade You to a Nice Suite?

A recent trend in the software business is bundling NLEs with related multimedia production and postproduction tools, forming an integrated suite of applications. From the manufacturer's viewpoint, promoting many or all of its acts under the same tent encourages brand loyalty. The consumer wins because the bundling concept doesn't work unless the integration is seamless. For example, when you use a special effects *filter* within Final Cut Pro, you shouldn't perceive that you've left the familiar boundaries of your editing desktop—even though you're accessing a plug-in module provided by a third-party vendor.

> **FILTER:** Software plug-in with a canned set of creative options involving colors, textures, or effects designed for artistic impressions or technical transformations.

A perfect example of this strategy at the entry level is Apple's iLife '04 suite, included now with all new Macs (and available as a modest-priced upgrade for older machines). At the professional level, Apple has introduced its Digital Production Platform, a suite of applications built around Final Cut Pro 4. Now targeting primarily the Windows platform, there's the Adobe Video Collection, built around Premiere Pro. The applications included in these suites are listed in **Table 11.1**.

Table 11.1 Digital Video Production Suites

Vendor and Suite	Product Name	Application
Adobe Video Collection Standard	Premiere Pro	NLE
	After Effects 6 Standard	Video motion effects
	Encore DVD	DVD authoring
	Audition 1	Digital audio workstation
Adobe Video Collection Professional	After Effects 6 Professional	
All other Standard applications		
	Photoshop CS	Digital photo editor
Apple iLife '04	iMovie	NLE
	iPhoto	Digital photo editor

Table 11.1 Digital Video Production Suites (*continued*)

Vendor and Suite	Product Name	Application
Apple iLife '04	iDVD	DVD authoring
	iTunes	Music library manager
	GarageBand	Music composition
Apple Digital Production Platform	Final Cut Pro 4	NLE (plus apps listed below)
	Shake 3	Compositing and effects for film and HD
	DVD Studio Pro 2	DVD authoring
	Logic Platinum 6	Music composition, notation, and audio production
Apple Final Cut Pro 4	LiveType	Title generation
	Soundtrack	Audio content creation
	Cinema Tools	Film and 24P HD NLE support
	Compressor	Streaming video encoder

Other software vendors, such as Pinnacle, Ulead, and Sony Pictures Digital, are also beginning to integrate their NLE products with postproduction tools, such as DVD authoring programs. There are far too many products and suites to cover here, but be aware that your choice of NLE now impacts more than just the editing function. And, as you might expect, vendors typically offer discounts and promotional pricing when you buy an application suite in a single purchase.

MAKING THE MAGIC INVISIBLE

Neither movie music nor visual effects should draw attention to themselves. Music should lend an unnoticed emotional dimension to the experience, subtly guiding the audience's emotions. And while movie publicists tout visual effects as "eye candy," and Dolby Surround Sound can shake you to your bones, all the tricks of the postproduction trade are wasted effort if they draw your attention away from the show's story or informational message.

When you hear that a feature-length motion picture took a year in post, it's generally not because the director, editor, and producer were cutting and recutting the story. No indeed, the most time-consuming part of finishing a movie is getting the technical stuff just right: repairing a dialogue track one syllable at a time, creating the song of a mockingbird that follows the same tune the actor is whistling, delivering on the screenwriter's promise of a spectacular sunset even though the sky was gunmetal gray when the scene was shot, or weaving in music that supports the mood and pacing of the story from one scene to the next.

And doing it so nobody notices.

Creating Sound Magic

As we discussed in Chapter 10, while editing progresses from the rough cut through a series of fine cuts, sound editors concentrate on refining the audio tracks. Garbled production dialogue must be repaired or replaced. Sound effects captured during production must be replaced with created ones—to achieve greater realism! Missing sound effects need to be added. While the final music score often arrives late in the editing process, *scratch tracks* and sample music must be laid into the late-version edits so studio executives and preview audiences will have a full film-going experience. At the end of the process, rerecording sound mixers bring all the audio tracks together at proper mix levels, free from distortion, with suitable equalizations and artful assignment to the movie theater's speaker array.

> **SCRATCH TRACK:** Soundtrack that contains sample music as a placeholder for an original music score; temp track.

All of these tricks cater to audience expectations, which have evolved throughout the history of film and television. For example, in the real world, a stalker on wet grass makes hardly any sound at all. But in a movie, the audience expects to hear the *squish-squish-squish* of his footsteps in the soggy earth, so the effect must be manufactured in post.

Creating Image Magic

Image postproduction concentrates on enhancing what was captured during production and can often create visions so fantastical as to defy capture in the real world. It also includes a complex process of quality assurance, as technicians make sure the picture is up to spec.

Preparing video for broadcast is particularly difficult because of standards imposed during the early days of analog transmission to keep stations' signals from interfering with one another. Preparing video for transfer to film and theatrical distribution forces you to deal with constraints such as the color reproduction characteristics of various film stocks.

MEET YOUR POSTPRODUCTION CREW

Postproduction people are artists in every sense of the word, but at the same time they can't avoid being technicians. This isn't a field where you can leave the technical details to others. Postproduction is *all about* the technical details.

In Chapter 10 you met a team of artists and technicians involved in the editing process, including editor, supervising editor, assistant editor, dialogue editor, music editor, sound effects editor, and visual effects editor. These people continue their work into the final postproduction phases, assisted by the following specialists.

Sound Designer

Just as a DP paints with light, a sound designer—working closely with the rerecording mixer—paints with sound, shaping the audience's impressions with dialogue, music, and effects. On many big productions a sound designer is hired to oversee creative audio decisions. If you don't employ a sound designer, your sound editor will step into the role.

Supervising Sound Editor

On a major production, where a team of editors and technicians work on different aspects of the soundtrack, the supervising sound editor coordinates the team, reporting to the lead editor.

ADR Supervisor

The ADR supervisor is in charge of hiring and directing the actors who must rerecord dialogue. If actors need to be called back, the ADR supervisor notifies the director and producers. On major productions, a certain number of ADR sessions are normally provided for in the actor's contract. Adding voice-over narration is also considered an ADR function. Unless you're planning to dub your production into another language, ADR isn't something you should strive to do—the best solution is to get good production sound in the first place.

Voice-Over Talent

Ideally, if dialogue has to be rerecorded, you'll get your actors into the studio to do it themselves. However, if that's impractical for some reason, you or your ADR coordinator will hire voice-over artists for this purpose. Some voice-over artists specialize in sounding just like big stars (because some screen actors hate doing ADR).

> **VOCALIZATION:** Using the human voice to produce postproduction sound effects.

Narration is another job for voice-over talent. It's generally not practical for a narrator to record a voice-over on the set, so typically this is done later in a sound studio. (One exception would be shooting a news segment on a short deadline, where a reporter might record a voice-over commentary on an auxiliary audio track.) Other voice-over jobs include singing and *vocalization* (vocal sound effects).

Foley Artist

Another group of postproduction specialists are called Foley artists, named for 1930s radio sound-effects magician Jack Donovan Foley, inventor of the stage that bears his name and on which these artists shuffle and hoof on cue. As they watch a scene projected in the recording studio, Foley artists supply footsteps, heavy breathing, body movement, rustling of clothes, hits, slaps, coughs and groans, even wind effects—to name just a few of their many tricks.

Composer

If a movie is going to have an original music score, the composer usually doesn't begin to work in earnest until the rough cut is complete. Even then, music recording must wait until the picture is locked because it's tied so closely to the final pacing of scenes.

Arranger

An arranger translates the composer's score into sheet music for each of the instruments in a studio orchestra. If a production is going to use new performances of old tunes, the arranger's job may also include setting that period music to a different tempo to make it sound more contemporary.

Musicians

Unless you're shooting a music video, musical artists won't play a note until postproduction. In most cases, having musicians on the set is a needless complication—the music will be difficult or impossible to separate from dialogue in post. If a music performance is on-camera and not part of a concert, it's usually pantomimed. If it's actually played, it becomes a guide track for production sound to be dubbed later.

Lead Mixer

Until a picture's soundtrack is mixed, it may contain 100 or more individual tracks, each carrying sections of dialogue, a musical instrument, or a layer of sound effects. Before the movie can be duplicated, all those layers must be collapsed into just two or four tracks. This process is called a *mix-down,* and it's performed by the lead mixer, who must pay close attention to the levels of each track so that the audio blending is just right (**Figure 11.1**).

> **MIX-DOWN:** Combining and blending multiple source audio tracks into one, two, or four output tracks.

Colorist

A colorist is a skilled technician who specializes in color correction, both for artistic effect and to meet technical standards of video or film distribution.

Title Artist

A title artist selects typography for the movie's titles and credits, sets the type using software tools, and applies animated effects such as scrolling.

Figure 11.1 Most professional editors have a small desktop mixing board (left) in their suite for handling audio inputs. Each vertical column of sliders and dials controls the level and equalization settings for one of the input or output channels. In specialized sound editing facilities, you'll find larger mixing consoles (right) capable of handling many more channels. If your production has a complex soundtrack, you'll do your mixdown at one of these consoles. Not shown is the most important instrument of all—a well-trained human ear.

Visual Effects Artist

This category of postproduction art can include a variety of specialists who work for the visual effects editor (or supervisor): matte painters (who create synthetic backgrounds), model makers, animators, and compositors.

POLISHING SOUND

Postproduction procedures for creating a finished soundtrack include replacing dialogue, repairing and enhancing production sound, adding sound effects, creating ambiance, and inserting music. Here's an overview of how it's done.

Replacing Dialogue

Garbled, unintelligible dialogue is unacceptable. Frustrated theater patrons who must turn to one another asking, "What did she say?" are not having a good time—or following the story.

Even so, replacing dialogue should be a desperate last resort. It's always cheaper and quicker to use production sound, even if you have to apply technical tricks to make the tracks viable. (See "Cleaning and Separating Dialogue Tracks" later in this chapter.)

Try Re-creating Production Sound

There are a couple of ways to avoid doing ADR—one of which is already too late to use this time, but might help next time:

- Try to get good production sound on the set. If your mixer/recordist advises you that an audio take is bad, *retake the shot*. If it's impractical to shoot the action again (for example, if the sun has set and daylight is gone, or the location owner insists you wrap for the day), record the sound wild. Capture the actors' wild lines as slated takes on the camcorder and/or DAT. Have the performers try it several times so you have some options in post. Then sync up the tracks in the edit.

- Go back to the location with the actors, and record wild audio tracks on camcorder or DAT. Chances are that the room tone or background noise won't match the original take perfectly, but these takes will probably be a better match than ADR tracks recorded in a studio. Bring a dub of the original cassette and play it back for the actors on the camcorder before they perform, so they can imitate their earlier line readings as closely as possible.

Why Resort to ADR?

Besides replacing garbled production dialogue you can't fix any other way, other reasons to do ADR include:

- Adding voice-over narration

- Recording offscreen dialogue not captured on the set, such as the unseen other end of a phone conversation

- Dubbing dialogue in a foreign language

- Creating an alternate version of the soundtrack to remove offensive language

- *Double-tracking* a vocalist who accompanies herself

- Using Foley artists to create sound effects, a process that can be done either in an ADR facility or on a special Foley stage

> **DOUBLE TRACKING:** Dubbing over a previously recorded track so a vocalist can sing harmony with herself.

Preparing for ADR

If dialogue replacement is your only option, here's how to use it.

Before the ADR session begins, the dialogue editor has a lot of work to do. He must prepare video dubs of the scenes that need additional or replacement dialogue, including the video track and all production audio tracks. The production dialogue will serve as a guide track.

> **STREAMER TRACK:** Audio track containing cueing beeps for the voice-over actor, used in ADR.

The editor must also create an additional reference track, called a *streamer track,* that contains a cueing tone (or sequence of tones) preceding each take. A typical streamer track will have eight beeps before the start of a take: The actor hears a series of three beeps at one-second intervals, then another three, then two—with the picture and sound cue occurring where the third beat would go.

If the ADR insert involves singing or matching to some rhythm other than lip movements, the material the sound editor prepares might also include a click track for the performer's reference during the take.

The ADR Studio

It's best to use an audio post house that specializes in ADR. Not only will it have all the required facilities, but also the technicians will have experience with the complexities of the process.

> **INTERLOCK STUDIO:** ADR facility in which film print and mag tracks can be synced, or interlocked.

ADR requires a specially equipped recording studio (**Figure 11.2**). Some people still call it an *interlock studio*, a holdover film term derived from the need to sync, or interlock, the picture, production mag-track playback, and ADR mag-track recording.

ADR facilities range in size from tiny soundproof booths to small stages. A booth is more appropriate for one or two voice-over artists; the stage is better for a larger cast. A booth will have virtually no room tone, but technicians can rig a stage with sound reflectors and baffles so it has just the right echo quality to match the room tone of the set. (Getting it right is largely a matter of trial and error—at hourly labor rates!)

> **TIP:** It's not worth the effort to reproduce location room tone in the ADR studio unless you are replacing audio for the entire scene. If you're just intercutting a few lines of ADR production dialogue, it's best to record the new dialogue flat, without echo, and mix room tone and background noise recorded on the set with the ADR track in post. To complete the effect, you may have to add some synthetic reverb to the voice.

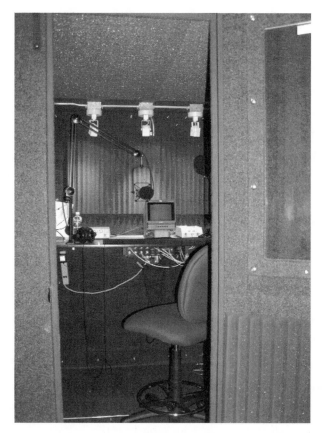

Figure 11.2 This small ADR sound booth is just the right size for recording narration. Its foam-coated walls will impart no room presence to the sound. Note the essential water bottle to prevent the narrator's occupational hazard—dry mouth.

FOLEY PIT: Stage with different walking surfaces and partitions for holding material to enhance the sound of footsteps; stage where Foley walkers work.

A variation on the ADR stage is a *Foley pit,* a recessed stage that has different types of floor surfaces, such as concrete and wood, to give just the right qualities to footsteps. Standard practice is to fill partitioned areas in the Foley pit with material that shapes the sound—corn flakes for the crunchy sound of walking in fresh snow and old mag tape for walking in grass. People who make their living stomping around in this stuff are called *Foley walkers.*

Looping

During an actual ADR session (in a process called *looping),* the actor watches the original take on a screen above the booth or stage and listens to the original line reading in her headphones. Then the recordist will replay the take, and after hearing a *two-pop,* or cueing tone on the streamer track, the actor will give her own reading while watching the picture in silent playback, attempting to match the lip movements precisely. This performance will be recorded on a new track.

LOOPING: Dialogue replacement process during which speeches recorded on the set are replaced with those of voice-over artists. Also, in audio editing, creating a repetitive music track by copying and pasting a waveform.

TWO-POP: Cueing tone that occurs two seconds before start of picture.

It's important to use the identical model mic you used during production and to place it in the same orientation to, and distance from, the actor that it was on the set.

For recording narration, it isn't always necessary for the narrator to see the video as he speaks. In that case, you don't need an ADR stage at all, and you can book your session in any good recording studio. But if the narrator is describing the details of some action as it unfolds on the screen, an ADR setup is advisable. No doubt you've seen wild-animal documentaries in which the narrator comments on an action just a bit too long before you see it. This is a common mistake, and an easy one to avoid.

TIP: If you're on a budget and can't afford an ADR facility, you can do a fairly good job on your own. Prepare by making DV dubs of required scenes and guide tracks, just as the dialogue editor would. Put your actor in a quiet room, and remember to use the same mic and audio perspective as on the set. Then play back the video and guide tracks from the camcorder to a field monitor and headphones while you record the dub track on the DAT. Use dual-system jam sync so you can match timecode in post.

Syncing ADR Tracks

It might seem that the whole point of ADR is to capture new audio that will be in perfect sync with the picture, particularly the actors' lips. But some fine-tuning is usually required.

The rule of thumb with lip sync is that it's OK for the ADR actor's voice to lag the lip movement slightly, but can never precede it. If it does, there are ways to tighten it in post.

This problem is particularly challenging when you're dubbing a movie into a foreign language. After the edit is locked, it's standard practice for a screenwriter/translator to do a foreign-language version of the script, attempting not only to convey the sense of the dialogue but also to use the *same number of syllables* in each line. If it's not possible to do both, the translation with the same number of syllables will probably prevail.

If the lip sync is close, syncing an ADR track on an NLE system needn't be any more complicated than aligning a dual-system DAT track. (For more information, see "Syncing Sound" in Chapter 10.)

The process gets trickier if the lip sync is off, which can happen even after repeated attempts to get it right in the ADR studio. If the voice-over artist's attack is even slightly inaccurate, the audience will notice. Then, too, you might want to use the most dramatically convincing take, even if it doesn't provide the best lip sync.

If lip sync is off, digital postproduction sound tools make it possible to fix it fairly easily. For instance, you can use keyframing on the ADR soundtrack to compress or expand the waveforms of audio tracks, aligning peaks in the dialogue (consonants) to the exact time-code locations of the corresponding lip movements.

Being able to manipulate sound this way is a great improvement over having to cut and splice mag tracks, but it's still tedious, forcing the dialogue editor to work one syllable at a time. And happily, it's no longer necessary.

For a Few Dollars Less

We've all seen horrible examples of bad dubbing, including those English-language versions of old Japanese horror movies. These low-budget pictures seem to ignore lip sync entirely (although the differences between the languages and the relatively fast tempo of Japanese speech do complicate the problem).

A radical refinement in the way people thought about ADR occurred in the 1960s. Italian film director Sergio Leone made a series of marvelous, low-budget westerns, mostly based on Japanese samurai movies, shot in the arid Spanish countryside, using multilingual, multinational casts—including a rising young American actor named Clint Eastwood. During the takes, each actor spoke the dialogue (or some version of it) in his or her own language. Leone produced foreign-language versions by looping everyone except the actors who happened to be speaking the native language of whichever region the version was being prepared for. This heavy reliance on post-dubbing is known as the "Italian system," and it was actually in use long before Leone brought it to international attention. (Federico Fellini, for instance, used it regularly.)

DUB TRACK: New audio track recorded during ADR.

Synchro Arts VocALign Project, an add-on (or plug-in) for NLE sound programs, automates the process of ADR alignment. (See *www.synchroarts.co.uk.*) This program processes the new audio track, or *dub track,* automatically compressing or expanding its audio waveform to achieve a best fit with the peaks of the waveform in the guide track (**Figure 11.3**).

What's the catch? As you'd expect, the guide track and the dub track must have the same number of syllables. You can also use VocALign to sync music and voice, or multiple voices singing in harmony.

Using Software Tools to Repair and Enhance Soundtracks

If the production dialogue sounds bad, and you don't want to do dialogue replacement with either wild sound or ADR, it's time to roll up your sleeves and get to work polishing the production sound. It's nasty work even with digital tools, but it beats forcing the audience to guess what the actors are saying.

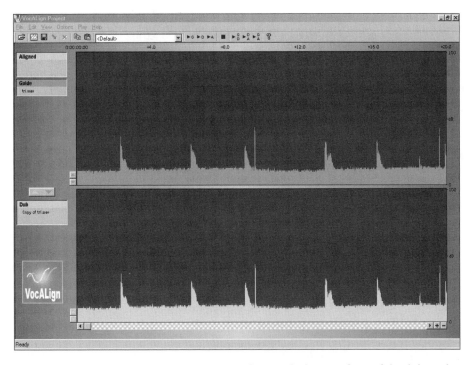

Figure 11.3 VocALign Project compresses and expands the waveform of the dub track to match the peaks and valleys of the guide track. The effect is to match the timing of syllables and lip sync in two different voice tracks, even if they're in different languages.

TIP: A common problem with production sound is bass rumble, or low-frequency noise from wind or traffic. To eliminate, or at least minimize, this problem using NLE software or a mixing board, adjust the equalization (EQ) settings on the audio track as follows: Set the 60 Hz slider to 0 percent, and the 150 Hz slider to 50 percent

> **BASS RUMBLE:** Persistent low-frequency audio noise due to wind or traffic.

Cleaning and Separating Dialogue Tracks

The first step in repairing production dialogue is to separate each actor's speech onto a separate audio track. This process is called *checkerboarding*, which describes the pattern it produces in the NLE timeline. You can achieve a checkerboard effect by making one copy of the soundtrack for each character in the scene, then deleting all the other characters' lines from each one.

> **CHECKERBOARDING:** Creating a separate audio track for each actor.
>
> **HANDLE:** Extra footage on either side of a clip for use in creating fades and other types of transitions.

After checkerboarding, you can add *handles* to either side of each audio take by dragging the timecode in and out points. Having handles will allow you to cross-dissolve between tracks, making differences in volume or equalization less noticeable (**Figure 11.4**).

TIP: In Final Cut Pro, you can set a default Handle Size parameter during clip capture that tells the program how much extra material should be included in the captured clip before and after your in and out points. A setting of one second on either side is about right for audio handles.

Checkerboarding helps you achieve clean production sound in several ways:

- By separating actors' dialogue onto separate tracks, you can replace them individually, if necessary, with better takes from the same scene. If the actor is off-camera, the replacement will be even easier because it doesn't have to match the picture. Otherwise, you may have to fix the lip sync or do a split edit to cover the problem. (For more information, see "Syncing ADR Tracks" earlier in this chapter, and "The Magical Split Edit" in Chapter 10.)

- Adding handles makes it possible to create smooth transitions between audio takes as *cross-fades* (audio dissolves) rather than as more abrupt, straight cuts. A cross-fade can disguise variations in room tone between takes, stifle noises such as intakes of breath and lip smacks, and help you tighten cueing between speeches.

  > **CROSS-FADE:** Audio dissolve in which the level of one track increases while the level of another decreases.

- Cutting in ADR dub tracks will be easier because you've already isolated dialogue you will be replacing.

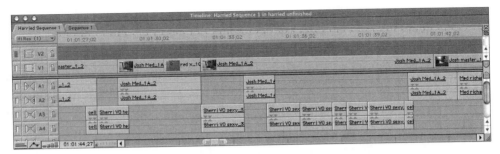

Figure 11.4 Checkerboarding segregates actors' dialogue onto different tracks, permitting you to do quick cross-fades for smooth transitions and to eliminate noises that occur just before or just after a line, such as throat-clearing, breaths, lip-smacks, and coughs.

Automatic Noise Reduction

A particularly handy tool for cleaning production sound is Bias SoundSoap Pro, a plug-in software module for removing or eliminating background noise. It's available for either Mac or Windows and plugs into a variety of applications, including many NLEs. While SoundSoap monitors audio input, you can play a sample of room tone and activate its "Learn Noise" function. It then digitally subtracts these signals from the rest of the production track. This simple processing step can remove or reduce hiss and rumble from air conditioning systems, electrical interference, and traffic.

And as much as we've preached against using your built-in mic, this trick can also remove its telltale camera whine. In an emergency, it might even make the guide track you recorded with the built-in mic suitable for production. (For more information, see *www.bias-inc.com*.)

Adding Sound Effects

Most sound effects aren't what you think they are. To take just one famous example, the laser blast effect in *Star Wars* is actually the sound of a mallet hitting one of the taut guy wires that hold up a radio tower.

These days, sound effects can also be entirely synthetic—audio waveforms manufactured within a computer by pure mathematics and digital tools rather than by recording some physical action. (You can also use a computer to transform the audio characteristics of any live effect you record.)

> **CANNED:** Describing a selection from a music or sound-effects library; a prerecorded tune or effect; not live.

A third alternative is to use a *canned* effect, a selection from a pre-recorded effects library. Canned effects may be live or may be built by sound designers; either way, they can be very convincing. However, searching through dozens of libraries for just the right one can take a lot more time than manufacturing the effect yourself. Even if you find the effect you're seeking, it might not be long enough or quite perfect in some other way, requiring you to use sound editing tools to modify it.

> **NOTE:** Canned effects may be copyrighted, just like music selections—which means you'll have to pay for using them. For more information, see "License Commercial Music" in this chapter.

In general, effects you steal from the real world sound better than canned or synthetic effects, but that doesn't mean what you see and what you hear are necessarily the same. For example, the most convincing body hits in fight scenes are created by a Foley artist breaking a celery stalk or a head of lettuce. If you were to simply record the sound of a fist striking a chin, all you'd get would be a brief, dull thud—not particularly impressive (and needlessly painful).

In fact, actors in fight scenes rarely touch one another; they swat the air, letting tricks of perspective and shallow depth of field make you think they connected. A well-timed sound effect convinces the audience the blow landed—and really hurt. As with any other aspect of movie magic, it's not about what's real but what the audience *expects*. This is why sound designers talk of the sound effect "selling" a stunt, in the same way sizzle sells steak.

> **BUTTON:** Visual and/or audio effect that punctuates the end of an action or scene.

In *Ten Ways to Shoot a Chair*, there's a musical "ding" on the track when Holly winks at the camera. (Filmmakers call the wink and its synchronized effect a *button*—a way to punctuate the end of an action or scene. A grimace, or even the punch line of a joke, are other examples of buttons.) Creating the sound of the ding wasn't easy. We rejected electronic sounds as not "sweet" enough, and the musical triangle we tried didn't sound right either. The effect we finally used was a recording of a spoon hitting the side of a wine glass, with the pitch tuned just right by filling the glass with water.

In some cases, it's possible to record wild effects and cut them in later, but syncing up wild sounds to actions the audience can see is incredibly time-consuming, if not impossible. Any money you save by not resorting to Foley will probably be eaten up in additional editing time. It's easier to record something like wild footsteps if the audience can't actually see the actor's feet in the shot. Be careful, though: You'll still have to sync the steps with the actor's upper-body movements.

Creating Ambiance

Creating the ambiance, or background noise, of a setting goes far beyond matching room tone from one take to the next. Sound editors spend a great deal of time constructing layer upon layer of subtle effects to convince the audience they're observing a slice of life rather than actors saying lines on a sound stage.

To give you some idea of just how complex this work can be, here's a list of layers a sound designer might use to create the ambiance for a short restaurant scene:

- Restaurant *walla*—a canned effect produced by actors' improvisational muttering, which sounds like the nonsense word "walla." The result is a low-level buzz of unintelligible conversations by a group of people.

> **WALLA:** Crowd murmur.

- Ringing phones and cell phones

- Snatches of conversation and cell-phone talk

- Laughter of people at other tables

- Coughing

- Clinking plates and silverware

- Clanging of pots in kitchen

- Waiters passing through kitchen swinging door

- Ice clinking in water glasses

- Gurgle of wine pouring

- Elevator gong and sliding door

- Keyboardist or strolling musicians

- Guests' and waiters' footsteps

- Exterior traffic noise, sirens, horns

- Exterior birds chirping

- Chair screeches

- Rustle of clothing

- Tinkle of jewelry

- Lips smacking

- Voice on public address system paging a guest

- Rolling of pastry cart

- Cash register or sales terminal

> **SPOTTING TABLE:** Listing of all music and sound-effect cues in a show.

Sometime after the rough cut is finished, the sound designer will lay out a *spotting table*, or chart of cues, for the scene (**Figure 11.5**). The majority of these cues will be background effects. Each cue will have a timecode, a notation of whether the event is the start of a music clip or a sound effect, and a description. The table is a want list for all the effects that need to be gathered or manufactured.

Production:	"For a Few Dollars Less"								Director: P. Shaner	
Date:	8/02/XX								Sound Designer: G. Jones	
Scene:	Saloon Fight				Scene In:01:05:06:21			Scene Out: 01:06:34:02		
Dialogue	**In/Out**	**Music**	**In/Out**	**Source**	**SFX**	**In/Out**	**Source**	**Ambience**	**In/Out**	**Source**
			01:05:06:21-						01:05:06:21-	
		Piano roll	01:05:38:11	Score				Walla	01:05:38:11	Library
					Breaking	01:05:38:11-				
					bottle	01:05:39:02	Foley			
"You!"	01:05:39:12									

Figure 11.5 The sound designer's spotting table shows all audio events (music or sound-effect cues) in the show, along with their timecodes.

THE INFINITE VARIETY OF MUSIC

The role of music in the movies goes back to the era of silent film, when every local movie theater employed a pianist whose job was to improvise on the emotional themes of the story as a film unreeled. Sometimes the movie distributors would send accompanying sheet music for a high-profile extravaganza, but mostly they relied on the skills of the vaudeville piano players who had standard ditties and riffs for most comedic or dramatic situations, as well as a collection of noisemakers like slide whistles and kazoos for special effects.

Even though real life has no musical soundtrack (except for people wearing headphones and carrying MP3 players), audiences expect their emotions to be guided and enhanced by a musical score as the scenes of a story unfold. Commercials rely on music as much as their stunning visual effects to impart a sense of excitement and motivate buying decisions. Even a training video will benefit from scoring to add interest and continuity.

Music and Copyright

Like many other forms of artistic expression, music is the private property of its composer, and it's protected by copyright law. In order to use an existing musical recording legally, or even to rerecord an existing score, you must first buy the right to use the copyrighted work.

In the United States copyright lasts for the author's life plus 70 years, or (in the case of a corporate author) 95 years from first publication of the work. However, these terms are under review by the U.S. Supreme Court and Congress. Since this field of law is changing rapidly to adapt to the new realities of digital distribution, be sure to consult an entertainment attorney before you use any copyrighted material. If you want to distribute your video production commercially, your distributors will insist on seeing written proof of copyright clearances for any music you use. (For more information, see "The Digital Millennium Copyright Act" in Chapter 12.)

Bottom line: You must clear (obtain legal permission to use) every piece of music you incorporate into your own work. Works more than a 100 years old are probably in the public domain. However, copyright can also apply to the arrangement of a piece of music or its performance. Don't assume you can use a recording of a Mozart sonata without clearing it just because the score is very old. Chances are, the performers that made the recording still hold copyright.

CLEAR: Obtain permission to use a copyrighted element you wish to incorporate in your work.

PUBLIC DOMAIN: Out of copyright; available for use by the public without fee.

So the question is not *whether* to use music, but how to find or create selections that fit your budget—and then how to incorporate them, legally and technically, into your production.

Where to Find Music

Your four options for finding music are:

- Copy recorded music into your show.

- Hire musicians to perform an existing composition.

- Hire a composer to write original music, along with an arranger to score it and musicians to perform and record it.

- Use music composition software to build tracks from canned loops.

Budget Levels and Music Sophistication

The least expensive way to find music is to use cuts from a music library. It's only a bit pricier to hire aspiring local musicians to record something original for you. If you've got lots of money to spend, you can license one or more hits by well-known performers, or hire a composer, an arranger, and an orchestra to create an award-winning original track. As with most postproduction decisions, it's mostly a matter of how much sophistication you're seeking—and how much you can afford to spend in direct costs and finishing time. And for some of these approaches, it will also depend on how much skill you want to develop using software tools for music capture and composition.

Use Library Music

Library music is available in a wide variety of genres, composed especially for use as soundtracks, from vendors including:

- DeWolfe Music (*www.dewolfemusic.com*)

- Opus 1 Music Library (*www.opus1musiclibrary.com*)

- SmartSound (*www.smartsound.com*)

At one time, library music was generally considered to be the audiovisual equivalent of elevator music—unoriginal and bland. That's not true anymore. Just as the digital revolution has brought an explosion in video production, it's done the same for the music world. There's a lot of material out there, much of it very good.

The main drawback to using library music is the time you'll have to spend searching for just the right selection. The main advantage is that fees are relatively modest; in fact, this is usually the most inexpensive way of providing your project with a professional-quality music track. Library music can easily rival the richness and power of commercial music and original scores. Furthermore, when you're dealing with a music library, you're one-stop shopping; you don't need to be concerned with tracking down all the rights holders.

> **TIP:** *Tracking down music rights can be a challenge. Licensing music actually involves two separate sets of rights: synchronization rights (permission from the composer to incorporate his music into your project) and a master recording license (permission from a performer to use her recording in your own copyrighted work).*

PER-DROP: License fee that applies to each use of a cut in a work; laserdrop fee.

UNLIMITED USE: Blanket license fee that covers all uses of a music/effects cut or library.

There are two basic ways to buy music from a library. The first way involves paying a *per-drop* fee; the term refers to the old practice of dropping a needle on an LP to select a cut. Today, it's called a *laserdrop*. A typical per-drop fee might be $50, and you'd owe it every time you place a new music clip in your edit.

The second way is an *unlimited use* fee, usually about $500, which you pay up front to purchase an entire CD full of library selections. You can use any clip on the CD as many times as you wish, and in as many different productions as you wish.

Deciding which way to go isn't difficult: After you've identified the selections you want, take a look at your spotting table and do the math. Since libraries group their cuts by CD according to musical genre, you'll save money with an unlimited use license if most of your cuts are in the same genre: dance, hip-hop, techno, industrial, pop, rock, jazz, blues, country, ambient, or classical/orchestral.

License Commercial Music

For many years it was relatively rare for movies to use commercial recordings on their soundtracks. Studios had staff composers, arrangers, and musicians, and most of the music was written expressly for the movies.

One of the reasons that changed was *American Graffiti,* released in 1973. For this nostalgic story, director George Lucas wanted to use 80 cuts of popular music from the 1950s and '60s. Eventually, the legal department at Universal Studios calculated that they could only afford licenses for 45 tunes, including golden oldies by Chuck Berry, Buddy Holly, and Booker T and the MGs. Of course the movie was a huge hit and sold millions of soundtrack compilations.

Like Lucas, many videomakers are tempted to use familiar cuts from commercial recorded music. We all have our favorites, each evoking a cherished time, place, person, or emotion. The problem is, those associations aren't the same for everyone. A popular song, for example, might make one listener think of his wedding day, another of her senior prom. Because popular music is so much a part of our daily lives, such strong emotional connections are unavoidable. If you use a popular piece in your video presentation, you risk evoking not the mood you want to create but the listeners' highly individual reveries. In short, familiar music will transport them out of your story and into theirs—not necessarily the effect you want.

ROYALTY: Licensing fee calculated as a percentage of sales for a particular use.

Another, bigger problem is that commercial music has become extremely expensive to license. It's much costlier than library music, and, depending on the artist, may cost more than you'd spend to hire a composer-keyboardist or a singer-songwriter to do an original score. For example, rights to use just one popular song can cost several thousand dollars, plus an ongoing *royalty* based on the revenue of your movie.

Unlike library music, for which there's a single rights holder, you might need to clear as many as four categories of rights for a commercial hit: composition, arrangement, performance, and synchronization. Fortunately, there are two licensing organizations that will help you do this: BMI (Broadcast Music, Inc.), online at *www.bmi.com,* represents about

300,000 songwriters. If BMI doesn't control the rights to the selection you want, chances are ASCAP (American Society of Composers, Authors and Publishers), online at *www.ascap.com,* does. Both Web sites have searchable databases of music selections. If you don't have specific cuts in mind, you can submit your want list to BMI and they will provide you with a list of tunes to consider.

When you finally obtain the rights to a piece of commercial music, you will receive a per-drop license. (As a rule, an unlimited use license for a commercial hit is outrageously expensive, unless the song's popularity peaked years ago.) If you want to cover the possibility that the soundtrack of your movie might be released on CD, or played over the Web, you'll have to pay additional fees for *ancillary* rights, which cover such *spin-off* usage.

ANCILLARY: Exploitation of a copyrighted work in different media, such as CD sales of a movie soundtrack; spin-off.

PERFORMANCE RIGHTS: Permission for musicians to perform a composer or songwriter's work.

If you absolutely must use a huge hit by some megastar performer, an affordable alternative to licensing the commercial cut is to obtain *performance rights* and rerecord the song. This is the same type of license a combo would get to perform an old standard in nightclubs. Your total cost for hiring musicians and getting both performance and synchronization rights could well be less than licensing the recorded version. (For example, recent big-budget pictures have featured new performances of Beatles songs.)

Employ Local Musicians

Songwriters who sing (possibly accompanying themselves on guitar or keyboard) can be excellent, inexpensive resources for creating an original music score. Or you might consider using public domain pieces, or obtaining performance rights to selections that can be performed by a local flutist, a small chamber orchestra, a rock band, or a jazz combo.

> **TIP:** By law, copyright vests with the author or performer, which means you would need to get the synchronization rights to any new performances. If you are paying the musicians, write agreements that specify the performance as a work for hire; this gives you exclusive rights for any purpose. Consult your attorney for details.

WORK FOR HIRE: Contractual arrangement between an author and an employer granting the employer all rights to a particular work. By law, copyright vests with the author unless a written agreement exists that specifies work for hire.

Musicians who know how to improvise will be particularly useful. An important technique for using any music clip is to sync it with the scene's in and out points, as well as its emotional beats and climaxes. Whether or not you do the recording on an ADR stage, some improvisational musicians, particularly jazz artists, can watch your scenes and get the timings pretty close, without the formality of a click track or even a written score.

Many composers and singer-songwriters package their tunes as music libraries. Their fees are often negotiable, and you can make good deals—just be sure the clearances are in writing. You can find these music sources by searching the Web.

Create an Original Score

Doing an original score involves a series of steps that hasn't changed much since the days of the old studio system.

Once the edit is locked, the music editor creates a click track for each scene guided by the spotting table. The click track indicates the desired in and out points for each music cue as well as its tempo. After conferring with the director on which emotional beats and dramatic effects should be punched up with music, the composer works from the locked version of the final cut and the click track to score each scene that requires music. The composer then collaborates with the arranger to voice the score for orchestra. The orchestra records the music on a very expensive, specially equipped scoring stage where the performers play as they watch the scenes on a large screen with a timecode indicator.

> **NOTE:** It's customary to retain composers, arrangers, and musicians by way of work-for-hire agreements, so you'll have exclusive control of all rights, including ancillary uses. However, these arrangements are negotiable. An alternative would be to pay less for a nonexclusive license specifically for movie use, permitting the composer to retain rights for all other uses.

A lower-cost alternative can be to employ a composer-keyboardist who can re-create the sounds of an entire symphony orchestra using a digital keyboard. For example, movie composer Vangelis is famous for his scores to *Chariots of Fire, Blade Runner,* and *1492: Conquest of Paradise*, which mix synthetic and sampled acoustic effects.

Build Music from Loops

Recent developments in digital sound editing have created another alternative for music scoring—*looping*. It combines the notion of library music with digital audio editing. You might call it "modular music," because you can assemble original-sounding compositions from these musical snippets.

LOOPING: Music construction from small modules of recorded or synthesized music that can be copied and pasted in audio editing software to form longer repetitive tracks.

Some music composition software, such as Sony Picture Digital Loops for ACID, rely on this notion of loops as the basic unit of composition. Other programs, such as Apple GarageBand and Steinberg Cubase, permit you to capture audio from your own musical performances, use it as source material, or combine it with loops.

Although loops can be lengthy music passages, they are more commonly small, repetitive musical units. In the language of musicians, they're intros, bridges, melodies, refrains, and codas. Perhaps the simplest example of a loop is a measure of drum backbeat. Using music composition software, you can copy and paste such a loop any number of times to create the drum track for an entire selection, or *song*.

SONG: In music composition, any complete musical selection, whether instrumental, vocal, or both.

TRANSPOSE: To translate from one musical key to another, involving raising or lowering the pitch of instruments and voices, *e.g.,* from the key of C to the key of G-sharp.

Getting a bit more complex, you could score the chorus of a song by mixing and matching loops for various instruments. Some music composition programs, such as Soundtrack, will even *transpose* all loops automatically to the same key and match tempo. Just as you duplicated the loops of the rhythm track, you can then copy and paste the entire chorus you've built, inserting it at the end of every verse. Or, you could build the instrumental accompaniment for one verse, then lay it underneath a different vocal lyric for every verse in a song.

While looping may not be as arduous as composing music from scratch, it does involve some knowledge of music theory and some skill using the software. Another modular approach, which requires less musical ability but achieves impressive results, is represented by SmartSound SonicFire Pro, which assembles finished selections for you after you've chosen some prerecorded modules. To score a scene, you select a tune from the library, and the software combines related modules to fit within the in and out points. Ultimately, it sounds like one coherent composition (**Figure 11.6**).

Looping and other forms of modular music can be an appealing way to go, particularly since it's cheap (amounting to an unlimited license). It also overcomes another common objection to library music—that you hear it everywhere. In the case of these ad hoc digital compositions, no two custom-generated pieces will be exactly the same.

How to Use Music

We've talked about the need to sync music clips to the ins, outs, beats, and climaxes of scenes. But short of asking your composer or musicians to make sure that happens when they lay down the track, we haven't suggested how to achieve it. Music editing is a big topic, both an art and a science. Here's an overview of tools and techniques.

The Digital Audio Workstation

Although NLE packages have some sound editing features built in, most sound editors prefer to use a separate set of tools specifically designed for manipulating audio. Today's counterpart of the NLE for audio is the *digital audio workstation (DAW)*. Compared to the audio editing capabilities of NLEs, these specialized sound editing programs offer increased flexibility and control, as well as better integration with *MIDI,* the working environment of digital musicians. Leading products, which include Digidesign ProTools, Sony Pictures Digital Sound Forge, and Abobe Audition, offer such capabilities as:

- *MIDI sequencer* (digital music generator and editor)

- Audio mixing for stereo and Surround Sound

- Device-control interfaces for mixers and decks

- Audio effects such as change tempo, change pitch, chorus, delay, distortion, reverb, and many more

DAW (DIGITAL AUDIO WORKSTATION): Audio editing software that usually also provides an integrated environment for music capture, looping, and music composition.

MIDI: Musical Instrument Digital Interface, a digital recording and editing standard.

MIDI SEQUENCER: Digital music generator and editor based on the Musical Instrument Digital Interface.

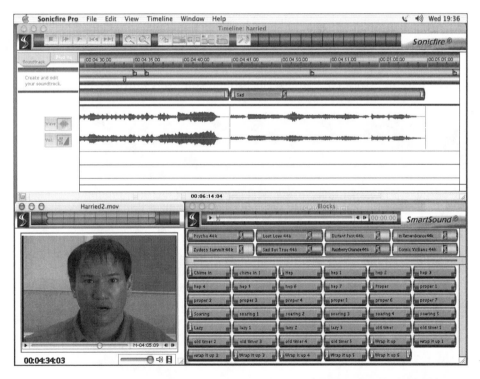

Figure 11.6 Sonicfire Pro constructs a custom digital music composition from its library of prerecorded modules to fit the length and dynamics of the scene you're scoring. The program provides video preview, permitting you to import and watch a video clip as you build the music track for it. This feature is a real time-saver, eliminating the need to export the music to your NLE program before you can sync it with the picture.

- *Automatic groove detection* for extraction of rhythm patterns from music clips

- *Region conforming* for graphic manipulation of audio waveforms

- Time compression/expansion of audio waveforms for fine-tuning sync with picture or other audio events

- *Edit smoothing* for blending waveforms at cuts

- Audio file import/export in multiple formats: WAV, Windows Media, QuickTime, MPEG 1 and 2, RealAudio, MP3

- Streaming audio outputs for the Web

- Support for audio plug-ins that add special features

AUTOMATIC GROOVE DETECTION: Sound editing feature that detects and extracts the musical beat from a clip.

REGION CONFORMING: Sound editing feature that permits graphic manipulation of audio waveforms.

EDIT SMOOTHING: Sound editing feature that blends audio waveforms at cuts.

CONTROL SURFACE: Device that provides tactile interface for controlling software settings.

All the products we've mentioned can be installed in your desktop NLE system. ProTools claims full compatibility with Avid NLE systems and also offers an extensive product line of hardware accessories for professional sound studios (**Figure 11.7**).

Figure 11.7 This console in a ProTools-equipped sound editing suite looks like a mixing board, and in fact that's what it's used for. But in NLE terminology it's a *control surface*, a kind of glorified mouse for controlling settings in the software—though to a sound editor it feels like a mixing board.

Backtiming

The time-honored technique of *backtiming,* or adjusting a music cue backwards from a key event, works amazingly well and can make a piece of canned music sound like it was scored just for your picture.

> **BACKTIMING:** Determining the insertion point of a music clip by timing backward from a desired sync point.

For example, let's say you've found a dramatic music clip that builds to a stirring crescendo. You want to use it in a scene to emphasize the hero's realization that he's being watched. To sync the clip using backtiming, you'd insert it in your NLE or sound editing program, identify the peak waveform of the crescendo in the timeline by playing back the clip, then line the peak up vertically with the visual cue (the hero's startled expression) on the video track.

So far so good. Now the crescendo coincides with the actor's stunned expression. But how do you determine where the music clip's in point should be? In analog sound editing, the technician would time the video clip up to the point of the climax, then back-time the music clip, rewinding it by the same number of seconds of running time and cueing it there. In digital NLE, you can simply insert the in point of the scene on the video track in the timeline and experiment with fading up the audio track gradually—just before, right on, or just after the cut. (Fading up music for the next scene just before a cut is a type of split edit, and it often helps the transition.) For the transition to sound right, you want to fade up on a *downbeat*

> **DOWNBEAT:** First beat of a musical measure.
>
> **SNEAKING IN:** Fading in an effect gradually.

at a point where a musical phrase seems to begin.

Or, if you have time in the scene, you can fade up the music even more slowly, giving the impression of building the mood gradually. This technique is called *sneaking in* the music cue.

POLISHING IMAGES

Putting the finishing touches on your images is a highly technical subject. When you get into this late phase of postproduction, you will rely increasingly on the engineering staffs of your subcontractors, clients, and distributors. Here's an overview of what's involved in making your show ready for prime time.

Color Correction

Tweaking the color of your screen images usually involves both technical and artistic decisions, and the process is actually more complicated than it might seem. Typically, you'll make an artistic judgment to adjust the color, which then requires a technical correction because you're out of broadcast spec. But then that doesn't look quite right. As you can imagine, color correction can get very tricky, which is how colorists stay employed.

Color-correction tools are already built into NLE systems like Symphony and Final Cut Pro. Also, color-correction tools like Boris FX are available as plug-ins, and Red Giant Magic Bullet has a fairly reliable broadcast-legal conversion function that requires little more than a click. Da Vinci Systems 2K Plus *(www.davsys.com)* is a bundled system that includes hardware and software for manipulating digital video and film images up to 2K x 2K resolution. If you're genuinely curious about the technical issues involved in preparing video for broadcast, see "Color Correction for Broadcast" in Appendix A.

Artistic Judgment in Color Correction

If you're adjusting colors for artistic effect, there are no rules—except that after you're done, make sure you've used broadcast-legal colors. (Perhaps you can't avoid that trip to Appendix A, after all.)

In achieving the effects you want with color correction, be aware of three different approaches, which should be available as options within your color-correction program:

- **Primary.** The color-correction procedures we've just described are all primary: they apply to the entire image. An artistic use of primary color correction might be to change the mood of a scene by shifting its overall cast to blue.

- **Secondary.** Color correction at the secondary level affects only pixels for which a selected characteristic falls within a certain range. For example, you could choose to adjust the chroma of all pixels above 70 percent saturation. This would give a garish quality to the brightest colors in an image. Obviously, experimentation will give you the best idea how this kind of color correction will affect your image.

- **Spot.** This kind of color correction changes the color parameters for a selected region of a picture. A good example is a shot you may have seen in *Schindler's List* in which the entire picture is black and white except for a little girl in a red overcoat.

Creating Titles and Graphics

Most NLE programs have the built-in capability for generating titles, but for really smooth animation we recommend using a plug-in such as Inscriber Technology TitleMotion Pro *(www.inscriber.com)* or LiveType, an animation-based titling application included with Final Cut Pro 4. Most NLE systems permit you to import the still images and animated sequences you create with these programs, adding the graphic files as additional video tracks in your scenes.

The most common type of animation for movie credits is vertical scrolling. The trick to achieving a smooth vertical scroll, without the type appearing to jump or flicker, is to move the titles up an even number of scan lines in each video frame—two, four, or eight. If your titling software doesn't have this setting, you'll have to render the title segment and play it back to make sure it's smooth.

When creating titles and graphics, remember to avoid noisy edges—which are all too easy to create when you're using computer-generated shapes and colors. (For more information, see "Basic Color Correction Steps," earlier in this chapter.)

As to color saturation in your titles, there's an easy way to check whether your computer-generated colors will be legal. The titling or graphics program typically uses an eight-bit color scheme, which means that RGB values can range from 0 to 255. To assure that your colors are legal, simply keep their RGB values between 16 and 235.

> **TIP:** Many videographers don't like the look of computer-generated titles. They prefer to shoot backlit typeset sheets called Kodaliths (named for lithographic sheet film) with a camcorder, then overlay the title clips on a background in the NLE process. This approach requires dealing with a photo lab to produce the sheets from your typeset printouts, but the distinct advantage is that the camcorder's edge-softening circuitry will eliminate video noise.

KODALITH: Kodak brand of opaque lithographic film, sold in paper-sized sheets.

LOWER THIRDS: Video titles positioned in the lower third of the frame.

An additional use of titles in video presentations is to superimpose information (for instance, the name and title of the person speaking) on the bottom of the screen. These titles are called *lower thirds,* because that's the area of the screen where they're usually supered. Here are some guidelines for preparing lower-third titles:

- Use text large enough for the audience to read easily. The rule of thumb is that text must be readable by an average person sitting at a distance from the screen equal to four times the height of the screen. (This formula works whether they are watching a movie in a theater or a TV set in their living rooms.)

- White, yellow, or yellow-orange text will super best whatever the background. If the background is busy or light-colored, you can add a drop-shadow effect to make the text "pop." Don't assume that dark-colored text will read better over light backgrounds. That works in print, but not in video.

- Don't add animation to lower-third titles. It's distracting and makes them harder to read.

- Don't cue the title until a few seconds into the take, giving the audience a chance to settle in. Ideally, cue the title at the speaker's first pause.

- Hold the title on the screen for either five seconds or the time it takes you to read the title aloud twice, whichever is longer. Then fade it off. If you don't have enough time before the next cut, consider finding a way to lengthen the video clip, or wait to super the title until you cut back to the person.

- On main titles as well as lower thirds, you must keep your titles within the broadcast-standard *safe title area*, which leaves a generous border around the image to avoid cutoff by variations in TV picture tubes. All video titling programs include templates for safe title areas. For example, in Photoshop, the name of the template file for 4:3 aspect-ratio TV is "title_safe.atn".

> **SAFE TITLE AREA:** Rectangular area within a video frame for positioning titles to avoid being cut off at the edge during display or projection.

Prepare Titles for a Master Tape

Videotape masters for broadcast or duplication require a special set of titles and graphics at the head of the program. All mid-level NLE programs can generate these effects.

The first 60 to 90 seconds of the tape should include standard color bars on the video track, and a continuous 1 KHz test tone on the audio tracks. For the next 20 seconds (until the program fades in), a *slate* should appear. Text on the slate should show the title of the program, the total running time in minutes and seconds, allocation of audio tracks (distributors usually require *split tracks*—dialogue on two stereo channels, music and effects on the other two), creation date, copyright notice, and producer's contact information.

> **SLATE:** Identifying card at the head of a master recording identifying the program, its details, and the producer. Also, in videography, a clapper board.

After the slate has been on the screen for 10 seconds, the audio track begins a countdown from 10 to 2, with a two-pop beep (a 1 KHz test tone with a duration of exactly one frame) at the two-second mark, followed by black and silence until program fade-in. At one-second intervals during the countdown, the number of seconds to the start of the program appears, supered and inset on the slate.

Postprocessing Filters

NLE systems and plug-ins provide thousands of filters, canned sets of creative options involving colors, textures, and effects designed for artistic impressions or technical transformations. You'll get the idea from the names of just a few of the filters out there: watercolor, fogged glass, neon glow, lens flare, paint daubs, torn edges, smudging, stained glass.

Applying Film-Look Filters

A major subset of these canned filters are "film-look" effects. Film-look filters include grain, dust, scratches, stains, shutter blur, even hairs in the projector gate. Another artifact of film projection that audiences notice only when it's entirely missing in video is called *bob and weave,* or *jitter.* As the sprockets in a film print become worn through repeated showings, the frames tend to move a bit in the projector gate, bobbing up and down and weaving from side to side. Curiously, this is another characteristic film audiences have come to associate with "quality," and many film-look filters now include the effect.

> **BOB AND WEAVE:** Jitter in film projection gate caused by worn sprocket holes in the film.

 To make Ten Ways to Shoot a Chair *look more like a 1950s training film, we applied a variety of film-look filters to simulate film grain, faded color, scratches, hair, and bob and weave.*

CineLook even offers a feature called StockMatch, which transforms video colors to more nearly match those of specific film stocks, including Kodak Ektachrome and Fuji FujiChrome. Be aware, however, that this transformation is largely an aesthetic one, designed to make your video look as if it were shot on film. It's not meant for film transfer, and applying it won't assure that these film stocks will reproduce your video colors any more faithfully.

What's the Best Way to Achieve 24 fps?

One of the main reasons that standard 30I NTSC video looks, well, like video is its interlaced mode, which samples each frame as two fields, 60 fields per second—more then twice the movie rate. As a result, video images seem crisper and motion appears less blurred than on film. To achieve a film look, one of the key objectives must be to match—or at least come close to—film's 24 fps frame rate.

There are a variety of ways to achieve film-look frame rate in video. Some affect the way you shoot, some rely on postprocessing, some involve a bit of both. The choices entail different tradeoffs of cost, practicality, and aesthetics. We'll describe your options briefly, then make some recommendations.

> ### Tints and Transfers
>
> *Amateurs tend to overdo digital postprocessing, but even big-name filmmakers use it from time to time. For example, the feature* Traffic *used a different overall color tint for each of three subplot sequences, each set in a different locale—San Diego, East Coast, and Tijuana. Tints for the first two locales were done photographically, but the pale brown of the footage shot in Mexico was achieved with digital color correction. In similar fashion, the movie* O Brother, Where Art Thou? *was shot on film in normal color, transferred to HD, postprocessed for a golden look, then transferred back to film for theatrical release.*

Your options for achieving film-look frame rate are:

Shoot in 24P mode. This is a straightforward choice and requires no postprocessing to achieve the desired frame rate. Its main disadvantage is that on a prosumer budget, you don't have many camcorders to choose from. If, for example, you use the Panasonic AG-DVX100, you'll have the option of shooting 24P, but without the aesthetic luxury of cinema-style lenses.

Shoot in 30P mode. Many more prosumer camcorders can shoot in this "movie mode," which turns off interlacing, samples the image 30 times per second, and more closely captures the motion effects of film. This is an "almost but not quite" choice, because 30P will still sample motion more smoothly than 24P and can't readily be converted to 24P in post.

Shoot in 30I and postprocess. If you shoot interlaced NTSC, plain-vanilla video, you'll actually have considerable flexibility in post, where you can go one of two ways:

- Within your NLE, apply a deinterlace filter to convert to 30P. This is an inexpensive option, because you don't need either a special camera or postprocessing software. This approach rivals shooting in 30P for its motion effects, but yields less resolution. Why? Because the NLE simply ignores and discards one of the fields to achieve 30P. It's therefore not a good choice for film transfers because the result will have even less detail than full-resolution DV.

- Use Red Giant's Magic Bullet (plug-in for After Effects) to postprocess and convert 30I to 24P. Unlike the NLE conversion just described, Magic Bullet doesn't just discard every other field. It interpolates, or blends, a pair of fields to generate a single composite frame. The result is much more like true 24P, at full DV resolution. (Magic Bullet will not convert 30P footage.)

Shoot in PAL. If you can put your hands on a PAL camcorder, you have some other good choices. However, in North America, rental rates for PAL camcorders can rival those of HD units, so it can be an expensive decision.

- Switch the PAL camera to "movie mode," if it has one, to shoot in 25P. You can convert from 25P to 24P within the NLE without much fuss. You'll also enjoy the somewhat higher spatial resolution of PAL over NTSC, which can be a factor if you'll do a film transfer later.

- Shoot in plain-vanilla PAL (25I) and deinterlace in the NLE. But you'll sacrifice resolution the same as if you were to convert 30I this way.

- Shoot 25I and postprocess with Magic Bullet. This is an excellent choice because the postprocessing interpolates the frames, and the spatial resolution will be superior to both 24P shot in-camera and converted 30I.

Quality of Results

Your choice of shooting and postprocessing method will also depend on whether your show will debut on television, in movie houses, or both. If the end result is intended primarily for television, the output of your NLE will be 30I NTSC, but with an aesthetically transformed look. Only a viewer with a keen technical eye will guess that you didn't shoot on film.

To achieve the best result when producing for television, avoid conversion steps that sacrifice resolution, but don't fret about shooting PAL to increase resolution—it won't show up on the screen. (Going PAL will, however, look better than NTSC if your end product is HDTV.)

It's a completely different story if your goal is film transfer. Blowing up DV to 35mm will show some telltale flaws. Closeups will look pretty good, but the backgrounds in long shots will lack detail. Leaves on trees, for example, will have an odd, geometric look—the result of both lack of resolution and DV compression. Shooting in PAL will improve resolution somewhat, but not nearly as much as shooting in HD.

> **NOTE:** *Ironically enough, actors' faces in closeups can look better in DV than in HD, even when projected on large movie screens. HD is notorious for picking up too much detail, disclosing every pore and blemish. DV's lesser resolution tends to soften these details. HD videographers typically use a diffusion filter on the camera lens to compensate.*

Some undesirable DV artifacts will be minimized when you postprocess with Magic Bullet and After Effects. Magic Bullet can correct some of the 5:1 compression artifacts of DV, storing the output as an uncompressed After Effects animation file. Although the DV compression would be re-applied if you output to NTSC, you needn't go through this step if you're transferring to film. You can submit the animation file to the transfer house instead.

DV-to-film transfer technology is getting better all the time. Interpolation is applied in the software conversion to improve resolution, and it's so good that you shouldn't see any scan lines on the big screen. But even so, you can still regard DV as the new 16mm, lending your production a kind of "cult-movie" cachet.

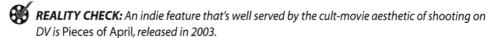 **REALITY CHECK:** *An indie feature that's well served by the cult-movie aesthetic of shooting on DV is* Pieces of April, *released in 2003.*

Ranking the Film-Look Approaches

Author Pete Shaner conducted several tests and ranks the approaches in **Table 11.2**, most desirable first.

See the results for yourself as side-by-side comparisons on the companion DVD in our instructional segment "How to Make Digital Video Look Like Film."

Table 11.2 Evaluating Film-Look Approaches

Rank (Best First)	Shooting Mode	Postprocessing Required	Result
1	24P	Film-look filters, if desired	TV or film transfer
2	25I (PAL)	Magic Bullet convert to 24P	TV or film transfer
3	25P (PAL)	Film-look filters, if desired	TV or film transfer
4	30I (NTSC)	Magic Bullet convert to 24P	TV or film transfer
5	30P	3:2 pulldown required for film	TV or film transfer
6	30I or 25I	Deinterlace in NLE	TV only

Adding Eye-Popping Special Effects

To create special effects through compositing, you need a sophisticated image-manipulation application like After Effects or Shake. However, there's been an explosion of software for "extra-special" special effects. Many of these are available as plug-ins for those bigger effects packages. Digital Anarchy is a vendor that offers a variety of these plug-ins. (For more information, surf to *www.digitalanarchy.com*.)

Combining Imagery: Using Analog Video and Film Sources

If you plan to draw extensively on archival sources—older videotapes or film—budget to have it transferred professionally to digital format. In particular, using a PC with a video capture card to import video footage will yield disappointing results. You'll end up with dropped frames because the PC's processor can't keep up with the video data rate, or you'll see annoying video artifacts from imperfect encoding. And there's no way to inexpensively transfer film to video: You must find a lab that has a digital telecine, an expensive piece of gear.

Ideally, you'll have these archival sources transferred to uncompressed digital video, then upload your DV to an uncompressed system, such as an Avid Meridien system, where it can all come together. This way, you won't introduce artifacts by first downconverting the footage to DV. If your release medium is television, you can probably get by with converting and editing everything in the DV realm. But if you plan to end up on film, here's one time when paying the hourly rate in the Avid suite may be justified.

TELECINE: Film or video lab system that scans film footage and converts it to video.

TIME BENDING: Applying variable video frame rates in postproduction for effects such as slow motion.

Just one example is Retimer SD, which applies variable frame rates smoothly in post. This process is called *time bending*. When you apply time bending in Final Cut Pro or After Effects, the result may be achieved by simply duplicating frames (to slow the rate) or dropping frames (to speed up). But Retimer SD interpolates the frames for a smoother result. Since only a few high-end camcorders permit you to shoot slow motion in-camera, one application of time bending is to achieve slo-mo in post.

Creating Virtual Realms

It might sound silly, but as more CGI tools become available for PCs, it's becoming increasingly possible for moviemakers to live like starving writers—producing works of art without ever leaving their garrets or seeing another human being.

Some software programs for this purpose that deserve mention are:

- Digital Anarchy 3D Assistants EZ, which enables easier manipulation of three-dimensional layers in After Effects

- The previously mentioned Aurora Sky, for creating synthetic sunrises, sunsets, and cloud banks

- E-on View d'Esprit 4 for synthetic scenery creation and its companion module Mover 4 to animate it *(www.e-onsoftware.com)*

These are just a few examples. There are tens, if not hundreds, more. As time goes on, watch for more postproduction and special-effect offerings to appear in the marketplace. Also, some will disappear—not because they failed, but because they will be acquired by larger brands and absorbed into their product offerings. For example, Apple's Logic audio editing software was originally developed and marketed by Emagic, and Adobe Audition began life as Cool Edit from Syntrillium.

THE MISSING INGREDIENT?

You may never be so discouraged as when you view your first rough cut, but don't be too depressed. The tedious, exacting work of postproduction makes all the difference, transforming the contrived into a convincing, lifelike story.

What do you need to get from here to there? Patience helps—and either plenty of money to hire the needed expertise, or lots of time to make your way by trial and error.

But the most important ingredient in postproduction is the magician's flair—a sense of artful trickery.

Think about it: In some early talkie, a cowpoke in a white hat swatted the air, and the audience believed that the low-down varmint in the black hat was dealt a crushing blow.

It took an insider to know that the real abuse was being directed at a crisp vegetable.

CHAPTER TWELVE

Distribution and E-Publishing

Whether or not you're looking to turn a profit, all video projects have the same ultimate goal—putting a story or message in front of the public. Digital video technology has already had a huge impact on production economics and aesthetics, but even greater and more far-reaching changes are on the way, thanks to ongoing developments in distribution technology.

GOING WIDE

In the language of motion-picture distribution, *going wide* means launching a movie in thousands of theaters nationwide all on the same day. This is an incredibly expensive process. Each print costs about $3,000, so you're looking at $3 million in duplication costs alone. Getting all those prints from the lab to the theaters in time for the big opening is a huge expense in itself, especially if you pay an air courier to ship each print to its destination. And costly as these expenses are, they are relatively small change in comparison to the advertising costs required to pack the theaters on opening weekend—typically, tens of millions of dollars.

> **GO WIDE:** Launch a major motion picture in thousands of theaters nationwide, or even worldwide, on the same day.

This scenario is going to change drastically within the next few years. Filmmakers may fret about the aesthetic trade-offs of film versus video, and theater owners may complain about the cost of retrofitting their venues for digital projection, but in the end, economics will rule. Conventional film-based distribution will fast become a totally unnecessary expense.

No one can predict how the media business will ultimately be transformed by these developments, but this chapter will give you a sense of what's coming—and how to prepare for it.

Currently, there are five primary distribution channels for digital video: videotape and DVD, commercial television, theatrical film, the Internet, and corporate networks.

MEET YOUR MASTERING AND DUPLICATION TEAM

Your team players at the distribution stage will be mostly vendors and subcontractors rather than individuals on your payroll. Technicians involved with mastering or preparing original recordings and duplicating them for distribution include the following.

Videotape and DVD

These are your human resources for videotape and DVD duplication.

Video Duplicator

Video duplicators work at video dubbing houses, where they take your master tape and copy it to multiple videocassettes, using a set of decks that run several times faster than normal speed. The dub house can also affix labels, insert cassettes in sleeves or albums, shrink-wrap, and ship.

DVD Author

Mastering a show for duplication on DVD requires an *authoring* process, which divides your presentation into *chapters,* and provides screen menus so users can select chapters for viewing. A DVD author must be able to think like a graphic artist (capable of creating attractive menus) and a computer programmer (to design the system of user interactions). But as DVD authoring tools are becoming more sophisticated, the technical aspects of these activities shouldn't be a worry. Creative flair is more important than ever—since the menu is the first thing a user sees.

> **AUTHORING:** Preparing a master presentation for output to DVD.
>
> **CHAPTER:** A single continuous sequence of video material on a DVD.
>
> **VIDEODISC:** Another term for DVD.

NOTE: *For reasons no one understands, computer disks are generally spelled with a k, videodiscs with a c. It's just another perplexing difference between video and computer cultures.*

DVD Duplication Technician

Some video dub houses and film labs have DVD duplication divisions; other suppliers specialize in making only DVDs. The facilities can be further subdivided into two categories:

- Short run (burning)

- Mass duplication (pressing)

> **PRESSING:** Stamping an optical disc, such as a CD or DVD, from a glass master.

A short-run house uses an electronic copying process much like videotape duplication, which burns multiple discs simultaneously on jukebox-style equipment. DVD *pressing* is much the same process found in record and CD factories—making a glass master disc and then physically stamping thousands of plastic copies. It's much faster to press DVDs than to dub videocassettes.

Like video duplicating houses, DVD duplicators can handle packaging and shipping.

Theatrical Film

Making film prints from digital videotape involves two major steps, and two kinds of technicians to handle them.

Video-to-Film Transfer Technicians

Transferring digital videotape to 35mm film happens at a specialized film recording service bureau. The transfer is done on a device called a *computer film recorder*, which creates a film *master negative*.

To preserve your options later, when a video is transferred to film, the resulting negative shouldn't necessarily include the soundtrack. The service bureau can transfer the digital audio tracks from your videotape master to analog *mag stripe* film stock, or to an optical track on a separate reel, whichever your lab or distributor prefers.

> **COMPUTER FILM RECORDER:** CRT or laser coupled to a photographic camera used to transfer digital video images to film.
>
> **MASTER NEGATIVE:** Film original used for creating an intermediate negative, from which release prints will be struck.
>
> **MAG STRIPE:** Sprocketed film stock coated with a magnetic oxide; used for mastering motion picture soundtracks.

Film Laboratory Technicians

Once you hand over the master negative to a film lab, skilled technicians will create a composite negative with an optical soundtrack that becomes the master for the film duplication process which creates *release prints*.

> **RELEASE PRINT:** Film to be projected in a theater made in a lab from film negative.

The lab might add your optical titles, and presumably, you've already done your fades, dissolves, and laser-weapons fire in digital post.

Although film laboratories can package and ship release prints, this isn't done much any more. Most of the time the lab simply stores your negative, awaiting further instructions. When you have a distributor, you authorize that company to order release prints from the lab and handle the details of shipping them to the theaters.

Television

When you're submitting a program to commercial television, you've got a couple of hard-headed groups to deal with. (In the case of an ad spot, the agency that produced it and paid for its placement will usually submit it, not you or your producer.)

Broadcast Engineer

The broadcast engineer of a local station, or the broadcast engineering department of a network, is responsible for making sure that the master videotape you submit adheres to technical standards. He doesn't care about the content. He doesn't even care much about whether its images are pretty. He just wants to be sure that the colors aren't oversaturated, the audio levels are right, the edges don't produce video noise, and you've done your slate, countdown, titles, and supers just so.

Broadcast Standards and Practices Director

This person *does* care about your content. She is often a lawyer, with an army of other lawyers and clerks in her employ, and is mostly concerned with whether you've filed your forms correctly. Do you have releases for actors? Did you clear the music? Did you check your facts? Does the content include strong language? Nudity? Violence?

Internet

If you intend to show your video on the Web, you'll need to hire at least one person (or firm) to get you online.

Web Designer

HTML: Hypertext Markup Language; original computer language used to create and process Web pages.

XML: eXtensible Markup Language; enhancement of HTML.

The Web designer is a combination graphic artist and computer programmer. His expertise lies in creating Web pages using *HTML* (Hypertext Markup Language) and *XML* (extensible Markup Language)—the programming methods of the Internet. To help you, he must also know about the file formats and bandwidth constraints that apply to digital video clips.

MEET YOUR DISTRIBUTION TEAM

When you're finally ready to put your show into the field, your assistants will be mostly vendors who specialize in one aspect or another of the distribution process. We'll present them here in the order you'll probably meet them.

Publicist

A publicist is a public-relations expert (showbiz types call her a *press agent)* who specializes in entertainment media. Many filmmakers don't think about retaining a publicist until a project is about to be released, in order to increase its exposure. But a publicist can be an essential early recruit for your team if you're an independent filmmaker seeking distribution.

PRESS AGENT: Showbiz term for a public relations professional; publicist.

A publicist will issue press releases announcing your project (perhaps as soon as you acquire a script or sign a star), get influential industry types to attend your screenings and sneak previews, and get you onto talk shows. A publicist might even connect you with a sales agent, who, in turn, will sell your show to distributors. And although you can do all this on your own, a publicist working with a sales agent can develop a winning strategy for submitting your project to film festivals, another way projects find distribution deals.

If you're working under contract to a movie studio or television network, a staff publicist or an outside public relations firm will probably be assigned to your project.

Corporate Marketing and Communications Department Staff

In a corporate environment, publicity for (as well as overall supervision of) your production will usually be handled by a marketing and communications, or "marcom," department. The staff in marketing and communications is responsible for creation and approval of all media materials (with the possible exception of advertising) produced for customers, stockholders, and the general public. It includes lawyers, marketing executives, and public relations experts.

Marcom departments rely heavily on focus groups and market surveys to test the popularity of their products and messages—and probably your video.

The marketing and communications department may hire outside contractors such as public relations and advertising agencies. In general, PR firms handle press relations while ad agencies create ads and place them in print or on the air. In a corporate setting, these agencies, not the sponsors themselves, may well be your contracting clients for video presentations.

Corporate sponsors seldom handle their own *traffic,* or media buys. Ad agencies perform this service, which requires extensive accounting to verify viewership and air times, as well as to pay royalties to actors and spokespersons. In their role as buyers of airtime for spots, ad agencies are a television network's most important and influential clients.

> **TRAFFIC:** Process of purchasing airtime from a network for advertising spots.

Sales Agent

A sales agent offers your completed (or, occasionally, partially completed) programs and movies to domestic and foreign distributors for licensing. The agent's turf may include television, theatrical exhibition, foreign, or combinations of these. It's possible to have multiple agents representing the same project.

The sales agent's strategy for selling foreign rights to a feature film usually involves attending three major trade shows: the Cannes Marché du Film on the French Riviera in the late spring, American Film Market (AFM) in Santa Monica, California, in the fall, and MIFED in Milan, Italy, also in the fall. Oddly enough, more foreign sales are made at AFM, which is widely attended by international distributors, than at either of the other events.

Domestic theatrical distribution in the U.S. is, for the most part, controlled by the major movie studios. To get their attention means getting a feature film into a major film festival that doubles as a film market; *e.g.,* Toronto, Sundance, Berlin, or Cannes.

Most network television deals that don't originate inside a studio are made at the National Association of Television Program Executives (NATPE) convention in January in Las Vegas.

Another function of the sales agent can be to obtain *finishing money,* financing for postproduction of your partially completed movie. Commitments from foreign distributors may convince investors to provide the necessary funds.

FINISHING MONEY: Investment funds for completing a movie that has been shot but for which some postproduction steps remain.

NEGATIVE FINANCING: Practice used by independent producers to secure production funding based on prior commitments of distribution.

NEGATIVE PICKUP: Commitment from a distributor, usually without advancing any cash, that it will release a movie if and when the filmmaker completes it.

BACK END: Any distribution revenue from a movie over and above domestic box-office receipts.

Sales agents occasionally make deals on movies that haven't been shot yet—a practice called *negative financing.* This is especially common on movies produced for television. When a network orders a movie from you, the typical fee is relatively modest—sometimes as little as $1 to $3 million—not quite enough to cover the cost of producing the film negative, or perhaps just enough to break even. (Salary for one star could easily eat up half that budget.) But the deal gives you the right to keep the income from any foreign sales. The sales agent then seeks commitments from foreign distributors, which will constitute your profit. In a variation on this practice, the network or studio may not put up any cash at all; it will just give you a *negative-pickup* deal, meaning if you deliver a finished negative, the network or studio will pick it up (distribute) it. The cash to actually produce the film comes from selling the *back end,* which includes foreign and video-store distribution. And until you get that far, you may need a loan from the bank to cover your production expenses.

Distributor

In the theatrical motion-picture market, a distributor basically wholesales films to the owner-operators of theaters. The distributor is the link between the movie studios and the theater chains. In the domestic market, studios have their own distribution divisions.

BOX-OFFICE GROSS RECEIPTS: Money collected from theatrical ticket sales, not including refreshment sales.

The math of theatrical distribution is discouraging to anyone who aspires to profit from making movies. The money a theater owner collects from ticket sales is called *box-office gross receipts.* Half of this revenue goes to the theater, half to the distributor. Unless the movie is a runaway hit, the theater owner's share is just enough to pay his expenses and break even. He gets his profit from selling drinks and snacks. In fact, that $3 soft drink you buy is practically all profit—the paper cup costs more than the fizzy stuff inside.

From his half of the box-office gross receipts, the distributor pays himself back for the costs of making film *prints* and taking out *ads (P&A)*. Then he takes another healthy cut as his profit, and returns what's left, called the *producer's gross*, to the studio.

> **P&A:** Distributor's term for prints and ads; marketing and release expenses above and beyond negative cost.
>
> **PRODUCER'S GROSS:** Portion of domestic gross remitted by distributor to the producing studio.

As a rule, before it returns any profit to the studio, a movie's box office gross must reach at least *three times* its production budget.

It doesn't take a studio head to see the bottom line: In today's movie business, theatrical distribution makes sense for one reason only—to stimulate public interest. That interest, in turn, stimulates sales and rentals of videotapes and DVDs, as well as licenses for television and foreign sales. If a movie is a hit, non-theatrical revenues can be equal to, or greater than, box-office receipts. Some movies with timeless themes can generate profits for years after their theatrical runs have come and gone.

Current Programming Department Staffers

If you're producing a television program under contract, you'll report to the network's current programming department. These people are in charge of making sure that regularly scheduled programs come in on time and on budget. Their role is quite different from the development department, where new movies and series are conceived and nurtured.

The staff of current programming is less concerned with creativity than with operational details. They want your videotape in time for the airdate, or they will have to schedule a rerun or replacement. They also help network executives make decisions about filling slots in the broadcast schedule.

Web Host Administrator

A Web host is a large, powerful computer server and the company that operates it, storing and providing access to the files for Web sites "hosted" there. Your Web host may or may not be the same entity as your Internet Service Provider (ISP); because of high bandwidth requirements, many ISPs refuse to host video content—or will support it only at premium rates.

If you use the Internet as a video distribution channel, technicians at your Web hosting service will assist you with any technical difficulties you may have. They will also monitor visitor traffic and your usage of network bandwidth and disk space on their servers—and they will charge you accordingly.

Host administrators don't care much about the content of your video, unless it can cause legal problems for the hosting company—by violating someone's copyright, for instance, or including pornography. (Most Web hosting contracts require material to have the movie equivalent of an R, if not a PG, rating. Hosting pornography is a specialty requiring, among other things, high bandwidth, credit-card authorization capability, and very high insurance premiums.)

Host administrators very much *do* care whether you've prepared your video files properly. If you don't, your visitors can bring a server crashing down—or at least block access so other visitors can't get through. (For more information on preparing video clips for the Internet, see "Creating Streaming Media Files" later in this chapter.)

DELIVERABLES FOR DISTRIBUTION

First-time producers can be shocked by the need to provide a complete set of *deliverables,* or contractually required submission items, to turn in along with their video program. They sometimes fail to keep records of production, can't produce actors' releases and music clearances, and don't prepare masters properly.

> **DELIVERABLES:** Items you are required to submit to your distributor.

The contract for any commercial distribution deal includes a list of required deliverables, including master format and paperwork. Read it carefully, and follow its guidelines.

Here's a list of typical deliverables for commercial movie distribution. The requirements for television won't include film negatives or prints, but most of the other elements will be the same.

> **TIP:** Like almost everything else in a movie deal, deliverables are negotiable. Many distributors will ask for the moon—your precious negative, for example. Try not to give it to them. Ask whether they'll be satisfied with an authorization granting access to the negative (or whatever item is under discussion). Customarily, the distribution agreement includes an addendum that allows the distributor to order prints from a lab where the negative is on deposit.

Film Items

Here are most of the elements the distributor will need to make release prints and videotapes from your original video:

- Access to the 35mm negative (or internegative) you made from the original video, with optical soundtrack or separate mag track, depending on requirements for release prints. (Remember, some theaters still have antiquated projection systems, especially in foreign markets.)

- 35mm print (typically, the most recent answer print, for purposes of judging quality)

- Digibeta NTSC master videotape (or PAL or SECAM, depending on the country of release)

- Dialogue list in English (dialogue-only version of the script)

- Music cue sheet (including selections, rights holders, and clearances—did you negotiate worldwide/universal rights or just North American?)

- Any foreign-language tracks made

Documentation

You must prove your right to license the movie to the distributor by supplying the following items:

- Employment list of all persons hired during production of the film (cast, crew, administration—everybody)

- Dubbing restrictions, if any, on rights to use actors' voices (agreements with artists may include clauses giving them the right to approve their foreign-language counterparts, or grant them additional fees for subtitled versions)

- Prior distribution history (disclosing any previous public exhibition, in any country)

- Distribution obligations and restrictions (agreements with artists may constrain the distributor or require additional fees)

- Contracts (literary rights, music and lyrics, service agreements)

- Notarized Certificate of Origin (country of authorship, determining applicable copyright laws); Certificate of Authorship (stating who holds rights, including script, life story, and motion picture); Short Form Assignment of Chain of Title (showing how original rights were acquired or licensed)

- Registered certificate of copyright (if U.S., Form PA with government seal)

Publicity and Ad Materials

You must also give the distributor the following tools to make it easier for her company to promote the movie:

- Promotional stills (frames from the movie to illustrate articles and ads)

- Production stills (behind-the-scenes photographs taken on the set for news stories)

- Photographic releases for stills

- Biographies of cast and crew (including height, weight, color of hair and eyes, and—it's a common requirement—clothing sizes)

- Synopsis of the film story

- Advertising materials (art for print ads and poster designs)

- Credits, including all required by contract with actors or technicians

- Cast list

- Technical crew list

- Trailer (35mm negative, print, and videotape master)

COPYRIGHT

Note that the list of deliverables includes registration of copyright. For media projects, copyright applies to both scripts and recorded works. Technically, your copyright begins the moment your project exists in tangible form (on paper or on tape), but it's difficult to defend your rights unless there's a public record of the work's existence—which is the purpose of copyright registration. The date of registration also establishes the term of copyright, which will expire eventually. At that time (many years after your demise), your work will belong to the public, along with *Little Women* and *Huckleberry Finn*.

To register a script or a completed video (which require separate registrations) in the United States, you must send a completed copyright form, a fee, and a copy of the work to the Library of Congress. (You can find forms and answers to questions about copyright at *www.loc.gov/copyright.*)

> **TIP:** Even though your script is a literary work, it requires a different copyright form than you'd use for a novel. The correct registration form for scripts and completed videos is Form PA (Performing Arts).

INTELLECTUAL PROPERTY: Any originally created material of value, such as a script, invention, artwork, computer program, or movie that can be protected by copyright.

As guaranteed by the U.S. Constitution, and World Intellectual Property Organization (WIPO) treaties, copyright law protects your rights as both a creator and a user of *intellectual property*, such as an original book or a video. As a creator, you have the right to control the making of copies and to profit from their sale. As a user, or owner of a copy, you have the right to use, lend, resell, or donate your copy.

All of this is pretty straightforward as long as you're dealing with books printed on paper. But the advent of digital media and electronic distribution systems has perplexed (and continues to perplex and vex) lawmakers, giant media conglomerates, computer users, surfers on the Internet, and the courts.

The problem is that not only is a digital copy easy to make, it's identical to the original; unlike a book, there's no such thing as a tattered and used copy. And it's all too easy to share that pristine, identical copy with millions of other Internet users.

The Digital Millennium Copyright Act: Your Rights in E-Space

As this book goes to press, lawyers all over the country are testing the courts' interpretation of the Digital Millennium Copyright Act (DMCA) of 1998, which Congress wrote to clarify copyright law for digital media. However, the DMCA begs more questions than it answers, and as fast as lawmakers propose revisions, the technology progresses another step and makes those revisions moot.

We won't attempt to define your rights in e-space, because, frankly, we don't know what they are, and neither does anyone else. Copyright is a rapidly changing area of the law. Pay close attention to new developments regarding copyright, because they will affect everything you do in the field of digital video.

Alterations to Your Work

Another contentious area of copyright law is the category of *moral rights:* the rights of an author to preserve the artistic integrity of his work, even after it's been sold or licensed to someone else. For example, some filmmakers contend that digital colorization of old black-and-white movies or editing them for "family" viewing should be considered violations of moral rights.

> **MORAL RIGHTS:** Rights of an author to preserve the integrity of her work, even after sale or licensing.

It's not clear whether U.S. copyright law covers moral rights, although some other countries do recognize them. However, if you sell your screenplay to a Hollywood studio, the contract will probably include a clause requiring you to waive your moral rights—just in case some court, someday, might hold that you ever had any!

Unauthorized alteration has become a hot issue with the Directors Guild. In response to situations in which video distributors were cutting scenes they considered offensive, past DGA president Martha Coolidge wrote:

Is it right to take finished films that have been created by someone else, change them to suit your whims, then profit by the commerce of these grossly altered products—and at the same time portray these versions as still being the works of their original directors?

Be warned: If your deal includes a waiver of moral rights, the buyer is reserving the option to alter your work without further permission. And, considering the mounting public pressure to censor works for all kinds of reasons—that's not a right you should willingly concede.

Decisions About Copyright

All of these issues are being hotly debated, but that doesn't mean you can do whatever you want. Get competent legal advice, understand the risks, and be impeccably careful about getting releases and clearances, registering your own copyrights, and so on.

For example, when you create a DVD, you have the option of applying electronic copy protection to the video files. That might seem a wise thing to do, especially if your work contains elements, such as music, licensed from other people. You'd be protecting their rights as well as yours. However, if you're making a video sales brochure, you might think it good business to encourage prospective customers to share it freely. But if you encourage sharing, are you making it easier for some people to violate the music copyrights you took such pains to license?

We don't know. But we believe they are important questions.

Releasing on Videotape and DVD

Whether you need to deliver a video recording to one person or millions, VHS videotape and DVD may be the media of choice. These familiar formats have a lot going for them: They're inexpensive, highly portable, and most people have players already in place.

These channels are especially important for distributing noncommercial and low-volume programs. If you can't (or don't want to) put your show on commercial TV, you can still distribute your project via the post office, parcel delivery service, or even by pounding the pavement and making deliveries yourself.

DVDs are quickly overtaking VHS tape for new film releases. In fact, the introduction of the DVD may well be the most rapidly accepted technological innovation in history. After just a few years on the market, DVD players can be found in a quarter to a third of the homes in the United States and Europe. Many new desktop computers now come with DVD drives.

The shift from LP and cassette to CD as the prime medium for distributing audio material moved music from an analog medium to a digital one. While the transition from VHS to DVD also takes movies from an analog to a digital medium, the DVD format is much more sophisticated than an audio CD, with a data structure that's ready-made for televisions with built-in computers. This development will have a major impact on how you prepare your shows for duplication, and also on how you design presentations for those "smart" TVs—including models yet to be invented.

Even so, you can't avoid dealing with studio-standard digital videotape if your show is headed for broadcast, or even for movie theaters. Although this requirement will change, for now digital tape is still the required format for submitting your show to networks, as well as to film-transfer services that prepare your show for theatrical release. And, for consumer use, VHS tape is still a viable distribution medium—although for how much longer nobody knows.

VHS Videotape Mastering

Videotape duplication facilities can handle both mastering and copying. They can also *upconvert* or *downconvert* your recording to other formats. For example, you'd need to upconvert a DV master to Digibeta for broadcast submission, downconvert it for VHS release. (For more information on recording formats, see "Non-DV Digital Formats" in Appendix A.)

> **UPCONVERT:** Transfer a video recording from a lower data rate or resolution to a higher one; upsample.
>
> **DOWNCONVERT:** Transfer a video recording from a higher data rate or resolution to a lower one; downsample.

Many dub houses require you to submit your show on Digibeta cassette, and if you have it on some other format they will charge you for the conversion. Remember that the maximum Digibeta cassette size is 120 minutes, so if your show is longer than two hours, you'll have to find a good break point to fit it onto two or more cassettes.

If the end product is going to be VHS cassettes, it's generally OK to submit your show on analog Betacam SP, as long as the duplicator will accept it that way. Since the duplication process is analog, you'll still get a quality product—and you might save some money on mastering, since the cassettes are less expensive than Digibeta. Even if you submit on Digibeta, the duplicator will make its own proprietary analog master, possibly as a continuous-loop tape, for use on high-speed copying decks.

MASTER-TO-SLAVE: Videotape copying process by which a player (master) controls recording by multiple VCRs (slaves).

The copying process is *master-to-slave*: One master player controls multiple slave recorders. Most facilities can copy your show onto tens or even hundreds of videocassettes at a time. Orders in the thousands usually take several days of continuous dubbing.

Pricing on videocassette duplication is very competitive. Get at least three bids, but when you're comparing prices, don't necessarily choose the lowest one. A big factor in videocassette duplication is the quality of the physical cassette—its mechanical characteristics and durability, as well as the grade of videotape inside. Cheap cassettes tend to break or jam in players, and the oxide coating will flake or rub off the tape with repeated use, causing dropouts. Or, the tape's silicone coating, which lubricates and protects the playback heads, will wear off too quickly.

Allow enough time for the duplicator to produce the quantity you need on a normal schedule. Even a small order of 100 cassettes can take two or three days, which includes mastering, duplication, quality control, and packaging. If you ask for rush service, the duplicator may be able to provide it by putting on extra shifts (to the limit of the number of recorders in the plant), but you'll pay a premium for it.

DVD Authoring

A DVD has a complex data structure much like a computer's hard disk. If you were to inspect the directory of a DVD on a computer, you would see a hierarchy of folders and file names (**Figure 12.1**). Although it's easy enough to use a DVD as a data storage medium and copy video clip files directly to it, DVD players won't be able to play them back unless the discs you create follow this strict data structure.

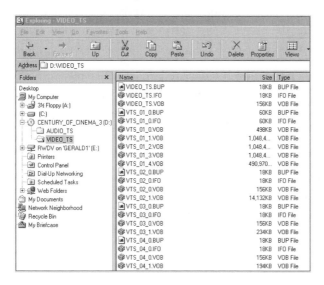

Figure 12.1 The directory of a DVD shows the VIDEO_TS folder, which contains all video clips, including their audio tracks and any subtitles.

Look at the directory in Figure 12.1, and you'll notice two folders: VIDEO_TS and AUDIO_TS. Normally, DVD players look for files only in these folders. The VIDEO_TS folder contains presentation files (.VOB), navigation files (.IFO), and media-information files (.BUP). The presentation files contain the video programming—video, audio, and subtitles. The navigation files contain programs (called *scripts*) that tell the player what to do when users make certain control selections. On DVDs that contain movies, the AUDIO_TS folder may be empty. It's there in case you want to include audio-only files such as AIFF, Wave, or SoundDesigner II files.

> **SCRIPT:** Computer program that automates a sequence of commands; stored program on a DVD for controlling the player.
>
> **HYBRID:** DVD that contains both video clips and other documents.

There may be other folders and files on the disc, but the player won't see them unless you specify a navigation program to instruct the player how to process them. DVDs that contain both video programming and data files are called *hybrid* DVDs. The DVD that accompanies this book is a hybrid because it contains both video clips and documents.

Happily, you don't have to build the DVD data structure by creating folders and copying files to them. You don't even have to know much about creating specialized files for handling user interaction. Your DVD authoring software takes care of those details.

DVDs include several technological features that are worth knowing about: Player levels and distribution controls.

Player Levels

The DVD recording standard includes specific categories, or levels, of player (**Table 12.1**). Corporate and educational network designers, as well as DVD authors, use these levels as a guide to make sure that players at multiple locations will respond to programming in the same way. In general, the higher the player's level, the more sophisticated its computerized functions and the higher its cost.

Most consumer DVD players on the market today are Level 1. They play menu selections the user picks by way of the keypad on a television-style remote control. Levels 2–4 support greater user interaction—typically via a keyboard and mouse—and are more suited to education, training, surveys, or tests. But except in some corporate networks, there hasn't been much exploitation of computer-based DVD capabilities. Some of the most interesting applications of these amazing machines are yet to be explored.

Many Level 2 and 4 players are rugged industrial models designed for continuous use in busy places, such as shopping malls and factory floors. Any desktop computer with a DVD drive can operate as a Level 3 player—so there are a lot of them out there.

Table 12.1 Levels of DVD Players

Level	Computer	Functions	Applications
1	Controller chip; no memory	User makes all selections	Home entertainment
2	Small internal with memory	Responds to programs on playback	Robot player; unattended continuous playback; in-store demonstrations
3	Interface to external	Combination of user selections and programmed operation	Education and training
1/2/3	Both internal and external	Combination of user selections and programmed operation	Multipurpose; home and office
4	Large internal with memory and computer disk storage	Combination of user selections and programmed operation	Education and training; corporate intranet

Distribution Controls

The last step in authoring a DVD requires you to set some restrictions on the distribution of the material and allows you to activate some optional controls:

Region code. Your authoring software might not allow you to burn a DVD without setting the disc's region code, which defines its authorized geographic area of distribution. This code not only controls the disc's default language but also restricts playback to specific players. When a user loads a DVD into the player, if its region code doesn't match the region code burned into a chip in the player, the DVD won't play.

Most people don't realize it, but one rationale behind the region code is so distributors can permit home viewing of movies only after the theatrical runs have ended in a particular region. It can also tell the player which language track, possibly including trailers and ads, to select for playback.

Digital scrambling. An optional copy-protection feature scrambles, or encrypts, the disc data. The disc can then only be read by players that have licensed decoding circuits. Attempts to copy the disc on a computer not equipped with a decoder won't work. The scheme is called the Contents Scrambling System (CSS) and is administered by the Motion Picture Association of America (MPAA, *www.mpaa.org*) and the DVD Copy Control Association (DVDCCA, *www.dvdcca.org*). You set this option when you create your master disc, but it's activated and applied by the commercial duplication facility in the copying process. You can be selective about which sectors are scrambled.

Analog copy protection. An optional scheme that discourages copying from DVD to analog videotape is called the Analog Protection System (APS). To activate this feature in your authoring software, you must buy a license from Macrovision (*www.macrovision.com*). If the author has applied APS to the disc, the DVD player adds noisy signals to its analog video output. Television monitors ignore these signals, but they interfere with VCRs, badly degrading the quality of any recorded picture.

Emerging protection schemes. Media companies are serious about implementing electronic safeguards to prevent loss of income from the pirating of copyrighted works. This is another area of technological development that will affect, and be affected by, any revisions to the DMCA. Congressional bills have been proposed to prohibit copying, while pending court cases test the limits of existing law. These issues will be hotly debated for a long time to come.

DVD Authoring Software

DVD authoring software ranges from "home-movie" level to professional versions. The home-movie products, intended mainly for building simple discs for Level 1 players, provide only a limited number of menus, audio tracks, and subtitle tracks. These products include:

- Apple iDVD 4 (included with, and requires, Mac OS X) Mac

- Pinnacle InstantCD/DVD 8; Windows

- Sonic Desktop MyDVD Studio Deluxe 5; Windows

> **MULTI-ANGLE TRACKS:** Parallel video tracks that show the same scene from different camera angles.

If all you want to do is release your feature on DVD with a simple chapter list and a few menu selections, any of these products will do the job fine. However, if you want to create *multi-angle tracks* that present the same scene from different camera angles, or need multilingual subtitles, or wish to provide lots of interactivity, you'll need a professional authoring application. These products include:

- Adobe Encore DVD; Windows

- Apple DVD Studio Pro 2; Mac

- Pinnacle Impression DVD-Pro; Windows

- Sonic Desktop DVDit! 2.5; Windows

- Ulead DVD Movie Factory 3 Disc Creator; Windows

The differences come down to personal taste and ease of use. For example, some of the packages come with ready-made templates for creating menus, and you'll prefer some designs to others. We used DVD Studio Pro 2 to create the DVD for this book. It was a logical choice because it's designed to work with Final Cut Pro, the NLE we used to edit the videos. For example, if you mark in and out points in Final Cut Pro, DVD Studio Pro will pick them up automatically. If your NLE application and authoring program don't work well together, you can't be assured all your settings will survive the translation.

Creating a DVD, Step by Step

We'll use DVD Studio Pro to provide examples as we survey the steps involved in creating a DVD, but the concepts are the same no matter which authoring program you use.

1. Convert your clips to MPEG.

   Start by converting your digital video files to the formats required for DVD. The recommended video format is MPEG-2 with the *VBR* (variable bit rate) option enabled. This selection gives the best quality images. To conserve space and maximize quality, the encoder will vary the data rate, generating more bits per second if frames contain a lot of detail or action, fewer if they don't (or if they don't differ much from previous frames). The maximum data rate for MPEG-2 is 9.8 Mbps, but as a rule you can count on an average of about 4 Mbps, which will eat up about 3.6 GB of disc space per hour of video. To achieve even greater compression, it's also possible to put your clips through the VBR process twice. The more compression you try to achieve, the more you will begin to affect playback quality. This isn't a science, and the results depend greatly on the content of the clip (amount of detail, speed of motion). In seeking the best VBR tradeoffs, let trial and error be your guide. In fact, for obscure technical reasons, the results of one encoding pass can look different from those of another, even with the same source material.

   > **VBR (VARIABLE BIT RATE):** "Intelligent" MPEG-2 encoding scheme that uses a variety of data rates to store the highest-quality picture in the smallest amount of space.

If you edited your clips in Final Cut Pro, you can use its QuickTime MPEG Encoder utility. If you're editing on a Windows system, your NLE software might have an export function that will convert your clips as well.

The maximum amount of data you can burn onto a single DVD-R disc on your PC is 4.7 GB—which will hold about 1 hour and 18 minutes of video in MPEG-2 format, depending on the complexity of your imagery. (However, Apple now claims iDVD 4 can fit 2 hours of material on the same disc. Higher-capacity disc formats are available, but you make your copies at a pressing plant.)

TIP: Remember that the maximum running time you can put on a DVD will be reduced if you choose to store interactive elements, such as menus, documents, or scripts.

CBR (CONSTANT BIT RATE): MPEG encoding scheme that uses a fixed data rate.

PCM (PULSE CODE MODULATION): One of several digital encoding schemes for audio.

AC-3: One of several digital encoding schemes for audio; Dolby Digital.

BUTTON: Graphic symbol on a screen menu that indicates a user selection.

If you need to fit a long show, or lots of separate clips, on a DVD disc, you can choose the MPEG-1 *CBR* (constant bit rate) video format instead. It runs at a fixed 1.8 Mbps and can fit more than twice as much running time as MPEG-2 on the same-sized disc. The picture quality will be lower, though—roughly comparable to VHS tape.

The MPEG conversion will automatically include the audio tracks of your video program. You can save audio-only clips as either Linear *PCM* (pulse-code modulated) or *AC-3* (also known as Dolby Digital). PAL players can play MP3 clips as well, but NTSC players can't. DVD Studio Pro uses a utility called A.Pack for converting audio-only tracks. Most sound editing applications, such as ProTools and Sound Forge, can export these files.

2. Create menus.

A DVD should have at least one main menu, which the viewer can use to select chapters and other material. Each selection on the menu is represented by a graphic *button* (**Figure 12.2**). Many authoring programs have built-in templates for creating these menus, which are bitmap images, or stills. You can also use a graphics program like Photoshop or Microsoft PowerPoint to create menus. However, the canned templates are becoming so attractive, with all kinds of complex motion built-in, that you'd have to be an ambitious designer indeed to build yours from scratch. These templates can make it easy to incorporate graphic animation and video clips in the menus, not just fancy button effects.

When you're creating menus, remember that computer-generated colors may be too saturated for video. Also, be aware that computer graphics use square pixels, but digital-video pixels are rectangular. As a result, you may see slight distortion of the menu when it appears on a television screen.

TIP: The Photoshop command to compensate for this distortion is Image > Resize > Image Size. To prepare NTSC graphics, create them in 720 × 540 resolution, then resize to 720 × 480.

3. Import Assets.

In DVD terminology, all video and audio clips, still-image files, and any other files you want to put on the disc are called *assets*. All authoring programs permit you to import assets, which is much the same process as capturing clips in an NLE. You identify the external file and give it a name by which you will refer to it during subsequent authoring steps. In DVD Studio Pro, imported material appears in the Assets folder.

Remember that you must first convert your digital video clips to MPEG-1 or MPEG-2. The resulting files will be type .M1V or .M2V.

> **ASSET:** Any clip or file that can be written to a DVD.

4. Add Chapter Markers.

Chapters are a logical method for organizing separate clips on a disc, or breaking your movie into a series of sections. Viewers can select a chapter to move instantaneously to a specific moment in the film.

The easiest way for feature filmmakers to create chapters is to put one at every reel change (roughly every 20 minutes). A more thoughtful authoring approach would be to start each chapter at a turning point in the story, such as "Josh Discovers His Mistake." Viewers will find this type of organization convenient, especially if they pause playback and want to resume later but don't know just where they left off.

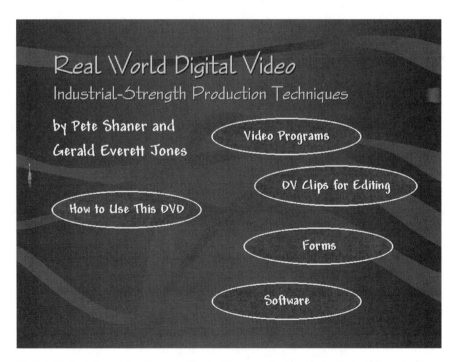

Figure 12.2 A DVD menu is composed of buttons for user selections. The authoring process must link buttons to actions the player will perform, such as playing video clips or executing computer programs, or scripts.

> **MARKER:** Timecode and label on a DVD indicating the in or out point of a clip; destination for a jump.

You'll need to identify the in and out points of each chapter for the player. To do this in your authoring application, you typically play back a clip and simply click to insert a *marker* at any desired point in the show. A marker contains both an explicit timecode and a label by which you can refer to it as you structure the disc, such as *Start of intro, End of intro, Start of chapter one, End of chapter one,* and so on.

Eventually, as more movies are produced specifically for the DVD medium, chapter organization may become a formal part of story structure, as it is in books. You'll know the dominance of DVD is complete when people expect to see chapter titles in theatrical movies!

5. Create interactive markers.

Not all markers need to be associated with chapters or full-screen menus. Buttons known as *interactive markers* can be supered on a scene as it plays. For instance, if you're creating a driver-education video, you might freeze the frame and ask the user to respond to a question on the screen: "In this situation, you should: 1) use your turn signal, 2) honk your horn, 3) swerve to avoid pedestrians, or 4) come to a full stop."

To provide these types of user selections, you must first create a bitmap file containing an *overlay image,* or thumbnail graphic, showing the buttons you want to float over the picture.

6. Create a story.

In DVD terminology, a *story* is a set of markers you want to play back in a particular order. A typical story would play back all the chapters in a movie, in the correct order, without pausing.

7. Specify buttons and button states in menus.

Once you've created menus with button graphics (or selected a template that contains buttons) and inserted markers in video tracks to correspond with those chapter selections, you're ready to define the actions the user will trigger by each selection. The action you usually want will be a *jump,* which starts playback at a specific marker. You then define each button and the marker to which it will be linked. You'll also select graphic effects to confirm the user's selection by highlighting the button.

> **INTERACTIVE MARKER:** DVD selection supered as a button over a video scene.
>
> **OVERLAY IMAGE:** Picture file to be supered, or overlaid, on another image.
>
> **STORY:** A set of markers defining a sequence of clips to be played back in a particular order on a DVD.
>
> **JUMP:** Programmed DVD operation that starts playback at a specific marker or timecode.

8. Specify a jump when each track is finished.

    You must tell the player what to do when it reaches the out-point marker of a given track. Most of the time you'll want to jump back to the main menu, but you can also jump to any named marker on the disc. A common source of errors is to forget to define end-of-track jumps, which can cause playback to hang—at which point the user will have to press the Menu button on the remote to manually recall the main menu.

9. Create multi-angled tracks.

    DVD allows the viewer to view a scene from different camera angles. Of course, to enable this feature you must have actually shot the scene from different angles and included each angle as a separate video track. You must also make sure that each angle has the same in and out markers—resulting in exactly the same timecodes and running times.

    Actually, this feature isn't restricted to camera angles. You can insert any set of video tracks with parallel action that will cut smoothly out of the preceding scene and into the following one. (This is an aesthetic requirement, not a technical one.) The only technical constraint is that the tracks must be identical in length.

10. Define scripts.

    As an optional feature for your presentation, you can create scripts, or computer programs, that process user responses and make decisions about what the player will do next. Scripts are text files containing instructions in a human-readable computer language. Computer programmers will be familiar with the IF...THEN statements of these scripts.

    Put in everyday language, a statement might say, in effect: IF the user presses 4, THEN play *Start of Intro*, OTHERWISE, after 20 seconds (or on any other key press) jump to *Review Questions* menu and wait for data input.

11. Build your finished project.

    When you've defined all the markers, menus, buttons, and actions for your disc, you're ready to *build*, or *multiplex*, the DVD.

    > **BUILD:** Write an authored video program to DVD; multiplex.

    The mastering process may take several hours. The more multilevel tracks you have and the more complex the interactions they involve, the longer it will take the computer to generate the files.

If you intend to duplicate high-capacity DVDs at a pressing facility, you shouldn't burn a disc at all. Just write your master to a DLT data tape drive, and bring the tape to the pressing facility.

Regardless of the output medium, all the files for a video show will end up in the VIDEO_TS folder, which the program will create for you on the disc or drive.

Once building is done, the authoring program will report any errors that occurred during the process. If you see any, you'll have to go back to look up the source of the errors in the help system or software manual, trace and fix them in the authoring program, then rebuild your disc.

DVD Mastering and Duplication

You'll need to decide whether to replicate your discs by burning or pressing. Here are the main considerations.

Disc Capacity

If you need a disc that will run longer than 1-2 hours in high-quality MPEG-2, the choice is easy: You'll have to order your copies from a pressing plant.

Discs intended for burners are designated DVD-5 and are *ss/sl* (single-side/single-layer). DVDs designed to hold feature-length programs (around 2.4 hours) are designated DVD-9 and are *ss/dl* (single-side/dual-layer). The dual plastic layers are bonded together in the pressing plant, doubling the disc's capacity. With either single-sided types, one side of the disc faces the laser head of the player, and a label can be printed on the unused side.

> **SS/SL:** Single-side/single-layer optical disc; DVD-5.
>
> **SS/DL:** Single-side/dual-layer optical disc; DVD-9.
>
> **DS/SL:** Dual-side/single-layer optical disc; DVD-10.
>
> **DS/DL:** Dual-side/dual-layer optical disc; DVD-18.

Pressing plants can also produce dual-sided disc copies. The *ds/sl* (dual-side/single-layer) type designated DVD-10 holds around 2.6 hours of video, while the *ds/dl* (dual-side/dual-layer) disc designated DVD-18 holds 4.7 hours. Obviously, neither double-sided disc can have a large label because the laser must be able to read both sides. (The duplicator can print a small amount of tiny text on the blank inner ring of the disc such as "Wide Screen Version," or "Standard Version." It's better than nothing.)

Order Quantity

If you need more than 1,000 disc copies, get bids from several pressing plants. The preparation of the glass master from which copies are pressed is an expensive process, which currently runs at least $4,000 (including one master and 1,000 copies). That's $4 per disc.

Industry rumor has it that pressing plant capacity was overbuilt during the dot-com boom, which means there's lots of extra capacity out there. So don't just get competitive bids, be prepared to haggle. You can find duplicators by searching the Web for "DVD Pressing" or "DVD Replication."

If you need hundreds of ss/sl discs, look for a supplier that uses jukebox-style burning machines. In fact, if you make multiple copies for corporate clients on a regular basis, you might invest one of these machines yourself. One advantage of this type of duplicator, which you don't have with pressing, is that each of the eight discs can have a separate data stream, so each disc in a batch can contain a different program. You can also intermix CDs and DVDs in a duplication run. (One model that burns eight CDs or DVDs at a time, at higher speeds than you can manage on a desktop computer, is the Rimage Producer Prostar: *www.rimage.com.*)

Beware of Poor Disc Quality

Disc prices are dropping all the time, and you can always save money by buying in bulk. But the quality of ready-made blank discs intended for burning varies considerably from one manufacturer to another. The lowest-priced ones will almost certainly give you problems.

RELEASING ON TELEVISION

If you want to reach as many people on the globe as possible, television is the way to go.

Today's channels of commercial television distribution are broadcast, cable, and satellite. In the United States, it's safe to assume that nearly every home has broadcast television, although in many of them the basic channels are actually being received via cable or satellite connections. Cable has dominated the market for upscale homes for years, but satellite service now appears to be luring some of those customers away.

Another distinction in commercial television is how the cost of programming is subsidized. In the traditional *ad-supported* approach inherited from radio, programs are interrupted periodically by paid advertising spots. So-called *premium* cable and satellite channels use a *subscription-supported* model with relatively little paid advertising; the cost of programming is defrayed by monthly fees paid by viewers. A third category is *public-access programming,* a community forum provided by a cable operator as a condition of its *franchise*, or governmental authorization.

AD-SUPPORTED: A communications channel subsidized by advertising revenue.

SUBSCRIPTION-SUPPORTED: A communications channel subsidized by user fees.

PUBLIC-ACCESS PROGRAMMING: Production facilities and airtime provided to the community by a cable operator as a condition of its federal broadcast license.

FRANCHISE: In cable television, a government license to operate in a specific metropolitan area.

TV Technicalities

If you're submitting a videotape for broadcast, the network's broadcast engineering department will tell you what's needed technically, and the current programming department will lay out all the other requirements, including paperwork. To get an idea of the submission details involved, take a look at "Deliverables for Distribution" in this chapter. Except for the film elements, ads, and posters, you'll probably need to provide just about everything on the list.

We've covered most of the technical requirements for preparing a broadcast-quality Digibeta master in "Converting DV Color to Broadcast-Legal" in Appendix A. Here's a quick checklist:

- Technically correct picture: 4:2:2 color space, colors no greater than 80 percent saturated, no noisy edges, lower-third and safe-title areas composed correctly with readable text, and correct aspect ratio (4:3 or 16:9 letterboxed)

- Slate, tone, and countdown preceding program

- Titles and credits checked against name spellings and contract requirements

- Split audio tracks: dialogue on tracks 1 and 2, music and effects on tracks 3 and 4

Producing for Cable TV

In general, preparing a show for cable or satellite is virtually indistinguishable from making it ready for broadcast. There are only two exceptions: local cable advertising and public-access programming—both of which have less stringent technical requirements.

Because cable operators want to encourage auto dealerships and furniture stores to air spots, even low-budget spots, it's common to find some of those spots produced on DV in consumer color space. (For more information on color space, see "What Is Color Space and Why Is It Important?" in Appendix A.) One reason that's possible is because the saturated colors that are typical of consumer color space are less likely to cause interference problems on cable than on broadcast channels.

As for public access, cable operators are legally obliged to provide studio and taping facilities at virtually no charge for use by the community. To use the studio, you usually have to qualify by taking a low-cost training course and booking well in advance. You must also demonstrate a noncommercial purpose for your show and pay the cost of tape stock. (You can save money by buying recycled stock from a dub house and bringing it to your taping session.)

As you might expect, the equipment in these almost-free facilities is often old and shopworn—old analog Type C or U-Matic gear. To put it politely, technical standards usually aren't an issue. If you produce your public access show on DV, you'll raise the bar on quality—but the cable company's analog studio cameras, sound mixer, switcher, and editing console will be of no use.

Movies and programs submitted to ad-supported networks must contain *act breaks* for insertion of advertisements. For programming you create under contract, the breaks will be determined in the early stages of preproduction—usually during script development. But if you're adapting your theatrical movie for TV broadcast, you'll have to find the breaks.

> **ACT BREAK:** Point in a video story with a pause for insertion of commercials.
>
> **CLIFF-HANGER:** Unresolved ending; plot technique used to sustain viewer interest through commercial breaks.

There are no hard and fast rules about the timing of breaks. However, it's important to end each act with a *cliff-hanger*—an unresolved plot point that makes the audience eager to stay tuned during the commercial to find out what happens. You'll also notice that the intervals between spots get shorter and shorter in the latter acts of a show, presumably because the audience is hooked by then and will tolerate more interruptions without switching channels.

RELEASING ON THEATRICAL FILM

The majority of projects intended for commercial theaters will be feature-length fiction movies, although feature documentaries are a small but increasingly significant segment of the market. Forget shorts, except on the festival circuit and in select art houses in a few major cities. (For more information, see the sidebar "Shorts" in Chapter 1.)

Remember, too, that the majority of people in movie theaters on weekends—the only time theaters are full—are young couples on dates. That means major box office successes are built, not by critical acclaim, but by enthusiastic younger viewers returning to see the same movie again and again. (Movies aimed at older adults occasionally succeed in spite of the odds—but no one can tell you why, or give you a formula for repeating the success.)

In any case, definitely forget about wide-releasing a film for exhibition in commercial movie theaters unless a distributor is footing the bill.

The worldwide theatrical film market breaks down into two major categories—domestic (U.S. box office) and foreign. About 80 percent of the movies on foreign screens were initially exhibited in the U.S. Ironically, that means a Swedish producer will have a better chance of getting her film shown in her own country if it runs first—however briefly—in the domestic U.S. market.

> **DIRECT-TO-VIDEO:** Movie produced with the intention of distributing primarily in video stores.

The same is true of movies intended primarily for the video store. The best strategy for a *direct-to-video* release requires at least limited theatrical distribution—and the accompanying expense of an advertising campaign—in domestic theaters.

Converting Video to Film: Should You Bother?

DV isn't really suited for exhibition on large theater screens, although it's been done. (For more information, see "Experimenting with Digital Video" in Chapter 1.) HD is the preferred digital video format for feature film production, but even it has its detractors. Currently, DV-to-film projects seldom break out of the art-house or cult-movie category— but now and then a DV project like *Tadpole* or *Pieces of April* will surprise everyone and go wide.

Converting a digital video production to film is an expensive and time-consuming process; a feature-length movie can easily take several weeks. So before you start, consider whether you need to do it at all.

For instance, if you have a feature but haven't yet found a distributor, don't be in a big rush to do the transfer. Many film festivals accept video submissions. And producer's sales reps often take videocassettes or DVDs with them when they call on distributors.

Some filmmakers don't even budget for film transfer during preproduction planning. They reason that if they're fortunate enough to find a distributor, they can either negotiate the film-transfer costs as part of the P&A allowance, or pay for the transfer from monies the distributor advances. Either way, this strategy relies on the distribution deal to pay for the negative. (Of course, some distributors will be reluctant to cut a deal unless they can verify the quality of the prints in advance.)

Preparing for Film Transfer

If you're under a production contract, you'll have producers, studio executives, and an army of experts guiding your steps during the transfer to film, and you'll be lucky if you have any input at all during late postproduction. But it always helps to know what's involved.

It's particularly important to establish a relationship with your film-transfer facility *before you shoot*. For example, although most film recording service bureaus will accept digital videotape in either NTSC or PAL formats, some specialize in one or the other. Some prefer you to shoot in progressive mode; others recommend shooting interlaced and then using NLE software or special utilities to convert the digital video file to progressive scan prior to doing the transfer.

> **ANAMORPHIC:** A cinema-style camera lens that optically distorts a wide-screen image to fit a standard aspect ratio.

Your digital video master should be in 16:9 aspect ratio, but if you shoot in NTSC or PAL and not in HD, you'll get the best possible DV-to-film resolution by shooting in 4:3 with an *anamorphic* lens. (For more information on aspect ratios, see "Aspect Ratio and Resolution" in Appendix A.)

TIP: *For best results, learn the technical requirements of the transfer facility, shoot some short tests, pay to have them processed, and examine the results—both under a magnifying glass and projected on a big screen. (You can use an old filmstrip projector to study individual frames.)*

PLATTER: Film reel for auto-mated motion-picture projec-tors that is large enough to hold an entire feature-length movie.

Theatrical release prints are shipped on multiple reels, so no mat-ter who does the transfer, a basic requirement for theatrical dis-tribution is to break your digital video recording into separate 20-minute videocassettes, corresponding to film reels. Older-style projection booths use a two-projector system, switching from one reel to the other during the show. Modern multiplexes splice all the reels together on *platters* for projection systems that require fewer personnel to operate.

You can break your movie into reels during NLE. No reel can exceed a running time of 20:30, although they can be shorter. Ideally, the break should occur at a pause in the action of your story. There must be a one-second pause—with no fades—on the audio track at the break point. That way, dialogue, music, or effects won't be cut off during the reel change. (The changeover on two-projector systems isn't precise.) Each videotape master for a reel will require a slate and countdown; check to see what format the transfer facility requires.

TIP: *If you're aiming to do a film transfer, be sure to look at your movie projected on a large screen before you lock your digital video master. For example, extreme closeups work well on television, but too many of them can make a movie audience uncomfortable. After you've looked at your picture on a wide screen, you may want to recut. Ideally, you should view your tape in a screening room equipped for electronic projection, but if you don't have access to one, you can use a big-screen TV in 16:9 mode and sit 8 to 12 feet back in a darkened room to simulate the experience.*

The Video-to-Film Transfer Process

Some film laboratories like DuArt and FotoKem perform video-to-film transfers along with conventional film services; other vendors specialize in this conversion. Currently, there are three transfer technologies, each offering a different level of cost and quality. In order of increasing cost and quality, they are:

- Kinescope

- Flying spot

- Laser

Kinescope

The *kinescope* process dates back to the early days of television. Before the introduction of videotape recording, it was the only way to make a permanent record of a live broadcast. The process simply involves using a film camera to photograph the program as it plays on a television screen.

> **KINESCOPE:** Process by which a program is filmed as it plays on a television screen.

Early kinescope recordings showed distortion at the edges of the picture because the faces of the old TV tubes weren't perfectly flat. Today's monitors virtually eliminate this problem, but kinescope recordings still show visible scan lines.

In fact, the quality of kinescope recordings is so poor that it's really not a viable technology for transferring your video to theatrical film. Its main use in recent years has been to provide low-cost transfers for film-festival submission, but now that festivals accept tapes or DVDs, there's no longer a reason to go to the expense.

Kinescope transfer for a feature-length movie costs around $10,000 to $15,000 and takes a few days.

Flying Spot

The *flying-spot* process refers to the scanning beam of a high-resolution CRT, which paints the video image three times—once for each primary color—onto a high-contrast video tube. The camera photographs the CRT and triple-exposes each frame of the film to create a full-color composite.

> **FLYING SPOT:** CRT imaging method; focused electron beam.

Quality is fairly good, since softness at the edge of the spot combines with the high resolution to blur the boundaries between scan lines—but the process is *slow*. Depending on the speed of the recorder, it can only crank out 12 to 60 minutes of film per day. At the slowest speed, that's 10 days of continuous recording for a feature—not including setup time for mounting each reel, handling, and quality control.

Flying-spot transfers can be done with 1K, 2K, or 4K scan lines. The 1K resolution might not be quite good enough for theatrical quality. The 2K option is optimal, since it's right at the limit of the resolution of 35mm film and so is sure to eliminate visible scan lines in the prints. At today's prices, transferring a feature in 2K mode will run you about $40,000.

The 4K option is used primarily for transferring HD and CGI movies to 70mm film. Transferring a feature in 4K mode costs about $80,000.

Transferring a DV original to film using a flying spot produces output roughly comparable to blowing up a 16mm film original to 35mm, only without the film grain. Service bureaus and labs that do flying-spot transfers currently include DVFilm *(www.dvfilm.com)*, E-Film *(www.efilm.com)*, FotoKem *(www.fotokem.com)*, and Swiss Effects *(www.swisseffects.ch)*.

Laser

The laser tape-to-film transfer process is similar to flying spot, except the color-separated monochrome images are painted directly onto the film by a laser beam. Laser transfers are available in 2K and 4K resolutions. Manufacturers of laser tape-to-film recorders are Arri *(www.arri.com)* and Cineon *(www.cineon.com)*. A film lab that offers ArriLaser transfers is DuArt *(www.duart.com)*.

Laser transfers are comparable in price and turnaround time to flying-spot transfers. However, some filmmakers think the definition of the laser beam is too sharp at 2K, and that the softer-edged flying spot actually produces a better-looking picture at that resolution. We don't recommend 1K laser transfers (if you can even find anyone who does them) because scan lines may be visible. Laser transfers are probably most common at 4K resolution for transfer to 70mm.

> **TIP:** One good reason for keeping picture and sound on separate reels is that soundtrack requirements for theatrical release prints vary. The most common soundtrack format is Dolby SR, which encodes stereo on an optical track of the release print. But DTS (Digital Theater Systems), used primarily for 70mm distribution with four-channel audio, puts the audio on separate optical discs.

Working with a Film Lab

Exactly how the transfer facility and the film lab work together will depend on the capabilities of each, and particularly on whether you have the transfer facility combine picture, sound track, and titles, or you choose to submit them to the film lab as separate elements and marry them there.

OPTICAL PRINTING: Film lab process of doing special effects (wipes, dissolves, fades) in the film printing stage.

For example, some transfer facilities prefer that you submit titles as a text data file, which they can image during film recording. Then they can super the titles on the picture master or create a separate negative, as you prefer. Or you can simply shoot titles on film. Either way, keeping images and titles on separate reels will give you some flexibility later if you or the distributor wants to prepare foreign-language versions. If you keep titles and picture separate, the film lab can combine them later via *optical printing* (the same process used to create traditional film effects, such as dissolves).

Keeping the soundtrack separate involves transferring it to analog mag stripe film or an optical sound negative.

One way or another, the lab must eventually combine the elements of picture negative, soundtrack, and titles in an optical printing process to create a *color master positive*. For volume orders, the lab will then make several *color duplicating negatives*, because those negatives are subject to wear and tear in the process of making lots of prints.

Before proceeding to make release prints, the lab will send you a one-off *answer print*. Some overall color correction is possible at this point. In a laboratory process called *color grading,* or *timing,* you can vary the color cast from scene to scene.

> **COLOR MASTER POSITIVE:** Optical print that combines picture, sound, and titles.
>
> **COLOR DUPLICATING NEGATIVE:** Negative made from master positive and used for making release prints.
>
> **ANSWER PRINT:** One-off positive film made by a lab for purposes of review and approval.
>
> **COLOR GRADING:** Film lab color-correction step affecting the overall color cast and brightness from scene to scene; timing.

Digital Projection

The complex video-to-film transfer process will go away forever once electronic movie projection becomes widespread. *DLP* (Digital Light Processing), a proprietary process developed by Texas Instruments *(www.dlp.com),* is just beginning to appear in theaters. DLP uses a matrix of tiny mirrors to vary the pixel values of a bright, reflected beam of light.

> **DLP (DIGITAL LIGHT PROJECTION):** Electronic theatrical projection method developed by Texas Instruments.
>
> **D-ILA (DIGITAL DIRECT DRIVE IMAGE LIGHT AMPLIFIER):** Holographic technology for electronic theatrical projection developed by JVC; DLP competitor.

A competing technology is JVC's *D-ILA* (Digital Direct Drive Image Light Amplifier), which Kodak is packaging in a new projector. (For more information, see *www.jvcdig.com/technology.htm.*) The JVC chip uses LCOS (liquid crystal on silicon).

A different technology, but a similar concept, is involved in the billboard-sized displays you see on Times Square and in Las Vegas. These are huge panels composed of red, green, and blue LCDs, three for each pixel, each about the size of a pencil eraser. The screens are so bright that if you ever get close to one (at a trade show, perhaps), we advise wearing sunglasses.

If and when digital projection becomes the norm, theatrical release will be via optical disc, high-capacity magnetic media, or direct transmission to computer storage devices in the theater by way of high-speed telecommunication lines or satellite. For example, using advanced data compression technology, it's now possible to fit an entire feature-length HD movie on a 50 GB magnetic disk. (For more information, see *www.evs-global.com.*) Some industry experts expect the winning distribution format for HD to be Sony's Blue Laser disc (**Figure 12.3**), which in its present format can hold 23.3 GB. However, raw discs were priced initially at $45 each, so don't expect it to be a consumer format any time soon.

Whether magnetic or optical media win the day, you can turn your digital videotape master over to the distributor and go fishing instead of sweating the details of the transfer.

RELEASING ON THE INTERNET

No one on the planet has the faintest idea what business models will succeed on the Internet. When the dot-com bubble burst in the late 1990s, the dream of being your own Internet movie studio and distributor tanked with it. For now, most of the video on the Web is limited to short clips in postcard-sized windows.

Figure 12.3 The Sony Blue Laser 5.25-inch optical disc, a suitable medium for HD, is sealed inside an airtight plastic cassette. The gallium nitride laser recorder creates such fine tracks and packs data so densely that even a microscopic amount of dust could cause significant data loss. (Photo courtesy Sony Electronics Inc.)

We *do* know that the biggest obstacle to commercial video distribution via the Internet is narrow bandwidth. What's needed to achieve commercial video quality is a huge increase in bandwidth, which the telecommunications industry is quietly working on while coping with its own growth pains. Universal access to big, cheap video bandwidth is on the way—but no one knows exactly when it will show up.

Nonetheless, some visionary companies are continuing to experiment with online video distribution. In fact, if you have a short subject or an animated video clip you want people to see, the Internet is one of the few places you can get it "on the air." Just don't expect to receive any money for your efforts. And don't expect it to look very good. Exhibiting on the Web is a lot like performing stand-up comedy: It's not exactly a paying gig—more like something you do to get visibility.

Producing video commercials for the Internet stands a better chance of making you a few dollars. Corporate marketers regard the Internet as a huge electronic trade show, a place to promote their products or services or provide supplementary information for presentations they distribute in some other channel. Short video clips of product demonstrations work well on the Web.

Putting DV on the Net

Preparing digital video clips for the Internet would be easy if you didn't have to accommodate the slow (narrow bandwidth) Internet connections most customers are still using. Surprisingly large numbers of people still use relatively slow dial-up modems to access the Net—and DSL or broadband cable aren't that much better.

If bandwidth weren't an issue, you could simply upload MPEG video to your Web site and be done with it. But recall that the DV data stream delivers 25 Mb of data every second. The best dialup modems run at 56 Kbps—450 times too slow! DSL connections may run 10 times faster, but that's still not nearly fast enough for DV.

So the problem is much like trying to put the output of a fire hose through a drinking straw: It can't be done, unless your viewers are willing to wait hours to download a video file before they play it. Or they don't mind waiting 15 seconds between video frames.

The solution—which degrades quality severely—is to reduce the volume of the data stream in several ways:

- Reduce the image on the screen to postcard, or even postage-stamp, size, reducing the number of pixels in each frame.

- Apply heavy data compression, which further reduces the number of bits to be transmitted.

- Reduce the number of frames per second; the lower the fps, the less data is required, and the jerkier the motion will appear.

- Reduce the number of audio bits per second; the lower the KHz, the less data is required, and the choppier the sound. Still, degraded audio is not as noticeable as picture degradation to many people.

- Render stereo sound as mono.

> **STREAMING VIDEO:** Video and audio data delivered more or less continuously over a network.

Some combination of these trade-offs is necessary to create a video file small enough to become *streaming video:* a format that allows Web servers to deliver video data in a relatively uninterrupted stream. (Some interruption still occurs, which is why the user's computer can't start playback until it writes enough downloaded data to a cache to accumulate a continuous clip.) The results are fairly disappointing, but these are the sacrifices you have to make if you want to see your video on the Internet. The good news is that the cost of putting streaming files on the Net is so modest anyone can do it.

There are a few catches, though. Many Web hosts either don't support streaming video at all or charge a premium for it. Also, continuous streaming to multiple online users at one time requires an expensive, high-capacity server. There's nothing (except possibly your contract with the hosting service) to prevent you from uploading streaming files to your site. However, it might not take many visitors to your site to crash the server—in which case the host would probably terminate your account and tell you not to come back. Even if you don't bring down the server, the host's system administrator will notice your high usage statistics and either raise your bill or invite you to depart.

Creating Streaming Media Files

Web users don't access video files directly. Everything the user experiences must be either embedded in, or linked to, Web pages, the documents displayed in browsers like Microsoft Internet Explorer and Mozilla (formerly Netscape).

If you have the talent and the patience, you can learn to build Web pages with applications like Adobe FrameMaker, Macromedia Dreamweaver, or Microsoft FrontPage. Or you can hire a Web designer to do it for you. In principle, building a page isn't much more complex than creating a document in a word processing application. However, once you start adding video clips and user interactions, things can get complicated.

If your site has a commercial purpose, either invest some time in learning to use the tools like a pro—or hire a pro.

Streaming Applications and File Formats

Currently, there are three major media players on the market, each with its own proprietary file format as well as the ability to play the other two—perhaps not quite as well as the native players would. All three applications are available as free plug-ins for your browser software—but only the players. Server (host) licenses cost money, and so do mastering and conversion programs. The vendors are trying to gain market share by cornering the player population, then selling tools to the people who need to communicate with them.

Sooner or later, one of the formats will probably prevail. The applications and their file formats are:

- Windows Movie Maker 2—Media Player (.AVI)

- Apple iMovie 4—QuickTime Player (.MOV)

- RealNetworks Real 10 Platform—RealPlayer (.RAM)

Exporting DV Clips

You can use any one of these applications to convert your DV clips to streaming media files, ready for uploading to the Net as part of your Web page. Even though each one of them will read the other formats, it will only write its own. To be absolutely sure all your Web visitors can open your movies, consider providing each and every clip in all three formats.

Some NLE programs can export one or more media formats. Also, discreet's Cleaner is widely used for creating streaming Web files.

When you're converting DV files to streaming format, you'll need to experiment with the following settings to give you acceptable playback. Each setting has an impact on quality, file size, required bit rate, and smoothness of playback. Here are some typical choices:

Image size. This setting defines the dimensions of the playback window on a computer screen. The smaller the image size, the smaller the output file—and all other factors being equal, a smaller file will play back more smoothly than a larger one at the same bit rate. Options are Email (postage-stamp size, for attachments), Web Small (between playing card and postcard sized, best for the Web), CD Medium, and CD Large (for making files for CD-R discs that don't use as much space as MPEG-1 or -2).

In most programs, selecting a given image size will set many of the other picture-display options. However, there's usually a set of Expert (or Custom) options you can use to fine-tune these other settings.

Screen format. If your DV file starts off as NTSC, the correct screen format will be 4:3. The typical dimensions for a Web Small window will be 320✕240 pixels, or about one-fourth the resolution of a TV screen.

Compression type. This setting selects the *codec,* or video encoder, used to generate the file. Cinepak is a commonly used one, but there are many, many others. Again, experimentation will be the only way to tell which one will give you the best results for the combination of options you've chosen.

> **CODEC (COMPRESSOR/ DECOMPRESSOR):** Computer hardware and/or software used to create or read compressed video.

Quality. This option can vary from Least to Best. The lower the setting, the smaller the file. Find the minimum setting that gives acceptable playback.

Frame rate. You can vary the video playback rate between 12 and 30 fps. A rate of 12 will be noticeably jerky, and of course 30 is TV rate. The higher the frame rate, the bigger the file and the more bandwidth will be needed to download it fast enough for playback.

Key frame interval. You can select how often the codec samples a full frame of video, rather than just looking at the differences between successive frames. Although the codec normally encodes a full frame whenever the scene changes drastically, decreasing this interval (expressed in the number of frames between full samples) can result in a sharper picture. For example, if you slow the frame rate down to 12 fps, forcing the codec to sample a full image every 12 frames, you might be able to improve quality.

Audio bit rate. You can vary the rate of streaming audio from 22.050 to 44 KHz. The top of this range is close to that of a CD recording.

Audio bit depth. You can select either 8-bit or 16-bit sampling. The higher sampling rate gives better sound but creates a bigger file.

> **TIP:** *Always choose the highest audio bit rate and bit depth if your clip contains music.*

Audio mode. You can select either mono or stereo. Obviously, mono creates a smaller file by encoding one less channel.

Bandwidth. The more bandwidth the user's connection supports, the higher the bit rate and quality can be. Because bit rate differs so greatly between dial-up modems and broadband, it's common practice on the Web to provide three different versions of the clip file—each optimized for a different speed. Your options are:

- 28 Kbps or 56 Kbps modem

- Single (128 Kbps) or Dual (256 Kbps) ISDN

- Various flavors of DSL/Cable (256, 384, or 512 Kbps)

   NOTE: *ISDN is more common than DSL in some parts of Europe.*

You can also choose a high-speed option if you'll be sharing clips within a private high-speed data network:

- Corporate LAN (highest speeds, such as T1, 1 Mbps+)

   NOTE: MXF (Multimedia eXchange Format) *is a proposed standard of ANSI/SMPTE. It's intended to simplify the job of preparing clip files for distribution over all types of networks. MXF doesn't use a single data structure. Rather, it defines a package that tells the receiving computer which application to use to open the data file it contains.*

   > **MXF (MULTIMEDIA EXCHANGE FORMAT):** Proposed universal data-file format for video, audio, and pictures.

Multipoint IP Distribution

When you set up a computer on a LAN or for DSL/Cable, you must provide an *IP (Internet Protocol) address*. It looks like this: 192.169.0.56, a string of numbers separated by periods. This is the computer's unique address on the network or the Internet. It's kind of a cross between a street address and a telephone number that's always connected. When a server responds to your request for data, it puts the information out on the network, tagged with your computer's IP address. When you're online, your computer is "listening" to the network all the time, but it only responds to data tagged with its address.

> **IP ADDRESS:** Internet Protocol; a computer's unique digital identifier on a network.

As the bandwidth available to users increases—and it surely will—the Internet can become a true broadcast medium for high-quality video. Computers subscribing to a particular channel would identify themselves to the server by their IP addresses and receive programming accordingly.

That scheme wouldn't be much of an improvement over conventional cable TV, except that using your IP address would permit servers to package programming specifically intended for you and no one else. Moreover, viewers would be able to watch whatever they wanted, whenever it was convenient for them. Such a video subscription service would resemble the current Replay and Tivo set-top boxes, which are basically computerized televisions with internal hard disks. However, with multipoint IP distribution, all the processing and storage would be on the server end, eliminating the complexity and expense of programming or local storage on the user's end.

Webcasting and Web Conferencing

Streaming video to users, rather than requiring them to download and store clip files, is called *Webcasting*. A related application that awaits more universally available bandwidth is *Web conferencing,* or two-way streaming of live video and audio to facilitate *virtual meetings.*

Many radio stations currently offer streaming audio of their programming over the Internet. This may be a model for video broadcasting in the future. In the U.S., the broadcast industry is strictly regulated by the federal government, but Webcasts can be picked up anywhere in the world and so far are not subject to the same laws.

WEBCASTING: Streaming media over the Net used as an alternative to broadcast transmission.

WEB CONFERENCING: Two-way Webcasting.

VIRTUAL MEETING: Real-time conference between participants at multiple locations, achieved by telecommunications.

PORTAL: Web site that provides a point of access for a vertical market.

If you're planning to use the Internet as a video distribution channel, you might consider submitting your work to a *portal*—a Web site that provides Internet access for people who are interested in a particular topic or group of products. The portal usually offers content of its own, along with links to remote Web sites related to users' favorite topics. An example of a portal for videophiles that hosts animation and documentary short subjects is Atom Films *(www.atomfilms.shockwave.com/af/home).*

> **TIP:** *Submitting clips to a portal usually involves completing an online application and uploading the file. A content administrator at the site will decide whether to post it. You'll receive an e-mail notifying you whether the work was accepted. When filling out the application, read the accompanying release form carefully—and then ask yourself if you're sure you want to do this. For no money at all, the release may grant the site worldwide exclusive rights—a very high price for the exposure you'll get.*

RELEASING ON CORPORATE NETWORKS

If you're making video pieces for a large company, the corporate network will be your primary distribution medium. Big companies have total control over their internal communications, which generally aren't subject to the government regulations or the commercial realities that constrain movies and television.

For years, many major corporations have had their own private, *closed-circuit television* systems. Early applications involved training presentations and live broadcasts of

CLOSED-CIRCUIT TELEVISION (CCTV): Private cable TV network.

meetings. Eventually, corporate customers extended their networks—some of them worldwide—linking their offices via leased phone lines, including microwave and satellite channels. The result was to pioneer live, two-way *videoconferencing,* which linked boardrooms with field offices and stockholder meetings.

When the Internet and MPEG video first made exchange of digital video feasible, public network connections weren't secure enough to carry sensitive corporate communications. But that's all changed. An innovation called *virtual private networking* (VPN) is now making the Internet an attractive alternative for highly secure traffic. Under VPN, data encryption technology is applied to create *tunnels,* or highly secure subchannels, within the public Net.

> **VIDEOCONFERENCING:** Two-way real-time video and audio communication over a network.
>
> **VPN (VIRTUAL PRIVATE NETWORKING):** Data encryption technology used to create private subchannels within the Internet.
>
> **TUNNEL:** Private Internet subchannel created by VPN.

Today, corporations are integrating their internal networks with the Internet and standardizing ways to exchange data with computers of customer and vendor companies—to automate orders, control inventories, and promote business-to-business sales. In this "always-connected" digital telecommunications environment, video files are just another type of document, exchanged as attachments to e-mails and embedded in other documents—along with digital photos, drawings, and audio clips.

As corporate networks continue to evolve, their reach is extending to the public. Businesses are now acutely aware that, anywhere customers are standing in line, they have a captive audience. Video monitors using various flat-screen technologies are appearing at bank teller windows (**Figure 12.4**), customer-service departments, and supermarket checkout lines. Eye-catching videos are offered there, presumably to help you pass the time, but also containing advertising messages to acquaint you with new services or simply to induce you to buy one more thing before you leave the store.

Preparing Clips for Corporate Nets

Distributing video files over a corporate network requires far less bandwidth than Webcasting—as long as there's no requirement for the experience to be live. (For more information on non-real-time distribution, see the accompanying sidebar, "Store-and-Forward Technology.")

In general, you'll use the same approach discussed in "Creating Streaming Media Files," earlier in this chapter. The main difference is the degree of compression required. If you're distributing over a high bandwidth network and the data stream doesn't have to traverse narrowband links such as VPN, you won't need to compress the files as much. You can use MPEG-1 (.m1v) or MPEG-2 (.m2v) files without having to impose streaming limitations such as small playback windows and reduced frame rates. However, if the distribution scheme includes the Internet, you're back to normal streaming video, with all its limitations and trade-offs.

The Future of Live Broadband

Because corporations command so much private bandwidth, they've begun to experiment with live digital transmissions in ways ordinary users of the Internet can only dream about.

For example, some banks are installing two-way videoconferencing at unattended ATMs so customers can have virtual conversations with customer service representatives and loan officers.

Figure 12.4 Messages on this video panel in a bank customer service area target customers waiting in line. Watch for a proliferation of screens in public places, as printed paper signs give way to moving electronic displays that carry public relations and advertising messages. (IMPART, Inc. photo courtesy Citizens Bank.)

Store-and-Forward Technology

For decades now, telecommunication satellites have been feeding programming from one central dish antenna to many receivers on the ground. Programs beam from television networks up to the satellites, which relay them back down to customers or to local stations and store them for later rebroadcast.

Now that television receivers can interface with computers, a new, lower-cost approach called store-and-forward is coming into use. Corporate users are beginning to think about using store-and-forward technology as a way to build inexpensive private television networks.

Video clip files are sent to computerized receivers via satellite using IP addressing. The receivers have large-capacity hard disks to store the incoming programs. Transmission can be scheduled during relatively inexpensive off-peak hours (satellite rates are lower during late-night and early-morning hours) because the files won't be played back right away. Furthermore, slower transmissions over less expensive, narrow bandwidth channels can be used because the files don't need to stream for real-time viewing.

Playback occurs at a time of the viewer's choosing, or when determined by corporate headquarters. To activate playback, a computer program in the local player processes a small text file called a playlist, *which specifies which files to select and when to display them (****Figure 12.5****). Applications include information kiosks in shopping malls, television monitors in airport departure lounges, and billboard-sized retail displays.*

> **STORE-AND-FORWARD:** Video communications achieved by sending files for later playback.
>
> **PLAYLIST:** Text file specifying display sequences on a computerized video player.

Delivering on the Democratization of Video

Digital production technologies have been a reality for years, but distribution systems for digital programs are still evolving. And all the issues revolve around bandwidth, bandwidth, and bandwidth.

What will the video world look like when we have all the bandwidth (and screen resolution) anyone could want?

Look what's happened to the music industry. Affordable MIDI systems and CD burners hit the market years before the current generation of DV tools did. Now aspiring musicians can not only create music, they can also self-publish their own professional-quality CDs. They can put up streaming Web sites to promote their bands. New services like Kazaa can test the limits of copyright protection as songs fly electronically hither and thither, and Apple can experiment with a new distribution model that sells downloaded songs for less than a buck a pop.

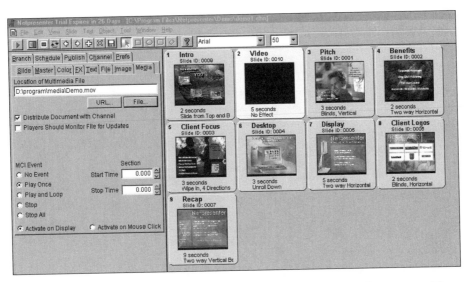

Figure 12.5 Netpresenter B.V. NetEd is a Windows application for creating store-and-forward video shows. This authoring program uses a slide-show format much like PowerPoint to define events in a playlist. Each event, or slide, can be any type of media file, including still image, video clip, audio clip, or animation. Receiving computers run a companion program called NetPlayer.

But have music publishers and record companies gone out of business? Has the digitally empowered rabble stormed the corporate gates and taken hold of the channels of distribution? Hardly. New business models *will* emerge. Perhaps media consumption will be sold increasingly as subscriptions, like magazines and cell-phone airtime. Or perhaps the entire Internet economy will be fueled by "micro-payments," garnering just pennies per click, but millions of them.

In any event, you can bet it won't be free. Expect television networks, cable companies, and movie studios to be around for a long time to come. And by virtue of the millions they can spend on advertising and promotion, they will continue to dominate access to consumers.

But increasingly, upstart videographers will be able to decide for themselves what stories they want to tell, and how, and to whom. And a wealth of new movies will find their way to viewers through a variety of known and unknown distribution channels.

Which ones will succeed? That part won't change: the ones with the best stories.

CHAPTER THIRTEEN
Coming Attractions

I'm going to direct all my films on film until they close the last lab down.

> —Steven Spielberg, quoted in the Kodak
> brochure "The Future of Cinema,"
> March, 2000

I think that I can safely say that I will probably never shoot another film on film.

> —George Lucas, Sony press conference at
> the National Association of Broad-
> casters convention, April 22, 2001

When Sony and Panavision first began to publicize the CineAlta camera, the high-definition, 24P camcorder that George Lucas used to shoot his most recent *Star Wars* feature, film manufacturer Eastman Kodak Company launched a public-relations campaign to tout the aesthetic superiority of photographic media. The brochure that contains this Spielberg quotation is downright defensive in tone. It was accompanied by a series of trade-magazine ads featuring prominent cinematographers and industry experts who declare that audiences deserve something better than cheap digital tricks that "almost look like film."

The release of *Star Wars: Episode II—Attack of the Clones* in May of 2002 quieted, if not silenced, the critics. Of the millions of fans who saw it, many did not even notice that it was produced in a new digital video medium.

Some veteran cinematographers saw the movie and grumbled that shooting HD was like using a plastic knife—not the tool you'd prefer for getting the job done.

But, while the techno-aesthetic debate rages on, studios are focusing on economics—as they have for over a century. Lucas calculates that eliminating the costs of film stock, processing, dailies, transfers, and answer prints saved him no less than $2.1 million—about *six times* what it cost co-author Pete Shaner and his investors to make their full-length movie *Nicolas* in HD.

Everyone in the industry is paying attention, whether they admit it or not. The film war isn't just about aesthetics or technology. It's a multibillion-dollar economic battle between worldwide corporations—including equipment manufacturers, content providers, and distributors—seeking to dominate the media industries of tomorrow.

Ironically, one company bidding to retrofit your local movie theater for digital projection is the same one that's boasting about the superiority of film: Eastman Kodak. That means even the high priests of film know the revolution is coming; they'd just like to sell a few more million feet of raw stock before the transition takes place.

Film is a mature technology. Although some enhancements can be expected, dramatic improvements are unlikely. But digital movie technology is accelerating at the same dizzying pace that's moved us from DOS, floppy disks, and Apple IIs to Linux, gigabyte-sized hard drives, and cheap palm-top computers in just a few decades.

The chips in digital camcorders will evolve at the same rate. Pretty soon, you won't be able to buy a consumer model that doesn't have HD resolution. It's a virtual certainty that the capabilities of digital video will surpass those of film in less than a decade.

In 1927, Warner Brothers released the first "talkie," *The Jazz Singer*, a hugely successful motion picture with synchronized sound starring Al Jolson. This technological advance caused major disruptions in the highly profitable silent film industry. The rate of film recording had to be speeded up so the soundtrack would sound good. Actors had to tone down their expansive gestures and begin exploring the subtleties of dialogue. Some silent-movie stars couldn't make the transition—their voices just weren't appealing. Recording dialogue made it necessary to place the noisy camera inside a soundproof enclosure—which made it much harder to move—and made the framing of shots more static and theatrical.

Managers of big theater chains and owners of small-town nickelodeons alike were forced to invest in the new sound projection equipment or go out of business. But ultimately theaters were retrofitted, movies flourished, and the memorable talkies of the 1930s created a giant worldwide entertainment industry.

The impact of digital video will be no less dramatic. In an interview on the set of *Nicolas*, a reporter asked Pete Shaner, "Do you have any sense that you're making HDTV's *The Jazz Singer*?" And the world's first director of a 24P feature replied:

> *I've said that to the crew to get them motivated, because God knows we're not paying them enough. There are probably things in this movie that, 60 years from now, people will look at and be horrified, because we crossed some line that hadn't even been drawn yet.*

In digital video, there's no use even trying to color inside the lines, because, as Shaner says, they haven't been drawn yet.

That's your job: Drawing new lines and painting new colors inside them.

What are you waiting for?

APPENDIX A

Digital Video Technology in Depth

Digital video can be a highly technical subject. However, as we've emphasized repeatedly, the better you know your tools the better your results will be. For example, videographers and editors in particular really do need to become proficient in the details of *recording formats*, file conversion, *compression* trade-offs, and color correction—to name just a few of the trickier topics. So, for those of you who enjoy working under the hood, this appendix supplements the discussions on camcorders in Chapters 3 and 4. For technical background on editing systems, see Appendix B: Selecting and Building an NLE System.

> **RECORDING FORMAT:** A technical standard for capturing pictures and/or sound on magnetic or optical media.
>
> **COMPRESSION:** Processing data to describe it with fewer bits and store it in smaller files. If you want even more information, take a look at the sources cited in the References and Web Links section at the end of the book, which are listed by chapter.

TYPES OF DIGITAL VIDEO: SORTING OUT THE CONFUSION

The term "digital video" is an umbrella that covers a variety of recording formats—some new and some more than a decade old. You may find some of the older equipment in broadcast studios and editing suites, but it's unlikely you'll want (or be able to afford) to use it. Still, you should know what the various formats are; you may end up needing *archival footage* from one of them.

> **ARCHIVAL FOOTAGE:** Film or video clips stored for use in future productions.

Non-DV Digital Formats

Let's start by taking a look at those digital video formats that are *not* DV:

- Digitized analog video

- Computer video files

- Legacy digital formats

- Digital Betacam (Digibeta)

- HD

Digitized Analog Video

Some analog video recording formats, many of which first appeared in the early 1980s, are still in use today. Analog formats include:

- 1-inch Type C (reel-to-reel tape used in studios)

- 3/4-inch U-Matic

- VHS

- SuperVHS (SVHS)

- Video8

- Hi8

- Betacam SP

The 8mm formats are still popular with home video enthusiasts, and professionals continue to use Betacam SP. The rest of these formats are beginning to look ancient.

If you want to incorporate archival analog footage into your digital video production, you'll need to digitize it using a video capture card. This conversion step requires a fast, powerful PC—and unless you do it just right, the results can be unreliable, with missing frames and compression *artifacts*. Most of the time the result won't look as good as DV.

> **ARTIFACT:** Visual glitch such as video noise or a digitizing error.

> **TIP:** When you use a video capture card to digitize an analog video source, the result won't necessarily be a valid DV file. If your video capture card was manufactured before the mid-'90s, it definitely won't be able to create a DV data file because the DV recording format didn't exist when it was built. (For more information, see "Digitizing Analog Sources: Video and Audio" in Chapter 10.)

Computer Video Files

While most of the video you see on the Web, or even on DVDs, is certainly digital video, it will be of virtually no use to you as source material for your video production.

Streaming video files you see on the Internet are highly compressed to keep download times as short as possible. If you import these files into your desktop editing system, they will be decompressed and may be editable, but they will look terrible. DVD files present similar problems. The compressed data file format used for most commercial DVDs gives disappointing results when imported and decompressed. On top of which, some DVDs use copy-protection schemes, which make them unsuitable sources for clips.

COMPUTER GRAPHICS:
Descriptive computer code of objects and their movement, commonly used for animation.

Strictly speaking, *computer graphics* and animation files are not digital video at all. They are coded descriptions of objects and movement. Your digital editing system may allow you to drop these animations into a digital video presentation, but you'll need to do a software conversion first.

> **TIP:** *Digital files uploaded from a camcorder to a Mac are a type of QuickTime, and those uploaded to a Windows PC are a type of Windows Media, but don't confuse Apple QuickTime files and Windows Media Player streaming files with the digital files uploaded from your camcorder. They are not the same. Streaming files are highly compressed, typically with greatly reduced resolution, so that they will play back as smoothly as possible over narrow bandwidths. Files uploaded from camcorders are full resolution and compressed only to the extent of DV's inherent and relatively lossless 5:1 compression.*

Legacy Digital Formats

Several uncompressed digital video recording formats were introduced in the 1980s:

- D-1
- D-2
- D-3

Because they require huge data storage and transmission capability, and because the equipment is very expensive, you won't find these formats used anywhere except network broadcast facilities and high-end editing suites.

Digital Betacam (Digibeta)

For almost a decade, Digital Betacam has been one of the mainstays of professional video production. Developed by Sony and usually referred to as Digibeta or "Digi," this ½-inch videocassette format got its start as a portable medium for field work but nowadays is used mainly for mastering and studio postproduction.

Digibeta has become almost mandatory for submitting your digital production to:

*   Videotape duplication houses

*   Networks and broadcast facilities

*   Film transfer laboratories

Digibeta gear—from camcorders to editing equipment and media—is very expensive even compared to professional DV equipment. That may be one reason Digibeta is being replaced by DVCPRO (a professional DV format technically defined as SMPTE D-7) and its high-bandwidth cousin DVCPRO-50. In any case, you should probably consider Digibeta primarily as a release or exhibition format, or an intermediate format for making transfers. (For more information on DV formats used in broadcast media, see "Proprietary DV Variants" later in this appendix.)

However, if you have access to a Digibeta camcorder, there's no reason you can't use it to make broadcast-quality digital video. Its output is as good as (some would say, better than) the best DV, and you can readily upload a Digibeta recording to your desktop editing system.

Digibeta cassettes are about the size of a hardcover book and range in length from 12 to 120 minutes. The 120-minute cassette costs about $70. (Compare this with about $5 for a 60-minute DV cassette the size of a matchbox!)

HD

With the exception of streaming computer files for Webcasting, all the digital formats we've discussed so far are compatible with SDTV (standard definition television) technology, the spec that defines TV pictures in the familiar 4:3 *aspect ratio*.

> **ASPECT RATIO:** The width (w) of a film or video picture compared to its height (h). Aspect ratios are usually written with a colon separating w and h. A TV picture that's 40 inches wide and 30 inches high has a 4:3 aspect ratio.

But SDTV is only one kind of television. The other is high-definition television (HDTV). The HDTV picture has a widescreen 16:9 aspect ratio, and delivers about four times the amount of picture detail as SDTV. Production tools and recording formats for this medium come under the broad heading of HD, or high-definition.

From a technical viewpoint, HD is a superset of DV, since HD existed first—on paper, anyway. Industry committees started planning HDTV back in the 1980s, well before they were sure there would be chips capable of handling the processing load. Then, in the early 1990s, they downsized the HDTV technology to come up with DV specs.

Compared to DV, HD cameras and camcorders are very expensive—although not when you stack them up against comparable Panavision film cameras. The Sony CineAlta, for example, which uses the proprietary Sony HDCAM tape format, lists for over $100,000. Panasonic's HD recording format is DVCPRO-HD, a 100 *Mbps* version of DVCPRO that runs on its AJ-HDC camcorders. JVC's HDTV camcorders use the HD-D5 format, an enhancement of the older D-5 studio standard. All of these recording formats provide broadcast-spec color space.

Mbps: Megabits per second.

At least one HD camera, the Thomson Viper FilmStream, uses no tape at all. Its high-end color space requires so much data that the camera output must be recorded directly to an array of computer hard drives. In fact, there are signs in the marketplace that tape may disappear altogether as a video recording medium, in favor of disks and memory cards. That transition will probably take several years, however.

To date, HD camcorders have been used mainly to shoot feature films like *Star Wars: Episode II—Attack of the Clones*, as well as network television series that air in HDTV. (Co-author Pete Shaner's low-budget independent feature, *Nicolas* was also shot on HD.) Over the next few years, HD quality will be migrating downward into the DV price range.

As you might expect, producing a film in HD is much more expensive than doing so in DV. The camcorders, editing systems, and media can cost 10 times more than their DV equivalents. For instance, a single 64-minute Sony HDCAM cassette costs about $92.

But there are still compelling reasons to shoot on HD if your project can afford it, just by eliminating costs of film stock, processing, and transfers. Even at its most expensive, an HD production will be a lot cheaper than shooting on film.

If you are producing for broadcast, there's another strong incentive to consider HD: Even if you don't intend your production to be aired on HDTV immediately, there will come a time in the not-too-distant future when *not* having your show in HDTV format will close off distribution opportunities and syndication deals.

You can edit HD on your current desktop editing system, as long as you add a few terabyte-sized, high-speed disk drives and a special high-bandwidth video board—but the upgrade raises the system price to about $30,000. Eventually, as the technology reaches into lower-priced gear, it will be hard to buy a camcorder or editing system that *doesn't* support HD.

PROPRIETARY DV VARIANTS

Manufacturers have come up with several proprietary DV enhancements in their bids to capture the lucrative prosumer and professional markets. All of them upload to valid DV files on your desktop editing system:

*   DVCAM

*   DVCPRO

*   Digital-S

DVCAM

Sony's proprietary enhancement of DV is DVCAM, which is also licensed to Ikegami Electronics, Inc. DVCAM cassettes come in both Mini DV or DVC form-factors. However, DVCAM cassettes use premium-quality, metal-evaporated (ME) magnetic tape and different recording characteristics intended to assure frame accuracy. (You can use a generic Mini DV cassette in a DVCAM camcorder, but you might not be pleased with the quality of the recording.) DVCAM can fit only 40 minutes of program on a Mini DV-sized cassette that would normally hold 60. And of course, if you want to shoot DVCAM, you must use a camcorder made by Sony or Ikegami.

Digital8 and Betacam SX: Hybrid Formats

Sony responded to the introduction of Mini DV by introducing Digital8, a consumer-oriented digital recording format that uses the same size cassettes as analog Video8 and Hi8. Hitachi also makes Digital8 camcorders.

Digital8 units can record and play back in either analog or digital modes. When you upload a Digital8 recording (analog or digital) to your editing system, the result is a valid DV file. Furthermore, if you play back a Video8 or Hi8 analog recording in a Digital8 camcorder, and connect it to a computer via i.LINK, the camcorder will upload a valid DV file with no need for a video capture card in the PC. This can be extremely useful if you want to include archival Video8 or Hi8 material in your digital video.

Nonetheless, Digital8 will likely be a transitional format. Mini DV already dominates the consumer marketplace, and sales of Digital8 camcorders will probably decline as the need to remain compatible with 8mm analog recordings disappears.

Sony took a similar approach in the professional market when it introduced its digital Betacam SX format along with machines that can read and write both SX and its still-prevalent analog brother, Betacam SP. Unlike Digital8, however, Betacam SX does not produce a valid DV file for uploading to your desktop editing system. (It's another of Sony's proprietary recording formats.)

DVCAM has a pair of advanced features aimed primarily at news gathering, designed to reduce the time required to upload your clips for editing—great when you're working on a tight deadline. The first is a tape indexing method that permits you to mark takes as OK or NG (no good) in the camcorder. The second is a 4X data transfer capability (brand-named i.LINK), which allows you to transfer one hour of camera material in just 15 minutes. Clearly, being able to transfer just the OK takes at 4X speed buys you more time for editing.

Oddly, while these features seem aimed at professional news videographers, DVCAM's color space follows the consumer spec. Presumably Sony's rationale is to make DVCAM gear price-competitive in the prosumer sector, leaving the upper end of the market to its Digital Betacam and Betacam SX, both of which offer professional color space. (For more information on Betacam SX, see the sidebar, "Digital8 and Betacam SX: Hybrid Formats" on the opposite page.)

DVCPRO

DVCPRO is Panasonic's enhancement to DV, which is licensed to Matsushita, Ikegami, Hitachi, and Philips. The generic term for DVCPRO is SMPTE D-7, and there's a movement afoot in the broadcast industry to make it the standard program submission format, displacing Digibeta.

DVCPRO is quite similar in features and performance to DVCAM, its prime competitor. For instance, both DVCAM and DVCPRO support locked audio and faster-than-real-time data transfers. And both formats use consumer-type DV color space.

One feature of DVCPRO that many editors really like is a supplementary *analog* sound track. It's not used as a program source, just as a reference: When the editor or assistant editor is uploading at faster-than-real-time, she can patch into the analog track and hear the audio shuttling by at chatterbox speed—just as it does on an analog deck. Many editors find it easier to locate the end of a take or a particular transition by listening for it.

You can buy camcorders and decks that use an enhanced version of DVCPRO called DVCPRO-50, which offers professional color space. It achieves this by doubling the data rate (number of data bits per second) in the digital recording—50 Mbps instead of the 25 Mbps used by DV, DVCAM, and DVCPRO.

DVCPRO-50 is a direct competitor of Digital Betacam and Betacam SX but uses the newer DV recording format. (For more information on Betacam SX, see the sidebar, "Digital8 and Betacam SX: Hybrid Formats" on the opposite page.)

Digital-S

The Digital-S format, also known as SMPTE D–9, is another direct competitor to Digibeta, aimed at professional electronic news gatherers. It's a proprietary development of Japanese Victor Corporation (JVC) and, unlike any of the other DV formats, it uses 1/2-inch magnetic tape and larger SVHS-sized cassettes. (In this respect, it departs from the DV spec, but its recordings use the professional DV data format.)

Like all the other enhanced-DV formats, Digital-S offers locked audio. And, like DVCPRO-50, it offers broadcast-spec color space at a data rate of 50 Mbps (twice that of Mini DV).

DV Technology: Under the Hood

If you're considering buying, renting, or even just *using* a DV camcorder, you need to know at least a little bit about what's going on inside.

> **FIELD:** One of two sets of horizontal scan lines (the odd-numbered lines or the even-numbered ones) that compose one frame of a video picture.
>
> **HELICAL SCAN:** Slantwise recording pattern on videotape created by the spiraling of record heads as the tape moves past them.

DV camcorders, analog camcorders, and VCRs all use much the same mechanism to make recordings on magnetic tape. Tape rolls past electromagnetic record and playback heads that are housed in a spinning cylinder, or drum. Fluctuating voltage in the record head causes changes in the magnetic properties of metal oxide particles on the tape. Whether the camera is analog or digital, a minimum of two heads is needed—one to record each of the two *fields* needed for one frame. (For more information on fields, see "What Are NTSC/PAL/SECAM Broadcast Formats?" in Chapter 3.) The pattern described by a head as it rotates past the moving tape is called a *helical scan*. As the head swipes across the tape, it records a single track with each rotation. The result is a series of tracks recorded diagonally across the tape (**Figure A.1**).

The DV Recording Format and Its Benefits

The heads in a DV camcorder spin much faster, and record more tracks per frame, than those in a VHS camcorder. The heads in a VHS unit spin at 1,800 rotations per minute (rpm), recording two tracks, or one pair of fields, per frame. By contrast, the heads in a DV camera spin at 9,000 rpm, rotating five times faster and recording 10 tracks, or five pairs of fields, for each frame.

Those ten tracks give DV its superior data loss prevention capability.

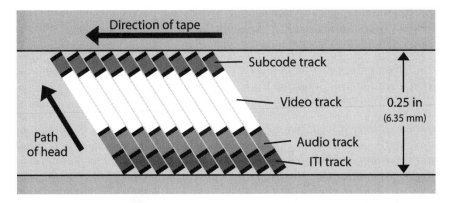

Figure A.1 **The DV tape recording pattern is the same, whether the cassette is a three-hour DVC or a one-hour Mini DV, consumer or professional spec.**

Even high-quality analog recordings, such as Betacam SP, are subject to dropouts: gaps in the recording due to tape imperfections and wear. The DV format employs a form of redundant data recording that is just as reliable on the cheapest DV camcorders as the most expensive. To achieve this, the camcorder shuffles, or distributes, video data and error- correction codes among all 10 tracks for a given frame. (Similar redundant recording schemes are used on CDs, DVDs, and RAID drives.) With redundant data recording you can retrieve a frame even if as many as two tracks in 10 are corrupted.

The tracks on a DV recording contain picture, sound, and a wealth of data that describe your camcorder, its settings, and its specific recording format. This extra information makes DV equipment "smart" enough that you can play tapes on a variety of hardware and still get good results. For example, a DVCAM deck "knows" that the track *pitch* on a DVCAM recording differs from one made on generic Mini DV. When you insert a Mini DV cassette into one of those decks, it makes all necessary adjustments and plays it back correctly—all without your having to touch a dial.

> **PITCH:** Degree of slant of the helical scan recording pattern on videotape.

Here's how the data is written to the tape: Each recorded track on a DV tape comprises four distinct signal areas, or sectors, of binary data (refer again to Figure A.1):

- Video
- Audio
- ITI
- Subcode

Video

This sector contains compressed image data, along with associated information like recording date, recording time, and camcorder settings. The camcorder also inserts an application identifier (APT) for the track as a reference for editing systems.

Audio

This sector contains digitized audio, auxiliary data, and APT. The DV format permits recording in a variety of mono and stereo modes and data rates. The default mode, even on the cheapest consumer camcorder, is higher than CD quality.

ITI

The Insert and Track Information on this sector includes track pitch, a redundant copy of the APT, and other positioning and location information. This data enables digital editing functions such as manipulating video and audio elements separately from one another—a trick that's almost impossible to do on analog systems. The ITI sector also contains information on whether the camcorder is a consumer or a professional model, which helps assure compatibility among DV formats.

Subcode

Timecode is recorded on this track along with the APT and the absolute track number (another reference point for editors). The track number also serves as an index for searches for scenes and still pictures. In professional DV recordings, user bits in the subcode area can include OK/NG take markers.

CCD TECHNOLOGY

If you think of a DV camcorder as an electronic eye, then the CCD chip is its retina (**Figure A.2**). (If you prefer to think of a camcorder as a camera, the CCD is the light-sensitive film emulsion.) The camera lens focuses light on the chip, which generates a flow of electrical impulses. Camcorder circuitry transforms these impulses to make a digital record of whatever the camera lens captured.

The surface of a CCD is an array of separate image-sensing areas—pixels—that divide the rectangular image into a grid (**Figure A.3**).

Figure A.2 The light-sensitive surface of this CCD chip is just ¹/₃-inch square. (Photo courtesy Canon U.S.A., Inc.)

Each image sensor on a CCD chip is a kind of photocell: Photons of light falling on the image sensor knock some of its electrons free. The more light that falls on the sensor, the more voltage it produces.

> **NOTE:** *The signals from a CCD are initially analog, not digital. The camcorder has to perform a separate analog-to-digital (A/D) conversion step to transform the fluctuating-voltage analog signal into a stream of binary ones and zeros. This binary data stream is manipulated by other circuits within the camcorder, which ultimately write it to tape in the DV format.*

CCDs only "see" in shades of gray. For a camcorder to capture a color image, it needs to take three separate measurements for each pixel in the finished image—one for each of the primary colors—red (R), green (G), and blue (B).

A/D CONVERSION: Analog-to-digital sampling.

Engineers use one of two methods for doing this trick. Method one uses a single CCD; method two uses three CCDs.

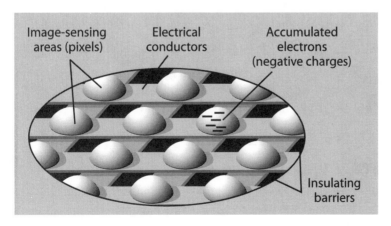

Figure A.3 Image-sensitive areas corresponding to pixels are positioned on a CCD chip in a two-dimensional matrix.

Single (Trilinear) CCD

To keep costs low, some consumer camcorders use a single CCD chip with R, G, and B sensor areas located side by side for each pixel. A tiny *dichroic filter* covers each sensor and allows only one of the primary colors to pass through (**Figure A.4**).

> **DICHROIC FILTER:** Optical barrier that permits only one primary color to pass through.

3CCD

Some consumer camcorders, and most prosumer and professional units, employ a 3CCD design (**Figure A.5**). Light coming through the camera lens passes through a *beam splitter*—a set of prisms or mirrors that separates the component colors and focuses the resulting monochromatic beams onto three separate chips. And yes, for the most part three CCDs are better than one: You'll generally end up with a brighter picture.

> **BEAM SPLITTER:** Set of prisms or mirrors that separates a light beam into its component primary colors.

> **TIP:** *Achieving better results at modest cost, some camcorders use a two-chip design, assigning one chip to brightness and the other to color information. Some still cameras use yet another technique—scanning the same CCD three times in quick succession through different color filters. (There isn't time to do this for each frame of video.)*

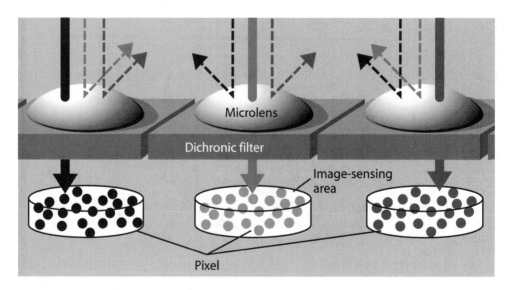

Figure A.4 In a single-chip, trilinear CCD camcorder, R, G, and B image-sensing areas are adjacent to one another at each pixel location.

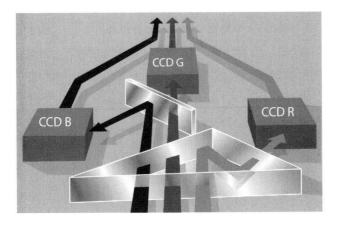

Figure A.5 In a 3CCD camcorder, a set of prisms or mirrors splits the incoming light into the primary colors and focuses the beams onto separate CCDs—one for each primary color.

Aspect Ratio and Resolution

The aspect ratio of your output medium will have a significant impact on how many pixels on the chip actually end up in the video picture.

Recall that SDTV has an aspect ratio of 4:3—essentially the same as the old Academy 1.33:1 motion picture format—and that the standard for HDTV is 16:9.

Most DV camcorders (and the CCDs inside them) are designed for the 4:3 aspect ratio of SDTV. However, many prosumer and professional models give you the option of switching to 16:9 mode. Beware of this switch! Most 4:3 cameras achieve wide-screen mode by *letterboxing*—chopping off the top and the bottom of the image area and throwing those pixels away. This sacrifices resolution.

> **LETTERBOXING:** Fitting a wide-screen image on a standard-sized screen by placing areas of black at the top and bottom.

> ## Foveon X3 Chip
>
> *The Foveon X3 chip will probably be the next significant step in camcorder technology.*
>
> *The first Foveon-based digital still camera was introduced in 2002. The technology has yet to appear in camcorders—but when it does, forget everything we've said about three chips being better than one.*
>
> *In chemical-based color film technology, a clear celluloid base is coated with multiple layers of light-sensitive emulsion. Each layer responds to a specific color of light. In a similar manner, Foveon X3 chips have three layers of electronic sensors—making it possible to measure each of the three primary colors at every pixel location. Potentially, the chip could provide three times the resolution of a CCD with the same pixel count.*
>
> *Cinematographers are particularly excited about Foveon technology, which could make it possible to capture video that's sharper and more film-like—at affordable prices.*

Another way to achieve 16:9 aspect ratio with a 4:3 camera is to use an anamorphic lens, which optically squashes a widescreen image into standard TV aspect ratio. Doing it this way, rather than switching to 16:9 mode in the camcorder, will give somewhat better DV resolution because you're using more of the CCD's available pixels. (If you use this approach, you must do the conversion to 16:9 in postproduction.) However, anamorphic lenses are designed for movie cameras, and you'll need a special adapter to be able to use one with a prosumer or professional DV camcorder. (For more information on these adapters, see *www.pstechnik.de.*)

By contrast, in an HD camera the CCD itself is designed for 16:9 format, so when you shoot a wide-screen picture you're using every pixel you can. You can choose to shoot in 4:3 mode with an HD camera, in which case the *sides* of the picture will be discarded (**Figure A.6**). However, because 16:9 chips start with more pixels in the first place, the resulting 4:3 image is at least as sharp, if not sharper, than the output from a DV camcorder with a 4:3 chip.

Bottom line: If you're shooting DV, stay in 4:3 mode; if in HD, use 16:9. You can always convert to the other aspect ratio in postproduction, and with more options and control than doing it in-camera.

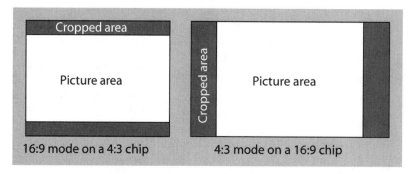

Figure A.6 Notice the difference in lost pixel area between shooting 16:9 with a 4:3 DV camera and shooting 4:3 with a 16:9 HD camera.

What Is Color Space and Why Is It Important?

In Chapter 3 we talked about color space in general terms to differentiate between output quality of consumer and professional DV camcorders. And we identified the specs as 4:1:1 (consumer) and 4:2:2 (professional). This is where we explain what these numbers mean, and why they matter to you.

SAMPLING: Conversion process during which fluctuating analog signals become streams of binary ones and zeros.

COLOR SAMPLE: The number of data bits used in one measurement of an analog R, G, or B picture signal; in DV and HD camcorders, usually 8 or 10 bits.

COLOR MODEL: A set of three primary colors (or data streams) that can be used in different combinations to reproduce a full spectrum of colors; color models include RGB, YIQ, and YUV.

Analog signals coming out of the CCDs are separate lines of R, G, and B. To become DV, they need to be digitized in a process called *sampling*. Most digital camcorders take 8-bit *color samples* of the analog picture signal; some high-end cameras, including HD models, use 10-bit samples. The more bits your camcorder uses, the wider the range of colors it can capture. For instance, if a camera uses 8-bit color, it can capture 256 levels of gray (2^8) for each monochrome pixel. A 10-bit camera can reproduce 1,024 levels of gray, or 2^{10}, levels.

If a 3CCD DV camcorder actually recorded the full RGB signal—which it doesn't—an 8-bit unit could capture 256 x 256 x 256, or 16.8 million, colors. However, digital camcorders only capture a half to a third that number in order to maintain compatibility with the *color model* used in analog television.

Color Models: RGB to YUV

When color television first appeared in the United States in the 1950s, the NTSC settled on a method of transmitting color that would permit black and white sets to display color broadcasts (in black and white, of course). Instead of R, G, and B, the NTSC standard uses a color model involving Y, I, and Q. Y stands for luminance, or perceived brightness, and is the only part of the signal used by black-and-white sets. Color, or chroma, information is carried in the I and Q signals.

In analog television broadcasting, the RGB signals from the video camera pass through an NTSC encoder, which transforms them to the YIQ model. Inside a color television set, the YIQ signal is converted back to separate R, G, and B signals, which drive three primary-color *electron guns*.

Today's DV systems take the RGB signal from the CCD and convert it into yet another color model, one called YUV, that's fairly similar to the old YIQ model. YUV includes a brightness component, Y (called *luma* in this model), and two chroma components, U and V.

Color Sampling and Subsampling

Converting analog R, G, and B into a digital signal is called *color sampling*. Converting RGB data to the YUV model is called *color subsampling*. The final subsampled signal is called *digital component* video.

ELECTRON GUN: Device in a television picture tube that directs beams of electrons to paint scan lines on the face of the tube.

COLOR SAMPLING: The process of converting analog R, G, and B signals to digital.

COLOR SUBSAMPLING: Deriving digital YUV values from RGB.

DIGITAL COMPONENT: The stream of video data composed of a specific number of data samples for Y, U, and V (*e.g.*, 4:1:1 or 4:2:2).

The 4:1:1 and 4:2:2 color-space ratios represent the relative number of times camcorder A/D circuitry samples Y, U, and V. At the rate of 4 (used for the Y samples), the converter takes 13.5 million samples per second. (The "4" means that sampling occurs at four times the analog subcarrier frequency.) The other numbers in the sampling ratio are fractions of the full rate: 2 means the system samples U or V 6.75 million times per second; 1 means the system samples U or V 3.375 million times per second.

> **NOTE:** *A more precise technical term for YUV is Y'CbCr. Among video engineers, YUV refers to analog and Y'CbCr (or YCC) refer to digital. Both terms describe the Y brightness, the blue difference chroma, and the red difference chroma. It's more common, if less exact, to see YUV used in reviews and product literature to mean either analog or digital video.*

Why do digital camcorders sample Y (luma) more often than U or V (chroma)? Y is mostly green (the G signal)—the brightness signal used by black-and-white sets. The human eye perceives picture detail best in the green part of the color spectrum. Sampling green more often devotes more data bits to picture detail, creating the sharpest picture possible with the bits available. (This is why the displays of night-vision infrared scopes are green: to give the best picture detail under low-light conditions.)

Tough critics of picture quality, like cinematographers and video engineers, will note one very interesting implication: The picture detail (the "4," or Y component) in a professional DV picture is *literally not one bit better* than that of consumer DV. The only differences lie in subtleties of color (the U and V chroma samples).

Color Space Requirements for Broadcast TV and Film Transfer

For most people, the differences in image quality between consumer and professional color space are quite subtle. The only time you need to worry about which color space your equipment uses is if you hope to sell your work to network or cable television—or if you're on assignment for those folks.

Color Space for Broadcasting

Digibeta delivers broadcast spec color space—4:2:2. But you can achieve the same result in professional DV formats like DVCPRO-50 or Digital-S, or even standard DV, at a fraction of Digibeta's cost.

Converting a 4:1:1 consumer DV recording to 4:2:2 broadcast color space is perfectly straightforward, provided that color is the only issue. One easy way to do this, for example, is to dub from a Mini DV cassette to a DVCPRO-50 deck. The circuitry in the DVCPRO deck will interpolate the 4:1:1 colors to create a valid 4:2:2 recording.

Now, the fact that the resulting 4:2:2 recording is valid for broadcast simply means it's up to the technical color-space spec. It doesn't mean it looks as good as a recording made with a 4:2:2 camera. In fact some video engineers insist that 4:1:1 recordings simply aren't suitable for commercial TV even after conversion. In reality, the differences in color rendition are mainly a matter of taste. (For more information on creating broadcast-legal output, see "Color Correction" in Chapter 11.)

> **TIP:** PAL (European) color space is 4:2:0. The "0" doesn't mean that the V component is ignored—just that it's sampled less frequently than 1, which produces the odd notation. Converting DV from NTSC to PAL is easy: Just pick the proper export format in your desktop editing program, and all the parameters (frame rate, scan rate, scan lines, color space) will be properly converted. However, you'll need a PAL deck to make a tape from the output file.

Color Space for Film Transfer

If you're aiming at a tape-to-film transfer, you don't need to worry about color space at all. Go ahead and concentrate on correcting colors so they work well on the screen. A digital video shot with consumer color space can look just as good as one shot with professional color space once it's transferred to film.

APPENDIX B

Selecting and Building an NLE System

By far the best approach to building an NLE system is to choose your software first, then make hardware purchases to match its requirements. Some software packages actually require you to buy specific makes and models of computers and video cards. So, picking hardware first actually risks wasting money on gear you don't need – or that won't work properly with the editing software you prefer.

Of course, if you have a recent-model machine already, you'll be taking on a retrofitting and reconstruction project. In particular, you may have to upgrade or replace the video display card or add a special rendering card, especially to enable neat tricks like 3D compositing.

But be warned – for DV editing and compositing, you'll want all the processing power and storage capacity you can afford. Even a computer that's just a year or two old might perform sluggishly, particularly when running the latest software.

CHOOSE YOUR PLATFORM

To evaluate software, you should begin by asking yourself a basic question about which side you're on (or intend to join).

One of your authors prefers Macs, the other prefers PCs. At one time this could have turned into a religious war, but these days the differences between these two kinds of computers aren't that significant. But you can't avoid the choice—early on—and it's one that will affect all the others that follow.

PLATFORM: Type of computer processor and operating system, *e.g.,* Intel/Windows or Motorola/Mac OS.

OPERATING SYSTEM: The "master" computer program that runs the hardware, generates images, and supports applications such as word processors and NLEs; *e.g.,* Windows or Mac OS.

You can get excellent results on either *platform* (the type of computer and *operating system*). If you already own a recent-model desktop computer, there's a lot to be said for sticking with what you're used to. (See the sidebar, "Upgrade or Buy New?" in this appendix.)

However, some NLE software only runs on one platform or the other, so unless you're prepared to switch, be sure to choose an NLE that runs on your computer.

NLE PRODUCTS: AN OVERVIEW

NLE solutions fall into three categories: high-end, mid-level, and inexpensive. Here's a survey of what's on the market as this book goes to press. Obviously, we don't have space to discuss every product in detail, but we'll try to give you an idea of what *kind* of products are out there. Check with dealers and surf the Web for current product versions and pricing.

High-End Professional Systems

If you're looking for high performance, this is where you'll find it. Professional NLE systems deliver fast rendering and smooth real-time playback thanks to proprietary hardware that often includes high-performance video cards, effects generators, and storage systems.

TURNKEY SYSTEM: Complete hardware and software solution, including accessories, support, sometimes even training.

Of course, you'll pay for the power. You can't buy this software without the hardware it runs on, and prices start around $10,000 for a *turnkey system*. The damage can easily rise to half a million dollars before you're done.

Traditionally, high-end editing systems have been hardware-intensive solutions. Custom-built display and rendering circuits are expensive to design, manufacture, and maintain, and they aren't as cheap as TVs or PCs because the market for this gear is relatively small: Consider that there are some thousands of professional editing facilities, but questionable potential for selling millions of consumer units. (Perhaps the true marketing potential for tools like Final Cut Pro depends on the success of the democratization of video as a cultural phenomenon: How many consumers will come to use their NLE as commonly as they do their word processor?)

Pros have three crucial reasons to demand fast hardware: 1) when they are working on tight deadlines and big money is at stake, 2) when they need to manipulate studio-quality video in uncompressed formats, and 3) when they must work alongside clients who expect to see real-time results.

> **Upgrade or Buy New?**
>
> *A rule of thumb in the computer industry is that any system or component more than three releases old is obsolete. If you own anything older than a G4, P4, or K7, donate it to a worthy charity and buy a nice, new NLE system.*
>
> *If your machine is a Mac G4, or PC with Pentium 4 or AMD K7 processor, an upgrade isn't out of the question. Compare your current setup with the hardware requirements listed on your NLE vendor's website, and do what you have to do to meet those requirements. Add only the specific models of video or FireWire cards the vendor recommends. If you're considering an upgrade to a dual-processor configuration, make sure the computer will support it, and let a dealer install it.*
>
> *You may have read articles in computer magazines about forcing processors to run faster than their rated speeds, a process called* overclocking. *We don't recommend overclocking unless you've got lots of time to diagnose and solve hardware problems. (And don't expect the manufacturers to support you.)*
>
> > **OVERCLOCKING:** Changing settings on the motherboard of a PC to force the processor to run at some multiple of its rated speed.

But all these assumptions are changing. Cheap general-purpose gigahertz-speed PCs and software-based solutions are closing the performance gap. And not only is software cheap to manufacture—but it's also easy to maintain. You can upgrade and enhance a software-based system over the Web with just a few clicks.

Avid has dominated the high-end market segment for years. Not so long ago, the company claimed that its editing systems are used on 85 percent of all feature films and 90 percent of prime-time television shows. Perhaps because the NLE market is so volatile and such specific claims are difficult to make, a more recent claim is "the de facto standard for video editing." Either way, Avid is still a major force in the industry.

In alphabetical order, high-end turnkey systems include the following. Prices start in the low five figures and can easily run to more than half a million bucks for a fully equipped suite.

- Àccom: Affinity Dimension 8.3, Axial 3000

- Avid: Avid | DS, Avid | DS HD, Film Composer, Media Composer, NewsCutter, Symphony

- Canopus: CWS100, RES

- discreet (division of Autodesk, Inc.): fire 6, smoke 6

- in-sync: Speed Razor HD 2

- Leitch: dpsVelocityQ, dpsVelocity Mid-Tower (turnkey)

- Lightworks: Touch (turnkey system)

- Matrox: DigiSuite

- Media 100: 844/X

- Pinnacle: Liquid Blue, Liquid Chrome, Liquid Silver

- Quantel: eQ, QEdit Pro

- Sony: XPRI 6

Many of these systems may be just as capable as a comparable Avid product, but two main things draw editors to Avid: compatibility with their peers and clients, and performance. Companies buy Avid like IT managers used to buy IBM—you won't get fired for picking what everyone else has. And an individual might choose Avid to equip a new postproduction house in order to tell his clients he has the same equipment they do.

DV is mostly about desktop tools, but if you're wondering what you're missing, we'll describe what you'd find in a fully equipped Avid facility.

High-End Avid Systems

The most widely used NLE system in the professional world is Avid's Media Composer, which comes in a variety of turnkey packages—now referred to collectively as Avid's

> **SYSTEMS INTEGRATOR:** Computer dealer that specializes in customizing hardware and software for special applications.

Meridien product line. There's only one way to buy one of these systems—through an Avid dealer, a *systems integrator* who specializes in building editing suites. (That's also the way most of the turnkey systems in the foregoing listed are sold.)

A related Avid product that's tailored to the requirements of film cutting is Film Composer, which is still the most commonly used editing tool in the movie industry. For compositing and finishing, you'll need Symphony, a separate system. And for building sophisticated soundtracks, you'll need Digidesign's ProTools (Digidesign is a division of Avid Technology, Inc.).

All are separate hardware-software turnkey systems, each with its own server and special-purpose peripherals. The exception is ProTools, which can be purchased either as a turnkey system (with mixing console), or as software for Windows or Mac.

Avid systems and their components are designed to work together smoothly. For major installations that require a team of editors working at the same time, Avid systems can be networked using high-speed fiber optic links so multiple workstations can share video file servers without slowing each other down. (This networking feature isn't exclusive to Avid, but given the complexity of an Avid installation, it's particularly useful.)

By the time you purchase all these complementary systems, install them under one roof, and link them with fiber, you could need a million-dollar loan from the bank (which might or might not cover a beefed-up air-conditioning system to keep all that equipment from overheating).

If you want to edit DV and only DV, you don't need to go here. Simply put, the main reason to consider high-end systems is to be able to work with various flavors of *uncompressed* video in a broadcast environment. For example, if you need to edit Digibeta or D-2 for broadcast, your peers are mostly using Avid Media Composer or Sony XPRI.

But for an all-DV production, using a desktop system will be far cheaper and less complicated technically.

However, don't expect high-end NLE systems to disappear overnight. Instead, the dividing line with desktop systems will probably become increasingly blurred. Perhaps indicating a change in this direction, Avid introduced its DNA product line in 2003. The concept is to provide a package of PC hardware add-ons for upgrading generic desktop systems to run each of its software products. The DNA package includes a set of plug-in cards and a breakout box that connects to the computer via a FireWire 400 cable. Each of the DNA packages has its own product name: Mojo for Xpress Pro, Adrenaline for Media Composer, and Nitris for Avid DS.

Mid-Level Desktop NLE Software

For most videomakers, these are the tools of choice for finishing the work they started with their DV camcorders. In fact, the latest mid-range NLE systems have become so powerful that many professionals consider them serious, cost-effective alternatives to the high-end solutions. These systems are based on DV editing software. The leading software-only packages are priced from about $300 to $2,500 and require relatively powerful, recent-model Macs or PCs for acceptable performance.

The most popular product in this category is Adobe Premiere (renamed Premiere Pro as of version 7). It's been on the market for several years, requires no special hardware, and is relatively low in price. When the product was introduced several years ago, it was available for both Macs and PCs. But in 2003, for reasons Mac devotees are still wondering and grumbling about, Adobe introduced version 7 for Windows but no new product for the Mac—effectively giving way to Apple's Final Cut Pro.

Final Cut Pro is perhaps the fastest-growing product in acceptance among Mac users, though it's more expensive than Premiere was. Professionals seem to prefer Final Cut Pro, mostly because its keyframe transformations can be applied to any effect. This makes the program more complex to learn and to use but much more flexible. In any case, Final Cut Pro is now Avid's most serious professional competitor.

REALITY CHECK: *Randy Ubillos, one of the former lead programmers of Premiere, left Adobe to join Macromedia, where he helped write the program that Apple now sells as Final Cut Pro. He once commented to a group of Mac users that Final Cut Pro is everything he hoped Premiere could be. Since that time, Adobe has enhanced its product considerably, both programs have continued to evolve, and yet they are remarkably similar in many ways. Now that Adobe no longer makes an NLE for the Mac, it's not too far wrong to think of Premiere Pro as Final Cut Pro for Windows.*

When professional editors started defecting from Avid's high-end systems to Final Cut Pro a few years ago, Avid introduced Xpress DV to keep them in the fold. It was available initially only for Windows, then a Mac version was introduced. As Apple continued to gain ground, Avid released Avid Free DV in the fall of 2003. It's a no-cost, entry-level, fully workable, downloadable NLE for Mac and Windows—which supports a limited number of effects and tracks. About the same time, Apple began to offer Final Cut Express, its entry-level product. It's a bit more robust—but hardly free at $299.

Different Approaches to Rendering

One way any desktop NLE can cut corners (at least compared to a hardware-packed Avid suite) is by handling rendering at two different levels. For instance, if you request playback during editing, rendering can be delivered in a lower-quality resolution to save processing time. The images are generally quite acceptable; in fact, you might not see the difference—as long as the playback is not analog and the screen isn't full size.

Another way these systems provide real-time playback during editing is to simply ignore some rendering requirements. For example, if a transition effect is so complex that the system can't generate it fast enough to keep up with the preview, you'll see an error message for the duration of the transition. The faster and more powerful your computer, the less often you'll see these messages.

Apple calls its software-based rendering and playback technology Offline RT, and you can adjust the playback and/or recording quality you want to High, Medium, or Low to match the capability of your hardware and the rendering performance you expect. In its latest enhancement in Final Cut Pro 4, RT Extreme can use dual processors to render multiple video streams, which Apple claims can deliver smooth playback even on a PowerBook.

As you might expect, Avid's comparable solution to the playback-and-rendering challenge involves not software but hardware. Offered as an add-on to Xpress DV Pro, Avid's Mojo is a paperback-book-sized hardware module that plugs into your computer to accelerate video rendering. It's small enough to toss into a briefcase with your laptop when you're on the road.

When the time comes to request finished-quality output—for downloading your show to a VCR, for example—the typical desktop NLE system will then take its own sweet time to do a full, high-quality job of rendering before it plays the edit. This can take many minutes, even hours, on the fastest systems, depending mainly on the complexity of effects and transitions.

> **NOTE:** We've seen ads for NLE systems claiming "no rendering required." That's just not true. The implied claim is that rendering is done fast enough to keep up with the playback, so you don't notice it's happening. However, most NLEs offer some "real-time effects," a different trick altogether. These transitions have been precalcuated and don't depend on transformations of specific images—the rendering is, in effect, instant and precooked.

Survey of Products

Here's a *partial* list of mid-range NLE software products. This crowded market is changing fast, and before the ink is dry on these pages, new products no doubt will be available and some of these (and possibly their manufacturers) will have vanished from the earth:

- Adobe: Premiere Pro; Windows

- AIST: MoviePack V6, MoviePack VE, MovieXone Plus; Windows

- Apple: Final Cut Express, Final Cut Pro 4; Mac

- Avid: Mojo, Xpress 5.8, Xpress DV 3.5, Xpress Pro; Mac or Windows

- Canopus: DVRaptor RT2 max, DVRex RT Professional, DVStorm 2, DVStorm 2 Pro+; Lets EDIT, Lets EDIT RT, Lets EDIT RT+;Windows

- discreet: Cinestream 3, EditDV 2; Mac and Windows

- Incite: Editor 3, Editor MAX, Editor Studio, Editor Suite; Windows

- in-sync: Blade 2.2, Speed Razor 5.5; Windows

- Leitch: dpsVelocity 8; Windows

- Lightworks: Touch 1.5 (software-only version); Windows

- Matrox (video hardware and software *bundled* with other NLEs): DigiSuite MAX with Incite Editor; Windows; RT.X10 Xtra and Xtreme Pro with Premiere Pro; Windows; RT Mac with Final Cut Pro; Mac

> **BUNDLED PRODUCT:** Software and compatible hardware components sold together as a package.

- Media 100: 100i 8.2; Mac; iFinish 4.6; Windows

- NewTek: VideoToaster VT(3); Windows

- Pinnacle: CinéWave card and software for Final Cut Pro; Mac; Liquid Edition; Liquid Edition PRO; Windows

- Ulead: Media Studio Pro 7; Windows

- Sony Pictures Digital (formerly Sonic Foundry): Vegas 4, Vegas+DVD 2; Windows

> **NOTE:** *Several of the mid- and low-cost packages offer discount pricing if you download their software from the Web rather than buying the retail boxed version.*

Mid-Level Market Leaders

Here's a quick overview of four mid-level packages: Xpress DV, Final Cut Pro, Premiere Pro, and Vegas. We're not necessarily saying these are the best products, but they are among the most popular. If you're shopping in this price range, you may want to look at Pinnacle Liquid Edition and Ulead Media Studio Pro, as well.

Here are some of the key differences between four leading NLE packages.

Avid Xpress Family: Most Professional

Avid introduced Xpress DV, a software-only NLE product that runs on both the Mac and PC platforms, in 2001. The idea was to make it possible for editors to work on desktop and notebook NLE systems using the same controls and interface they were used to on the dedicated Avid hardware—and to output files that would be directly compatible with Avid's high-end systems.

Hence, the main reason to select Xpress DV is compatibility with the rest of the Avid world, which still represents the majority of high-end workstations in professional editing suites. This is no small consideration, and it's why we list Xpress DV as the most professional mid-level choice.

The internal workings of Avid systems are proprietary, and the company has no incentive to make integration easy for its competitors. That means, until recently, that using Xpress DV was your only assurance of being able to move projects from your desktop into high-end systems without technical difficulties. Other manufacturers, especially Apple, are working hard to resolve any incompatibilities, but, as you might expect, Avid isn't helping them.

> **TIP:** *Xpress DV's compatibility advantage is receding. There are now a number of third-party tools for exchanging projects between Final Cut Pro and Avid systems, but they aren't yet trouble free. (See www.automaticduck.com.)*

Of the products shown in **Table B.1,** Xpress DV was the first to let you to assign program functions to any combination of keys you like—a feature called "soft keys." Avid makes a lot of this, and rightly so because veteran editors love it. (Apple added this feature to Final Cut Pro in version 4, and Adobe followed suit in Premiere Pro.)

To provide a range of capabilities and prices, Avid has expanded Xpress DV into a family of products. As we've mentioned, Free DV is the entry-level product, permitting just two video and two audio tracks, with 16 effects. Xpress DV supports eight video and audio tracks and more than 100 effects. Significantly, Free DV is the only Avid product that doesn't support uploading your project to its professional systems.

Avid combined the features as the add-on PowerPack, a suite of utilities, to create Xpress DV Pro. It's aimed at film editors and 24P videographers. Xpress DV Pro can handle 24 video and audio tracks and more than 115 effects. It can also generate cut list instructions for film negative cutters (mainly useful if you're editing film dailies), supports complex effects and title animation (which you can do with many less expensive tools), and 24 fps editing (but not in HD resolution, so this is currently useful mainly for film work). If you plan on making editing your career (or are already doing so), especially with a concentration on film projects, Xpress DV Pro is probably the way to go.

If you need to work with uncompressed video, want real-time digital output, or spend much time editing on a laptop, plug in the Mojo hardware accelerator. A professional-level Avid desktop or laptop solution is going to cost you more than a comparable Final Cut Pro system, but that's the price you pay for joining the "broadcast club."

Final Cut Pro 4: Most Powerful in One Package

Final Cut Pro 4 is a powerful and popular package. Its main disadvantage (at least for PC users) is that it's strictly a Mac product, and runs best on recent high-end models like the G5. For film-oriented work with Final Cut Pro, Apple once offered Cinema Tools, an add-on package comparable to Xpress PowerPack. These capabilities are now included in Final Cut Pro 4.

With the release of version 4, Apple incorporated new capabilities that formerly required other, standalone applications: LiveType generates animated titles, Soundtrack helps you compose music scores from clips, and Compressor converts video output to various formats you'll need for authoring DVDs or creating video Web sites. This strategy is quite the opposite of Adobe's, which is to segregate functions among multiple, complementary products, as we'll explain shortly. However, Apple does offer more sophisticated separate applications, including DVD Studio Pro 2 for disc authoring, Logic Platinum 6 for music composition and audio production, and Shake 3 for compositing and effects for film and HD—all designed to work well with Final Cut Pro.

Table B.1 Leading Mid-Level NLE Software Packages

	Avid Xpress DV 3.5	Final Cut Pro 4	Adobe Premiere Pro (v.7)	Vegas 4
Overall impression	Most professional	Most powerful	Most popular; best Web tool	Budget choice
List Price	$695	$999	$699	$559.96
Approx. cost including hardware	$4,500–$7,500	$5,000–$7,000	$2,700–$4,000	$2,000–$3,500
Platforms	Windows XP Pro Mac OS X 10.1.4+	Mac OS X 10.2.5+	Windows 98 SE/ME/W2K/XP	Windows 98 SE/ME/W2K/XP
Hardware Requirements	Specific PC/Mac makes and models	Specific Macs	Most recent PCs	Most recent PCs
HD support	No. Separate product: Avid | DS HD	Yes	Yes	Yes
Required processor	P3 750MHz min/Dual P4 recommended	G4 400MHz min G4 350MHz Dual G4 450MHz+ recommended	P3 800 MHz or Dual P4 recommended	P3/K6 400MHz min
System RAM	256MB min/384MB recommended	384MB min/512MB recommended	256MB min/1GB recommended	128MB min
Program disk space	20GB total internal drive	1–14GB	800MB available	30MB available
Soft Keys	Yes	Yes	Yes	No
Color Correction	Yes	Yes	Yes	Yes

Among Mac users Final Cut Pro is far more common than Xpress DV, partly because it's been on the market longer (Xpress DV for Mac didn't appear until late 2002), and partly because it lets you control and customize effects more easily. In addition, Final Cut Pro offers more flexibility, especially in mixing and matching digital formats such as NTSC and PAL.

Final Cut Pro 4 requires a powerful Mac to run on, and by the time you factor in the hardware costs you'll end up spending at least $5,000 to get started. If you opt for all the bells and whistles, you can end up dropping close to eight grand. At prices like these, Final Cut Pro isn't a system for people who are less than fully serious about doing their own editing.

If you want to edit in HD, there's good news and bad news. Unlike Xpress DV, Final Cut Pro is ready for HD out of the box—but you'll need to upgrade your hardware to the tune of about $20,000. (For more information, see the sidebar "Upgrading Final Cut Pro to HD," later in this appendix.)

Premiere Pro: Most Popular with Windows Users and Web Developers

When you include pros, amateurs, and students, Adobe Premiere probably has the largest user base of any NLE application. Even now that a Mac version is no longer available, Adobe could well hold onto this leadership position just because the Windows market is so much larger.

At one time, professional video editors felt that Premiere worked more like a computer application than an editing console, but recent releases—and a variety of third-party plug-in modules —have made it much more sophisticated. Also, Premiere is much less picky than either Xpress DV or Final Cut Pro about your computer hardware. As the specs in Table B.1 show, Premiere Pro will run on most PCs—not just a few expensive, name-brand models. (Of course Premiere Pro's specs also make it clear that you need a faster processor and more memory for real-time playback.)

Bottom line: With Premiere Pro, you can get into the video editing business for as little as $2,500–$4,000, hardware and software included. (As we'll show shortly, Vegas 4 is also an attractive alternative for a budget system, also for PCs.)

Unfortunately, there are some bothersome gaps in Premiere's feature set. For example, it has only limited titling capabilities and lacks color correction—gaps that can be filled only if you buy one or more of Adobe's other software products. If you want a one-stop solution, Adobe markets a suite of video-production tools called the Video Collection. It comes in two versions: 1) Standard includes Premiere Pro, After Effects 6 (standard version, for video postproduction effects), Encore DVD (disc authoring), and Audition (audio editing). To this package, the Video Collection Professional adds Photoshop CS (digital photography and still graphics), and the upgraded After Effects 6 Professional. Either collection delivers a more extensive set of animation and graphics capabilities than any other single NLE package—but for a total system cost that's as much or more than you'd spend on Xpress DV or Final Cut Pro.

Moreover, if you're doing multimedia or Webcasting that involves lots of graphics and animation, you'll want to add one or two additional packages: TitleMotion 4.2, a plug-in for creating animated titles, and LiveMotion 2.0, for programming interactive presentations. By the time you add up all these extra software modules, the Adobe video production suite is no longer particularly cheap, but it's still the right set of tools for the Internet—and it does a very nice job of editing DV.

Sony Pictures Digital Vegas 4: Serious Software on a Budget

If you're looking for a mid-level NLE package that's low in total system cost but provides a strong set of editing features and a professional-style editing environment, take a look at Sony Pictures Digital Vegas 4. It's even less picky about hardware than Premiere, so your total cost for an entry-level system can be the lowest of the four mid-level NLEs we've described. Moreover, because it was developed by Sonic Foundry, a company that also developed sound editing tools and music libraries, the audio capabilities of Vegas 4 rank with the best in the business. But like Premiere Pro, it won't run on a Mac.

Vegas 4 even includes some professional features you won't find in any other NLE at its price level: support for 24P and film-style EDLs, HD video, color correction, an unlimited number of tracks, and 100 levels of undo. It can also translate any format it handles to any of its other formats.

That said, users of Vegas 4 are definitely in the minority. Many videomakers don't even know about it. Back when it was offered by Sonic Foundry (as Vegas Video 3), some users might have feared not having the big-corporate support of one of the three A's (Avid, Apple, or Adobe). But now that the product is backed by Sony Pictures Digital, perhaps more professionals will give it serious consideration.

Inexpensive Home-Movie Packages

These inexpensive software packages generally cost less than $100, run on most recent-model computers without any special hardware, and are primarily aimed at editing home movies. They include most of the basic NLE functions but offer fewer types of transitions, a limited number of video/audio tracks, and don't allow you to customize effects. They achieve reference-quality video playback much the same way Internet media players do—by reducing the image to a playing-card-sized window.

Nonetheless, if you're making a home video or an experimental piece and your main goal is to have fun while building your skills, one of these inexpensive software packages could be perfect for you. Start small, save money, and get your feet wet before you move up to an expensive, professional system.

If your computer doesn't already have an IEEE 1394 port, you'll need to spend about $50 to add one to handle DV uploading from your camcorder. Eventually you might want to add another hard drive for video data storage so you can edit longer shows.

Some of these low-end products are de-featured, "training-wheels" versions of mid-level packages and offer upgrade pricing when you're ready to move up.

- AIST: Movie DV 4.5

- Apple: iMovie 4; Mac

- discreet: introDV; Windows

- Pinnacle: Studio 9

- Roxio: VideoWave Movie Creator, VideoWave 5 Power Edition; Windows

- Sony Pictures Digital (formerly Sonic Foundry): Screenblast Movie Studio 3; Windows

- Ulead: VideoStudio 7; Windows

WHICH MAC OR WHICH PC?

We hope our lengthy survey of NLE software packages has helped you form at least a preliminary opinion about which one best fits your needs and work style. Once you've chosen an NLE, it's time to buy or build a computer that will run it. Check the manufacturers' recommended hardware specs, but feel free to exceed them if you can afford it. Any NLE program you buy will be a very greedy beast.

Choosing an NLE Package

As you get to know more about the various NLE applications and their respective features, your preferences for hardware and software will probably become more sophisticated, depending mostly on what you intend to use your editing system for. Ask yourself:

- *Do you intend to hire out your services as an editor? If so, compatibility with high-end systems, particularly Avid-equipped suites, will be extremely important.*

- *What types of projects will you specialize in? For example, do you intend to produce for film, television, or the Web? Different products excel in each of these media.*

- *How much sophistication do you want—and how much can you afford? Do you need complex transitions and animated effects? Multi-layered soundtracks? If you're producing animation, special effects sequences, or commercials, you'll want extensive compositing and finishing tools, either as built-in features of your NLE or as plug-ins.*

- *What's the running time of your typical project? The answer will tell you how much disk storage you require (Remember, you'll need 13 GB for every hour of stored video.)*

Comparing Computer Hardware

It's safer to let a dealer with experience building computers for NLE configure your system for you. Such dealers know which components work and which may give trouble. You'll probably end up paying a bit more for the hardware than you would if you bought it online and pieced it together yourself, but you'll be less likely to make an expensive mistake. And if you run into a problem or something doesn't work right, you'll have somewhere to turn for support.

> **TIP:** The price of your NLE system will depend mainly on how much expensive, special-purpose hardware it includes. Remember, though, that extra hardware doesn't necessarily add features—just processing speed. Don't pay a premium for high performance until you have some idea of what you want your system to do.

Even if you let a dealer put together the hardware for you, you should be knowledgeable enough to discuss the options with him—and to notice if he's spending your money needlessly. Here are some of the technicalities you should be aware of.

Processor Type and Speed

Check your NLE vendor's Web site for the latest processor requirements. Manufacturers are fairly specific about which processor they require because *processor speed* (the number of instructions the processor can perform per second) is crucial to system performance. If the processor isn't fast enough, playback will appear jerky on the screen, and some effects won't be reproduced at all.

> **PROCESSOR SPEED:** Number of instruction cycles your CPU is capable of executing every second, expressed in millions (MHz) or billions (GHz).

However, beware of salespeople who try to tell you that processor speed is the only hardware benchmark that counts. In many cases, RAM will have just as big an impact on system performance; in other instances the speed of your video board will be the bottleneck. Overall system performance depends on a balance of components and peripherals, and different applications demand different combinations. This is why an experienced dealer is so important.

RAM

Random access memory (RAM), also called system memory, is the computer's main temporary storage area, where it loads data to and from the hard disk as it flows into the processor. Processor speed and RAM capacity are the two single most important factors in a computer's performance. Specs for NLE systems show minimum RAM (necessary for the software to run at all) and recommended size (required if you want real-time playback). Some NLE manufacturers even advise a specific type of RAM chip, such as *SDRAM* (synchronous dynamic random access memory), which is both faster and more expensive than other types of RAM.

> **RAM (RANDOM ACCESS MEMORY):** Computer memory chip; system memory.
>
> **SDRAM (SYNCHRONOUS DYNAMIC RANDOM ACCESS MEMORY):** High-speed computer memory chip.

Video Display Card

Your video display card paints the picture you see on your monitor. Its capabilities limit the number of pixels in an image, the number of possible colors for each pixel, and the speed with which the computer can update the image as it generates a sequence of video frames. The video card that comes standard in most desktop computers may not be up to the job of displaying video in acceptable resolution at real-time speeds. That's why NLE software manufacturers recommend specific high-performance models, usually equipped with extra large amounts of on-board video RAM. Check your NLE vendor's Web site for the latest word on video requirements, or ask your dealer. And remember, you need two video outputs in order to have a dual-screen desktop. Some cards offer dual outputs.

Video Editing Card

A few video cards have NTSC or PAL composite video outputs you can use to connect a video monitor to view the full-screen television picture on playback. However, most video cards don't include such an output, and in any case you'll get smoother playback if you add a separate *video editing card* that handles both computer and television output and does

> **VIDEO EDITING CARD:** High-performance video card that computes video effects to ease the load on the computer processor and speed up playback.

much of the processing required to display video effects—freeing the CPU for other tasks. These cards aren't cheap; prices may run between $500 and $1,000, compared to $100 for a good video card. Manufacturers like Matrox and Pinnacle sell video editing cards, often in combination with NLE software.

Two Processors Are Better Than One

Several NLE manufacturers recommend dual processors for best performance. A dual-processor configuration means that the computer actually has two matched processors that work in tandem. Typically when you play back your edit on a dual-processor NLE system, one chip handles the transition effects while the other generates video. The result is smoother playback, particularly if transitions are complex. (For more information, see the sidebar, "Why Is Rendering So Hard?" in Chapter 10.)

Most video editing cards work alongside your regular video card, controlling the studio monitor, handling IEEE 1394 input and output, analog video capture (composite and S-video in), and composite out. (If you're working in HD, a high-resolution video editing card is mandatory.)

Hard Drive Type, Speed, and Capacity

Video files are huge, so you should buy the biggest hard drives you can afford. You'll need 13 GB of disk space for every hour of video. So for even short projects, you'll probably need 20–40 GB total storage.

NLE specs include the manufacturer's recommended size for free space on the computer's primary hard drive. This spec applies to the application itself and its support files only, and *doesn't* include disk space for video data storage. For best performance, data should be stored on a separate drive, or at least on a separate partition of the primary drive. (See "Preparing Your Drives Before Installing NLE Software" later in this appendix.)

Some hard disks don't read or write fast enough to enable smooth real-time video play-back. You'll get the best results from EIDE, Ultra ATA, or Ultra SCSI drives, which spin at 7200 RPM or faster. External drives that use the IEEE 1394 connection and operate at this higher speed are called fast FireWire.

Upgrade Final Cut Pro to HD

Upgrading a Final Cut Pro system to handle HD will run upwards of $30,000 for a system that might include:

- *Power Mac dual G5 system (the same components listed for the high-performance Xpress DV system in Appendix A)*
- *Pinnacle CinéWave HD video editing card, software, and breakout boxes (hardware interfaces to video and TV monitors)*
- *RAID controller card*
- *Rorke Data Galaxy-i 640 GB 7200 RPM RAID storage system*

The Rorke Data Galaxy disk array listed here will store 640 GB (about half a terabyte) of data, which may seem excessive—but it's only enough for about two hours of HD video. Some high-end edit suites equipped for HD use 9 terabytes of RAID storage.

Unless you're a video engineer, don't try configuring this system yourself. HD systems are as finicky as champion racehorses. Consult a systems integrator who specializes in building these high-end Final Cut Pro systems. (One such vendor is www.promax.com.)

> **BREAKOUT BOX:** Hardware junction between a video editing card and digital and analog monitors.

REALITY CHECK: *The hard drives in consumer-level PCs typically run at 5,000 RPM, which is too slow for smooth video playback at anything but low resolution. You need at least 7,200 RPM. Some newer drives are rated at 10,000 RPM, which is impressive. But, depending on the speed and capacity of the rest of the computer's electronics, you might not see a noticeable difference, except perhaps with HD.*

There's no way to describe the utter despair you'll experience if you lose all the work you've put into your editing project due to a hard disk failure. *RAID* drives are the most reliable way to store data in a desktop system. Data is copied to multiple locations on mirrored disks, enabling its recovery even if one of the disks crashes. RAID is pricey technology, but if you can afford it, it's worth it to avoid down-time on projects with close deadlines.

> **RAID:** Acronym for redundant array of independent disks; set of drives that act as a single storage system and can tolerate the failure of a drive without data loss.

TIP: *Using an external fast FireWire drive to store your video data is a good idea, since you can easily plug the disk (and your data) into any NLE system with a FireWire port.*

CONFIGURING AN EDITING SYSTEM: THREE EXAMPLES

We're not in the business of building NLE systems—or endorsing products—but you may find it helpful to consider three examples of system configuration, including an economy desktop setup, a high-end desktop setup, and a notebook. The costs listed below are both current and approximate; they may have changed drastically by the time this book reaches your hands.

Configure for Lowest Cost

Here's a sample configuration designed to run Vegas 4 on a Windows PC. Many PC manufacturers, including IBM, Sony, Compaq, Dell, and Gateway, now offer specially configured "DV workstations," including fast processors and hard disks, high-performance video and sound cards, and FireWire connections. The example shown in **Table B.2** is based on one of those bundled systems. It includes two high-speed hard drives, one for programs and the other for video data.

For doing one-off DVD releases, you might consider adding a DVD burner and authoring software, although many desktop PCs now include them. Remember that CD burners can't create DVDs, and some PCs are too slow to support the high data rates of DVD burners.

To record your show on videocassette, you don't need any other hardware. Simply connect the TV Out and Audio Out signals to your home VCR.

Table B.2   A Sample Budget-Priced NLE System

Component	Description	Price
Processor	P4 2+ GHz	$ 1,200
Operating system	Windows XP	
Memory	250 MB	
Internal hard drive	100 GB Ultra ATA 7200 RPM	
Video display card	NVIDIA GeForce FX 5700 with TV Out	
Sound / FireWire	32-bit Sound Card with IEEE 1394 I/O port	
External hard drive for video data	160 GB 7200 RPM 1394 external HD	$ 250
NLE software	Vegas 4	$ 560
	Approx. **Total Price**	$ 2,000

This budget-priced NLE system is built around Vegas 4. The external FireWire drive is not included in the computer package and must be ordered separately.

 REALITY CHECK: *If you need to cut a few hundred dollars from the hardware expense, consider buying a recent-model PC refurbished by the manufacturer, with a factory warranty. These are often business machines that have been leased for short periods, discontinued models, or assembly-line rejects that needed repair. You'll generally have a more reliable machine—and better service—than if you purchased a discount "white box" unit.*

Configure for Best Performance

The system shown in **Table B.3** is designed to run Xpress DV on an Apple Power Mac. It delivers real-time playback of uncompressed DV using dual processors for best speed. Like the low-end system we just discussed, it also has two hard drives. It includes dual 17-inch flat-panel computer monitors, as well as a 14-inch television studio monitor and a set of high-quality speakers for judging output quality.

Since this is a high-end system designed for a pro, we've included a color-coded keyboard for often-used Avid commands. (See *www.postop.com*.) At this level, where mass production is the goal, you'll probably give a Digibeta master tape to a DVD duplication house for authoring—or a DLT tape if you've done the authoring yourself. However, the $500 cost of a 40 GB internal DLT drive isn't included in our example system. (For more information, see "DVD Authoring" in Chapter 12.)

Table B.3 A Sample High-Performance NLE System

Component	Description	Price
Processor	Dual Power Mac G5 2.0 MHz	$ 2999
Operating system	OS X 10	
Memory	1 GB upgrade	$ 250
Internal hard drives	2 x 250 GB Serial ATA 7200 RPM	$ 525
Video display card	(Built into Power Mac)	
Sound / FireWire	(Built into Mac)	
TV preview monitor	Sony 14-in studio monitor	$ 690
Audio speakers	JBL Creature	$ 129
NLE software	Avid Xpress DV Pro	$ 990
Two 17-in computer monitors (for dual-screen desktop)	Apple Studio Display	$699 x 2
Color-coded NLE keyboard for Xpress DV	Post-Op Video EZ keyboard USB for Mac	$ 150
	Approx. **Total Price**	**$ 7,100**

Configure a Notebook

Apple's 17-inch PowerBook G4 shown in **Table B.4** comes out of the box loaded with everything you need to run Final Cut Pro in OffLineRT mode. Add a fast FireWire external hard drive to store video data and you have a highly portable system: a powerhouse that's still small enough to fit on the meal tray of an airplane. Add editing software and a 160 GB external drive—a package your Apple dealer can assemble for you.

Table B.4 A Sample Notebook NLE System

Component	Description	Price
Processor	17-inch SuperDrive PowerBook G4 800 MHz	$ 2,999
Operating system	OS X	
Memory	1 GB upgrade	$ 300
Internal hard drive	80 GB Ultra ATA 5400 RPM	$ 125
Auxiliary hard drive (for video data)	LaCie d2 160 GB 7200 RPM external FireWire drive	$ 219
NLE software	Final Cut Pro 4	$ 999
	Approx. **Total Price**	**$ 4,600**

Preparing Your Drives Before Installing NLE Software

Follow these tips prior to doing the installation:

- For best performance, including the smoothest possible real-time playback, segregate programs and data onto separate disks or partitions. All things considered, it's best to run two physically separate disks. This buys you faster performance and a better margin of crash protection.

- If you don't already have one or two big hard drives installed, stop now and install them. If you're planning on using a single disk, get the biggest one you can find. If you're planning on running two disks, size the first one by calculating how much storage space you'll need for the operating system, the NLE program, and any other programs, such as postproduction tools, you plan to use. Then add at least another 50 percent as a cushion for expansion. Since this calculation is at least partially theoretical, it's a good idea to make that primary partition as big as possible.

- Calculate the size of the second drive based on the running time of the typical project you will be editing. For DV, you'll need 13 GB of storage for every hour of program. Multiply that by one more than your typical shooting ratio (for instance, if you shoot 4:1, multiply by five) to arrive at your minimum requirement. So if your movie will run two hours and you have an average of four takes for every shot, you'll need:

  13 GB/hr × 2 hr × 5 versions = 130 GB total

- Put the operating system on the primary drive; eventually you'll put data on the other. (Any external drives should always be the data disks.)

- If you must run your system on just one hard disk, you'll need to partition it into two *logical drives*. (Since this will wipe out all existing data, be sure to make and verify a full backup first.)

- The size of your partitions will be limited by the size of your hard disk. This makes the following calculations a bit complex; work out the numbers on paper before you proceed, and make any adjustments and compromises necessary.

> **LOGICAL DRIVES:** Partitioning procedure by which a single physical hard disk appears to the user as two or more separate disks.

- Base the ideal size of the secondary partition as just described for a secondary drive—allowing 13 GB of storage per hour of video data.

- Put the operating system on the primary (boot) partition; eventually you'll put your data on the second partition.

The following instructions apply whether you're installing dual disks or dual partitions:

- Unless you're formatting brand new drives, use a diagnostic utility like Symantec Norton Disk Doctor to check hard disks for errors. Then use a disk utility like Symantec Norton Speed Disk to defragment the disks.

- Before installing the NLE software, make sure that all *device drivers* (support software for video cards and accessories) are up to date, including QuickTime and Windows Media Player. You can download the latest drivers from the technical support sections of the device manufacturers' Web sites. Check the NLE software manual and/or its home Web site to see which devices and drivers are supported. In some cases, the NLE manufacturer will specify whether you should use the driver supplied by the device manufacturer or the version distributed with the operating system (it can make a difference).

- Just before installing the NLE application, disable virus protection temporarily and do a *clean boot*. Make sure no other programs are running. (You can restore the system to normal after you've completed a successful installation.)

> **DEVICE DRIVER:** Hardware-specific control program that handles communication between a peripheral device, the operating system, and application programs.
>
> **CLEAN BOOT:** Starting a computer with just the operating system and device drivers and no other programs.

GLOSSARY

Glossary

24P: 24 fps, progressive (video camera scanning mode that most simulates film). *Chapter 3.*

30I: 30 fps, interlaced (video camera scanning mode used for normal NTSC). *Chapter 3.*

30P: 30 fps, progressive (video camera scanning mode used for "film-look" video). *Chapter 3.*

A

Abby Singer: The second-to-last shot of the day. *Chapter 9.*

AC-3: One of several digital encoding schemes for audio; Dolby Digital. *Chapter 12.*

Accessory shoe: Bracket on a camera for mounting floodlights or flash accessories; if it also provides power, it's called a "hot shoe." *Chapter 3.*

Act break: Point in a TV program with a pause for insertion of commercials. *Chapter 12.*

A/D conversion: Analog-to-digital sampling. *Appendix A.*

Add-in: Software module that runs inside another application to extend its capabilities; plug-in. *Chapter 10.*

ADR: See Automated dialogue replacement. *Chapter 7.*

Ad-supported: Communications channel (like broadcast TV) subsidized by advertising revenue. *Chapter 12.*

AE shift: Semi-automatic camcorder function that adjusts by one or two f-stops from a setting calculated by the camera's autoexposure circuit. *Chapter 4.*

Air: Cinematographer's term for empty space within the composition of a shot. *Chapter 5.* Also, as used by sound engineers, distance between a subject and the microphone. *Chapter 7.*

Airdate: Scheduled broadcast date for a television or cable show. *Chapter 10.*

Ambient light: Naturally occurring light. *Chapter 6.*

Anamorphic: Cinema-style camera lens that optically compresses a wide-screen image to fit a standard aspect ratio. *Chapter 12.*

Ancillary: Exploitation of a copyrighted work in a different medum, such as CD sales of a movie soundtrack; spin-off. *Chapter 11.*

Answer print: One-off positive film made by a lab for purposes of review and approval. *Chapter 12.*

Aperture: Size of lens opening used to control exposure; iris. *Chapter 4.*

Archival footage: Film or video clips stored for use in future productions. *Appendix A.*

Artifact: Visual glitch such as video noise or a digitizing error. *Appendix A.*

Aspect ratio: The width (w) of a film or video picture compared to its height (h). Aspect ratios are usually written with a colon separating w and h. A TV picture that's 40 inches wide and 30 inches high has a 4:3 aspect ratio. *Appendix A.*

Asset: Any clip or file that can be written to a DVD. *Chapter 12.*

Assistant editor: Postproduction professional who prepares video and audio material for assembly by the editor. *Chapter 10.*

Attenuator: Variable-gain junction box for connecting audio cables that can also compensate for electrical mismatch in the lines; pad. *Chapter 7.*

Audio perspective: Apparent direction, volume, and distance of an audio source in relation to screen action. Also includes the distinctive spatial quality of a particular room or space. *Chapter 7.*

Audiovisual (A/V) format: Two-column script format traditionally used for corporate video and commercials; director's format. *Chapter 2.*

Authoring: Preparing a master presentation for output to DVD. *Chapter 12.*

Auto: Camcorder full automatic mode in which most if not all critical camera settings are determined by logic circuitry. *Chapter 4.*

Autocapture: Ability to automatically identify and segregate clips during a DV upload; DV scene detection. *Chapter 10.*

Automated dialogue replacement (ADR): Rerecording sync-sound dialogue in post-production; looping; dubbing. *Chapter 7.*

Automatic groove detection: Sound editing feature that detects and extracts the musical beat from a clip. *Chapter 11.*

Axis: Stage Line. *Chapter 5.* Imaginary line through a mic defining the core of its pickup pattern. *Chapter 7.*

B

Back end: Any distribution revenue from a movie over and above domestic box office receipts. *Chapter 12.*

Back light: In a three-point lighting plan, light that falls on the subject from behind and separates it from the background. *Chapter 6.*

Background lighting: General illumination of a set, particularly the back wall, rather than specific objects or players in it. *Chapter 6.*

Backtiming: Determining the insertion point of a music clip by timing backward from a desired sync point. *Chapter 11.*

Balancing color: Compensating for different color temperatures within a lighting setup to achieve consistent overall color rendition. *Chapter 3.*

Ballast: Starter/regulator for fluorescent lights. *Chapter 6.*

Barn doors: Hinged panels on the front of movie light housings that can be adjusted to control the beam angle of the light. *Chapter 6.*

Bass rumble: Persistent low-frequency audio noise due to wind or traffic. *Chapter 11.*

Beam angle: A light's area of coverage, measured in degrees, within which intensity is at least half of the light's rating. For example, a narrowly focused spotlight might have a beam angle of 20 degrees. *Chapter 6.*

Beam splitter: Set of prisms or mirrors that separates a light beam into its component primary colors. *Appendix A.*

Beat: In writing, acting, or editing, a change of an actor's mood or intention in a scene; also, a momentary pause in pacing. *Chapter 10.*

Beauty shot: Highly flattering, meticulously lit closeup of a star in a movie or a product in a commercial. *Chapter 6.*

Best boy: On a movie crew, the second grip, or assistant to the key grip. *Chapter 6.*

Bin: In Final Cut Pro, a folder used to group and store DV clips. *Chapter 10.*

Black balance: Camcorder color compensation adjustment when red, green, and blue signals are all effectively zero. *Chapter 4.*

Black level: Minimum pixel value in a video picture, defined as 7.5 IRE for NTSC and 0 IRE for PAL; pedestal; setup. *Appendix A.*

Black wrap: Dull, black foil that can be wrapped around the barn doors of movie lights to narrow the beam angle. *Chapter 6.*

Blimp: Canister-like windscreen that fits around a microphone. *Chapter 7.*

Blocking: An actor's movements within a scene. *Chapter 5.*

Blog: A succession of daily Web page postings, exchanges between Web site operator (author of the blog) and other users with common interests; Web log. *Chapter 1.*

Blown out: White area within a video image that is totally overexposed and contains no picture detail. *Chapter 4.*

Bob and weave: Jitter in film projection gate caused by worn sprocket holes in the film. *Chapter 11.*

Boom arm: Dolly-mounted crane. *Chapter 5.*

Boom operator: On the set, the audio technician responsible for holding and positioning the boom pole and its attached microphone. *Chapter 7.*

Boom pole: Long pole to which the microphone is attached; microphone boom. *Chapter 7.*

Booming: Raising (booming up) or lowering (booming down) the camera on a boom arm; crane shot. *Chapter 5.*

Box-office gross receipts: Money collected from theatrical ticket sales, not including refreshment sales. *Chapter 12.*

Breakdown: Process of deconstructing a shooting script into production elements such as locations, sets, interior or exterior, day or night, cast, props, and so on. *Chapter 2.*

Breakout box: Hardware junction between a video editing card and digital or analog monitors. *Appendix B.*

Browser: In Final Cut Pro, a window that displays a directory of captured clips. *Chapter 10.*

Build: Write an authored video program to DVD; multiplex. *Chapter 12.*

Bundled product: Software and hardware components sold together as a package. *Appendix B.*

Business: Physical action by an actor. *Chapter 9.*

Button: Visual and/or audio effect that punctuates the end of an action or scene. *Chapter 11.* Also, graphic symbol on a screen menu that indicates a user selection. *Chapter 12.*

C

C-47: Movie-grip term for a common clothespin. *Chapter 6.*

C-stand: Movie grip's adjustable metal stand, a multipurpose holder for devices that diffuse, filter, mask, or reflect light. *Chapter 6.*

Cache: Temporary storage area in a computer's memory, on disk, or both. *Chapter 12.*

Call sheet: List of cast and crew assignments and reporting times, as well as equipment requirements, instructions, and contact numbers for the next shooting day. *Chapter 9.*

Camera log: A written record of what's been recorded on each reel (DV cassette) and track (DAT cassette), with corresponding timecodes for each take. Also camera and sound log; daily editor's log. *Chapter 9.*

Camera operator: Person on a movie crew who has physical control over the camera; on a fully crewed shoot, takes direction from the cinematographer and directly supervises the work of other crew members responsible for focusing during a take or executing complex camera moves. *Chapter 1.*

Canned: A selection from a music or sound-effects library; a prerecorded tune or effect; not live. *Chapter 11.*

Canvas: In Final Cut Pro, a window showing the frame at the current position of the play-head in the timeline; also displays playback of sequence. *Chapter 10.*

Cardioid: Typically short style of microphone that is sensitive mainly to the sound directly in front of it, often used by singers and interviewers. *Chapter 7.*

Catering: Meals served to cast and crew on the set. *Chapter 8.*

CBR: See Constant Bit Rate. *Chapter 12.*

CCD (Charge-Coupled Device): Image-sensing chip in camcorder and digital camera. *Chapter 3.*

CGI: See Computer generated imagery. *Chapter 1.*

Chapter: Single continuous sequence of video material on a DVD. *Chapter 12.*

Checkerboarding: Creating a separate audio track for each actor's dialogue. *Chapter 11.*

Chewing the scenery: Overacting. *Chapter 9.*

Chromatic resolution: The number of colors a camcorder or video display is capable of recording or showing. *Chapter 3.*

Cinema-style lens: Photographic lens designed for a motion-picture camera. *Chapter 3.*

Cinematographer: The crew member primarily responsible for both the technical and artistic aspects of lighting and photography or videography; sometimes called the director of photography (DP), even if the production is on video. *Chapter 1.*

Claiming the set: Assuming authority over operations on the set at a particular time; during shooting, a responsibility alternately held by the director and the first assistant director. *Chapter 9.*

Clapper: The hinged part of a slate that makes a clapping sound when snapped shut; image and sound of clapping provide easily identified simultaneous events so the editor can sync the picture and soundtrack. *Chapter 7.*

Clapper board: Another term for a filmmaker's slate. *Chapter 7.*

Clean boot: Starting a computer with just the operating system and needed device drivers, with no other programs running. *Appendix B.*

Clean single: Closeup (or one of its variations) that frames one actor exclusively, in contrast to a "dirty single," in which some part of another actor's profile is showing as well; single. *Chapter 5.*

Clear: Obtain permission to use a copyrighted element you wish to incorporate in your work. *Chapter 11.*

Click track: Music guide track for use by composers and/or performers that marks tempo as a series of audible clicks. *Chapter 10.*

Cliff-hanger: Unresolved ending; plot technique used to sustain viewer interest through commercial breaks. *Chapter 12.*

Clip: Any short segment of recorded video. *Chapter 1.*

Clock wipe: Spiraling wipe transition effect; radial wipe. *Chapter 10.*

Closed-circuit television (CCTV): Private cable TV network. *Chapter 12.*

Close-mic: Placing microphone near the subject, appropriate for a closeup shot. *Chapter 7.*

Closeup (CU): Shot that frames an actor's head and shoulders. *Chapter 5.*

CMYK: Color model used in film and print, composed of four primary colors: cyan (C), magenta (M), yellow (Y), and black (K). *Appendix A.*

Codec (compressor/decompressor): Encoder/decoder; computer hardware and/or software used to create or read compressed audio and video. *Chapter 12.*

Color balance: Compensation for different color temperatures within a lighting setup to achieve a pleasing overall color rendition. *Chapter 6.*

Color cast: Overall tint in a picture. *Appendix A.*

Color duplicating negative: Film negative made from master positive used for making release prints, also dupe negative. *Chapter 12.*

Color grading: Film lab process for correcting color casts. *Chapter 12.*

Color master positive: Optical print that combines picture, sound, and titles. *Chapter 12.*

Color model: Set of three primary colors (or data streams), which can be used in different combinations to reproduce a full spectrum of colors; color models include RGB, YIQ, YUV, and CMYK. *Appendix A.*

Color sample: Number of data bits used in one measurement of an analog R, G, or B picture signal; in DV and HD camcorders, usually 8 or 10 bits. *Appendix A.*

Color sampling: Process of converting analog R, G, and B signals to digital. *Appendix A.*

Color space: The range of colors a camcorder or video device can reproduce. *Chapter 3.*

Color subsampling: Deriving digital YCC values from RGB. *Appendix A.*

Color temperature: Tint of white light, measured in degrees on the Kelvin scale (°K). *Chapter 6.*

Compositing: Combining two or more video images to create a new image. *Chapter 1.*

Compression: Processing data to describe it with fewer bits and store it in smaller files. *Appendix A.*

Computer film recorder: CRT or laser coupled to a photographic camera; used to transfer digital video images to film. *Chapter 12.*

Computer generated imagery (CGI): Synthetic pictures, special effects, or animation produced by manipulating graphic objects (including previously captured digital pictures) in software. *Chapter 1.*

Computer graphics: Descriptive computer code of objects and their movement, commonly used for animation. *Appendix A.*

Condenser: Type of microphone that senses sound by the compression of a material such as crystal. *Chapter 7.*

Constant Bit Rate (CBR): MPEG encoding scheme that uses a fixed data rate. *Chapter 12.*

Continuous zoom: Changing camera lens magnification or demagnification via the semi-automatic zoom control. *Chapter 4.*

Control surface: Device that provides tactile interface for controlling software settings. *Chapter 11.*

Cove: On a studio set, curved boundary between a background wall and the floor, for purposes of eliminating shadows that would be created by a hard corner. *Chapter 6.*

Coverage: Taking a complete enough set of shots for a scene so the editor has every angle she needs to make the edited scene work. *Chapter 5.*

Craft services: Snacks and beverages made available to cast and crew on the set. *Chapter 8.*

Crane: Counterweighted lever for raising or lowering a camera. *Chapter 5.*

Crew call: Call time for anyone who doesn't have a separately specified reporting time on the call sheet. *Chapter 9.*

Cross dissolve: Gradual transitions from one image to another by momentarily blending the images. Also called "cross-fade" or "dissolve." *Chapter 10.*

Cross-fade: A visual dissolve. *Chapter 10.* Audio dissolve in which the level of one track increases while the level of the other decreases. *Chapter 11.*

Cukie: Sheet of opaque material such as metal or wood with a pattern of holes cut into it so that light casts a pattern when projected through it. Movie lore has it that cukie is short for "Cucalorus," name of the gaffer who invented it. Pronounced "cookie." *Chapter 6.*

Cutaway: Any shot that interrupts or follows a scene, relieves its tension, or comments on it. *Chapter 5.*

Cutting in-camera: Shooting just one good take of every shot you need; shooting only the portions of scenes from a given setup you expect to use in the edit (*e.g.,* not shooting a master all the way through if you'll cut to closeups instead). *Chapter 8.*

D

D-ILA (Digital Direct Drive Image Light Amplifier): Holographic technology for electronic theatrical projection developed by JVC. *Chapter 12.*

Daily progress report: During a shoot, the first assistant director's statistical account of what was accomplished that day. *Chapter 9.*

DAT: Digital audiotape; cassette tape format. *Chapter 7.*

Data bit: Basic unit of binary digital computer code; a 0 or a 1, represented by switches in electronic circuits or by memory locations in storage devices that are set to "off" or "on," respectively. *Chapter 3.*

DAW (digital audio workstation): Audio editing software that usually also provides an integrated environment for music capture, looping, and music composition. *Chapter 11.*

Day for night: Practice of shooting night scenes during the day by placing a dark blue filter over the camera lens. *Chapter 6.*

Day-out-of-days report: During a shoot, the second assistant director's record of cast scheduling and actors' time attendance. *Chapter 9.*

Day player: Actor whose services are hired for one specific shooting day. *Chapter 8.*

Daylight blue: A light source color-balanced for use outdoors, to supplement or simulate sunlight. *Chapter 6.*

Deal memo: Letter of agreement used to hire members of the cast and crew. *Chapter 8.*

Deliverables: Items you are required to submit to your distributor. *Chapter 12.*

Device driver: Hardware-specific control program that handles communication between a peripheral device, the operating system, and application programs. *Appendix B.*

Dialogue editor: Postproduction professional on an editorial team who works exclusively with production sound, especially dialogue recorded on the set. *Chapter 10.*

Dichroic filter: Optical barrier that permits only one primary color of light to pass through. *Appendix A.*

Differential: Referring to an electrical circuit that relies on differences in parameters between two electrical signals. *Chapter 7.*

Digital component: Stream of video data composed of a specific number of data samples of Y, U, and V (e.g., 4:1:1 or 4:2:2). *Appendix A.*

Digital matte: Special effect achieved by compositing two scenes, such as superimposing a real subject over a fantasy background. *Chapter 6.*

Direct-to-video: Movie produced with the intention of distributing primarily in video stores. *Chapter 12.*

Director of photography (DP): The crew member primarily responsible for both the technical and artistic aspects of lighting and photography, or videography; cinematographer, whether the production is film or video. *Chapter 1.*

Director's format: European term for two-column A/V script format. *Chapter 2.*

Dirty single: Variation of the closeup or single in which all of the featured actor, as well as part of the profile of his listener, is framed in the shot. *Chapter 5.*

Dissolve: Gradual transition from one image to another by momentarily blending the images. Also called "cross dissolve" or "cross-fade." *Chapter 10.*

DLP (Digital Light Projection): Electronic theatrical projection method developed by Texas Instruments. *Chapter 12.*

D, M, E: Abbreviations for dialogue, music, and sound effects. *Chapter 7.*

Dolly counter-zoom: Zooming out while dollying in; zooming in while dollying out. *Chapter 5.*

Dolly in: Shot during which the camera is wheeled in toward the subject. *Chapter 5.*

Dolly out: Shot during which the camera is wheeled away from the subject. *Chapter 5.*

Doorway dolly: Rolling platform that accepts a camera tripod and rides along sectional, tubular track. *Chapter 9.*

Double tracking: Dubbing over a previously recorded track so a vocalist can sing harmony with herself. *Chapter 11.*

Downbeat: In a musical score, first beat of a measure. *Chapter 11.*

Downconvert: Transfer a video recording from a higher to a lower data rate or resolution; downsample. *Chapter 12.*

Drop: Release of an actor (usually a weekly player) from the shooting schedule and from the payroll. *Chapter 9.*

Drop-frame mode: Standard NTSC frame rate of 29.97 fps. *Chapter 4.*

Ds/dl: dual-side/dual-layer optical disc; DVD-18. *Chapter 12.*

Ds/sl: dual-side/single-layer optical disc; DVD-10. *Chapter 12.*

Dual processor: Computer with two processors working in tandem. *Chapter 10.*

Dual-system sound: Simultaneously recording sync sound on an external tape recorder and the camcorder. *Chapter 7.*

Dub: An audio or videotape copy. *Chapter 1.*

Dub track: New audio track recorded during ADR. *Chapter 11.*

Dump-truck director: Pejorative term for a director who overshoots and lets the editor worry about which takes to use. *Chapter 8.*

DV scene detection: Ability to automatically identify different shots on a camera tape during a DV upload; autocapture. *Chapter 10.*

Dynamic: Type of microphone that senses sound by the movement of a diaphragm within an electrical coil. *Chapter 7.*

E

Edit decision list (EDL): Text file identifying all clip files, sequences, and transitions in an edited show, including instructions for assembling the finished presentation. *Chapter 10.*

Edit point: Position in the NLE timeline at which the next edit will occur. *Chapter 10.*

Edit smoothing: Sound editing feature that blends audio waveforms at cuts. *Chapter 11.*

Effective pixel count: Number of pixels on a CCD that show up in the active picture area— the image on the screen. *Chapter 3.*

Electron gun: Device in a television picture tube that directs beams of electrons to paint scan lines on the face of the tube. *Appendix A.*

Equalization: Adjusting frequency response of audio lines in relation to one another. *Chapter 7.*

Establishing shot: Image that introduces the audience to a new setting in which the next action will take place. *Chapter 5.*

Eye cup: Rubber shield surrounding the eyepiece of the camera viewfinder. *Chapter 4.*

Eye line: Imaginary line connecting two actors' eyes as they look at one another. *Chapter 5.*

Eyelight: A narrowly focused spotlight aimed at an actor's eyes for the purpose of adding sparkle, interest, and personality. *Chapter 6.*

Extreme closeup (ECU): Shot of an actor's head that shows only a portion of the face, cutting off either the chin or the forehead. *Chapter 5.*

Extreme long shot (ELS): Shot that looks at the subject from very far away, as if the viewer were spying unobserved from a great distance. *Chapter 5.*

F

F-stop: A numeric index defining aperture size. Camcorder f-stop settings generally range from f/1.6 (the widest opening, allowing the most amount of light to enter the lens) to f/16 (narrowest opening, least light). *Chapter 4.*

Fall: Single performance of any type of stunt, even if it doesn't involve falling. *Chapter 8.*

Feedback: Undesirable whine in an audio circuit, usually caused by locating a mic too close to a loudspeaker. *Chapter 7.*

Field: One of two sets of horizontal scan lines (the odd-numbered lines or the even-numbered ones) that compose one frame of a video picture. *Appendix A.*

Fill light: In a three-point lighting plan, the light that softens and fills in shadows created by the key light. *Chapter 6.*

Filter: Software plug-in with a canned set of creative options involving colors, textures, and effects designed for artistic impressions or technical transformations. *Chapter 11.*

Final cut: Producer's approved edit of a show. *Chapter 10.*

Fine cut: Any near-finished version of an edit in progress. *Chapter 10.*

Finishing money: Investment funds for completing a movie that has been shot but for which some postproduction steps remain. *Chapter 12.*

First cut: Director's approved edit of a show. *Chapter 10.*

First day of principal photography: First shooting day for the first unit of a movie production; the official start date of the production for contractual purposes. *Chapter 9.*

Flag: Opaque cloth panel stretched on a frame that can be mounted on a C-stand for the purpose of masking light. *Chapter 6.*

Flash memory module: A solid-state storage chip that can be inserted into digital photographic cameras and video camcorders for purposes of holding still images and short video clips; Memory Stick. *Chapter 3.*

Fluid head: Swivel mount on a camera tripod that contains hydraulic fluid to dampen jarring and assure smooth movement. *Chapter 9.*

Fluorescent: Tube-style light with no filament, filled with gaseous metal that glows when electricity passes through it; in movie terminology, a "Kino Flo," named for one manufacturer. *Chapter 6.*

Flying spot: CRT imaging method used for video-to-film transfer; focused electron beam. *Chapter 12.*

Focal length: Range of distances over which a lens can achieve a sharp picture. *Chapter 4.*

Foley artists: Postproduction specialists who watch a scene projected in the recording studio and supply sounds of footsteps, heavy breathing, body movement, rustling of clothes, hits, slaps, etc.; Foley walkers. *Chapter 8.*

Foley pit: Stage with different walking surfaces and materials to create sounds of footsteps and other sound effects added during postproduction; stage where Foley walkers work. *Chapter 11.*

Foveon chip technology: Single-chip digital-camera image sensing that relies on the optical principle that red, green, and blue light penetrate the chip's silicon layers at different depths—possibly emulating the behavior of conventional film stock better than three-chip CCD designs. *Appendix A.*

Fractals: Mathematical formulas used in CGI systems to create synthetic fog, clouds, trees, and mountains. *Chapter 1.*

Frame: One still image within a motion sequence captured by a movie camera or camcorder; it takes 24 (or 30) of them to comprise one second of motion picture for film or NTSC video. *Chapter 3.*

Frame left/frame right: Screen direction based on the viewpoint of the audience. *Chapter 9.*

Frame rate: The number of still images a film or video camera captures every second; frames per second (fps); picture rate. *Chapter 3.*

Franchise: In cable television, government license to operate in a specific metropolitan area. *Chapter 12.*

Fresnel: Halogen movie light equipped with a glass lens for focusing the beam; sizes from small to large include: "pepper," "inkie," "betweenie," "tweenie," "baby-baby," "junior," "senior," and "tenner." Pronounced: freh *–nel. Chapter 6.*

Front office: In the studio system, the executive suite on the lot. *Chapter 9.*

G

Gaffer: Electrician on a movie set; selects and adjusts lights as directed by the DP. *Chapter 6.*

Gamma: A constant color-correction factor applied to a video signal to compensate for nonlinear response of output devices such as television picture tubes. *Appendix A.*

Gamma knee: Controllable subset of gamma color-correction values. *Appendix A.*

Gel: Transparent optical material that changes the color of light passing through it. *Chapter 6.*

Generator operator: Gaffer who operates a gasoline-fueled electrical power source on a movie set. *Chapter 6.*

Gimbal: Mechanical device that allows a camera to remain level even if its mount is tipped. *Chapter 9.*

Go wide: Launch a major motion picture in thousands of theaters nationwide, or even worldwide, on the same day. *Chapter 12.*

Grandfather: To obtain union authorization retroactively, usually just prior to distribution. *Chapter 8.*

Grip: A crew member who deals primarily with the equipment that doesn't plug in. *Chapter 6.*

Grip clip: Spring-loaded hand vise used by grips to fasten accessories such as flags to C-stands or to each other. *Chapter 6.*

Guerilla filmmaking: Shooting with one camera and a minimal budget and crew, typically done outside the movie studio system by independent producers who want to tell unconventional stories; film-style shooting done as if by a news crew. *Chapter 1.*

Guide track: Sync sound track (usually the original production track) that serves as a template for a replacement track built during postproduction or recorded during ADR. *Chapter 7.*

Gyro: Continually spinning, weighted mechanical disc assembly that resists movement perpendicular to its axis of spin. With a gyro-equipped camera stabilizer pole, the operator must exert some effort to tip the camera; short for *gyrostabilizer. Chapter 9.*

H

Halogen-quartz: Incandescent lamp with tungsten filament and filled with a mixture of halogen gas and vaporized quartz. The gas glows brightly and helps prevent the filament from combining with oxygen so as not to burn up at high temperatures. *Chapter 6.*

Handle: Extra footage on either side of a clip for use in creating fades and other types of transitions. *Chapter 11.*

Hard light: Bright illumination emanating from a point source, such as a single, bare lamp; causes sharp shadows. *Chapter 6.*

HD / HDTV: See High definition. *Chapter 1.*

Head: The mechanism on top of a tripod or dolly that holds the camera and allows you to move it. *Chapter 4.* Recording / playback element in video cameras and tape recorders, *e.g.,* record head, playback head. *Appendix A.*

Headshot: Actor's publicity photo, typically with a resume printed on the back or stapled to it; photo and resume (P&R). *Chapter 8.*

Helical scan: Slantwise recording pattern on videotape created by spinning record head as tape moves past it. *Appendix A.*

High Definition (HD / HDTV): High-resolution digital video producing a wide-screen (16:9) display with resolution at least four times that of standard video. Also called *hi-def.* *Chapter 1.*

High key: In a three-point lighting plan, a bright primary light on the subject, suitable for comedy. *Chapter 6.*

Histogram: Graph showing statistical distribution of values; pixel counts at various levels of intensity in a picture. *Appendix A.*

HMI lights: Daylight-balanced, incandescent lamps with tungsten filaments and filled with hydragyrum medium-arc iodine gas, which glows brighter than the halogen-quartz type. *Chapter 6.*

Honey wagon: Rolling portable toilet facility for use on movie locations. *Chapter 8.*

Hot set: Movie set where camera and sound are rolling. Also, any idle set that's not to be disturbed because it will be used later. *Chapter 9.*

HTML: See Hypertext Markup Language. *Chapter 12.*

Hunting: Fluctuating camcorder performance due to logic circuits' inability to compensate for fast-changing conditions. *Chapter 4.*

Hybrid: DVD that contains both video clips and other documents. *Chapter 12.*

Hypercardioid: Type of microphone with an extremely narrow axis and long focal distance; shotgun; a typical boom mic. *Chapter 7.*

Hypertext Markup Language (HTML): Computer language used to create and process Web pages. *Chapter 12.*

Hz (Hertz): Cycles per second. *Chapter 3.*

I

IC index: Feature on some camcorders that logs a take's starting point and timecode location on the tape by creating an electronic table in an embedded chip, or integrated circuit (IC), in special Mini DV cassettes. *Chapter 4.*

Improvisational approach: Permitting experimentation on the set in terms of actors' performances and/or shot design. *Chapter 5.*

In and out points: Pointers that mark the beginning and end of that part of the clip you'll use in the final sequence. *Chapter 10.*

In the can: Successfully capturing a desired shot; cinematographer's term for a completed take. *Chapter 1.*

In-betweening: Creating a transformation within a video sequence by changing the starting and ending frames and letting the computer calculate how to change, gradually, from one to the other; keyframing; interpolation process. *Chapter 10.*

Incandescent: Any lamp whose light comes from a glowing wire or filament. *Chapter 6.*

Incident light meter: A photocell device that measures the intensity of light falling on the subject, rather than the overall level of light reflected into the camera lens. *Chapter 6.*

Indication: An acting performance intended to please the director or audience by producing a particular result or impression. *Chapter 9.*

Insert: Shot briefly intercut with a longer scene, usually showing some meaningful detail. *Chapter 5.*

Insert stage: Small sound stage on a movie lot used primarily to shoot inserts, or tight closeups of props and gestures; small stage in a television studio used for remote interviews and field reporting, typically with the local cityscape added electronically in the background. *Chapter 5.*

Installation: Museum exhibit by an artist that may include multimedia elements. *Chapter 1.*

Intellectual property: Any originally created material of value, such as a script, invention, artwork, computer program, or movie that can be protected by copyright. *Chapter 12.*

Intensity: Absolute measure of the brightness of a light source. *Chapter 6.*

Interactive marker: DVD selection supered as a button over a video scene. *Chapter 12.*

Intercut: Insert one shot into another; also, cutting back and forth repeatedly from one shot to another. *Chapter 5.*

Interlaced scanning: Method used by NTSC and PAL/SECAM to capture and display one video frame as two alternating field patterns. *Chapter 3.*

Interlock studio: ADR facility in which film print and mag tracks can be synced, or interlocked. *Chapter 11.*

Interpolation: Mathematical approximation process by which digital circuitry estimates the values of missing pixels. *Chapter 3.* Also, the process used to derive intermediate frames in editing and animation keyframing, or in-betweening. *Chapter 10.*

IP address: Internet Protocol; a computer's digital identifier on a network. *Chapter 12.*

Iris: In videography, another term for "aperture." *Chapter 3.* In editing, a traditional spiraling transition effect. *Chapter 10.*

ISO/ASA: In photography, a numeric index of film speed, or sensitivity to light. *Chapter 6.*

J

J-cut: See Split edit. *Chapter 10.*

Jam sync: Multiple-device timecode synchronization technique by which one device serves as the master timecode generator and all linked devices serve as slaves. If the master signal becomes unstable for any reason, the slave uses its internal timecode, then resynchronizes with the master when the signal is restored. *Chapter 7.*

Jump: Programmed DVD operation that starts playback at a specific marker, or timecode. *Chapter 12.*

K

Key grip: Head lighting technician on a movie crew. *Chapter 6.*

Key light: Primary light source in a scene; central point of a classic, three-point lighting plan; "Rembrandt" lighting. *Chapter 6.*

Keyframing: Creating transformation within a video sequence by changing the starting and ending frames; in-betweening; interpolation process. *Chapter 10.*

Keying: In video postproduction, compositing process that substitutes portions of a second scene for every instance of a value (luminance key) or color (chroma key) in the first scene. *Chapter 6.*

Kick: In lighting terminology, any bright reflection off an object. *Chapter 6.*

Kinescope: Film transfer from video made by photographing a program as it plays on a television screen. *Chapter 12.*

Kodalith: Kodak brand of opaque lithographic film, sold in paper-sized sheets; used to make title artwork to be filmed as an optical effect. *Chapter 11.*

L

L-cut: See Split edit. *Chapter 10.*

Lamp: The bulb or light-producing device within a movie light. *Chapter 6.*

Lamp operator: Gaffer who replaces burned out bulbs or other lighting elements. *Chapter 6.*

Lap dissolve: Prolonged dissolve. *Chapter 10.*

Laserdrop: See Per-drop. *Chapter 11.*

Lavalier microphone: Small mic worn by the subject, clipped to a tie or pocket, or concealed in clothing or hair; lav. *Chapter 7.*

LCD (Liquid Crystal Display): Device that shows the current view through the lens of a camcorder. The LCD may be either internal (seen through the viewfinder) or external (on a small door that flips out from the camera body). *Chapter 4.*

Lead gaffer: Chief electrical technician, or just "the gaffer." *Chapter 6.*

Letterboxing: Fitting a wide-screen image on a standard-sized screen with bands of black at the top and bottom. *Appendix A.*

Line-item budget: Detailed budget that supports the top sheet, or summary page. *Chapter 8.*

Line level: Voltage level of audio output signals, measured in decibels (dB). *Chapter 7.*

Line producer: A movie professional who develops, or supervises development of, schedules and budgets, then contracts for crew, equipment, supporting actors, extras, and postproduction services. *Chapter 1.*

Location: A physical space where you plan to shoot, such as a park, an office building, or your own living room. *Chapter 1.*

Location scout: Movie professional who identifies and travels to prospective locations to judge and report back to director and producers on their suitability. *Chapter 8.*

Locked: Approved, edited version of a show, to which no further picture changes are made. *Chapter 10.*

Locked down: Immobilized camera on a stationary mount, such as a tripod. *Chapter 4.*

Logical drives: Partitioning procedure by which a single physical hard disk appears to the user as two or more separate disks. *Appendix B.*

Logline: One- or two-sentence description of a screen story; idea for a movie; concept. *Chapter 2.*

Long shot (LS): Shot showing the actor's entire body along with a good deal of her environment. *Chapter 5.*

Looping: Dialogue replacement process during which dialogue recorded on the set is replaced by the actor recording dialogue later on a sound stage; see Automated dialog replacement. Also, in audio editing, creating a repetitive music track by copying and pasting a waveform. *Chapter 11.*

Low key: In a three-point lighting plan, a subdued primary light on the subject, suitable for drama. *Chapter 6.*

Lower thirds: Video titles positioned in the lower third of the frame. *Chapter 11.*

M

Mag stripe: Sprocketed film stock coated with magnetic oxide, used for motion picture soundtracks. *Chapter 12.*

Manual production board: Color-coded production schedule in which each vertical paper strip holds the information for one scene, and scenes are arranged in the calendar order in which they will be shot; first AD or second AD has custody of the board on the set; strip board. *Chapter 8.*

Marker: Timecode and label on a DVD indicating the in or out point of a clip; also, the destination for a jump. *Chapter 12.*

Martini: Last shot of the day. *Chapter 9.*

Master negative: Film original used for creating an intermediate negative from which release prints will be struck. *Chapter 12.*

Master shot: Continuous take of an entire scene, showing all the actors. *Chapter 5.*

Master-to-slave: Videotape copying process by which a player (master) controls recording by multiple VCRs (slaves). *Chapter 12.*

Matte: In filmmaking, a cardboard or metal cutout placed over the lens of a motion picture camera to mask part of the frame from exposure. *Chapter 6.*

Matte painting: In traditional filmmaking, a fake background done as a painting on glass to be double-exposed with a live scene. *Chapter 6.*

Mbps: Megabits per second. *Appendix A.*

MD (MiniDisc): Small magnetic disk for digital audio recording. *Chapter 7.*

Medium closeup (MCU): Wider variation of a closeup shot of an actor's head and shoulders. *Chapter 5.*

Medium shot (MS): Shot showing the actor from the waist up. *Chapter 5.*

Memory effect: Tendency of rechargeable batteries to recharge only to the same degree they've been discharged. *Chapter 9.*

Mic: Microphone. *Chapter 3.*

MIDI: See Musical Instrument Digital Interface. *Chapter 11.*

MIDI sequencer: Digital music generator and editor based on the Musical Instrument Digital Interface. *Chapter 11.*

Mini: Mid-range in power but compact in size and therefore highly portable, an open-face halogen-quartz movie light; in smaller sizes, "teenie weenies" or "betweenies"; in larger, "redheads," " Mickeys," "blondes," or "mighties." *Chapter 6.*

Mix-down: Combining and blending multiple source audio tracks into one, two, or four output tracks. *Chapter 11.*

Mixed lighting: Lighting setup containing light sources of varying color characteristics. *Chapter 6.*

Mixer: Audio module for connecting multiple sources (channels) and controlling their volume levels; also, the person who operates it. *Chapter 7.*

Monitor: External display device connected to a camcorder that shows the viewfinder image on a larger screen so you can frame the shot and judge its quality. *Chapter 4.*

Monophonic: Single-channel audio track: left (L) or right (R) channel of a stereo track. *Chapter 7.*

Montage: From the French word meaning "to assemble," an edited sequence of rapid, usually related, shots. *Chapter 1.*

Moral rights: Rights of an author to preserve the integrity of his or her work, even after sale or licensing. *Chapter 12.*

Morphing: Visual transformation in which the shape of one object seems to blend continuously into the shape of another. *Chapter 1.*

MOS (Mit Out Sound): Hollywood term for shooting picture without recording sound, supposedly derived from German émigré director who yelled: "Ve zhoot it mit out sound!" *Chapter 7.*

Motion blur: Software filter that simulates motion of the camera or subject; softens detail by making groups of pixels appear fuzzy. *Appendix A.*

Motivating a light source: Convincing the audience that your movie lights mimic real-world lighting sources. *Chapter 6.*

Multi-angle tracks: Parallel video clips that show the same scene from different camera angles. *Chapter 12.*

Multimedia eXchange Format (MXF): Proposed universal data-file format for video, audio, and pictures. *Chapter 12.*

Multiscan: Referring to computer and television monitors and TV sets that can operate at a variety of scanning modes, or frame rates. *Chapter 3.*

Music editor: Postproduction professional on an editorial team who keeps lists of cues and creates click tracks to assist the composer. *Chapter 10.*

Musical Instrument Digital Interface (MIDI): Digital recording and editing standard. *Chapter 11.*

MXF: See Multimedia eXchange Format. *Chapter 12.*

N

Negative conforming: Process of editing a film negative to match frame-for-frame the final locked workprint, or Edit Decision List. *Chapter 10.*

Negative cutter: Laboratory technician who cuts, or conforms, the original camera film negative. *Chapter 10.*

Negative financing: Practice used by independent producers to secure production funding based on prior commitments of distribution. *Chapter 12.*

Negative pickup: Commitment from a distributor, usually without advancing any cash, that it will release a movie if and when the filmmaker completes it. *Chapter 12.*

Non-Linear Editing (NLE): Digital editing, as in Final Cut Pro, Avid, and so on. *Chapter 1.*

Nondestructive editing: Editing a clip without affecting the source material. *Chapter 10.*

NTSC (National Television Standards Committee): North American analog broadcast television standard. *Chapter 3.*

O

Off-axis sound: Weak audio signals emanating from outside a mic's pickup pattern. *Chapter 7.*

Off-mic: Referring to a speaker who is off the axis of the microphone. *Chapter 7.*

Omnidirectional: Type of microphone that picks up sound equally well from all directions. *Chapter 7.*

On call (O/C): Cast or crew member assigned to work for the day but with no set call time. *Chapter 9.*

On speculation: Practice of working (usually writing) for a producer with payment conditional on some future event or decision; writing a spec script; on spec. *Chapter 8.*

One-off: Single, custom-made video copy (called a "dub") of a tape or DVD, as opposed to multiple dubs made from a master tape or data file. *Chapter 1.*

Open face: Movie light fixture with no focusing lens. *Chapter 6.*

Operating system: Master computer program that runs the hardware and supports applications such as word processors and NLEs; Windows or Mac OS. *Appendix B.*

Optical printing: Film lab process of doing special effects (wipes, dissolves, fades) in the film printing stage. *Chapter 12.*

Outline: One- or two-sentence descriptions of major scenes of a script, often numbered. A feature-length movie will have about 30-40 major scenes. *Chapter 2.*

Overclocking: Changing settings on the motherboard of a PC to force the processor to run at some multiple of its rated speed. *Appendix B.*

Overlay image: Picture file to be supered, or overlaid, on another image. *Chapter 12.*

Overscan: Camera viewfinder function showing a larger image area than will actually be recorded. *Chapter 4.*

Over-the-shoulder (OTS): Closeup of one character, shot from behind another character in the scene. *Chapter 5.*

P

P&A: See Prints and Ads. *Chapter 12.*

Painting with light: Term coined by cinematographer Rudolph Maté to describe his expressionistic approach to single-camera lighting. Painting with light generally makes creative use of highlights and shadows to create a powerful mood. *Chapter 6.*

Panning: In cinematography, pivoting the camera in a horizontal plane during a shot. *Chapter 5.* In audio terminology, mixing Left and Right stereo signals; adjusting audio balance. *Chapter 7.*

PCM: See Pulse Code Modulation. *Chapter 12.*

Pension and health (P&H): Fringe benefits stipulated by union contracts for actors and crew. *Chapter 8.*

Per diem: Daily pay rate; also, daily allowance for personal expenses such as meals and parking. *Chapter 8.*

Per-drop: License fee that applies to each use of a cut in a work; laserdrop fee. *Chapter 11.*

Performance rights: Permission for musicians to perform a composer or songwriter's work. *Chapter 11.*

Performance video: One-person theatrical show, often confessional or intimate in nature. *Chapter 1.*

Phantom power: External electrical voltage supplied to a microphone for the purpose of powering its pickup head. *Chapter 7.*

Phase: Timing of the continuous cycling of alternating current (AC) electricity. *Chapter 7.*

Phase Alternating Line (PAL): British analog broadcast television standard. *Chapter 3.*

Photoflood: Cone-shaped tungsten light with built-in reflector used to provide area lighting for photography. *Chapter 6.*

Pickup: Restoration of an actor (usually a weekly player) to the shooting schedule and to the payroll after having been dropped. *Chapter 9.*

Pickup head: Portion of a mic containing its audio sensing component. *Chapter 7.*

Pickup pattern: Locus within which a microphone is most sensitive to sound. *Chapter 7.*

Picture editor: Lead editor, primarily responsible for assembly of a movie; cutter. *Chapter 10.*

Pitch: Degree of slant of the helical scan recording pattern on videotape. *Appendix A.*

Pixel: Picture element; smallest area of color in digital video picture. *Chapter 3.*

Pixellation: Enlargement and exaggeration of the individual picture elements, or pixels, that make up a digital image for a block-picture effect. *Chapter 1.*

Places: Request for actors to assume their starting positions in a scene. *Chapter 9.*

Plant mic: Cardioid or hypercardioid microphone with swivel pickup head that can be hidden, or planted, in or near an object, such as a centerpiece, on the set. *Chapter 7.*

Platform: Type of computer processor and operating system, *e.g.,* Intel/Windows, or Motorola/Mac OS. *Appendix B.*

Platter: Film reel for automated motion-picture projectors that is large enough to hold an entire feature-length movie. *Chapter 12.*

Playhead: In Final Cut Pro, a cursor that marks the position on the timeline of the video frame currently being displayed in the canvas. *Chapter 10.*

Playlist: Text file specifying display sequences on a computerized video player. *Chapter 12.*

Plosive: Sound made in human speech by expelling a small blast of air. *Chapter 7.*

Plug-in: Software module that runs inside another application to extend its capabilities; add-in. *Chapter 10.*

Point of attack: Point at which the audience is introduced to a new scene. *Chapter 10.*

Point Of View (POV): Shot showing what one character is seeing. *Chapter 5.*

Popped p: A speaker's overdone plosive, which causes distortion in the audio recording. *Chapter 7.*

Portal: Web site that provides point of Internet access for users with similar interests. *Chapter 12.*

Positive/negative space: Amount of space in front of (positive) or in back of (negative) an actor in a frame. *Chapter 9.*

Post: Slang for "postproduction." *Chapter 1.*

Postproduction: Everything that happens to a movie between the last day of production and its initial release. *Chapter 1.*

Practical: A working light source visible in the scene; any working appliance on a set that must have electrical power. *Chapter 6.*

Press agent: Showbiz term for public relations professional; publicist. *Chapter 12.*

Pressing: Stamping an optical disc, such as a CD or DVD, from a glass master. *Chapter 12.*

Prints and Ads (P&A): Distributor's term for marketing and release expenses above and beyond negative cost. *Chapter 12.*

Processor speed: Number of instruction cycles your CPU is capable of executing every second, expressed in millions (MHz) or billions (GHz). *Appendix B.*

Producer's gross: Portion of domestic gross remitted by distributor to the producing studio. *Chapter 12.*

Progressive scanning: Capturing the entire video frame in one scan, as opposed to dividing it into fields. *Chapter 3.*

Project Change Notice (PCN): Documented request for change to a project; requires signed authorization before the change can be implemented. *Chapter 9.*

Project file: In Final Cut Pro, a document that contains all the data in the browser, which you can use to reconstruct a project from the original camcorder tapes. *Chapter 10.*

Prop: Object used by an actor in some on-camera action. *Chapter 8.*

Protocol: Data communication specification for the sequence of transmission; set of rules that defines the sequence of commands required for one data device, such as a modem, to communicate with another. *Chapter 3.*

PSA (Public Service Announcement): Informational television spot presented on behalf of a government agency, charity, or nonprofit organization; normally aired at no charge to the advertiser. PSAs air off-peak—late night and weekends. *Chapter 1.*

Public access programming: Production facilities and airtime provided to the community by a cable operator as a condition of its federal broadcast license. *Chapter 12.*

Public domain: Out of copyright; available for use by the public without fee. *Chapter 11.*

Pulse Code Modulation (PCM): One of several digital encoding schemes for audio. *Chapter 12.*

Pumping: Erroneous operation of automatic audio gain control in which the circuit keeps adjusting the level up and down as it seeks to compensate for sudden conditions of loudness or quiet. *Chapter 7.*

Pull out: Zoom out. *Chapter 5.*

Push in: Zoom in. *Chapter 5.*

R

Rack focus: To change focus during a shot; named for the flat gear called a "rack" (half of the rack-and-pinion focusing mechanism on old-style movie cameras). *Chapter 5.*

RAID: See Redundant Array of Independent Disks. *Appendix B.*

RAM (Random Access Memory): Computer memory chip; system memory. *Appendix B.*

Ramping: Smoothly changing the playback speed of a clip; for instance, from normal speed to slow motion to fast motion and back again. *Chapter 1.*

Raster: Zigzag pattern painted by the electron beam as it scans the photosensitive phosphors on the inside face of a cathode ray tube (CRT). *Chapter 3.*

Reaction shot: A shot that shows an actor's facial expression or body language in response to some dialogue or action. *Chapter 5.*

Recording format: Technical standard for capturing pictures and/or sound on magnetic or optical media. *Appendix A.*

Redundant Array of Independent Disks (RAID): Set of hard drives that act as a single storage system and can tolerate the failure of one or more drives without data loss. *Appendix B.*

Region conforming: Sound editing feature that permits graphic manipulation of audio waveforms. *Chapter 11.*

Rehearsal for the keys: On-set run-through for department heads. *Chapter 9.*

Release print: Film to be projected in a theater made in a lab from film negative. *Chapter 12.*

Rendering: Mathematical calculations required to display digital imagery on a computer screen; playback of your movie, with effects, in NLE software. *Chapter 10.*

Resolution: Sharpness and detail in a film or video image; spatial resolution. *Chapter 3.*

Reverb: Echo effect; short for *reverberation. Chapter 7.*

Riding gain: Adjusting audio levels at the mixer on the set while a take is in progress. *Chapter 7.*

Rig: Run electrical power lines to lights or sound equipment; adjust or attach accessories to lights. *Chapter 6.*

Rigging gaffer: Electrician on a movie set responsible for stringing, connecting, and securing power lines to lights. *Chapter 6.*

Rim light: Back light that adds a pleasing glow to an object's outline. *Chapter 6.*

Ringing: Video noise resulting from too-sharp edges in a picture. *Appendix A.*

Roll off: Audio engineer's term for turning equalization control down, filtering out lower frequencies. *Chapter 7.*

Room tone: Audio recording of a silent set or studio, to be used during the edit for putting in pauses or covering sound holes; also called presence. *Chapter 7.*

Rough cut: Editor's early version of a show, usually without special effects or music. *Chapter 10.*

Royalty: Licensing fee calculated as a percentage of sales for a particular use. *Chapter 11.*

Rule of screen direction: Motion of actors within the frame must preserve continuity from one shot to the next. *Chapter 5.*

Rule of thirds: Guidelines for visual composition that divide a frame into horizontal and vertical thirds. *Chapter 9.*

Run of show: Type of employment contract extending for the duration of a shoot, requiring the worker to be on call every day. *Chapter 8.*

S

Safe title area: Rectangular area within a video frame for positioning titles so they won't be cut off at the edge during display or projection. *Chapter 11.*

Sample reel: Highlights of an actor's (or videographer's) work, typically a series of edited clips, usually not more than a few minutes in length. *Chapter 1.*

Sampling: Conversion process during which fluctuating analog signals become streams of binary ones and zeros. *Appendix A.*

Saturation: Intensity of color. *Appendix A.*

Scanning mode designations: Video camera scanning modes are delineated with a combination of a frame rate (usually 24 or 30) and a letter that refers to scanning method ("I" for interlaced, or "P" for progressive). For instance: 24P, 30I, 30P. *Chapter 3.*

Scene: Basic unit of visual storytelling that advances the plot or imparts useful information to the audience. *Chapter 1.*

Scratch track: Soundtrack that contains sample music as a placeholder for an original music score; temp track. *Chapter 11.*

Scrim: Saucer-sized disk of wire mesh that reduces the intensity of a light. *Chapter 6.*

Script: The full, correctly formatted, screen story; can also be deconstructed into a script breakdown for production planning. *Chapter 2.* Computer program that automates a sequence of commands; stored program on a DVD for controlling the player. *Chapter 12.*

Script breakdown sheet: List of production items and budgetary elements specified in a script for one scene. *Chapter 8.*

Script supervisor: Production staff member who observes shooting to assure compliance with the script, and to avoid breaks in continuity; also provides the editor with shot-by-shot script notes and the director's preferred takes. *Chapter 5.*

SDRAM (Synchronous Dynamic Random Access Memory): High-speed computer memory chip. *Appendix B.*

SECAM: See Système Electronique Couleur Avec Mémoire. *Chapter 3.*

Second unit: Often used on large-scale movie productions, auxiliary director and location crew that may shoot concurrently with the main production to save time and expense by capturing establishing shots, backgrounds, inserts, and so on. *Chapter 5.*

Servo: Electric motor that translates applied voltages to discrete motion in precisely controllable steps. *Chapter 4.*

Set: In traditional moviemaking, a constructed performance area, a sound stage; a specific room or playing area on location where shooting is taking place; generally speaking, wherever you happen to be shooting. *Chapter 1.*

Set dressing: Furnishings and decorations on a movie set. *Chapter 8.*

Set wireman: A gaffer who specializes in bringing electrical power to the set. *Chapter 6.*

Setting: In a script, the description of a location, including whether action takes place exterior (outdoors) or interior (indoors), and whether it's day or night. *Chapter 2.*

Setup: Camera placement within a particular setting and scene. *Chapter 1.*

Shim: Wooden wedge used to level dolly track. *Chapter 9.*

Shooting call: Approximate time the first AD expects the camera to roll for the first take. *Chapter 9.*

Shortie: Cardioid dynamic microphone popular with singers and interviewers. *Chapter 7.*

Shot: Single, continuous film exposure or tape recording. *Chapter 1.*

Shot list: List of individual shots, including settings, subjects, and key actions. *Chapter 5.*

Shot plan: Diagram showing camera setups and positions of actors required to capture all shots needed for a scene. *Chapter 5.*

Shotgun: Hypercardioid microphone with characteristically long barrel, often used as a boom mic. *Chapter 7.*

Shutter angle: Video camera setting that emulates staccato-motion effect of varying the physical angle of a motion-picture camera shutter. *Chapter 4.*

Shutter speed (motion-picture camera): Varies the frame rate (fps). *Chapter 4.*

Shutter speed (still photography): Varies length of time film is exposed to light. *Chapter 4.*

Shutter speed (video camcorder): Varies length of time CCDs are exposed to light during each frame; does *not* affect the frame rate. *Chapter 4.*

Side: An actor's script page showing only the character names and dialogue; any script page. Also refers to script pages used on the set, sometimes even reproduced on half-size paper, with only that shooting day's scenes, in their shooting order. Easy to fold up and stick in your back pocket while working. Probably derived from the German word for page *(Seite). Chapter 2.*

Signal-to-noise (S/N) ratio: Strength of the information-carrying signal in an audio line in relation to the amount of noise; the higher the ratio, the better the quality of the audio signal. *Chapter 7.*

Signatory: Producer who signs an agreement to abide by a union's working rules. *Chapter 8.*

Silk: Panel of translucent cloth stretched on a frame that can be mounted on a C-stand for the purpose of diffusing light. *Chapter 6.*

Single: Shot that frames one actor; or, "clean single." *Chapter 5.*

Single-system sound: Recording sync sound on the camcorder only. *Chapter 7.*

Slate: Hand-held chalk or marker board—nowadays a digital LED device—for recording the scene and take number, held in front of the lens to mark the beginning of a take for the editor and clapped to establish sync; clapper board. *Chapter 7.* Also, card at the head of a master recording identifying the program, its details, and the producer. *Chapter 11.*

Slo-mo: Slang for "slow motion." *Chapter 4.*

Slug: Slang for scene heading in a movie script. *Chapter 2.*

Smart slate: Electronic clapper board, or slate, with numeric LED display of timecode. *Chapter 7.*

Sneaking in: Fading in an effect gradually. *Chapter 11.*

Soft light: Diffuse illumination coming from a large, bright area like a reflector. *Chapter 6.*

Song: In music composition, any complete musical selection, whether instrumental, vocal, or both. *Chapter 11.*

Sound board: A type of audio mixer that can control both levels and equalization for many audio lines. *Chapter 7.*

Sound effects editor: Postproduction professional on an editorial team who lays in sound effects from multiple sources—production, synthetic, and Foley. *Chapter 10.*

Sound mixer: Audio technician responsible for monitoring sound levels and operating mixer equipment on the set; also used to mean re-recording mixer, the person operating the mixing board for the final sound mix at the conclusion of postproduction. *Chapter 7.*

Sound recordist: On the set, an audio technician who operates a tape recorder external to the camcorder. *Chapter 7.*

Spatial quality: Amount of echo, or apparent depth, and other noise characteristics of a room or space. *Chapter 7.*

Spatial resolution: The number of pixels used by a camcorder or video display. *Chapter 3.*

Spike: Mark an actor's final position with tape on the floor of the set. *Chapter 9.*

Split edit: Transition in which the picture of the incoming scene precedes the sound cut (L-cut), or the sound of the incoming scene precedes the picture cut (J-cut). *Chapter 10.*

Split tracks: Preferred four-track audio configuration for distributor; segregating music and effects on two separate tracks, with dialogue on two other tracks. *Chapter 11.*

Splitter: Electrical connector that branches one input to form two output lines; Y-connector. *Chapter 7.*

Spot: Advertising industry term for a television or radio commercial, usually referred to by its length (30-second spot, 60-second spot). *Chapter 1.*

Spotlight: Intense beam, a very hard light, on a specific object or area in a scene; also called a "spot." *Chapter 6.*

Spotting table: Listing of all music and sound-effect cues in a show. *Chapter 11.*

Spy cam: Webcam used for continuous surveillance of a remote location. *Chapter 1.*

Squib: Small explosive charge worn by an actor; when fired by remote control, simulates a gunshot wound. *Chapter 8.*

Ss/dl: single-side/dual-layer optical disc; DVD-9. *Chapter 12.*

Ss/sl: single-side/single-layer optical disc; DVD-5. *Chapter 12.*

Stage line: An imaginary line drawn between two actors on the set to assure visual continuity; camera setups are on the same side of the line, often called "the axis," or "the 180 degree rule." *Chapter 5.*

Stand-in: Substitute for an actor who has the same build and wears similar clothes. Stand-ins walk through a scene to assist the DP in setting lights. *Chapter 9.*

Stationary matte: Static composited scene in which the subject and background don't move, or move only slightly in relation to one another. *Chapter 6.*

Status display: Alphanumeric readouts that appear in the camcorder viewfinder (and sometimes on a field monitor) showing f-stop, battery level, timecode, Rec/Pause/Standby, and more. *Chapter 4.*

Store-and-forward: Video communications achieved by sending files for later playback. *Chapter 12.*

Story: The basic narrative in a script or fiction movie ; the single most important element of any video presentation. *Chapter 2.* Set of markers defining a sequence of clips to be played back in a particular order on a DVD. *Chapter 12.*

Storyboard: Series of hand-drawn illustrations of the director's intended shots, based on his or her visual interpretation of the script. *Chapter 1.*

Strain relief: Rigging technique in which cables are looped or taped in place to prevent connectors from separating if someone trips or tugs on the cable. *Chapter 7.*

Streamer track: Audio track containing cueing beeps for the voice-over actor, used in looping. *Chapter 11.*

Streaming video: Video and audio data delivered more or less continuously over a network or the Internet. *Chapter 12.*

Strike: To take down a set and pack up equipment in preparation for moving to another location. *Chapter 8.*

String-out: Editor's preliminary assembly of clips. *Chapter 10.*

Structured approach: Adhering strictly to a storyboard or shot plan. *Chapter 5.*

Subscription-supported: Communications channel mostly subsidized by fees paid by users. *Chapter 12.*

Supercardioid: A type of microphone that is more narrowly sensitive to sounds directly in front of it than the cardioid type. *Chapter 7.*

Supervising editor: On large projects such as movies and TV specials, a postproduction professional who manages a team of editors, some of whom are assigned to specialized tasks, such as music and special effects. *Chapter 10.*

Switcher: Control console in a TV studio where the director selects which camera's image will be recorded or transmitted. *Chapter 3.*

Sync sound: Audio recorded during a take that corresponds to video action; frame-accurate soundtrack. *Chapter 3.*

Synopsis: A short summary of a script or screen story, typically a few pages or less. *Chapter 2.*

Système Electronique Couleur Avec Mémoire (SECAM): French and Asian broadcast television standard; translates as "electronic color system with memory." *Chapter 3.*

Systems integrator: Computer dealer that specializes in customizing hardware and software for special applications. *Appendix B.*

Swing gang: Team within a set construction crew that assembles a set. *Chapter 8.*

T

Tail-slating: Shooting an upside-down slate at the end of a take. *Chapter 9.*

Take: Each recorded attempt to capture a shot. *Chapter 1.*

Talk-back circuit: On some sound mixers, output jacks for headsets with earphones and mics to be worn by the mixer and boom operator so they can communicate. *Chapter 7.*

Tech rehearsal: Last run-through before the first take. *Chapter 9.*

Telecine: Film or video lab system that scans film footage and converts it to video. *Chapter 11.*

Telephoto shot: Done with a long lens, a narrow-angle closeup taken from a great distance. *Chapter 5.*

Texturing: Adding a synthetic surface to a 3D graphic object. *Chapter 10.*

Theatrical movie: Feature-length motion picture intended for exhibition in commercial movie houses. *Chapter 1.*

Throw: Distance a beam can cover before becoming too faint for lighting purposes. *Chapter 6.*

Time bending: Applying variable frame rates in postproduction for effects such as slow motion. *Chapter 11.*

Timeline: In NLE systems, the graphic representation of the edited sequence of video and audio tracks. *Chapter 10.*

Timing: Film lab color correction step affecting overall color cast and brightness from scene to scene. *Chapter 12.*

Top sheet: Summary budget page showing subtotals for each department and major budget category. *Chapter 8.*

Total pixel count: Number of pixels on a single CCD, whether the camcorder uses one or three chips. *Chapter 3.*

Traffic: Purchasing airtime from a network for advertising spots. *Chapter 12.*

Transfer: Conversion of film or analog material to digital video, or vice versa. *Chapter 2.*

Transpose: To translate from one musical key to another, involving raising or lowering the pitch of instruments and voices, *e.g.* from the key of C to the key of G-sharp. *Chapter 11.*

Traveling matte: In filmmaking, a double-exposure matte that moves along with its subject. In video, a key process involving a moving subject. *Chapter 6.*

Treatment: Narrative describing the plot and essential elements of a screen story, perhaps with excerpted dialogue. A form for presenting movie projects to executives and investors who may not want to deal with the details of a formatted screenplay. *Chapter 2.*

Trim: Mark the in (starting) and out (ending) timecodes of a clip. *Chapter 10.*

Trucking: Moving the camera parallel to a moving subject while keeping a constant distance. *Chapter 5.*

Tungsten: Particular type of incandescent light with filament made from this metal; European crews may call it *wolfram. Chapter 6.*

Tunnel: Private Internet subchannel created by Virtual Private Networking (VPN). *Chapter 12.*

Turnkey system: Complete hardware and software solution, including accessories, support, sometimes even training. *Appendix B.*

Two-pop: Cueing tone that occurs two seconds before start of picture. *Chapter 11.*

Two-shot: Shot that frames two actors. *Chapter 5.*

U

Unlimited use: Blanket license fee that covers all forms of distribution for a music/effects cut or library. *Chapter 11.*

Upconvert: Transfer a video recording from a lower to a higher data rate or resolution; upsample. *Chapter 12.*

Upload: Process of transferring data from a smaller computer or device to a larger one or to a network; *e.g.,* from camcorder to PC or from PC to Web; opposite of *download*. In the DV format, upload time can range from 1:1 (that is, one hour of transfer time per hour of program) to 4:1 (one hour of program takes just 15 minutes of transfer time) with expensive, high-performance gear. *Chapter 1.*

V

Variable Bit Rate (VBR): "Intelligent" MPEG-2 encoding scheme that uses a range of data rates to store the highest quality picture in the smallest amount of space. *Chapter 12.*

Video chat: Two-way conferencing via linked webcams. *Chapter 1.*

Video editing card: High-performance video card that computes video effects to ease the load on the computer processor and speed up playback. *Appendix B.*

Video gain: Degree of amplification of CCD output, measured in decibels. *Chapter 4.*

Videoconferencing: Two-way, real-time video and audio communication over a network. *Chapter 12.*

Video diary: Uncensored streams of autobiographical material captured with a webcam or camcorder. *Chapter 1.*

Videodisc: Another term for DVD. *Chapter 12.*

Viewer: In Final Cut Pro, a window showing the clip you're working with. *Chapter 10.*

Viewfinder: Device that lets you see the current view through the lens of a camcorder. Status information is usually displayed as well. *Chapter 4.*

Virtual meeting: Real-time conference between multiple locations, achieved by telecommunications. *Chapter 12.*

Virtual Private Networking (VPN): Data encryption technology used to create private subchannels within the Internet. *Chapter 12.*

Visual climax: Nonverbal resolution of a screen presentation that gives it a sense of completeness or finality. *Chapter 2.*

Visual effects editor: Postproduction professional on an editorial team who creates or supervises video compositing and titling. *Chapter 10.*

Vocalization: Using the human voice to produce postproduction sound effects. *Chapter 11.*

VPN: See Virtual Private Networking. *Chapter 12.*

VTR: Videotape recorder. *Chapter 3.*

VU meter: Audio level indicator marked off in a range of volume units (VU), which is equivalent to the dB scale. *Chapter 7.*

W

Walk-through: Informal rehearsal on the set in which actors say (but don't perform) their lines and go through their blocking with the director. *Chapter 9.*

Walla: Crowd murmur. *Chapter 11.*

Warner's closeup: Closeup shot of an actor's face, so tight that it cuts off either the chin or the forehead. *Chapter 5.*

Wattage: Measure of electrical power consumption. *Chapter 6.*

Web conferencing: Two-way Webcasting. *Chapter 12.*

Webcam: Any video camera equipped to output compressed video (MPEG2) for distribution on the Internet. *Chapter 1.*

Webcasting: Streaming media over the Internet as an alternative to broadcast transmission. *Chapter 12.*

Wild sound: An audio-only take of a sound on the set, recorded with no corresponding picture; the sound of a slap, for example; wild track. *Chapter 7.*

Wipe: Transition effect that gradually reveals the next scene as the current scene is wiped off the screen. *Chapter 10.*

Work for hire: Contractual arrangement between an author and an employer granting the employer all rights to a particular work. By law, copyright vests with the author unless a written agreement exists that specifies work for hire. *Chapter 11.*

X

XML (eXtensible Markup Language): Enhancement of HTML used to create Web pages and facilitate exchange of data and processes among networked computers. *Chapter 12..*

Z

Zebra pattern: A feature on some prosumer and all professional camcorders, a slanted-bar symbol that appears in the camcorder viewfinder superimposed on overexposed areas in the scene. Also called "zebra stripes," or "zebra." *Chapter 4.*

Zoom lens: Lens with continuously variable focal length. Zooming in increases magnification and makes the subject seem closer, while zooming out does the opposite. *Chapter 3.*

REFERENCES

References and Web Links

1. All You Can Achieve with Digital Video

American Film Institute (AFI) *(www.afi.com)*

Filmmakers Alliance *(www.filmmakersalliance.com)*

Footage [documentary] *(www.footage.net)*

Independent Feature Project *(www.ifp.org)*

International Documentary Association (IDA) *(www.documentary.org)*

Laporte, Leo [blog and webcams] *(www.leoville.com) (www.techtv.com)*

Media Access Project [free-speech issues] *(www.mediaaccess.org)*

Media Communications Association International [corporate communicators] *(www.mca-i.org)*

RE: Vision Effects, Inc. [animation] *(www.revisionfx.com)*

Rees, A. L., *A History of Experimental Film and Video* (London: British Film Institute, 1999)

Squires, Malcolm, *Video Camcorder School: A Practical Guide to Making Great Home Videos* (Pleasantville: Reader's Digest, 1992)

Tvcameramen.com *(www.tvcameramen.com/index.html)*

Utz, Dr. Peter, "How-To Info and Books for Videographers" *(http://videoexpert.home.att.net/index.htm)*

2.   Yes, You Need a Script

Egri, Lajos, *The Art of Dramatic Writing*
(New York: Touchstone/Simon and Schuster, 1960)

Final Draft [screenwriting software] *(www.finaldraft.com)*

Hunter, Lew, *Lew Hunter's Screenwriting 434* (New York: Perigee/Penguin Putnam, 1995)

InkTip.com (formerly Writers Script Network) [writer-to-producer mart]
(www.inktip.com)

National Creative Registry [script registration service] *(www.protectrite.com)*

Seger, Linda, *The Art of Adaptation: Turning Fact and Fiction into Film*
(New York: Henry Holt, 1992)

U. S. Copyright Office *(www.loc.gov/copyright)*

Writers Guild of America *(www.wga.org)*

WriteSafe [script registration service] *(www.writesafe.com)*

3.   DV Technology and the Camcorder

Billups, Scott, *Digital Moviemaking: A Butt-Kicking, Pixel Twisting Vision of the Digital Future and How to Make Your Next Movie on Your Credit Card* (2nd ed., Studio City: Michael Weise Productions, 2003)

Collier, Maxie D., *Digital Video Filmmaker's Handbook* (Hollywood: ifilm Publishing/Lone Eagle, 2001)

Foveon, Inc. [advanced CMOS chips] *(www.foveon.com)*

Grotta, Sally Weiner, "Anatomy of a Digital Camera: Image Sensors," *ExtremeTech,*
June 12, 2001, Ziff Davis Media, Inc. *(www.extremetech.com/article2/0,3973,15465,00.asp)*

Silbergleid, Michael and Mark J. Pescatore, *A Guide to Digital Television,* 3rd ed.
(New York, United Entertainment Media, 2002)
(www.digitaltelevision.com/publish/dtvbook/toc.shtml)

VCDHelp.com [digital format comparisons] *(www.vcdhelp.com/comparison.htm)*

Williamson, Glen A., "Television" *(www.williamson-labs.com/480_tv.htm)*

4. Using Your Camcorder Like a Pro

American Society of Cinematographers (ASC) *(www.theasc.com)*

B-Roll.net: The Television Photography Web Site *(http://b-roll.net)*

Eastman Kodak Company, "More on 'Telephoto Lenses' Depth of Field," *(www.kodak.com)*

Hall, Conrad L., *Visions of Light: The Art of Cinematography*
(Los Angeles: Image Entertainment, 1993)

Johnson, Bruce A., "Camera Accessories," *Digital Video Magazine*, April 2002
(www.dv.com)

Kapoor, Dave, "Filters for Digital Cameras," Spectra Cine, Inc.,
"Determining the ASA/ISO Rating or Exposure Index of a Video Camera"
(http://spectracine.com/determiningtheexposureindexo.htm)

P+S Technik [cinema lens adapters] *(www.pstechnik.de)*

Reichman, Michael, "The Luminous Landscape: The Understanding Series"
(www.luminous-landscape.com)

Sony Electronics Inc., *HDTV Production: Arrival of a 24-Frame Progressive Scan HDTV
Production System—Implications for Program Origination* (Park Ridge: Sony, 2001)

5. Shots and Shot Plans

Block, Bruce A., *The Visual Story: Seeing the Structure of Film, TV, and New Media*
(Boston: Focal Press, 2001)

Famous Frames, Inc. [storyboard artists] *(www.famousframes.com)*

St. John Marner, Terence, *Film Design* (New York: A. S. Barnes, 1974)

Storyboard Quick! [software] *(www.storyboardartist.com)*

6. Lighting for DV

Airstar Space Lighting *(www.airstar-light.com)*

B&H Photo-Video Pro Audio Corp., "Glossary for Professional Video"
(www.bhphotovideo.com)

Birns & Sawyer, Inc. [rentals] *(www.birnsandsawyer.com)*

Clairmont Camera Film & Digital [rentals] *(www.clairmont.com)*

Kino Flo Lighting Systems *(www.kinoflo.com)*

Lowel-Light Manufacturing, Inc. *(www.lowel.com)*

Mole-Richardson *(www.moletown.com)*

Paskal Lighting [rentals] *(www.paskal.com)*

Studio 1, Article Index *(www.studio1store.com/articles.htm)*

Studio Depot *(www.studiodepot.com)*

7. Sound on the Set

Audio-Technica U.S., Inc., "Resolving Interference Problems"
  (www.audiotechnica.com/using/wireless/advanced/resolve.html)

Audio-Technica, U.S., Inc., "Setting Up Wireless Microphone Audio"
  (www.audiotechnica.com/using/wireless/basics/setup.html)

Audio-Technica U.S., Inc., "Using Multiple [Wireless] Systems"
  (www.audiotechnica.com/using/wireless/advanced/multi.html)

Internet Newsgroup (Audio Professionals), "rec.audio.pro FAQ"
  (www.vex.net/~pcook/RecAudioPro/index.html)

PolderbitS Sound Recorder and Editor (Windows), Sound Sculptor II (Mac)
[audio recording software] *(www.tucows.com)*

Rose, Jay, "Big Mistakes," *Digital Video Magazine*, July 2002

Sennheiser Electronic GmbH & Co., KG [mics] *(www.sennheiser.com/sennheiser/icm.nsf)*

Shure, Inc., "Shure Model FP33 User Guide"
  (www.shure.com/pdf/userguides/guides_audiomixers/fp33_en.pdf)

Tech Target, "Whatis.com Definition: Jam Sync"
  (http://whatis.techtarget.com/definition/0,,sid9_gci213624,00.html)

8. Preproduction

Academy Players Directory [casting guide] *(www.playersdirectory.com)*

Casting Society of America (CSA) *(www.castingsociety.com)*

Daniels, Bill, David Leedy, and Steven D. Sills, *Movie Money: Understanding Hollywood's (Creative) Accounting Practices* (Los Angeles: Silman-James, 1998)

Donaldson, Michael C., Mimi Donaldson, and David Frohnmayer, *Negotiating For Dummies®,* (New York: Wiley, 1996)

Entertainment Partners [scheduling and budgeting software] *(www.entertainmentpartners.com)*

Filmmaker.com [forms and tips] *(www.filmmaker.com)*

Gaines, Philip and David J. Rhodes, *Hollywood on $5,000, $10,000, or $25,000 a Day: The Survival Guide for Low-Budget Filmmakers* (Los Angeles: Silman-James, 1994)

Goodell, Gregory, *Independent Feature Film Production: A Complete Guide from Concept to Distribution* (New York: St. Martin's Press, 1982)

Independent Feature Project, *Make Your Movie (www.ifp.org/nav/makeyourmovie.php)*

Industry Labor Guide [software tables] *(www.scriptdude.com/production.html#IndustryLaborGuide)*

Maier, Robert G., *Location Scouting and Management Handbook* (Boston: Focal Press, 1994)

Producers Guild of America *(www.producersguild.com)*

Rodriguez, Robert, *Rebel Without a Crew: Or How a 23-Year-Old Filmmaker with $7,000 Became a Hollywood Player* (New York: Plume/E. P. Dutton, 1996)

Schmidt, Rick, *Feature Filmmaking at Used-Car Prices: How to Write, Produce, Direct, Film, Edit, and Promote a Feature-Length Film for Less than $10,000* (New York: Penguin/Viking, 1988)

Schreibman, Myrl A., Gilbert Cates, and Lew Hunter, *Indie Producers Handbook: Creative Producing from A to Z* (Hollywood: Lone Eagle, 2001) *(www.indieproducing.com)*

Singleton, Ralph, *Film Scheduling: Or, How Long Will It Take to Shoot Your Movie?* (Hollywood: Lone Eagle, 1991)

Vogel, Harold L., *Entertainment Industry Economics: A Guide to Financial Analysis, 5th Edition* (Cambridge: Cambridge Univ., 2001)

9.   On the Set

American Federation of Television and Radio Artists (AFTRA) *(www.aftra.org)*

Crew Net *(www.crewnet.net)*

Digital Cinema: A creativePLANETCommunity *(www.digitalcinemamag.com)*

Directors, The: The Essential DVD Collection (Los Angeles: Fox Lorber, 2001)

International Alliance of Theatrical Stage Employees (IATSE) *(www.iatse.org)*

Jeffords, Bob, *Jeffords' Rules and Regulations,* Directors Guild of America *(www.dga.org)*

Ohio, Denise, *Five Essential Steps in Digital Video: A DV Moviemaker's Tricks of the Trade* (Indianapolis: Que, 2001)

National Association of Broadcast Employees and Technicians (NABET)/Communications Workers of America (CWA) *(www.nabetcwa.org)*

Rose, Jay, "The Wrong Line," *Digital Video Magazine,* June 2002 *(www.dv.com)*

Screen Actors Guild *(www.sag.org)*

10. In the Cutting Room

American Cinema Editors (ACE) *(www.ace-filmeditors.org/index.htm)*

Apple Pro [training] *(www.apple.com)*

Ondattje, Michael, *The Conversations: Walter Murch and the Art of Editing Film* (New York: Knopf, 2002)

Sony Pictures [audio and video editing software, music library] *(http://mediasoftware.sonypictures.com)*

Wilson, Michael Henry (dir.), *A Personal Journey with Martin Scorsese Through American Movies* (Burbank: Miramax, 1995)

11. Polishing Sound and Images

Allied Post Audio [audio postproduction services] *(www.alliedpost.com)*

American Society of Composers, Authors and Publishers (ASCAP) [music licensing] *(www.ascap.com)*

Averbuch, Nir [composer] *(www.muzikhead.com)*

BIAS, Inc. [audio software] *(www.bias-inc.com)*

Broadcast Music Incorporated (BMI) [music licensing] *(www.bmi.com)*

Carlsson, Sven E., "Sound Design of *Star Wars*" *(www.filmsound.org/starwars)*

Charly [music licensing] *(www.licensemusic.com)*

DeWolfe Music [library] *(www.dewolfemusic.com)*

Digital Anarchy [NLE plug-ins and software] *(www.digitalanarchy.com)*

Dolby Laboratories Inc., "Surround Sound: Past, Present, and Future" *(www.dolby.com/ht/430.l.br.9904.surhist.pdf)*

E-On Software [NLE plug-ins and software] *(www.e-onsoftware.com)*

Film Music magazine *(www.filmmusicmag.com)*

Frederick, Paul [composer] *(http://home.earthlink.net/~pfrederick2/)*

Inscriber Technology [NLE plug-ins and software] *(www.inscriber.com)*

Josephs, Mark [singer-songwriter] *(www.mark-josephs.com)*

Opus 1 Music Library *(www.opus1musiclibrary.com)*

Recording Industry of America (RIAA) *(www.riaa.org)*

Rose, Jay, "Welcome to the Digital Playroom!" *(www.dplay.com/index.html)*

Rose, Jay, "Sounds of the Silver Screen: How to Make Digital Video Sound Like Film," *Digital Video Magazine*, May 2001 *(www.dv.com)*

SmartSound Software [music software tools, library] *(www.smartsound.com)*

Synchro Arts VocALign [sound sync software] *(www.synchroarts.co.uk)*

12. Distribution and E-Publishing

Advanced Media Technologies, Inc., "DVD Pressing" *(www.amtone.com/dvdpress.html)*

American Film Marketing Association (AFMA) *(www.afma.com)*

Arri [ArriLaser film recorder] *(www.arri.com)*

Atom Films [e-distributor] *(atomfilms.shockwave.com/af/home)*

Box Office Results *(www.the-numbers.com/movies)*

Campbell, Russell, *Photographic Theory for the Motion Picture Cameraman* (New York: A. S. Barnes, 1980)

Celco [film recorders] *(www.celco.com)*

Cineon [laser film recorder] *(www.cineon.com)*

Coolidge, Martha, past president of DGA, letter quoted in Bob Baker, "Who Can Edit a Movie? Directors Guild Files Suit," *Los Angeles Times*, September 21, 2002

Da Vinci Systems [color correction systems] *(www.davsys.com)*

Disc Makers [DVD duplication hardware and services] *(www.discmakers.com)*

Digital Film Group, "FAQs" *(www.digitalfilmgroup.net)*

Duart [film transfers and lab] *(www.duart.com)*

DVD Copy Control Association (DVDCCA) *(www.dvdcca.org)*

DVFilm [film transfers], "Top Ten Most Commonly Asked Questions"
    (www.dvfilm.com/faq.htm)

Eastman Kodak Company, "Motion Picture Printing"
    (www.kodak.com/country/US/en/motion/support/h1/printingP.shtml)

E-Film [film transfers] *(www.efilm.com)*

EVS [HD compression technology] *(www.evs.tv)*

Film Festivals [listing] *(www.filmfestivals.com)*

FotoKem [film transfers and lab] *(www.fotokem.com)*

Internet Movie Database *(www.imdb.com)*

JVC D-ILA [digital projection] *(www.jvcdig.com/technology.htm)*

Kagan World Media [media marketing research] *(www.kagan.com)*

Lancaster, Kurt and Cynthia Conti, *Building a Home Movie Studio and Getting Your Films Online* (New York: Billboard Books/Watson-Guptill, 2001)

Lasergraphics, Inc., "Video to Film Transfer" *(www.lasergraphics.com/pages/videotofilm.htm)*

Leunig, Sheila M., Esq., "Will Your Web-Based Business Benefit from the Digital Millennium Copyright Act?" *(www.witi.org/wire/feature/sleunig/index.shtml)*

Macrovision [APS copy protection license for DVDs] *(www.macrovision.com)*

Motion Picture Association of America (MPAA) *(www.mpaa.org)*

National Association of Broadcasters (NAB) *(www.nab.org)*

Rimage [DVD duplication equipment] *(www.rimage.com)*

Rose, M. J. and Angela Adair-Hoy, *How to Publish and Promote Online* (New York: St. Martin's Griffin, 2001)

Streitfeld, David, "The Cultural Anarchist vs. the Hollywood Police State," *Los Angeles Times Magazine,* September 22, 2002

Swiss Effects [film transfers] *(www.swisseffects.ch)*

Texas Instruments DLP [digital projection] *(www.dlp.com)*

U.S. Library of Congress [copyright information and forms] *(www.loc.gov/copyright);* "Executive Summary Digital Millennium Copyright Act Section 104 Report" *(www.loc.gov/copyright/reports/studies/dmca/dmca_executive.html)*

Wilkinson, Jim and Bruce Devlin, "The Material Exchange Format (MXF) and its Application," *SMPTE Journal*, September, 2002

Without a Box, Inc. [film festival submission service] *(www.withoutabox.com)*

13. Coming Attractions

DLP Projection *(www.dlp.com)*

Eastman Kodak Company, *The Future of Cinema: Leaders of the Entertainment Industry Share Their Views of Tomorrow* (Los Angeles: Eastman Kodak, 2000)

Eastman Kodak Company, *The Future of Filmmaking* (Los Angeles: Eastman Kodak, 2000)

Lucasfilm, Ltd., "Star Wars II: The Next Generation of Digital," June 10, 2002 *(www.starwars.com/episode-ii/news/2002/06/news20020610.html)*

A. Digital Video Technology in Depth

Advanced Television Systems Committee (ATSC) *(www.atsc.org)*

Hecht, Marvin, "Hecht's HDTV Links" *(www.geocities.com/marvin_hecht/hdtv.html)*

Hullfish, Steve, "Color Correction Plug-Ins," *Digital Video Magazine*, January 2002; "Color Correction Techniques," February 2002; "Fundamentals of Color-Correction," January 2002 *(www.dv.com)*

Jackman, John, "Creating Broadcast-Legal Stills," *Digital Video Magazine*, December 2001 *(www.dv.com)*

Long, Ben, "Digital Video 101: Choosing the Right Video Format," September 6, 2000 *(www.creativepro.com/story/feature/8455.html)*

Murray, James D. and William D. vanRyper, *Encyclopedia of Graphics File Formats,* 2nd ed. (O'Reilly & Associates, Inc., Sebastopol, Calif., May 1996) *(www.oreilly.com/catalog/gffcd/noframes.html)*

National Semiconductor, "LM9627 Product Folder" [CMOS technical description] *(www.national.com/pf/LM/LM9627.html)*

Poynton, Charles, "Color Links" *(www.poynton.com)*

"Professional Digital Video Tape Recorder Comparison" *(http://kensystem.com/kensys/vtr.htm)*

Rule Broadcast Systems, "Tech Tips: All Digital Video is NOT Created Equal" *(www.rule.com/techtip.cfm?techtipID=19#top)*

Society of Motion Picture and Television Engineers (SMPTE) *(www.smpte.org)*

Sony Corporation, "Guidance of Sony Semiconductor Data Sheet" *(www.sony.co.jp/~semicon/english)*

Wilt, Adam J., "The DV, DVCAM, & DVCPRO Formats" *(www.adamwilt.com/DV.html)*

B. Selecting and Building an NLE System

Adobe Premiere Pro [NLE training] *(www.adobe.com/products/premiere/training.html)*

Adobe Systems Incorporated, "Support Knowledgebase Document 322499: Using Locked and Unlocked DV Audio in Premiere 5.x" *(www.adobe.com/support/techdocs/25dce.htm)*

Automatic Duck [NLE import/export tools] *(www.automaticduck.com)*

Avid [NLE training] *(www.avid.com/training/index.html)*

Capria, Frank, "Software NLEs," *Digital Video Magazine*, May 2002

Dvcreators.net [training] *(www.dvcreators.net)*

EZ Keyboard Products [NLE keyboards] *(www.postop.com/SelectEZproduct.htm)*

Sundance Media Group [Vegas training] *(www.sundancemediagroup.com)*

Vegas Resources [NLE downloads] *(www.creativecow.net/articles/vegasvideo.html)*

INDEX